US–Japan–North Korea Security Relations

This book examines the major security and related issues between the United States, Japan and North Korea (officially, the Democratic People's Republic of Korea – DPRK).

The central purpose of the book is to analyze the policymaking processes of Washington, Tokyo and Pyongyang with respect to the DPRK's nuclear weapons and other important security issues, and ultimately to provide practical ways to improve the security environment in Northeast Asia. Ongoing security-related issues examined here include nuclear and missile testing by the DPRK; its removal from the US list of states sponsoring terrorism, and the abduction of Japanese nationals by North Korean agents that occurred during the 1970s and 1980s. Unlike many other books, which typically take the position that North Korea is a rogue state run by an irrational, belligerent and autocratic leader, this book reveals the fundamentals of Pyongyang's security concerns in the region.

This book will be of great interest to students of Northeast Asian politics, Asian security studies, US foreign policy and security studies/IR in general.

Anthony DiFilippo is Professor of Sociology at Lincoln University in Pennsylvania, US. His most recent publications include *The Challenges of the U.S.–Japan Military Arrangement: Competing Security Transitions in a Changing International Environment* and *Japan's Nuclear Disarmament Policy and the U.S. Security Umbrella*.

T0347286

Asian Security Studies

Series Editors: Sumit Ganguly, *Indiana University, Bloomington* and Andrew Scobell, *US Army War College*

Few regions of the world are fraught with as many security questions as Asia. Within this region it is possible to study great power rivalries, irredentist conflicts, nuclear and ballistic missile proliferation, secessionist movements, ethnoreligious conflicts and inter-state wars. This book series publishes the best possible scholarship on the security issues affecting the region, and includes detailed empirical studies, theoretically oriented case studies and policy-relevant analyses as well as more general works.

US–Japan–North Korea Security Relations

Irrepressible interests

Anthony DiFilippo

LONDON AND NEW YORK

First published 2012
by Routledge
4 Park Square, Milton Park, Abingdon, Oxon OX14 4RN
605 Third Avenue, New York, NY 10017

*Routledge is an imprint of the Taylor & Francis Group,
an informa business*

First issued in paperback 2013

British Library Cataloguing in Publication Data
A catalogue record for this book is available from the British Library

Library of Congress Cataloging in Publication Data
DiFilippo, Anthony, 1950-
US-Japan-North Korean security relations : irrepressible interests / Anthony
DiFilippo.
p. cm. -- (Asian security studies)
Includes bibliographical references and index.
1. United States--Military relations--Korea (North) 2. Korea (North)--
Military relations--United States. 3. United States--Military relations--
Japan. 4. Japan--Military relations--United States. 5. Korea (North)--
Military relations--Japan. 6. Japan--Military relations--Korea (North)
I. Title. II. Title: United States-Japan-North Korean security relations.
UA23.D535 2011
355'.0310973095193--dc22
2011004693

ISBN13: 978-0-415-78297-5 (hbk)
ISBN13: 978-0-415-72395-4 (pbk)
ISBN13: 978-0-203-80706-4 (ebk)

Typeset in Times
by Taylor and Francis Books Ltd

Contents

Preface

In this book I do my best to analyze objectively the policy positions developed in Washington, Tokyo and Pyongyang, and when necessary Seoul, Beijing and Moscow, as they relate to specific security concerns that each of these governments have in Northeast Asia, a region where the Cold War still has not been laid to rest. With respect to security policies developed for this region, it is important to underscore that the political beliefs of policymakers and those determined to influence them are typically driven by ideologies that have been formed and sustained by the hostilities of the Cold War and sometimes even before this period. Thus, the political beliefs and ideologies that have caused tensions to run high, and solutions to problems to be the perennial reliance on military threats and readiness continue to exist. And so Washington and Pyongyang remain bitter adversaries, as do Tokyo and Pyongyang, which has as its staunchest ally Beijing and to a lesser extent Moscow; at the same time, the Korean War is still not over. Far too often then confrontational policies continue to trump reasoned diplomacy and rapprochement.

During the course of my work on this book, I had lengthy discussions in Japan with many individuals, both in and out of government, who hold widely varying political perspectives. I choose to maintain the anonymity of these individuals, some of whom were especially helpful to me. The exception to anonymity is Professor Sachio Nakato, who during my sabbatical in the 2010 spring semester, very kindly arranged for me to spend time at Ritsumeikan University's Graduate School of International Relations in Kyoto. Accepting an invitation from the Korean Association of Social Scientists in the Democratic People's Republic of Korea afforded me the opportunity to have lengthy discussions with a number of prominent North Koreans during my six-day visit there in January 2009. Several South Korean officials were also helpful to me in one way or another during the time I spent researching and writing this book. To all of these individuals, I extend my warmest thanks and appreciation.

On several occasions, I received research awards from Lincoln University in Pennsylvania, United States. This funding was very helpful in that it enabled me to offset the costs of doing research in Japan for this book. In my judgment, this book has been improved because of some of the comments made by its reviewers. Much thanks to Marguerite Hoberg for her painstaking work in preparing the index for this book.

This book is dedicated to those who recognize that nonconfrontational diplomacy, when practiced with diligence, can resolve problems in foreign affairs.

Anthony DiFilippo, January 2011

1 Introduction

This book mainly examines the recent security-related policy issues involving Japan, North Korea, whose official name is the Democratic People's Republic of Korea (DPRK), and the United States. When appropriate and necessary, however, the security interests of South Korea, China and Russia are incorporated into the analysis. Although the relationship between the United States and Japan, which is built on a more than half-century-old bilateral security alliance, remains in good shape, serious problems still exist between Tokyo and Pyongyang and between the latter and Washington. Because each of these governments have perceived security interests and objectives, the security environment of Northeast Asia very remains unsettled. To better understand the recent problems that have shaped the security policies of Japan, North Korea and the United States, we will first briefly look at some historically important background issues.

The historical context

Apart from the few exceptions where analysts have questioned how the Korean War (1950–53) started,[1] the typical thesis is that in June 1950 North Korean forces crossed the 38th parallel and invaded South Korea.[2] Less known, particularly in the West, is that the DPRK maintains that in the early morning hours of June 25, "The south Korean puppet army, under the direct command of the 'AMAG' [American Military Advisory Group], launched an armed invasion all along the 38th parallel on a preconceived war plan."[3] That each side has blamed the other for the onset of the Korean War, and that there is arguably no scholarly or political consensus on this matter, is far less important than stressing that the Cold War created fierce animosity between the advocates of capitalism and communism. It was this fundamental problem that led to the heightened military environment on the Korean Peninsula and the readiness to use force on both sides. This readiness inevitably resulted in a war that caused millions of deaths, both combat and civilian. Also important to understand is that the armistice agreement that ended the actual fighting made clear that Cold War politics created barriers so high that a permanent peace treaty was then not possible.[4] Without a permanent peace treaty, the

Korean Peninsula has technically been in a state of war for more than a half a century, and during this time the United States and the DPRK have remained – quite often bitter – adversaries.

Japan's annexation of the Korean Peninsula by its imperial forces from 1910 to 1945 left permanent scars on South and North Korea, causing both countries to harbor strong resentment toward the Japanese. Formally established in 1953, South Korea's security alliance with the United States, though not the political equivalent of the US–Japan military arrangement,[5] eventually made it easier for some tolerable amount of amity to exist between Tokyo and Seoul, with normalized relations taking place between them midway through the 1960s. That Tokyo and Pyongyang maintained opposite political allegiances during the Cold War ensured that a condition of mutually enmity prevailed in Japan and North Korea.

The end of the Cold War and the dissolution of the Soviet Union and the Eastern Bloc created serious economic problems for the DPRK.[6] Exacerbating North Korea's economic problems, severe flooding and drought crippled the country during the 1990s and led to widespread starvation and loss of life. Feeling threatened because of the collapse of the Soviet Union, which provided both economic and military assistance to North Korea,[7] Pyongyang became increasingly concerned about the security of the DPRK. The first North Korean nuclear crisis during the early 1990s brought Pyongyang and Washington into a bitter dispute. The DPRK's plutonium production and threatened withdrawal from the Nuclear Nonproliferation Treaty in 1993 noticeably heightened problems existing between Washington and Pyongyang. However, these problems abated somewhat when they signed the Agreed Framework in October 1994, the bilateral accord that froze five of North Korea's plutonium-related production facilities, four at Yongbyon and one at Taechon.[8]

Still, all was not well. In August 1998, the DPRK, without giving prior notification, launched a rocket, a Taepodong-1, which had a longer range than the Rodong missile that it launched in 1993. Although Pyongyang stated that it had launched an artificial satellite, the *Kwangmyŏngsŏng-1*, because the rocket flew over Japanese territory, bilateral relations between Japan and the DPRK were adversely affected.

By the end of the Clinton administration's second term in office, relations between Washington and Pyongyang had improved somewhat. Identified by the US State Department in 1983 and again in 1988 as a country sponsoring terrorism, Pyongyang wanted very much for the DPRK to be removed from this list by the Clinton administration.[9] In early October 2000, Washington and Pyongyang issued a joint statement on global terrorism. The Clinton administration's position in this document was that "as the DPRK satisfactorily addresses the requirements of U.S. law, the U.S. will work in cooperation with the DPRK with the aim of removing the DPRK from the list of state sponsors of terrorism."[10] Less than a week after this, the United States and the DPRK agreed to the Joint Communiqué, which stipulated that both countries will "work to remove mistrust, build mutual confidence, and maintain an atmosphere in which they can deal constructively with issues of central concern."[11] Later in the month, Secretary of State Madeleine Albright made an unprecedented trip to the DPRK.

In the meantime, Japanese conservatives, many of whom were nationalists, were ratcheting up the abduction issue in Japan. In the 1970s and 1980s, North Korean agents abducted a small number of Japanese nationals, flagitious acts intended to gain knowledge about Japanese ways and to learn the Japanese language so that the DPRK could gain some political advantage during the turbulent times that characterized the Cold War. For a number of years, Pyongyang repeatedly denied the DPRK's involvement in the abductions, claiming that it knew nothing about them. Pyongyang was much more concerned with the large number of deaths and the widespread destruction, plundering and human rights violations, including the use of Korean "comfort women" or *juugun ianfu*, as the Japanese called them, perpetrated by Japan during its imperial colonization of the Korean Peninsula.

Largely ignoring these concerns, Japanese nationalists and their conservative sympathizers continued to press the abduction issue. By 2000, with the help of the Japanese media, which increasingly sensationalized the kidnappings, the abduction issue was Japan's major foreign policy concern with respect to North Korea, noticeably surpassing both the missile and nuclear issues. After North Korean leader Kim Jong Il admitted to Prime Minister Junichiro Koizumi during their summit in September 2002 that unauthorized DPRK agents – said by Pyongyang to be "people in special organizations [who] by themselves kidnapped the Japanese [because] they believed that there was no problem kidnapping people from an enemy state"[12] – were responsible for kidnapping Japanese nationals, things changed. Japan's Cabinet Office surveys showed that a very big majority of Japanese respondents indicated that they were concerned about the abduction issue, more so than the nuclear and missile issues.

Before the abduction issue made its way to the top of the Japanese foreign policy agenda, Tokyo had embarked on a course to make Japan a "normal country," or *futsu kokka*, in the mid 1990s. Having Japan become a normal country would free it from the restraints of its pacifist constitution, permit involvement in international security, legitimate its growing military power, including its strengthened security alliance with the United States, and make easier the efforts to employ ancillary actions, such as the imposition of economic sanctions. The strengthened US–Japan security alliance that started to take shape in 1996 created additional worries in North Korea.[13] Already very concerned about the overwhelming military power of the United States, Pyongyang increasingly railed at what it saw as Japan's intention to launch a "reinvasion" of Korea.

In the mid 1990s, shortly after Tokyo began working to make Japan a normal country, the DPRK launched *songun*, its military first policy. Coming in the wake of the first North Korean nuclear crisis, Pyongyang fully embraced *songun*, despite the DPRK coming on very hard economic times, including famine that led to many deaths between 1995–2000.[14]

Promoted mainly by nationalists and their conservative sympathizers, Japan's quest to become a normal country and all that this entails eventually dovetailed with the abduction issue, something that has been ignored by some analysts who have simply connected the kidnapping problem to the strengthening of the US–Japan security alliance.[15] The convergence of the abduction issue with efforts to become a normal state gave Japanese nationalists and their sympathizers the opportunity to identify North Korea as a real and impending threat to Japan's national security, which they took advantage of as best they could,[16] especially since they could also point to the DPRK missile issue and emerging new nuclear crisis. After getting over the initial reservations that missile defense violated Japan's pacifist constitution, many Japanese policymakers began to accept the importance of increasing the country's involvement with the United States in building a missile defense system.

The end of the Cold War prompted Tokyo and Pyongyang to hold several rounds of normalization talks. Because they remained far too apart with respect to their differences, these talks were unsuccessful.

Recent imbroglios

The second North Korean nuclear crisis broke out in October 2002, with US claims that North Korea was concealing a uranium-enrichment program to build nuclear weapons, which for years Pyongyang repeatedly said did not exist. With the support of traditional conservative hawks, the neoconservatives within George W. Bush's first administration succeeded in getting the president to accept a hard-line North Korean policy.[17] Pyongyang considered this policy very hostile to its national interests, particularly since it carried with it the possibility of a preemptive, perhaps even a nuclear, attack on the DPRK. Guided by the suppositions of the neoconservatives and hardliners, the Bush administration's North Korean policy literally went nowhere for years. Because the political tides had changed by late 2006, the Bush administration adopted a relatively conciliatory North Korean policy that eventually was able to make some progress toward the goal of resolving the North Korean nuclear issue – at least until a major verification impasse emerged in the second half of 2008. Through all of this and to the present, the level of military preparation and readiness has remained high for the United States, Japan and North and South Korea.

By the fall of 2002, US–DPRK relations were visibly bad and remained this way for several years. As a result, the six-party talks between the United States, the two Koreas, Japan, China and Russia, which had been created in the summer of 2003 to resolve the North Korean nuclear problem, made little progress, at best, for some time. During the second half of 2006, Pyongyang authorized a series of missile tests and eventually conducted its first underground nuclear test.[18]

Tokyo came to embrace fully the US hard-line policy, and the failure to make significant progress on the abduction issue combined inauspiciously with Pyongyang's determination to develop *songun* to worsen Japan–North Korean relations.

Despite two visits by Prime Minister Koizumi to the DPRK, the first in 2002, which yielded the promising Pyongyang Declaration, and the second in 2004, Japan–North Korean relations continued to deteriorate. Poor bilateral relations brought a new wave of troubles to some *zainichi* Koreans, the name that applies to all Koreans who have resided in Japan for many years. While *zainichi* Koreans have long experienced discrimination in Japan, those that view the DPRK as their homeland, the *zainichi chōsenjin* have also had to contend with the repercussions of giving their political allegiance to the North.

The Bush Administration's change to a conciliatory policy offered an olive branch to Pyongyang. The DPRK would be removed from the US list of states sponsoring terrorism if it would give an account of its nuclear programs and disable its nuclear facilities. This was in addition to the assistance package that the participants of the six-party talks, with the exception of Japan, extended to the DPRK in exchange for denuclearization in February 2007. However, the transition by the Bush administration to a more DPRK conciliatory policy came too late to repair the growing animosity that existed between Japan and North Korea.

Tokyo insisted that, because Pyongyang had not attempted to make progress on the abduction issue, this unequivocally made North Korea a terrorist state. Tokyo's position was analogous to that of the US hawks and neoconservatives, who not only had consistently pushed for a hard-line North Korean policy but also maintained that the DPRK remain listed as a terrorist state. Although Tokyo did not want the Bush administration to remove the DPRK from the US list of states sponsoring terrorism, it was the resurgence of US hardliners, who took charge of verifying the DPRK's nuclear capabilities in July 2008, that precipitated a temporary impasse in the multilateral process designed to resolve the North Korean nuclear issue.

Appearing concerned about the DPRK's international image, which included wanting to convince the Bush administration that the de-listing process should go forward, Pyongyang agreed to bilateral meetings with Tokyo in June and August 2008. During these talks, Pyongyang agreed – not for the first time – to a reinvestigation of the abduction issue. Japan, for its part, agreed to ease up somewhat on the sanctions that it had imposed on North Korea once there was evidence that Pyongyang had begun the reinvestigation. Neither of these things happened.

In September 2008, Tokyo called Pyongyang's announcement, which was that it was delaying the reinvestigation to see who would replace moderate Prime Minister Yasuo Fukuda, "extremely disappointing and deplorable."[19] At about this same time, DPRK Vice-Minister of Foreign Affairs Pak Kil Yon called Japan a "war criminal state that beautifies the history of aggression and massacre of millions of innocent peoples in Korea and other Asian countries."[20]

Pyongyang's determination to be removed from the US list of states sponsoring terrorism finally paid off. In fall 2008, the Bush administration suddenly announced that it had de-listed North Korea. Responding to the de-listing, Pyongyang indicated that it would resume disablement activities at Yongbyon and permit inspectors from the United States and the International Atomic Energy Agency to continue their work in the DPRK, all of which had stopped during the impasse.[21]

Although Japan's new Prime Minister Taro Aso initially tried to minimize the Bush administration's perfunctory notification gesture to Tokyo just prior to the de-listing of North Korea, this quickly changed. Within days of the US announcement, Aso stressed Tokyo's "dissatisfaction" with Washington for de-listing North Korea. Aso also emphasized his government would "continue to demand" that Pyongyang promptly start the "promised reinvestigations" of the abduction issue and restated Japan's position "not to join economic and energy assistance under the six-party framework."[22]

In early 2009, the new Obama administration made clear that it wanted to retain the six-party framework to resolve the North Korean nuclear issue, even though some senior officials had been openly critical of the approach that the Bush White House had taken toward the DPRK. Pyongyang had expected the Obama administration to be open to direct dialogue and was dissatisfied when this did not materialize right away. Displeased with the Obama administration and with the reaction of the UN Security Council to its demonstration of *songun*-based activities, Pyongyang, after its rocket launch in April 2009, eventually detonated a second nuclear device late in the spring of 2009.

As Pyongyang eventually saw it, the Obama administration's DPRK policy was no less hostile than that of its predecessor. Making matters worse, the conservative governments in Tokyo and Seoul had gotten the Obama administration's ear and were thus able to exert some influence on Washington's policymaking with respect to the DPRK.

By early 2010, Pyongyang on several occasions proposed replacing the 1953 armistice agreement with a peace treaty. Pyongyang stated that one option would be to hold discussions for a peace accord within the "framework of the six-party talks,"[23] which had not taken place since December 2008 when the participants failed to agree on a verification protocol. The Obama administration disregarded Pyongyang's proposals for a peace treaty, deciding instead to remain focused on denuclearization before anything else could occur, a position it continued to maintain with the support of its Japanese and South Korean allies.

A note on methodology

This book treats the beliefs and sentiments of government officials largely (but not exclusively) in the United States, Japan and the DPRK as the basis of policymaking. It demonstrates that these countries' respective security interests are not only paramount to policymakers in each state but also that these interests are often conflicting and, especially between the DPRK and the United States, along with its allies in Japan and more recently South Korea, they are confrontational. At the same time, this work does not ignore the influence that political organizations outside of government have on policymaking processes.

The methodological approach frequently employed in this book uses an empirical spotlight to highlight the myriad nuances and the manifest changes of policymaking, which, because it has too often been based on policymakers' ideological predispositions and credulous political beliefs, has too many times led to irrational, or rationally dubious, responses to prevailing conditions. Thus, the methodological approach employed in this book often shows empirically how policymaking processes develop from policymakers' political convictions, as well as others determined to influence policy, or sometimes as in the case of the DPRK in the words of the official state apparatus that directly reflects the positions of those making policy. The problem is that in too many instances policymakers and others rely too much on what they believe, somewhat analogous to religious doctrinaires, rather than on a full and objective examination of the available facts and then proceeding rationally to allow their reasoned beliefs and judgments to form and execute policy.

Perhaps the best example of this is the Bush administration's North Korean policy and Pyongyang's reaction to it. The Bush administration's North Korean policy was in the formative stage prior to the president's and his top advisors' decision to allege publicly that the DPRK was maintaining a clandestine uranium-enrichment program to build nuclear weapons.[24] The neoconservatives and hardliners that populated the Bush Administration's first term insisted that the irredeemably roguish North Korean regime led by Kim Jong Il could not be trusted and that it was determined to build nuclear weapons.[25] Early on, Bush branded North Korea part of an "axis of evil," which, like others of this nefarious ilk, is determined "to threaten the peace of the world." Soon thereafter, Bush added a personal touch by calling Kim a "pygmy" in October 2002 and, though he had never met or talked to the DPRK's Dear Leader, Bush proclaimed a few months before this, "I loathe Kim Jong-il."

Reactions from the DPRK were emotive as well. Not to be outdone, Pyongyang got into the name-calling game early. Reacting to the appointment of hardliner John Bolton to the position of Undersecretary of State for Arms Control and International Security and to his "bellicose and provocative remarks" to a Senate committee, Pyongyang stated that this left no doubt that the Bush administration has the "criminal aim" to destabilize the Korean Peninsula and the Asia-Pacific region.[26] Shortly after the onset of the second North Korean nuclear crisis, the DPRK called Bush "an incompetent and rude president who is senseless and ignorant," even about basic diplomacy.[27]

In early February 2003, Pyongyang called Bush a "political imbecile" and a "despicable swindler."[28]

Attempting to counter what they repeatedly called the US' "hostile policy towards the DPRK," Kim Jong Il and his policy advisers who supported demonstrating a hard-line response helped the Bush administration fulfill the prophecy that the 1994 Agreed Framework between Washington and Pyongyang was a dead deal. In short, rather than maintain the freeze, Pyongyang advanced its *juche*-based *songun* policy, which included a nuclear-weapons program.

Hardly any of these moves by Pyongyang and Washington can be categorized as the elements or basis of objective, rational policymaking. Thus, in October 2006 one of the worst possible scenarios became a reality: the DPRK detonated its first *plutonium*-based nuclear device; less than three years later, it performed a second underground nuclear test.

Japan's obsession with the abduction issue and the DPRK's reaction to it illustrates still another case of policymaking that is not replete with objectivity and rationality. Contrary to the prediction that the public would not rally around a new policy issue associated with the DPRK,[29] the abduction issue, strongly backed by a sympathetic public, became and remained Japan's principal foreign policy concern with North Korea, rather than its nuclear weapons program. Typical of Japanese hardliners, Shigeru Ishiba, the hawkish head of the Japanese Defense Agency, stated in October 2002 that because of the abduction issue, the "Japanese people have come to realize that North Korea is a horrible terrorist state."[30] For its part, Pyongyang – referring to the Kim–Koizumi summit in 2002 – has repeatedly insisted that the abduction issue "has already been resolved" and has commonly stated that Japan – pointing to its history of militarism and imperialism – is a "criminal state." In short, mutual sentiments of animosity and distrust have precluded Tokyo and Pyongyang from rationality and objectively approaching a solution to the abduction issue, policy postures that have also prevented the resolution of other bilateral problems.

This book whenever possible makes frequent use of primary-source data, including interviews and meetings. The regular use of primary-source data is intended to capture the evolution and regression of policymaking, mainly in Washington, Tokyo and Pyongyang and, more recently, in Seoul, showing how policymakers act and react to events and issues that they perceive relate to the security interests and objectives of their respective countries. Methodologically speaking, this is critically important, since this approach permits the reader to see unequivocally the often self-serving development of security policies that emanate from policymakers' sentiments, and that too many times have led to regional instability in Northeast Asia.

Purpose and arrangement of the book

This book differs from others that have analyzed the most recent North Korean nuclear and related security issues of concern to several governments with interests in Northeast Asia.[31] Thus, this book examines the security-based approaches of Washington, Tokyo, Pyongyang, to a lesser degree Seoul, and even Beijing and Moscow, and shows that those of the United States, Japan, North Korea and more recently South Korea continue to foster regional instability, mainly because their policies remain ineffective in two important ways. First, the enduring and often overbearing political commitment of these governments to their national and security interests has precluded the solution of serious problems. Second, the United States, Japan and North Korea have typically demonstrated the predilection to marginalize the importance of rapprochement. This is also true of South Korea, especially beginning in 2008 when Lee Myung-bak became president and quickly abandoned the diplomatic engagement policies of the two previous administrations – Kim Dae-jung, known for his "sunshine policy,"[32] and Roh Moo-hyun. In other words, these countries have been far more willing to let military and related power strategies color the formation and implementation of their policies, not too dissimilar from the Cold War.

Chapter 2 explains the ideological basis of the DPRK's policymaking – specifically *juche* and *songun* – and demonstrates that the current security problems and threats perceived by Pyongyang have given it reason to defend the advancement of *songun* and its possession of nuclear weapons. Viewing the protection of the DPRK's sovereignty as being of utmost importance, Pyongyang maintains that it is perfectly justifiable to advance its military capabilities to protect "the country from the U.S. imperialists' reckless moves for provoking a new war."[33]

Chapter 3 shows that while Japan's postwar political culture emphasized the importance of retaining the war-renouncing constitutional clause – Article 9, the basis of the country's anti-militarism – it has been slowly but steadily moving off of this pacifist trajectory, working hard to become a normal country. Along with the influence of Japanese nationalists and their conservative sympathizers on the policymaking process, the security interests and concerns of the United States and those of the DPRK have been pushing Japan in the direction of remilitarization.

Part of the justification for the existence of the US–Japan security alliance is because Washington and Tokyo continue to view North Korea as a threat to regional stability. Chapter 4 examines the recent developments in US and Japanese policies with respect to North Korea. When the second DPRK nuclear crisis materialized during the fall of 2002, Washington and Tokyo were at least within a few pages of each other with respect to how to handle Pyongyang. However, as Chapter 4 shows, Washington's and Tokyo's policies, after becoming largely indistinguishable, became somewhat divergent as security interests shifted – in the United States, because of changes in the Bush Administration's DPRK policy, which included the removal of North Korea from the State Department's list of countries sponsoring terrorism, and in Japan because of the abduction issue. Chapter 4 also analyzes the early months of the Obama's administration's policy toward North Korea.

Chapter 5 examines the problems that *zainichi chōsenjin* or Chongryon Koreans have had to contend with in Japan. That Japan and North Korea have been unable to establish normal diplomatic relations has made life difficult for their association, known as Chongryon, as well as for Chongryon Koreans. While historical issues are discussed, Chapter 5 focuses mainly on the problems Chongryon and Chongryon Koreans have faced in recent years because of the noticeable deterioration in Japanese–North Korean relations.

Chapter 6 analyzes several different reasons why Japan and the DPRK have been unable to improve their bilateral relationship, ultimately leaving serious problems unresolved. In Japan, partisan politics has contributed to the poor relations it has with North Korea. Making this matter worse, Pyongyang has often succumbed to the policy prescriptions of hardliners in the DPRK. Together, partisan politics in Japan and the influence of hardliners in the DPRK have militated against the improvement of bilateral relations. Moreover, Japan's instinctual-like readiness to support US security initiatives, even though Tokyo's interests have not always been the same as Washington's, has further complicated the improvement of Japanese–North Koran relations.

Finally, after making some concluding remarks, Chapter 7 examines the important matter of rapprochement between the United States and North Korea and between the latter and Japan. It argues that new trust-building policy approaches are necessary, most especially a permanent peace treaty to end the Korean War, to enable the United States, Japan and the DPRK, as well as South Korea, to lay the groundwork for peaceful co-existence.

Notes

1 I. F. Stone, *The Hidden History of the Korean War, 1950–1951* (Boston: Little, Brown, 1988), esp. p. 43; Bruce Cumings, *The Origins of the Korean War: The Roaring of the Cataract*, vol. 2. (Princeton, NJ: Princeton University Press, 1990), pp. 568–621; Channing Liem, *The Korean War (6.25, 1950 – 7.27, 1953) – An Unanswered Question* (Pyongyang: Foreign Languages Publishing House, 1993), reprinted in *The People's Korea*, 1998, www1.korea-np.co.jp/pk/054th_issue/koreanwar/98080502.htm (accessed on April 5, 2011).

2 William Stueck, *The Korean War: An International History* (Princeton, NJ: Princeton University Press, 1995), pp. 10–13; Dean Acheson, *The Strategy of Freedom*, speech to the United Council of Churches, Cleveland, Ohio, delivered by radio broadcast from the Secretary of State's office in Washington, DC, November 29, 1950; Richard Whelan, *Drawing the Line: The Korean War, 1950–1953* (Boston: Little, Brown and Company, 1990), pp. 100–01.

3 Ho Jong Ho, Kang Sok Hui and Pak Thae Ho, *The US Imperialists Started the Korean War* (Pyongyang: Foreign Languages Publications House, 1993), p. 178.

4 Anthony DiFilippo, "The Peace Deal Obama Should Make: Toward a U.S.–North Korea Peace Treaty," 7-4-10, *Asia-Pacific Journal*, February 15, 2010.

5 Cheon Seongwhun, "North Korea and the ROK-U.S Security Alliance," *Armed Forces & Society*, vol. 34, no. 1, October 2007, pp. 5–28.

6 Korea Development Institute, *North Korean Economy from the Perspective of FRG* (Federal Republic of Germany), Seoul, 2004.

7 Don Oberdorfer, *The Two Koreas: A Contemporary History* (Addison-Wesley, Reading, MA, 1997), pp. 11, 153–60.

8 United States General Accounting Office, *Nuclear Nonproliferation: Difficulties in Accomplishing IAEA's [International Atomic Energy Agency] Activities in North Korea* (Washington, DC: General Accounting Office), July 1998; Leon Sigal, *Disarming Strangers: Nuclear Diplomacy with North Korea* (Princeton, NJ: Princeton University Press, 1998); Joel Wit, Daniel Poneman and Robert Gallucci, *Going Critical: The First North Korean Nuclear Crisis* (Washington, DC: Brookings Institution Press, 2004).

9 Anthony DiFilippo, "North Korea as a State Sponsor of Terrorism: Views from Tokyo and Pyongyang," *International Journal of Korean Unification Studies*, vol. 17, no. 1, 2008, pp. 1–40.

10 US Department of State, *Joint U.S.-DPRK Statement on International Terrorism*, Washington, DC, October 6, 2000, http://statelists.state.gov/scripts/wa.exe?A2=ind0010b&L=uskorea-kr&P=74 (accessed March 25, 2011).

11 US Department of State, *U.S.-DPRK Joint Communiqué*, Washington, DC, October 12, 2000, http://usinfo.org/wf-archive/2000/001012/epf407.htm (accessed March 25, 2011).

12 Author meeting with researcher in the DPRK Foreign Ministry specializing in Japanese issues, Pyongyang, January 8, 2009.

13 Anthony DiFilippo, *The Challenges of the U.S.-Japan Military Arrangement: Competing Security Transitions in a Changing International Environment* (Armonk, NY: M.E. Sharpe, 2002).

14 Between 600,000 and 1 million deaths were likely to have resulted from famine in North Korea. See Daniel Goodkind and Loraine West, "The North Korean Famine and Its Demographic Impact," *Population & Development Review*, vol. 27, no. 2, June 2001, pp. 219–38.

15 For example, see Kenneth Pyle, *Japan Rising: The Resurgence of Japanese Power and Purpose* (New York: Public Affairs, 2007), p. 297.

16 Some scholars in South Korea also recognize that Japanese conservatives have used Japan's problems with North Korea to bolster their political agenda. See Han Chung Sook, "Il Bon kwa 6 Cha Hoe Dam" ("Japan and the 6-party Talks"), *Hankyoreh*, October 23, 2009.

17 Jacob Heilbrunn, *They Knew They Were Right: The Rise of the Neocons* (New York: Doubleday, 2008), pp. 228–80; J. Peter Scoblic, *Us vs. Them: How a Half Century of Conservatism Has Undermined American Security* (New York: Viking, 2008), pp. 235–45.

18 From October 2002 until October 2006, a North Korean nuclear crisis existed. After Pyongyang detonated a nuclear device, the nuclear crisis became simply the nuclear issue. The crisis was effectively over, since US policy neither prevented North Korea from demonstrating its nuclear weapons capability nor lead to its disarmament. Whether or not Washington recognizes the DPRK as a nuclear weapons state is irrelevant. That the DPRK has demonstrated its nuclear weapons capability and that it can build nuclear weapons makes this an issue of grave international concern, just like it is for any other nuclear weapons state, among them India, Pakistan and Israel, all of which, like North Korea, are not parties to the Nuclear Nonproliferation Treaty.

19 Government of Japan, Headquarters for the Abduction Issue, *Newsletter (No.2) from the Headquarters for the Abduction Issue*, Tokyo, September 30, 2008.

20 *Statement by H.E. Pak Kil Yon, Vice-Minister of Foreign Affairs, Chairman of the Delegation of the Democratic People's Republic of Korea*, General Debate, Sixty-third Session of the United Nations General Assembly, New York, September 27, 2008.

21 "Foreign Ministry Spokesman on DPRK's Will to Cooperate in Verification of Objects of Nuclear Disarmament," *Korean Central News Agency*, October 12, 2008.

22 "Aso Expresses 'Dissatisfaction' over U.S. De-listing of N. Korea," *Kyodo News*, October 14, 2008.
23 "DPRK Proposes to Start Peace Talks," *Korean Central News Agency*, January 11, 2010.
24 Anthony DiFilippo, "Security Trials, Nuclear Tribulations and Rapprochement in Japan-North Korean Relations," *The Journal of Pacific Asia*, vol. 11, 2004, pp. 7–31.
25 Anthony DiFilippo, "U.S. Policy and the Nuclear Weapons Ambitions of the 'Axis of Evil' Countries," *New Political Science*, vol. 28, no 1, March 2006, pp. 101–23.
26 "KCNA and the Appointment of New U.S. Deputy Secretary of State," *Korean Central News Agency*, April 3, 2001.
27 "Bush's Remark Assailed," *Korean Central News Agency*, October 29, 2002.
28 "Bush's Anti-DPRK Vituperation under Fire," *Korean Central News Agency*, February 7, 2003.
29 Tsuneo Akaha, "Japan's Policy Toward North Korea: Interests and Options," in *The Future of North Korea*, ed. Tsuneo Akaha (London: Routledge, 2002), p. 87.
30 "Ishiba Says Japanese View N. Korea as Terrorists State," *Kyodo News*, October 11, 2002.
31 Mike Chinoy, *Meltdown: The Inside Story of the North Korean Nuclear Crisis* (New York: St. Martin's Press, 2008); Charles Pritchard, *Failed Diplomacy: The Tragic Story of How North Korea Got the Bomb* (Washington, DC: The Brookings Institution, 2007); Yoichi Funabashi, *The Peninsula Question: A Chronicle of the Second North Korean Nuclear Crisis* (Washington, DC: Brookings Institution Press, 2007); Victor Cha and David Kang, *Nuclear North Korea: A Debate on Engagement Strategies* (New York: Columbia University Press, 2003).
32 Chae Kyung-suk, "The Future of the Sunshine Policy: Strategies for Survival," *East Asian Review*, vol. 14, no. 4, Winter 2002, pp. 3–17.
33 "U.S. Unabashed Design for Aggression Under Fire," *Korean Central News Agency*, March 24, 2009.

2 Nuclear armed to the teeth

This chapter explains how Pyongyang came to the conclusion that powerfully increasing its military capabilities, specifically by ultimately acquiring and demonstrating its nuclear weapons capability, was the best choice for the survival of the Democratic People's Republic of Korea (DPRK). To provide a solid foundation to the explanation, this chapter examines the DPRK's *juche* idea and the *songun* policy. After a brief discussion of some important security-related issues, this chapter also shows the connection of *juche* and *songun* to the first and second DPRK nuclear crisis and provides some perspective to Pyongyang's relations with Washington and Tokyo.

The familiar, the not so familiar and the overlooked

One of the most common images of North Korea in Japan and in the United States – and for that matter, throughout much of the world – is that it is a highly militarized society. While North Korea has an active military force that exceeds one million troops, DPRK defense spending is considerably less than it is in the United States and Japan.

In 2006, military expenditures by the United States, the world's top spender by far, amounted to $522 billion.[1] In this same year, Japan ranked sixth in the world, spending $41.1 billion on defense.[2] Although the Central Intelligence Agency (CIA) no longer publishes information on North Korea's military spending, its data indicate that the DPRK spent approximately $5.2 billion in 2002, which would rank it about twenty-fourth or so in the world.[3]

According to the US State Department, the DPRK spends about 25 percent of its gross domestic product (GDP) on the military.[4] Using the CIA's estimate of the DPRK's GDP for 2008, this would put North Korea's military spending at about $6.55 billion for that year.[5] With an estimated population, according to the CIA, of 23.5 million people in 2008, per capita military spending in the DPRK therefore would be about $279. In contrast, US per capita military spending came to $1,799 in 2007 and in Japan it was $339.[6] For sure, the DPRK's struggling economy elevates the percentage of military spending to GDP. But the available data, as imperfect as it is, certainly does not make the DPRK more militarized than the United States and Japan.

The demise of the Soviet Union, in particular, and the end of its subsidies to the DPRK, followed by floods, drought and famine during the mid 1990s were devastating to the North Korean economy and society.[7] Owing especially to the devastation caused by the floods and famine, many North Koreans died. The argument that by making the right policy decisions Pyongyang could have averted the food crisis,[8] despite facing serious external problems and devastating floods and drought, is based on a politically biased assumption, which is simplistic and incapable of being proven empirically. No government is immune from making bad decisions. But more importantly, there is just no way to determine with absolute certainty exactly what "right" decisions are or how many of these Pyongyang would have had to make to offset major economic disruptions – the demise of the Eastern Bloc and the Soviet Union and cataclysmic flooding and drought – from turning into a famine. Moreover, the DPRK long had to contend with the imposition of economic sanctions by the United States, which along with Japan has opposed North Korean membership in international financial institutions, such as the International Monetary Fund, the World Bank and the Asian Development Bank.[9] Perennially concerned about compromising the sovereignty of the DPRK, Pyongyang's judgments related to the famine should not be viewed as right or wrong from a Western perspective, but rather as political decisions made to sustain the nation's socialist revolution.

It has been commonly maintained that international food aid to the DPRK did not reach the starving North Korean population,[10] but rather that it had been diverted by public and party officials and by the military to its personnel.[11] However, there is compelling evidence to show that the diversion of food resources was not a *fait accompli*. In consultation with the North Korean government, which initially had been reluctant to cooperate with foreign organizations, nutritional surveys conducted by the World Food Program, the European Union and the United Nations Children's Fund in 1998 and then again in 2002 showed that malnutrition had very noticeably declined for children under the age of seven.[12]

Songun (military first)

This, however, did not mean that Pyongyang has not prioritized the military. The DPRK maintains that *songun* "is based on the viewpoint that military strength plays a leading role in the struggle for independence against imperialism. It, therefore, puts up military affairs as the concern of paramount importance in state administration and gives topmost attention to the building of military preparation."[13] This became especially true since 2002 with the onset of the second DPRK nuclear crisis.

Songun is widely accepted by North Koreans as indispensable to the preservation of the DPRK. Similar to South Korea, military service is obligatory for North Koreans once they reach the age of 17.[14] A North Korean college student points out that it is the "obligation of every citizen of the Republic, who has grown under the state care [free education and health care], to defend the country." This college student emphasizes that his father has always said, "he cannot lay down the weapon as long as there exists the enemy with a covetous ambition of conquering our country."[15]

In the mid 1990s, when Kim Jong Il, affectionately known as the Dear Leader, came to power, *songun* became inextricably linked with the DPRK's evolving *juche* (self-reliance), the ideology that had been developed and popularized during the time when his father the Great Leader and eternal president, Kim Il Sung, held power. However, the North Koreans maintain that although the official establishment of *songun* occurred under the leadership of Kim Jong Il, it originated during the 1930s when Kim Il Sung was in Manchuria fighting the Japanese.[16] Not too long after the Great Leader's death in 1994 and the consolidation of political power into the hands of his son Kim Jong Il, the younger Kim drew on his relationship with the military to reconfigure *juche,* which is considered a man-centered socialist ideology. Even before his father's death, Kim Jong Il had acquired a top position in the restructured National Defense Council and had secured control of the military. The younger Kim's implementation of *songun* prompted the diminution of the Korean Workers' Party's influence in state affairs and the ascendancy of *songun*, which soon became the core component of preserving North Korean socialism.[17] In a speech given in January 2003 to top officials of the Central Committee of the Workers' Party, Kim Jong Il, moving away from a central precept of Marxism, stated "our Party has given prominence to the People's Army over the working class."[18] However, at least one analyst contends that North Korea's claim that *songun* has taken the place of workers and even the communist party is exaggerated.[19]

Pyongyang had to face the fact that the DPRK's military and economic relationship with the Soviet Union had indeed ended after the Cold War. After some of the dust had settled in North Korea from the first nuclear crisis in the early 1990s, Pyongyang came to believe that security threats from the hegemonic policy practiced by the United States left it with only one rational choice: to strengthen the DPRK's military capabilities. Less than three months after Pyongyang and Washington signed the Agreed Framework in October 1994, the accord that effectively resolved the first North Korean nuclear crisis, Kim Jong Il took what he believed was a significant step in the direction of helping to guarantee the security of his country.

Begun in earnest on January 1, 1995 when Kim visited the Takabasol military facility, *songun* places the army in the vanguard to defend the DPRK's continuing socialist revolution and the nation's sovereignty mainly against American imperialism, supposedly necessary given the deterioration in US–North Korean relations.[20] Based on the *juche* principle of self-reliance and independence, *songun* predisposes the DPRK to deal with its problems, especially with the United States but also with Japan and South Korea, by emphasizing the need for military preparedness. Today, a common sentiment in North Korea is that the hostile policy of the United States, as one prominent North Korean social scientist stated, "made the DPRK develop nuclear weapons." In other words, "political events in the DPRK are greatly related to U.S. policy."[21]

Thus, Pyongyang believes that the purpose of *songun* is "to solve all the problems arising in the revolution and construction [of the country] on the principle of giving a preference to the military affairs." This means that the DPRK works "to strengthen the army as an invincible force so that it can frustrate any aggressive moves of the imperialists." It also means, according to policymakers in Pyongyang, that because of *songun* "today the Korean people are vigorously building a great prosperous powerful nation."[22]

A little over a year after Kim officially inaugurated the DPRK's *songun* policy, Washington and Tokyo began what became a series of steps to strengthen the US–Japan security alliance. Created during the early years of the Cold War to forestall the aggressiveness of the Soviet Union and to contain the communist threat, the US–Japan military alliance, rather than end with the demise of the Soviet Union, was placed on a course that has led to it being continuously strengthened by officials in Washington and Tokyo.[23]

Although Washington would have preferred the demise or implosion of Kim Jong Il's government, this has not happened. The strengthened influence of the hardliners in the DPRK, at least for a time, was a direct result of what they viewed as the policy of the Bush administration to eliminate the government of Kim Jong Il,[24] which they also believed Tokyo fully supported. Reflecting the ideological sentiment attached to *songun*, DPRK Defense Minister Kim Il Chol stated in early August 2006, "Comrades, we can live without candles, but we can't live without bullets."[25] Shortly after this Kim Yong Chun, head of the General Staff of the Korean People's Army, stated that it is imperative that North Korea closely observe the actions of the United States "and its followers including Japan." Kim went on to emphasize that we must "do our utmost to bolster our self-defensive war deterrent, unhindered by anything, tightly holding the revolutionary banner of Songun."[26]

The DPRK maintains that today *songun* is beneficial for Koreans everywhere, since it functions as "an invincible shield which reliably safeguards the peace on the Korean Peninsula and the security of the nation and a powerful driving force" that "vigorously accelerates the advance of an era of independent reunification."[27] In September 2008, Kim Jong Il explained in detail the purpose of *songun*. Writing that the formal institution of *songun* resulted from the incessant threats to the nation's sovereignty caused by "US-led imperialist reactionaries," Kim stresses that his country has "frustrated all the challenges of the imperialists reactionaries and all their schemes to isolate and stifle [the DPRK], and demonstrated its invincible military might to the world." According to Kim, *songun* is directly responsible for preventing the invasion of the DPRK by the imperialist forces and that it must be continuously strengthened to provide for the security of the DPRK, making it the "decisive military guarantee for building a great prosperous and powerful socialist country." Because Pyongyang also sees *songun* as a policy that supports national reunification, Kim Jong Il attributes much credit to it for bringing about the historic June 2000 Joint Declaration and the October 2007 Declaration between North and South Korea and argues that the "national spirit for reunifying the country independently has been raised to an unprecedented height."[28]

However, Pyongyang's relations with Seoul became noticeably acrimonious beginning in early 2008 when Lee Myung-bak became president of South Korea. Given the unresolved nuclear issue and the threat Pyongyang's perceives, mainly from the United States, the protection of the DPRK's sovereignty has become more important than the unification of the peninsula.[29] Today, *songun* reflects the unresolved problems of the Cold War between Washington, Tokyo and Seoul.

Juche foundation

Kim Il Sung's *juche* idea called for "self-defense in national defense." The elder Kim, who had fought against Japanese imperialism for years, reasoned that national security required a strong military built on revolutionary zeal. When the Korean People's Army was established in 1945, Kim Il Sung stressed the difference between the militaries of capitalist societies and his army. Couched in the principles of Marxist-Leninism, he emphasized that the militaries of capitalist societies are designed to maintain the oppression and exploitation of the working classes so that the small capitalist class can continue to reap significant economic rewards, calling the US military "the prototype of the predatory imperialist army." In contrast, Kim maintained that his army was made up of members of the working classes and peasants and that its purpose was to create a liberated and independent Korea that provided protection to the masses from the foreign imperialist threat and from internal reactionary forces.[30]

Kim Il Sung warned against becoming a victim of what he called a "pacifistic mood," stressing that it is important "to arm the entire people more adequately." He emphasized that it is necessary for every member of the society to become knowledgeable of military issues so that they can maintain "revolutionary vigilance" against the threats to the nation's security. The elder Kim maintained that the DPRK was a nonaggressive state that only wanted peace; however, it was not afraid of war and it was fully prepared to fight imperialist intervention. Kim Il Sung claimed in 1970 that the DPRK was not interested in competing with the technically sophisticated militaries of the advanced countries. Rather, he argued that the all-consuming dedication of the members of the People's Army to freedom and liberation was sufficient to defeat the enemies of the state and to ensure national security.[31]

Concerned about military modernization in South Korea, which the United States encouraged and supported, under Kim's leadership the North began a defense build-up of its own that lasted throughout the 1970s and that included the acquisition of all kinds of advanced equipment, such as tanks, aircraft, submarines and missiles.[32] Kim Il Sung believed, especially after the Korean People's Army in January 1968 captured the *Pueblo*, the "US armed spy ship" attempting to appear as an "oceanic electron ship," and shot down the American reconnaissance plane, the EC-121, in April 1969,[33] that "US imperialist maneuvers to provoke a new Korean war in Korea have already reached an advanced stage. They have made full preparations in South Korea for another war, committing military provocations more openly against the Democratic People's Republic of Korea."[34] Washington's posturing in the South and the strengthening of Seoul's military with US support were only part of what worried Kim Il Sung, who maintained in 1970 that, "Under the wing of the U.S. imperialists, the Japanese militarists are also stepping up their renewed aggressive maneuvers against Korea."[35]

Although Kim Jong Il's *songun* became a force that drew too much of North Korea's available resources away from satisfying the core human needs of a socialist society and toward the military, Kim Il Sung's *juche* provided the ideological bedrock for this policy. Unlike any other DPRK official, Kim Jong Il could and did interpret *juche* as he saw fit. One major interpretation related to his position on Marxist-Leninism.[36] Because *juche* was constructed by the Great Leader to fit the unique historical realities of the Korean revolutionary movement, Kim Jong Il argues that its development moves beyond Marxist-Leninism. Although invaluable in the past, the younger Kim maintains that Marxist-Leninism is not completely germane to contemporary revolutionary movements. Kim Jong Il carefully separates his views from the revisionists of Marxist-Leninism, which he maintains has "historical limitations." Only the *juche* idea, which allows individuals to "develop from subordination,"[37] can move man beyond the historical constraints of Marxist-Leninism to fashion a true revolutionary movement.[38] Kim also stresses that the man-centered focus of the *juche* idea found in *chajusong* (independence or autonomy), which together with creativity and consciousness, forms the essence of man's social being. The younger Kim points out that Kim Il Sung developed the *juche* idea subsequent to his realization that in the "new era when the oppressed and humiliated masses of the people became masters of their own destiny" and that the recognition of this along with *chajusong* moves socialism "onto a higher plane" than Marxist-Leninism. Significantly, *chajusong* must be constantly defended; says Kim Jong Il, "it is an absolute requirement of man as a social being and his inalienable fundamental right."[39] However the most significant change in Kim Jong Il's treatment of Marxist-Leninism stems from his *songun* policy, which as mentioned above gives the soldier precedence over the worker. In other words, "army first, workers next."[40]

Similar to his father, Kim Jong Il connected "independence in politics," which is responsible for the creation and existence of *chajusong*, and "self-reliance in defense." Also like his father, the younger Kim emphasizes that the *juche* idea relies fundamentally on "economic self-sufficiency." Together, the three lead to the well being of the people. Integral to a self-sufficient national economy for Kim Jong Il is "technical independence," which is necessary to remedy the inevitable problems that emerge "in economic and defense construction." Kim Jong Il moves well beyond his father's position that everyone must be knowledgeable of military issues. He stresses that the DPRK must rely on technological modernization and "build its own defense industry" so that it can sustain an "unconquerable revolutionary army" that can protect the nation from "imperialist aggression."[41]

Today, the DPRK's diplomatic policy stems from the *juche* idea, which holds that "people can be liberated from Japan and the United States." Pyongyang believes that because of the threat of imperialistic war, *songun* "is the necessary policy of the DPRK."[42] Therefore, *juche* and *songun* together provide the DPRK with the ideological and policy tools needed to deal with the perceived intimidations and threats coming from the United States and Japan, as well as from South Korea.

The need for political reassessment

The end of the Cold War forced the DPRK to reassess its political situation. Pyongyang knew that, besides the economic and foreign trade problems that it had to contend with, because of the dissolution of the Eastern Bloc and the break up of the Soviet Union,[43] political conditions had drastically changed. Feelings of betrayal and isolation complicated Pyongyang's perception of its political situation. Although opposed by Pyongyang, Moscow and Beijing normalized diplomatic relations with Seoul in the early 1990s and, in 1995, Russia ended its bilateral military accord with the DPRK.[44] Even though the 1961 treaty of mutual assistance between China and North Korea had not been abrogated,[45] Pyongyang reasoned that the changes ushered in by the end of the Cold War meant that the DPRK had to assume additional independent responsibility for the nation's security.

From the United States, the DPRK wanted a peace treaty to replace the armistice agreement and the removal of American troops from South Korea. Some, however, alleged that what Pyongyang claimed to want was only a pretext concealing its real objective, which was to have the DPRK fulfill its socialist plan to invade the South and unify the peninsula.[46] If in the past Pyongyang may have been contemplating using its *juche* brand of socialism and revolutionary stratagem to force a unification of the Korean Peninsula, this certainly became a very remote possibility with the end of the Cold War. From Japan, Pyongyang wanted, as much as Tokyo did, normal diplomatic relations, particularly once it realized that Moscow was warming up to Seoul.[47]

Although Pyongyang recognized the United States as the single biggest threat to DPRK security, it remained very leery of Japan's intentions and constantly vigilant – sometimes to the point of exaggeration – of Japanese remilitarization. Pyongyang viewed the US–Japan security alliance as an ever-present threat to DPRK security, as it did the US–South Korean security alliance. While the US–Japan security alliance troubled Pyongyang because of its level of military sophistication, from the North's perspective, the US–South Korean alliance gave America's imperialist forces a military foothold on the Korean Peninsula.

Pyongyang understood that the DPRK's military expenditures came nowhere close to what the United States and Japan were spending, and Seoul's defense budget only added to its anxiety. In 1992, the United States spent $305 billion on its military; Japan about $36 billion; and South Korea approximately $10.6 billion. Most of the US' 1992 defense budget was not intended to deal with problems associated with North Korea, since, like today, Washington believed that it had to fulfill its global security objectives. Still, Japanese and South Korean military expenditures in 1992 exceeded $46 billion dollars, considerably more than $30.5 billion spent by the DPRK.[48]

The first nuclear crisis

North Korea became a party to the 1970 Nuclear Nonproliferation Treaty (NPT) as a nonnuclear weapons state in December 1985. Soon after this, Pyongyang's troubles with the UN's International Atomic Energy Agency (IAEA) began brewing. NPT's Article III requires that nonnuclear weapons states that accede to the accord 180 days after it came into force have 18 months to negotiate and finalize a safeguards agreement with the IAEA. The DPRK failed to meet this 18-month deadline, but did request and receive an extension of an additional 18 months from the IAEA. When the DPRK failed to meet this new deadline, Pyongyang later stipulated that it was necessary for the United States to remove all of its nuclear weapons from South Korea.[49] Still technically at war with both the United States and South Korea and uneasy with Washington's regional security alliances with Seoul and Tokyo, the DPRK was deeply concerned about the existence of US nuclear weapons in South Korea. Pyongyang also worried about Team Spirit, the US and South Korean joint military exercises, and wanted these to end before it signed a safeguards agreement with the IAEA.[50]

Although Pyongyang remained very skeptical, the first Bush administration maintained at the end of 1991 that the United States had removed all nuclear weapons from South Korea. Shortly after this, Pyongyang and Seoul signed the *Joint Declaration of the Denuclearization of the Korean Peninsula* in January 1992. The joint declaration prohibited the North and the South from developing or manufacturing, possessing, stockpiling, testing or using nuclear weapons. To forestall the development of nuclear weapons research and development, the joint declaration prohibited the North and the South from maintaining nuclear facilities for reprocessing plutonium or for uranium enrichment. However, in accordance with the NPT the joint declaration permitted the North and the South to use nuclear energy for peaceful purposes.[51]

The DPRK's safeguards agreement finally came into force in April 1992. Because of problems with the information that Pyongyang sent to the IAEA, most notably the agency's suspicion that the DPRK had reprocessed more plutonium than the small amount that it reported, tensions began to mount. US satellite images provided to the IAEA of two unreported DRPK nuclear facilities worsened the situation, especially after Pyongyang refused to allow the agency to inspect the sites. Maintaining that they were military buildings, Pyongyang later rejected the agency's demand for a special inspection of the two sites. In late February 1993, the IAEA's Board of Directors gave the DPRK three months to permit the inspections. About two weeks later, on March 12, 1993, the DPRK announced that it was withdrawing from the NPT, which the accord permits three months after official notification.[52]

In the March 1993 letter from the DPRK's Ministry of Foreign Affairs to the president of the UN Security Council, Pyongyang indicated its reasons for giving notice of its intention to withdraw from the NPT, all of which were subsequently rejected by Washington and Seoul. Pyongyang stated that the US–South Korean resumption of Team Spirit was nothing short of an exercise for nuclear war, a threat to the DPRK's national security and an attempt to disarm it. The letter further stated that Washington and Seoul had been instrumental in persuading the Board of the IAEA and other member states to pass the February resolution that demanded the special inspection of the two military sites. In the letter the DPRK Ministry of Foreign Affairs stressed that the military sites had nothing to do with nuclear work and that inspections would be an infringement of North Korea's national security. The letter also pointed out that Pyongyang's decision to withdraw from the NPT would stand until the United States stopped its nuclear threats and the IAEA ended its unjust treatment of the DPRK. In April 1993, the Security Council received a letter from the IAEA's director-general indicating that the agency had recently adopted a resolution that stated that the DPRK had not complied with its safeguards agreement and that the agency could not verify that Pyongyang had not diverted some fissile material. In May, the Security Council passed a resolution, which was cosponsored by eight countries, including the United States and Japan. Although a DPRK representative, who had been invited to the Security Council meeting as a guest, urged members to oppose the resolution, it nonetheless was easily adopted. The resolution called on the DPRK to recommit to the NPT and to comply with its IAEA safeguards agreement.[53]

On June 11, 1993, just before the official deadline, Washington persuaded Pyongyang not to withdraw from the NPT.[54] Still, for months after this, things did not improve. Convinced that the IAEA was under Washington's thumb, Pyongyang's relationship with the agency and the United States remained very strained. Because of its continuing problems with the IAEA and in direct response to the agency's resolution of June 10 that sanctioned the DPRK, Pyongyang decided to withdraw North Korea's membership in the IAEA. In the letter announcing its withdrawal, North Korea called the June resolution "another unjust resolution," charging that the director-general of the IAEA "has pursued the dishonest political purposes of stifling the DPRK under the pretext of its inspections rather than seek a fair resolution of the nuclear issue."[55]

That the Clinton administration had been pressing for economic sanctions from the UN Security Council and had drawn up plans to launch a pre-emptive attack on DPRK nuclear facilities indicates that the situation had reached the crisis point. Subsequent to the DPRK's announcement of withdrawal from the IAEA, former President Jimmy Carter visited Pyongyang and in discussions with Kim Il Sung found a way to avoid further problems and perhaps avert war.[56] A few months later, in October 1994, Washington and Pyongyang signed the Agreed Framework, which shut down the DPRK's plutonium-reprocessing facilities at Yongbyon, as well as a smaller one at Taecheon. The Agreed Framework stipulated that IAEA inspectors would monitor the freeze of the DPRK's graphite-moderated reactors, that Washington and Pyongyang would begin taking steps to normalize relations, and that the United States would not threaten to use or use nuclear weapons on North Korea. If fully implemented, the Agreed Framework would also bring the DPRK into full compliance with its IAEA safeguards agreement, which would occur after much of the work on the light-water project had been done.[57]

Republican politicians in Washington were especially critical of North Korea and did not believe that Pyongyang ever intended to bargain in good faith.[58] After returning from a trip to South Korea in June 1994, Senators John McCain and Phil Gramm showed no reluctance in making clear their views about North Korea's leadership and the DPRK's objectives. Referring to Carter's trip to North Korea, Senator McCain maintained that "he didn't see anything new in Kim Il Sung's offers" to the former president. McCain stated that Kim Il Sung's "record is full of empty promises," of "misleading deception and of outright lies concerning his nuclear program." Senator Gramm remarked that, "Carter talked about giving them light water reactors as a substitute to generate electricity. They're not generating electricity with nuclear power plants. The whole objective is weapons." Serving largely to confirm what Pyongyang had long feared, Senator McCain stated that they should try economic sanctions first, which he believed were unlikely to work, but then "air strikes to disable the North Korean nuclear capability must be a serious consideration." Senator Gramm took a somewhat different approach, deciding to emphasize that US troops in South Korea were "at the highest state of readiness" and that he and Senator McCain had identified several ways that they were about to communicate to the Pentagon to "raise our level of readiness."[59]

Although concerned about the DPRK nuclear issue, through all of this Tokyo's position stood in stark contrast to the hard-line one it would assume during most of the second North Korean nuclear crisis that began several years later. Japan believed during the first DPRK nuclear crisis that diplomacy was the key to settling the issue. Fearing political problems and backlash in Japan, Tokyo opposed the imposition of economic sanctions on the DPRK.[60]

North Korea's nuclear activities, which date back a number of years before its run-in with the IAEA, should not, as too often has been the case, be cause to conclude definitively that it had been working full bore to develop nuclear weapons. Its reluctance to accede to the NPT and its subsequent long delay in agreeing to a safeguards agreement with the IAEA indicate only that Pyongyang was uncomfortable with the accord and with the safeguards agreement, and nothing more. Moving from the existence of nuclear equipment, which was initially supplied by the Soviet Union, and facilities, to the position that the DPRK was then attempting to develop nuclear weapons is a presumption.

The DPRK is certainly not the first country to have reservations about the NPT and the required safeguards agreement with the IAEA. It took Japan, which has repeatedly maintained that it has a moral obligation to take the lead in abolishing all nuclear weapons, more than six years, from the time it signed the NPT in February 1970, to ratify the accord in June 1976.[61] Moreover, it is unlikely that Moscow, which at the time pressured the DPRK to accede to the NPT, believed that Pyongyang had an imminent plan to develop nuclear weapons. Moscow is thought to have continued to train DPRK nuclear scientists in the Soviet Union until its dissolution at the end of 1991, and both Soviet and East German nuclear and missile scientists remained in the DPRK during the 1990s.[62] It makes little sense for Moscow to have pressured the DPRK to accede to the NPT as a nonnuclear weapons state and at the same time be involved in helping Pyongyang develop nuclear weapons. That the NPT's Article IV guarantees all parties the right to work on and develop nuclear technology for peaceful purposes and that such activities can be performed in a cooperative and collaborative manner provides a plausible explanation of Moscow's nuclear assistance to the DPRK after 1985.

It has been commonly pointed out that the secrecy of the DPRK – often disparagingly labeled the hermit kingdom[63] – makes it almost impossible to know what Pyongyang is up to and what its position is on important political matters. It is therefore interesting to note that in 1991 Kim Il Sung gave a speech during a conference in Pyongyang in which he endorsed a nuclear-free Korean Peninsula and repudiated the existence of nuclear weapons, stating "The testing and production of nuclear weapons must be banned."[64] About two years later when a Japanese delegation visited the DPRK in May 1993, one member asked Kim Il Sung if his country was building nuclear weapons. Kim replied emphatically, "No we are not producing nuclear weapons." Kim also told the Japanese delegation that the DPRK has no plans, no ability and no money to produce nuclear weapons.[65]

In any case, serious political problems persisted. While Pyongyang was determined not to have the United States and its alliance partners, Japan and South Korea, undermine or jeopardize DPRK socialism, Washington was equally resolute in its efforts to arrest what it saw as the inherent aggressiveness of a revolutionary communist system. Fundamentally, Washington wanted the absolute certainty that North Korea was not attempting to develop nuclear weapons, since this would further destabilize Northeast Asia and undermine the NPT regime.

The unraveling

The 1994 Agreed Framework followed by the creation of KEDO (Korean Peninsula Energy Development Organization) in March 1995 put in motion the mechanisms to freeze and eventually dismantle the DPRK's plutonium-based nuclear facilities. The United States, Japan and South Korea were the original members of KEDO, the consortium whose primary purpose was to facilitate and implement the Agreed Framework between Pyongyang and Washington. The Agreed Framework stipulated that the United States would establish a consortium to provide 500,000 metric tons of heavy oil annually to the DPRK until the first light-water reactor (there were to be two) promised to the North was completed. Subsequently, with its formation, the consortium assumed these responsibilities; however, the United States remained, especially with respect to the light-water project, the DPRK's "principal point of contact."

At the end of May 2006, KEDO's executive board, which by then included the European Union, ended the DPRK's light-water project after two, one-year suspensions. KEDO maintained that it ended the light-water project because for a protracted period the DPRK had not met the conditions of the KEDO-DPRK Supply Agreement,[66] which incorporated many of the Agreed Framework's key points. Thus, in both the Agreed Framework and the KEDO-DPRK Supply Agreement, Pyongyang committed North Korea to remaining a party to the NPT, to accepting IAEA monitoring, and to the freezing of its graphite-moderated nuclear reactors.[67]

Approximately one month after the signing of the Agreed Framework, IAEA inspectors arrived in North Korea and established that the DPRK, as stipulated in the framework, had indeed frozen its plutonium-reprocessing activities. However, IAEA inspectors were not as confident about everything associated with the DPRK's nuclear program. Some differences between what the IAEA understood to be its monitoring responsibilities and Pyongyang's explanations continued, for several years after the signing of the Agreed Framework.[68]

By 2003, Pyongyang had abandoned all of its obligations, including compliance with its IAEA safeguards agreement. The Bush administration and KEDO maintained that the DPRK had admitted to having a clandestine uranium-enrichment program to develop nuclear weapons when a US delegation visited Pyongyang in October 2002. Because of pressure from the Bush administration, KEDO stopped shipments of heavy fuel oil to North Korea in December 2002. It was subsequent to KEDO's decision to stop deliveries of heavy oil to the DPRK that Pyongyang demanded IAEA inspectors leave North Korea, that it restarted nuclear-reprocessing activities at Yongbyon and that it withdrew from the NPT in April 2003.[69]

Looking back, since at least December 1996, Pyongyang expressed concern that the hostilities it perceived coming from Washington and Seoul could undermine the Agreed Framework.[70] Less than three weeks after the signing of the Agreed Framework in October 1994, the midterm elections put the Republican Party in the majority in both the House and the Senate beginning in January 1995. Many Republicans saw the Clinton administration's North Korean policy as conciliatory and not surprisingly had considerable disdain for the Agreed Framework. Pyongyang was well aware of this and stated in January 1997, "the anti-DPRK hostile policy of the U.S. conservative hardliners who have tried to stifle it, hating the DPRK–U.S. agreed framework."

In June 1997, Pyongyang was starting to show signs that it was becoming impatient with the progress that was being made on the implementation of the Agreed Framework. Again stressing that a peace treaty needed to take the place of the 1953 armistice agreement, Pyongyang also stated that if Washington really wanted peace "it should implement the DPRK–U.S. framework agreement with sincerity."[71] One problem that existed early on was that the Agreed Framework stipulated that Washington would take responsibility for the leadership of the international consortium (i.e., KEDO). This meant the United States "will make best efforts" to have a supply contract for the light-water project with Pyongyang within six months from the signing of the accord. However, a supply contract did not happen until December 1995, 14 months later.

Although the subsequent groundbreaking ceremony for the light-water project in August 1997 pleased Pyongyang, some uncertainty also existed in the DPRK. The Agreed Framework included a "target date of 2003" for the completion of the light-water project. On the day of the ceremony, Pyongyang noted that the groundbreaking occurred two years and 10 months after the signing of the Agreed Framework and one year and eight months after the KEDO-DPRK Supply Agreement. At the ceremony Ambassador Ho Jong of North Korea's Ministry of Foreign Affairs and the official who signed the KEDO-DPRK Supply Agreement noted, "We have a long way to go until the project is finished."[72]

But whatever optimism Pyongyang might have had about the light-water project, it began to sour by March 1998. At this time, Pyongyang noted that while it quickly froze its nuclear program, Washington had not been meeting its responsibilities under the Agreed Framework. The framework stipulated that within three months the United States and the DPRK would lower trade and investment obstacles. Pyongyang complained that Washington had not taken significant steps to reduce sanctions and that not much work had been done on the light-water project.[73] When KEDO suspended the light-water project for the first time on December 1, 2003,[74] rather than being completed as the Agreed Framework stipulated, it was, according to KEDO, "approximately 34.5% complete."[75] Regarding trade obstacles, US exports to North Korea in 1995 increased sharply to $11.6 million, up significantly from 1994 when they stood at $200,000. However, in 1996, US exports to North Korea markedly declined, totaling $500,000, then grew to $2.5 million and $4.4 million in 1997 and 1998. That Washington did not have normal trade relations with North Korea showed up, most especially, in DPRK products imported by the United States, of which there were none between 1992 and 1999.[76] By the end of March 1998, Pyongyang was noticeably more frustrated, complaining that the Agreed Framework cannot be unilaterally implemented. Pyongyang warned that if the United States "continues to delay the frame-work agreement under groundless pretexts and conditions, it will have to be held wholly responsible for all consequences to be entailed by its perfidious misdeeds."[77]

Pyongyang complained constantly about problems in the delivery of heavy oil shipments that the United States promised to the DPRK in the Agreed Framework. According to a US analysis that mainly relied on KEDO data, for three years after the signing of the Agreed Framework, KEDO had problems gaining sufficient funds to pay for the heavy oil shipments to North Korea but that beginning in 1998 deliveries were occurring on a more regular basis.[78] However, Pyongyang did not see it this way. In May 1998, Pyongyang complained both about the delay in the light-water project and that the United States "has not set forth the timetable for heavy oil supply this year and is not supplying heavy oil to the DPRK in time."[79] In mid August, Pyongyang stated that the inadequate supply of heavy oil has "plunged our economy into a great confusion."[80]

It is hard to ascertain the extent to which KEDO had sufficient funds to send regular shipments of heavy oil to the DPRK from 1995–97. Indeed, contributions for heavy oil more than doubled between 1997 and 1998, reaching $48.2 million in the latter year. Nonetheless, there were sizeable funds available for heavy oil between 1995 and 1997. Significantly, in 1995, KEDO picked up three new members – New Zealand, Australia and Canada, in 1996 another three – Chile, Argentina and Indonesia – and in 1997, two more – the European Community and Poland. What is more, other states that are not members made financial contributions to KEDO, typically giving what KEDO termed "unrestricted funds." KEDO had $12.2 million available for heavy fuel oil in 1995, $24.6 million in 1996 and $22.9 million in 1997. These contributions for heavy oil did not include those designated as unrest-ricted funds, which amounted to $1.5 million in 1995, $2.7 million in 1996 and $28.6 million in 1997.[81]

In 1995, the United States was largely responsible for supplying the heavy oil to the DPRK. Especially with the new Republican-controlled Congress in place, the Clinton administration believed that getting approval for funds to provide heavy fuel oil to the DPRK would have been difficult in 1995. To circumvent Congress, Secretary of Defense William Perry used funds from the Department of Defense. Perry maintained that between $10 and $15 million came from the Defense Department's "emergency funding category" in 1995, which generally corresponds with the KEDO figure for that year cited above.[82] However, the big unanswered question is why the United States and KEDO could not find the funds needed to purchase and deliver the heavy oil to North Korea, especially after 1995, since KEDO's membership had grown and many of its members were wealthy.

Unlike problems with the delivery of shipments of heavy oil, the delay in the light-water project is harder to explain by relying on the lack-of-funds argument. To a considerable extent, funding for the light-water project would come from Japan and South Korea. In 1995, the first year of KEDO's existence, Japan contributed $3 million to the organization for the light-water project, with the money specifically designated for "pre-project services and site survey." In 1996, South Korea contributed $6 million dollars for the same type of preliminary work on the light-water project.[83] Yet, as indicated above, the groundbreaking ceremony for the light-water project did not occur until August 1997. Between 1995 and 2003 contributions for the light-water reactors amounted to about $1.5 billion.[84] Well before 2003, the expectation was that the light-water project, rather than being completed as promised in 2003, would not be finished until 2007 or later.

Pyongyang also continued to worry about protecting the DPRK's sovereignty from what it perceived as external threats. Along with the strengthening of the US–Japan security alliance, Pyongyang strongly condemned the Ulji Focus Lens, an annual military exercise between the United States and South Korea that began on August 18 and ended on August 29, 1998. Having previously condemned the Ulji Focus Lens, Pyongyang this time pointed out that the joint military exercise was equivalent to the "Team Spirit" exercises and that it violated the Agreed Framework the DPRK has been sincerely implementing. Pyongyang also stressed that Ulji Focus Lens shows that Washington talks about peace and the importance of the Agreed Framework but that this "is just hypocrisy for covering up its aggressive policy towards the DPRK."[85] In late August 1998, two days after the end of Ulji Focus Lens, the DPRK without giving any advance notice launched a Taepodong-1 that flew over Japanese territory.

Pyongyang indicated that it was not at all comfortable with the strengthened US–Japan military relationship and eventually stated that the Taepodong-1 was not a missile but rather an artificial satellite, the *Kwangmyŏngsŏng-1*, which the DPRK, as a sovereign state, had every right to launch. Tokyo stated that it would continue with research on a missile defense system, which it shortly thereafter committed Japan to with the United States, and indicated that the new defense guidelines with Washington would soon become law. In addition to cutting off food aid to North Korea because of the Taepodong-1 launch, Tokyo also announced that it was ending its financial contributions to KEDO, a penalty that did not last too long.[86]

In February 2000, Pyongyang claimed that it was experiencing the most severe power shortage in the DPRK's history, although it did note that natural disasters also contributed to the DPRK's energy problems. Pyongyang maintained that its graphite-moderated nuclear reactors, which had been built for the peaceful purpose of producing electrical power, would have been up and running by now but that Washington had demanded a freeze. Pyongyang maintained that the freezing of North Korea's nuclear facilities had cost the DPRK dearly and now cannot be made up by heavy oil shipments.[87] Soon after this, Pyongyang stressed that US conservative hardliners were demanding "verification devices" claiming that they were still suspicious of the DPRK's freezing of its nuclear activities and that they are unacceptably pushing for changes to the Agreed Framework. Pyongyang again indicated that the light-water project had been delayed and that now "it is hard to tell when the project is expected to be completed."[88]

The next year, in February 2001, Pyongyang expressed its concerns about the changes in US policy toward the DPRK. Although President Bush was only in office for one month, Pyongyang pointed to his administration's "hardline stance" on foreign and security policy toward the DPRK. Pyongyang rejected the administration's talk of "phased access" and "conditional reciprocity," arguing that what the new administration wants is for the DPRK to disarm before the US fulfills its obligations under the Agreed Framework. Pyongyang noted that even though the new fiscal year had begun the preceding October, it still had not received a timetable for the delivery of the heavy oil, and stated the light-water project "is unlikely to become a reality."[89]

Pyongyang's perspective

Some contradictory things were simultaneously happening in the second half of the 1990s. Creating some optimism for a while was the four-party talks between North and South Korea, the United States and China. With the stated objective of bringing a permanent peace accord to the Korean Peninsula,[90] there were six rounds of the four-party talks held between December 1997 and August 1999, though they finally ended without making progress.[91] On the other side, in 1996 Washington and Tokyo began the process of strengthening the US–Japan security alliance; several years later they accomplished this objective. Pyongyang viewed the process of strengthening the US–Japan security relationship as specifically aimed at the DPRK.[92] As Pyongyang saw it, the DPRK faced the prospect of military confrontation with its powerful Cold War nemesis, with its previous colonial ruler, and perhaps with South Korea.

Implemented to deal with the perceived threat of an external attack and in part to offset domestic opposition to Kim Jong Il, whose leadership inauguration roughly coincided with economic malaise, famine and massive starvation,[93] the initial problem with *songun* was that Pyongyang did not have the funds to devote to it. DPRK military expenditures, according to the CIA, were estimated to be $5 to $7 billion dollars between 1995 and 1997. However, the CIA's estimates of DPRK defense spending are much higher than what Pyongyang has reported. For example, Pyongyang reported that the DPRK's military expenditures were $2.2 billion in 1994, while the CIA estimated that three years earlier, in 1991, North Korea's defense spending was $5 billion. Thus, while Pyongyang has maintained that DPRK defense spending constituted approximately 12 percent of GDP, the CIA has estimated that it was at least twice as high. These differences aside, it does appear that the DPRK's

GDP declined between 1995 and 1996 and that it was virtually the same in 1997 and 1998 as it was in 1995.[94] With a per capita GDP that stood at about $900 in 1997, it is a moot matter whether DPRK military spending was 12 percent, 25 percent or more of GDP, since even the lower figure is far too high, especially for a poor society.

Beginning around 2002 there were for awhile modest improvements in the DPRK's economy.[95] Despite subsequent economic problems, the DPRK still spends a disproportionately large amount on the military. Pyongyang continues to believe that it has legitimate security concerns. The combined military power evident in the strengthened US–Japan security relationship, plus South Korea, is something that Pyongyang has not been able to overlook. As Pyongyang sees it, lest the DPRK's imperialist enemies prevail, the revolutionary *juche* ideology that reinforces and sustains *chajusong* has to be protected by *songun* at any cost.

An argument posited in Beijing is that Pyongyang decided to initiate *songun* because Washington had dragged its feet in fulfilling its commitment to the Agreed Framework.[96] Certainly, Washington's failure to fulfill its commitment to the Agreed Framework did not please Pyongyang. Because Pyongyang had frozen the DPRK's plutonium-producing facilities, it expected timely deliveries of heavy oil, the completion of the light-water project, and "full normalization of political and economic relations" with the United States. Additionally, as we saw above, Pyongyang continued to express its concerns about the military threats it perceived coming from Washington, Tokyo and Seoul. All of this together has allowed Pyongyang to rationalize *songun*.

Although established two years before, it was not until 1997 that Pyongyang clearly indicated the primacy of *songun*. Referring to the efforts of Kim Jong Il, a *Rodong Sinmun* editorial in April 1997 stated, "Never before have the status and role of the People's Army been so extraordinarily elevated as today." The Korean People's Army, the Workers' Party of Korea and the Kim Il Sung Socialist Youth League did not use the term *songun* in DPRK political statements until January 1999 when it appeared in a joint editorial.[97] Moreover, the *Korean Central News Agency*, the official news outlet of both the North Korean government and the Workers' Party of Korea, did not use the term *songun* in its articles until early April 2003, six months after the second nuclear crisis emerged in October 2002 and after both Pyongyang and Washington had considered the Agreed Framework dead. Since April 2003, the term has been used regularly by Pyongyang. It is certainly plausible that by the latter part of the 1990s, because Pyongyang was becoming increasingly worried about Washington's commitment to the Agreed Framework, it devoted more resources to the military than it would have otherwise done if the United States had appeared committed to the accord and to signing a peace treaty. Big military expenditures and the frequent use of *songun* in official North Korean news articles, especially after the emergence of the second DPRK nuclear crisis,[98] appear as mechanisms intended to counteract the perceived threat from the United States, particularly in light of its strengthened military alliance with Japan.

From nuclear allegations to a nuclear weapons test

Many people in Washington were not politically committed to the Agreed Framework, particularly after the Republicans gained control of Congress. It was an open secret that many in Washington also believed that Kim Jong Il's North Korea would inevitably collapse, making for no need to rush to fulfill the United States' obligations to the Agreed Framework.[99] Still, the improvement in US–DPRK relations toward the end of Clinton's second term provided reason for some optimism. This optimism, however, proved to be short-lived.

The trip to North Korea by US Assistant Secretary of State for East Asian and Pacific Affairs James Kelly in early October 2002 demonstrated that the new Bush team was not going to adhere to the same engagement policy as that employed by the Clinton administration.[100] This, however, is certainly not the impression the Bush administration had given a little over year earlier. In July 2001, Charles Pritchard, US special envoy for North Korean issues, told the House of Representatives' Subcommittee on East Asia and the Pacific that the Bush administration had studied its predecessor's position and that it would be "incorporating into [its] policy those items that we believe were successful and that we want to continue to carry.[101] Having already been greatly annoyed by President Bush's designation of the DPRK as one of the countries making up the "axis of evil," officials in Pyongyang reacted angrily to Kelly's accusation that North Korea had a clandestine uranium-enrichment program from which it intended to develop nuclear weapons.

Pyongyang had become very skeptical of the Bush administration's commitment to the Agreed Framework almost from the start. Issued in late 2001, the Bush administration's *Nuclear Posture Review* identified North Korea as "among the countries that could be involved in immediate, potential, or unexpected [nuclear] contingencies" with the United States.[102] When it was revealed in early March 2002, this threat heightened Pyongyang's security concerns. Moreover, this threat unequivocally violated the 1994 Agreed Framework, which explicitly stated, "The U.S. will provide formal assurances to the DPRK, against the threat or use of nuclear weapons by the U.S."[103] Compounding Pyongyang's worries was the announcement by the Bush administration of its preemptive strike strategy.

After Kelly's visit to the DPRK, Pyongyang made several decisions that put the Agreed Framework in jeopardy, which as we saw above unraveled by early 2003. This led the Bush administration and some government agencies to add to the discussion relating to the status of North Korea's nuclear-weapons efforts. During the Clinton years, it was said that the DPRK, at best, could have stored a very small amount of plutonium, thus implying that North Korea could conceivably manufacture one or two nuclear weapons.[104]

Similarly, in January 2001 at the very end of the Clinton administration, the Department of Defense reported that the DPRK "may have enough plutonium for at least one nuclear weapon."[105] This, however, changed during the Bush administration. In February 2003, the Defense Intelligence Agency told a Senate committee that it thought that the DPRK had "a full range of WMD" [weapons of mass destruction], which includes "perhaps two nuclear weapons."[106] The CIA was much more explicit, reporting to the same Senate committee that North Korea "has produced one or two simple fission-type nuclear weapons."[107] What is more, CIA Director George Tenet was unambiguous when he told this Senate committee that North Korea's nuclear weapons programs "includes developing the capability to enrich uranium."[108]

It is important to note that the Bush administration was not the first to become concerned about uranium-enrichment activities in the DPRK. There were suspicions circulating within the Clinton administration in the late 1990s or at least by 2000, that Pyongyang had been concealing a uranium-enrichment program.[109] At about this same time, the Clinton administration also suspected that the DPRK had a plutonium-producing facility at a secret underground site at Kumchang-ri. After some resistance from Pyongyang, Washington inspected the site and concluded that there had been no violation of the Agreed Framework.[110]

Regarding the Bush administration's claim that Pyongyang was concealing a uranium-enrichment program to develop nuclear weapons, the DPRK Foreign Ministry maintained that Washington repeatedly invents things, such as it did with the "secret underground nuclear facilities discovered" in the 1990s at Kumchang-ri. The DPRK Foreign Ministry stated, "At that time the U.S. peddled what was called 'information' only to find the tunnel in Kumchang-ri empty. So, the U.S. had to grant 600,000 tons of food to the DPRK in compensation for such groundless mockery of it. This is a serious lesson that the U.S. should have drawn." Pyongyang felt that it was important to provide its side of the story after it became public that Kelly and his delegation maintained that the DPRK admitted to having a uranium-enrichment program. Pyongyang stated that though "producing no evidence," Kelly's attitude was "so unilateral and high-handed" the DPRK told him that it "was entitled to possess not only [a] nuclear weapon but any type of weapon more powerful than that so as to defend its sovereignty and right to existence from the ever-growing nuclear threat by the U.S." Pyongyang also stated that Kelly informed the DPRK that unless it ends its uranium-enrichment activities, North Korea–Japan and North–South relations would be in peril. Later, Pyongyang stated that, because of arrogance that he exhibited during his visit, the DPRK "took the attitude of neither denying it nor confirming" the uranium-enrichment program.[111]

The Bush administration never provided solid evidence that the DPRK had a uranium-enrichment program to develop nuclear weapons, nor did it identify the program's whereabouts. Even an official in the ultra-hawkish vice president's office, Stephen Yates, who served as Cheney's deputy assistant for national security affairs, stated in an interview after leaving his position that what the Bush administration had on the DPRK's uranium-enrichment program "was not necessarily a slam dunk but overwhelming circumstantial evidence that tells us for sure that they're pursuing this."[112] However, this is not how Pyongyang portrayed things, given that it eventually maintained that the DPRK has "no secret nuclear program" that enriches uranium.[113]

That the DPRK had aluminum tubes, as Chapter 4 points out, is hardly solid evidence that it had plans to establish a program to enrich uranium for nuclear weapons, since aluminum tubes have other uses. Although the DPRK may have had some equipment that could be used to enrich uranium, there is no compelling evidence that it then had either the facilities or the program needed to produce highly enriched uranium for nuclear weapons.[114] The Bush administration could have employed a far less hostile and hubristic policy toward the DPRK to ascertain its objectives, and thus conceivably have avoided the second North Korean nuclear crisis. Specifically, the Bush administration could have attempted to find out whether any equipment the DPRK might have had other than aluminum tubes, which may not have been used to enrich uranium, was intended for a uranium-enrichment program to build nuclear weapons and, if so, to work with reasoned diplomacy to remove it.[115]

The good information on the DPRK's clandestine uranium-enrichment program that the Bush administration repeatedly said it possessed was not seen this way by the Obama administration.[116] Referring to the Bush administration's allegation of the DPRK possessing an uranium-enrichment program to develop nuclear weapons, Secretary of State Hillary Clinton stated in an interview while visiting Seoul in February 2009 that no one has been able to identify "any specific location" or "any specific outcome of whatever might have gone on, if anything did."[117]

In any case, before Secretary Clinton's telling remark the Bush administration maintained for years, although with varying degrees of intensity, that the DPRK had a uranium-enrichment program to develop nuclear weapons. If this were true, the DPRK would have been in direct violation of the North–South 1992 *Joint Declaration of the Denuclearization of the Korean Peninsula*. This, in turn, meant that the DPRK would have contravened the 1994 Agreed Framework, which recommitted North Korea to the 1992 Joint Declaration. Unlike Beijing, which retained doubts about the existence of a clandestine DPRK uranium-enrichment program to build nuclear weapons, as did Seoul but to a much lesser extent, the Japanese government was more willing to accept Washington's proof. Although from time to time skepticism was heard coming from some Japanese officials about North Korea's alleged uranium-enrichment program, officially Tokyo accepted its existence. At a press conference given by the Japanese Ministry of Foreign Affairs in February 2003, Press Secretary Hatsuhisa Takashima stated that Japan had been encouraging North Korea to stop and dismantle "in a visible and verifiable way the new nuclear development program using enriched uranium."[118]

The US-led invasion of Iraq in March 2003 put Pyongyang on high alert. Baghdad's claims that it did not have any weapons of mass destruction fell on the deaf ears of the Bush administration. Pyongyang quickly reasoned that it was not about to let the DPRK become susceptible to invasion. Having already accused Japan of being the first nation to support the US-led invasion of Iraq,[119] Pyongyang indicated that the DPRK was not Iraq or Afghanistan, proclaiming that, "We have the invincible and powerful army-based policy."[120] Pyongyang later charged that the mere accusations of terrorism, the existence of weapons of mass destruction, and "nuclear suspicion" were sufficient justifications for Washington to attack a country, even without the authorization of the United Nations. Pyongyang reasoned that the lesson learned from the US-led invasion of Iraq is that the DPRK can protect itself only if "it has a physical deterrent force."[121] Pyongyang continued to maintain that a preemptive attack launched by the United States and supported by Japan could occur at any time, warning that American policy makers and Japanese reactionaries should be mindful of retaliation by the DPRK.[122] Stating that the situation in Iraq proves that "disarmament leads to war," Pyongyang stressed that the "DPRK has the right to build up a nuclear deterrent force for self-defence" and that it will never yield to Washington's "demand that it scrap its nuclear weapons program first."[123]

Washington and Pyongyang had been at odds over how to resolve the North Korean nuclear problem. The Bush administration wanted multilateral talks, given its position that the bilateral discussions that produced the Agreed Framework had been a failed attempt by the Clinton White House to eliminate North Korea's ambitions to acquire nuclear weapons. Pyongyang believed that resolution of the crisis could only occur through bilateral discussions, stressing that it was not a multilateral problem but rather one between the DPRK and the United States. Because of the diplomatic initiative by the Chinese, Washington and Pyongyang agreed to hold trilateral talks in Beijing in late April 2003, with China serving as both the host to and participant in the discussions.

Pyongyang later agreed to participate in multilateral discussions. In August 2003, the first round of the six-party talks between the United States, North and South Korea, Japan, Russia and China, which just a few years earlier had renewed and strengthened its relationship with the DPRK,[124] took place in Beijing. Two more rounds of the six-party talks occurred in 2004. Still, the North Korea nuclear crisis worsened. In February 2005, North Korea's Ministry of Foreign Affairs explained why Pyongyang decided to suspend indefinitely its participation in the six-party talks. Citing hostile bilateral relations, specifically the Bush administration's nuclear threat against the DPRK, its suggestion that military force could be used to depose Kim Jong Il's government, and Secretary of State Condoleezza Rice's labeling of the DPRK as an "outpost of tyranny," Pyongyang decided that its involvement in the six-party talks was serving no purpose. Noting also at this time that Japan's hostility toward the DPRK had increased in accordance with US policy, the North

Korean Ministry of Foreign Affairs announced that the DPRK had built nuclear weapons for defensive purposes.[125] Kim Jong Il's *songun* and its defense of North Koreans' *chajusong* had seemingly reached a new security level with the DPRK's claim that it had produced nuclear weapons.

The threat perceived by Pyongyang, especially from the United States and Japan, meant that the DPRK's military preparedness now apparently included the creation of a nuclear deterrent. When reviewing the DPRK's budget for 2004 and 2005, Pyongyang stressed the need to increase military spending. Referring to 2004, Pyongyang indicated that, "to cope with the more frantic moves of the U.S.-led imperialists to isolate and stifle the DPRK, the DPRK government allotted 15.6 percent of its total budgetary expenditure as military spending." As for 2005, Pyongyang stated that it "will allocate 15.9 percent of the total state budgetary expenditure as military spending with a view to bolstering the People's Army, developing defence industry and implementing to the letter the Party's policy of placing all people under arms and turning the whole country into a fortress."[126]

With pressure from Beijing, the DPRK decided to rejoin the six-party talks in July 2005. However, in November, remonstrating against the US' freezing of DPRK funds deposited in the Banco Delta Asia (BDA) in Macau, Pyongyang again decided to boycott the six-party talks.

In the fall of 2006, Pyongyang demonstrated that its repeated claim that it had a nuclear deterrent force was not just bluster. Thus, by choice and because of the maladroit, hard-line policy of the Bush administration, a policy that Tokyo fully endorsed, Pyongyang decided to detonate an underground nuclear device in October 2006. Pyongyang had demonstrated its use of the *juche*-based *songun* policy to move the DPRK from a state with a disproportionately large number of military personnel to one that possessed the technical capability to detonate a nuclear device.

All the time in the world

The fact that the DPRK had detonated a nuclear device changed the political equation for Pyongyang and for Washington as well. By incorporating a nuclear deterrent into *songun*, Pyongyang believed that it had created the assurance that the DPRK's *juche*-based socialist system would be less likely to face the same fate as Iraq. The Bush administration failed to understand Pyongyang's commitment to the *juche* idea and to *songun*, which originated in part from Kim Il Sung's insistence that the DPRK not subscribe to the "pacifistic mood." Moreover, along with Pyongyang demonstrating that it had a nuclear deterrent, it showed that it could now wait out Washington.

As we will see in more detail in Chapter 4, the Bush administration suddenly moved away from its hard-line position and adopted a recognizably conciliatory approach toward North Korea. Because of this changed approach, the February 2007 six-party talks were hailed as a somewhat of a success; they were seen as the implementation phase of the September 2005

Joint Statement that came out of these talks in which Pyongyang committed the DPRK to complete denuclearization, to returning to the NPT, and to accepting IAEA safeguards. After years of deadlock, the only significant difference then observable between the Agreed Framework and the denuclearization action plan reached in February 2007 was that the Bush administration was stressing that its agreement was multinational.[127]

An important concession made by the Bush administration was that it had changed its position on the BDA issue. Assistant Secretary of State for East Asian and Pacific Affairs and head of the American delegation to the six-party talks Christopher Hill made clear the US position on the financial sanctions associated with the BDA, the same ones that for months Washington had repeatedly insisted were not connected to the DPRK nuclear crisis. Hill pointed out in Beijing after the conclusion of the February discussions that the "United States is committed, and we've told the Chinese chair and we told the other participants that we will resolve the matter of the financial sanctions pertaining to the BDA within thirty days."[128] A little over three weeks later, the DPRK's head negotiator to the six-party talks Kim Kye-gwan stated, "The U.S. has promised the North that it would scrap its financial sanctions on the Banco Delta Asia and the North is keeping a close eye on the promise."[129] However, when the six-party talks convened in March 2007, the BDA problem had still not been resolved, which caused the DPRK delegation to leave Beijing. What was repeatedly said to be a technical problem, whose solution was imminent, dragged on for months. Despite strong suggestions that it should implement the initial phase of the February 2007 agreement, Pyongyang refused to budge, maintaining that before it would comply the BDA problem had to be resolved.

The neoconservatives' hard-line influence on US policymaking had noticeably diminished by 2007 but it had not been altogether eliminated, especially given President Bush's predisposition to this line of thinking. Although only ephemeral, vestiges of neoconservativism reappeared now and then throughout the remaining time of the Bush administration. One such time was in April 2007, two weeks after the deadline passed for Pyongyang to shut down the Yongbyun nuclear facility, when President Bush was asked at Camp David if he was "going soft on North Korea." With Japanese Prime Minister Abe by his side, Bush remarked that he was prepared to get tough with Pyongyang, including the use "of more sanctions," stating also that, "our patience is not unlimited." Abe then commented that unless Pyongyang complies "we will have to take a tougher response on our side."[130] Later, US Secretary of Defense Robert Gates chimed in, repeating Bush's remark that Washington would not have unlimited patience with North Korea.[131]

Just before the sixth round of the six-party talks began in March 2007, IAEA Director General Mohamed ElBaradei visited Pyongyang. While there North Korean officials told ElBaradei that the DPRK would shut down its Yongbyon facility as promised during the February six-party talks in 60 days – that is, on April 14 – once the BDA issue had been settled.[132]

Especially now since it possessed a *songun*-based nuclear deterrent, Pyongyang was not going to be forced or persuaded into compliance until it got what it wanted from Washington. In May, Pyongyang stated that the reason it did not fulfill its pledge to shut down the Yongbyon nuclear facility was because the BDA problem had not been fully resolved – an unambiguous demonstration of its unwavering commitment to the principle of "simultaneous action" or "action for action" when dealing with Washington on the nuclear issue. The North Korean Ministry of Foreign Affairs stated at this time that the DPRK would completely comply with the commitment it made at the February talks: to close down the Yongbyon facility once it is able to use the funds previously frozen at the BDA as it did before the imposition of financial sanctions.[133] That the frozen BDA funds amounted to only $25 million strongly suggested that for Pyongyang it was more of a matter of achieving an "action for action" result than of gaining access to the money.

Fallout: nuclear deterrence and the worsening Japan–DPRK relationship

Meanwhile, relations between Japan and the DPRK hit rock bottom. With a nuclear deterrent to wait out Washington and because the Bush administration had begun to see that its previous hostile policy toward North Korea had failed, Pyongyang could now play political hardball with Japan. Unlike in the first DPRK nuclear crisis during the 1990s, Japan assumed an active role from the outset in the second one.[134] Pyongyang reasoned that because Japan was becoming a political outlier, owing to the increasing Japanese obsession with the abduction issue, it could use this to the DPRK's advantage. This was made much easier since in September 2006 the nationalist Shinzo Abe had become prime minister.

One outcome of the action plan for denuclearizing North Korea that came out of the February 2007 six-party talks was the creation of five working groups, which were to convene within one month.[135] One of these working groups was charged with the normalization of Japan–DPRK relations. Although the normalization talks between Japan and North Korea occurred within 30 days, these discussions accomplished nothing. Pyongyang was highly critical of Tokyo's decision not to contribute to the DPRK's energy-assistance package that the other participants, including Japan, had agreed to at the February six-party talks,[136] unless progress had been made on resolving the abduction issue. Tokyo was unequivocal: "Japan is going to pay nothing in terms of energy support to North Korea."[137]

Less than a week before the start of a new round of normalization talks between Japan and North Korea that were held in Hanoi in early March 2007, Japanese Prime Minister Abe created an international controversy. Appearing determined to push his nationalist agenda forward, Abe asserted, "The fact is, there is no evidence to prove there was coercion"[138] of the "comfort women," the women that were widely believed, including by many historians, to have been forced by the Japanese military to serve its troops as sex slaves during the Second World War. Abe's comment reflected his and the far right's intention to assuage, at the very least, Japan's culpability with respect to the comfort women. Some interpreted the prime minister's comment as contradicting the formal statement made by Chief Cabinet Secretary Yohei Kono in 1993, which offered an apology by the Japanese government to the comfort women. Kono's statement acknowledged that the "Japanese military was, directly or indirectly, involved" in the dreadful conditions that the comfort women experienced and that often they had been "recruited against their own will, through coaxing[,] coercion, etc." Kono's statement further pointed out that many of the comfort women were from the Korean Peninsula, which Japan had annexed, and that they became comfort women "generally against their will, through coaxing, coercion, etc."[139] Although Abe maintained that he would not abandon the Japanese government's commitment to the 1993 statement, he insisted that while there is not evidence proving the direct involvement by the Japanese military in forcing the comfort women to serve as sex slaves, "there were cases in which brokers serving as middlemen in effect coerced them. So I think there was coercion in a broad sense." By creating the feigned dichotomy between direct and broad coercion,[140] Abe attempted to justify his refusal to offer a new expression of remorse to the comfort women, notwithstanding a US House resolution submitted in early 2007 seeking an official apology from the Japanese government.[141]

While both Beijing and Seoul took umbrage at Abe's remarks and his government's position with regard to the comfort women, Pyongyang was incensed. The DPRK's Ministry of Foreign Affairs issued a statement on the same day the Japan–North Korean normalization talks began in Hanoi, lambasting Abe for his leading role in steering the Japanese government away from Japan's proven historical connection to the comfort women issue. The ministry's statement also stressed that, "No matter how desperately the Japanese authorities may try to whitewash the crime-woven past of Japan and cover up the crimes related to the 'comfort women' for the imperial Japanese army, the worse flesh traffic in the 20th century, they are historical facts that Japan can neither sidestep nor deny." For Pyongyang, this behavior by Abe and his government further demonstrated Tokyo's efforts to remilitarize Japan.[142]

The political tensions at the normalization talks in Hanoi were palpable. While Japan remained focused on the unresolved abduction issue, the DPRK insisted that the most pressing problems stemmed from the Japanese annexation of Korea. At the conclusion of the troubled, two-day talks, the DPRK representative Song Il-Ho stressed that Japan demonstrated "unreasonable insistence" on the abduction issue and, repeating Pyongyang's past position on this matter, stated that it has been "completely resolved." Responding to the far-from-promising outcome of the normalization talks, Tokyo's representative Koichi Haraguichi emphasized, "I hope they understand the consequences."[143]

It is important to understand that Pyongyang had its confidence level raised after the DPRK detonated a nuclear device and it was quick to recognize the apparent willingness of the Bush administration to employ appeasement rather than hostility. This gave Pyongyang more leeway in dealing with Japan, especially since Tokyo had suffered a major blow at the February 2007 six-party talks when the Bush administration agreed to start the process of removing the DPRK from the US State Department's terrorism list.

Adding to its problems, Tokyo's insistence that the abduction issue be incorporated into the six-party talks worried some of the other participants to these multilateral discussions. Not too dissimilar from what Pyongyang maintained, Beijing, Moscow and even Washington understood that the six-party talks could be jeopardized if the abduction problem became inextricably linked to resolving the North Korean nuclear issue, especially since the United States had agreed to release the DPRK's previously frozen BDA funds.[144]

With *songun* now bolstered by a nuclear deterrent, Pyongyang maintained in June 2007 that, unlike in the past, military hostilities initiated by Japan or by any other country could not threaten Korean sovereignty. Referring the colonization period, Pyongyang stressed that Korea "wailed bitterly and loudly when the country's sovereignty was usurped by the Japanese imperialist aggressors as it could hardly equip itself even with firelocks in the past. But thanks to the Songun politics of the Workers' Party of Korea it is demonstrating its dignity as a nation with tremendous military power which no foreign enemy on earth dare provoke."[145]

North Korea's lingering suspicions and reliance on *songun*

Pyongyang remained very suspicious of Washington's and Tokyo's military objectives. The North Korean Ministry of Foreign Affairs maintained that Washington's determination to establish a worldwide missile defense system for protection against DPRK and Iranian missiles was a subterfuge that would only cause Pyongyang to increase it defense capabilities.[146] Expressing its concern about the forward progress of the US–Japanese missile defense system, Pyongyang also identified a number of reasons why it was convinced that Japan has been hard at work becoming a major military power, like the United States.[147]

On June 25, 2007, the North Korean Ministry of Foreign Affairs officially announced that the BDA problem had been settled to Pyongyang's satisfaction and that the DPRK was ready to move forward with the denuclearization process it had committed to at the February six-party talks.[148] Very soon after this, Pyongyang launched three short-range missiles. Although Washington and Tokyo had not shown much concern over the previous missiles the DPRK launched in the spring of 2007, calling them simply routine military exercises, this time they both were noticeably critical of Pyongyang. Despite the fact that the Pentagon again viewed the late-June missile launches as routine, the US National Security Council emphasized that it was "deeply troubled that the DPRK has decided to launch several missiles during a delicate time in the six-party talks."[149] Prime Minister Abe stated that Pyongyang had violated the UN Security Council resolution that called "on North Korea to abandon its ballistic missile programs" though, at the same time, indicated that the launches did not pose a threat to Japan's security.[150]

Whether just another routine military exercise or not, Pyongyang had nonetheless established two things: its willingness to comply with its end of the bargain made at the February six-party talks, and that it was also going to do what it could to assure an "action for action" approach to resolving the nuclear crisis. Now possessing a nuclear deterrent, the missile launches showed Pyongyang's determination to maintain *songun*, despite how officials in Washington and Tokyo interpreted them.

Conclusion

When the Cold War ended, Pyongyang understood that the DPRK's revolutionary socialism, nurtured by the *juche* ideology, was confronting new and major changes. A contracted trade environment, brought on by the demise of the Eastern Bloc countries and the Soviet Union, and the same perceived political threats that existed during the Cold War, meant that serious struggles lay ahead for the DPRK. Adding to existing problems, the DPRK was forced to contend with floods, drought and widespread starvation. The first North Korean nuclear crisis during the early 1990s put the Clinton administration at odds with Kim Il Sung. Convinced that the energy-needy DPRK was at work developing nuclear weapons, the Clinton administration pressed hard to shut down North Korea's plutonium-reprocessing facilities, which it accomplished with the 1994 Agreed Framework.

There is no definitive evidence that the Clinton administration intentionally procrastinated in fulfilling its obligations specified in the Agreed Framework because it expected the DPRK to collapse. However, the Clinton administration did drag its feet, particularly with respect to the construction of the light-water reactor project that would give the DPRK some energy independence and the means to build its economy.

By the 1990s, Pyongyang's uncertainty with Washington and the possibility of internal dissension set off by serious economic problems coincided with the formal institution of Kim Jong Il's *songun* policy that emanated from the antecedent *juche* ideology of independence and self reliance. The official institution of *songun* left no doubt that the North Korean leadership had concluded that increasing the effectiveness of the sword was the best way to deal with the perceived threats to the survival of the DPRK. What is more, DPRK's missile development gave the cash-starved nation a source of foreign funds.

Delays by Washington in meeting its obligations made in the Agreed Framework increasingly frustrated Pyongyang. However, it is unclear whether these delays angered Pyongyang enough to cause it to initiate a clandestine uranium-enrichment program for energy, weapons or both. In any case, the allegation that the DPRK had such a program to build nuclear weapons led to the collapse of the Agreed Framework and to the second North Korean nuclear crisis. While Pyongyang often maintained that the DPRK had no uranium-enrichment program to develop nuclear weapons, at the same time it repeatedly claimed that the Bush administration's adoption of a hostile policy toward the DPRK had added to its security concerns. Together, both Washington and Pyongyang took very deliberate steps that prolonged nuclear problem.

Although in the past there had never been any definitive proof that the DPRK had nuclear weapons, the enduring North Korean nuclear crisis proved that Pyongyang had at some point obtained the capability to detonate a plutonium-based nuclear device. The consensus view holds that the DPRK's first nuclear test was a crude nuclear device, which raises three important questions. Did the DPRK have this capability in 2002 or even before then and chose to do little or nothing to improve its competency in building nuclear weapons? If the North's first nuclear test was, relatively speaking, substandard, why did Pyongyang not immediately detonate another device to prove that it had mastered this technology? Did the DPRK's perception of a hostile US policy that had been supported by Japan give Pyongyang the justification it needed to build a nuclear deterrent, which it added to *songun's* portfolio?

If the DPRK developed a nuclear deterrent after October 2002, then the Bush administration's policy was an important factor that contributed to North Korea conducting its first nuclear test and, before this, did a lot to help end the Agreed Framework. Moreover, by encouraging Japan's heightened interest in security, Washington was giving Pyongyang more fodder to add to its justification of why the DPRK had to advance *songun*. Still, Pyongyang ultimately made the decision to disregard the Agreed Framework and to develop and demonstrate its *songun*-based nuclear deterrent.

Having spurned a pacifist posture since its birth, the DPRK has always taken the position that a strong and committed military will sustain the sovereignty of the revolutionary state. While it is certainly debatable just how effective this has been, it is clear that by typically making *songun* the first response to problems Pyongyang has at times too quickly eliminated other diplomatic options and strategies. Thus, the Bush administration's hostile policy played right into the hands of DPRK military hardliners who wanted to move the North's nuclear weapons program forward. Said a prominent North Korean, because of Washington's hostile policy, it was the United States that "made the DPRK develop nuclear weapons to defend the nation and its sovereignty."[151] By repeatedly deciding to demonstrate and strengthen *songun*, Pyongyang has helped its critics justify the inauspicious image of the

DPRK as a rogue state that relies on provocation as a first response to international problems.

Notes

1 US Bureau of the Census, *Statistical Abstract of the United States: 2009*, Table 486, www.census.gov/compendia/statab (accessed on March 25, 2011).
2 Center for Arms Control and Non-proliferation, Washington, DC, www.armscontrolcenter.org/policy/securityspending/articles/fy09_dod_request_global (accessed on April 5, 2011).
3 Central Intelligence Agency, *CIA World Factbook 2004*; GlobalSecurity.org, www.globalsecurity.org/military/world/spending.htm (accessed March 25, 2011).
4 US Department of State, Bureau of East Asian and Pacific Affairs, *North Korea*, August 8, 2008, www.state.gov/r/pa/ei/bgn/2792.htm#econ (accessed March 25, 2011).
5 Central Intelligence Agency, *The World Factbook*, www.cia.gov/library/publications/the-world-factbook/index.html (accessed on April 5, 2011).
6 Stockholm International Peace Research Institute, *The 15 Major Spender Countries in 2007*, www.sipri.org/contents/milap/milex/mex_major_spenders.pdf (accessed on April 5, 2011).
7 Hyung Gu Lynn, *Bipolar Orders: The Two Koreas Since 1989* (London: Zed Books, 2007), p. 5.
8 Stephan Haggard and Marcus Noland, *Famine in North Korea: Markets, Aid, and Reform* (New York: Columbia University Press, 2007).
9 Bradley Babson, "The International Financial Institutions and the DPRK: Prospects and Constraints," North Pacific Policy Papers, #9, University of British Columbia, March 14, 2002.
10 The United States has not been immune to food-distribution problems; thus, sometimes comparing apples to oranges can be informative. In 2007, 13 million households in the United States officially experienced "food insecurity," a condition that means that at some point in the year they had a problem obtaining enough food. Of this amount, 4.7 million households experienced "very low food security," which means that during the year some of the people in these households had to decrease their food consumption and change their normal eating behavior because of food insecurity. In 2007, 691,000 children were in "very low food security" households, up significantly (by 261, 000) from 430,000 in 2006. See Mark Nord, Margaret Andrews and Steven Carlson, *Household Food Security in the United States, 2007* (ERR-66), US Department of Agriculture, Washington, DC, November 2008. In 2008, food insecurity in the United States increased to 17 million households, the worse it had been since 1995 when annual food surveys began. See Mark Nord, Margaret Andrews and Steven Carlson, *Household Food Security in the United States, 2008* (ERR-83), US Department of Agriculture, Washington, DC. November 2009.
11 Haggard and Noland, *Famine in North Korea*, pp. 108–25.
12 UNICEF (United Nations Children's Fund), *Child Nutrition Survey Shows Improvements in DPRK, But UN Agencies Concerned About Holding onto Gains*, UNICEF, Pyongyang/Geneva, February 16, 2003, www.unicef.org/media/media_3878.html (accessed on April 5, 2011); Hazel Smith, *Hungry for Peace, International Security, Humanitarian Assistance, and Social Change in North Korea* (Washington, DC: United States Institute of Peace, 2005); Tim Beal, *The Struggle Against American Power* (London: Pluto Press, 2005), pp. 154–57; Bruce Cumings, *North Korea: Another Country* (New York: The Free Press, 2004), p. 182.

13 "Politics for Independence against Imperialism," *Korea Today*, no. 1, 2009, Pyongyang, p. 32.
14 Central Intelligence Agency, *The World Factbook*, www.cia.gov/library/publications/the-world-factbook/index.html (accessed on April 5, 2011).
15 "On Duty for National Defence," *Korea Today*, no. 1, 2009, Pyongyang, p. 17.
16 Author meeting with two members of the Korean Association of Social Scientists, Pyongyang, January 9, 2009; "Creation of Songun Idea, Turning Point of History," *Korean Central News Agency*, June 28, 2007.
17 Ilpyong Kim, "Kim Jong Il's Military-First Politics," in *North Korea: The Politics of Regime Survival*, eds. Young Whan Kihl and Hong Nack Kim (Armonk, NY: M.E. Sharpe, 2005), pp. 59–74.
18 Kim Jong Il, *The Songun-Based Revolutionary Line is a Great Revolutionary Line of Our Era and an Ever-Victorious Banner of Our Revolution* (Pyongyang: Foreign Languages Publishing House, 2007).
19 Alexander Vorontsov, "North Korea's Military-First Policy: A Curse or a Blessing?" Center for Northeast Asian Policy Studies (Washington, DC: The Brookings Institution, May 26, 2006).
20 Dermot Hudson, "Songun Politics in the Context of the Anti Imperialist Struggle of the Korean People and the World People," *Red Banner of Songun*, February 11, 2006, www.songunpoliticsstudygroup.org (accessed on August 9, 2006).
21 Author meeting with the president of the Korean Association of Social Scientists, Pyongyang, January 6, 2009.
22 "Songun Politics based on Juche Idea," *Korean Central News Agency*, September 1, 2006.
23 Following the US–Japan Joint Declaration on Security in April 1996 came the new Guidelines for Japan–US Defense Cooperation, then the cooperative effort on missile defense, which has been followed by other bilateral security initiatives. See Anthony DiFilippo, *The Challenges of the U.S.-Japan Military Arrangement: Competing Security Transitions in a Changing International Environment* (Armonk, NY: M.E. Sharpe, 2002).
24 Selig Harrison, "Getting Around Pyongyang's Hard-Liners," Nautilus Institute, *Policy Forum Online*, July 5, 2005, www.nautilus.org/fora/security/0555Harrison.html (accessed on September 29, 2006).
25 "Pyongyang Pushes 'Army-First' Policy," *International Herald Tribune*, August 8, 2006.
26 "DPRK will Bolster War Deterrent with Utmost Efforts: KPA General Staff," *Korean Central News Agency*, August 24, 2006.
27 "All Koreans Called Upon to Work for Independent Reunification," *Korean Central News Agency*, February 11, 2009.
28 Kim Jong Il, "The Democratic People's Republic of Korea is a Juche-Oriented Socialist State with Invincible Might," *Rodong Sinmun* and *Minju Joson*, September 5, 2008, republished in *Study of the Juche Idea*, no. 81, February 2009 by the International Institute of the Juche Idea, Tokyo, 2009.
29 Park Myung Rib, "Yuk Sa Sok Ui Hankook Munjewa Buk Hae Munje" ("Korean and North Korean Nuclear Problem in History,") *The Hankyoreh*, September 20, 2009.
30 Kim Il Sung, *Revolution and Socialist Construction in Korea* (New York: International Publishers, 1971), p. 88; Kim Il Sung, Excerpted from *The Creation of the People's Liberation Army*, speech presented at the review of the Korean People's Army, February 8, 1945.
31 Kim Il Sung, *Revolution and Socialist Construction in Korea*, pp. 211–14.
32 Hideshi Takesada, "Military Trends in North Korea," in *North Korea at the Crossroads* ed. Masao Okonogi (Tokyo: Japan Institute of International Affairs, 1988), pp. 73–76.

33 For an account of the EC-121 incident see, Richard Reeves, *President Nixon: Alone in the White House* (New York: Simon and Schuster, 2001), pp. 67–69.

34 Ho Jong Ho, Kang Sok Hui and Pak Thae Ho, *The US Imperialist Started the Korean War* (Pyongyang: Foreign Languages Publishing House, 1993), pp. 246–47.

35 Kim Il Sung, *Revolution and Socialist Construction in Korea*, p. 211.

36 Masao Okonogi, "The Ideology and Political Leadership of Kim Jong Il," in *North Korea at the Crossroads*, ed. Masao Okonogi (Tokyo: Japan Institute of International Affairs, 1988), pp. 1–21.

37 Author interview with representatives of the International Institute of the Juche Idea, Tokyo, July 27, 2007.

38 "Comrade Kim Jong Il Defies Revisionism: On Marx, Engels, Lenin, and Stalin," Excerpted from *Respecting the Forerunners of the Revolution is a Noble Moral Obligation of Revolutionaries*, Pyongyang, 1996, pp. 13–16.

39 Kim Jong Il, *On the Juche Idea*, Document sent to the National Seminar on the *Juche* Idea to commemorate the seventieth birthday of Kim Il Sung, March 31, 1982, published by *The People's Korea*, 1998, www1.korea-np.co.jp/pk/062nd_issue/98092410.htm (accessed on April 5, 2011).

40 "What is Songun? Statement by the Anti Imperialist National Democratic Front (AINDF), Response to Answers Put Forward with Regard to Songun Politics," *Red Banner of Songun*, www.songunpoliticsstudygroup.org (accessed May 20, 2007).

41 Kim Jong Il, *On the Juche Idea*; Jo Song Baek, *The Leadership Philosophy of Kim Jong Il* (Pyongyang: Foreign Languages Publishing House, 1999); Kim Il Sung, *The Life of a Revolutionary Should Begin with Struggle and End with Struggle*, Speech Made at a Banquet Given by the Central Committee of the Workers' Party of Korea and the Government of the Democratic People's Republic of Korea (Pyongyang: Foreign Languages Publishing House, 1990); Kim Il Sung, *Revolution and Socialist Construction in Korea*, pp. 92–93.

42 Author interview with representatives of the International Institute of the Juche Idea, Tokyo, July 27, 2007.

43 "North Korea's Foreign Trade Remains Bleak [June 1995]," in *North Korea: Uneasy, Shaky Kim Jong Il Regime* (Seoul: Naewoe Press, 1997), pp. 63–66.

44 Young Whan Kihl, "Staying Power of the Socialist 'Hermit Kingdom'," in *North Korea: The Politics of Regime Survival*, pp. 3–33.

45 This treaty remains in effect even today. See Dingli Shen, "North Korea: The Chinese View," *Le Monde Diplomatique*, November 2006.

46 "Does Pyongyang Really Want Peace? [August 1995]" in *North Korea: Uneasy, Shaky Kim Jong Il Regime* (Seoul: Naewoe Press, 1997), pp. 11–14.

47 Hong Nack Kim, "Japanese–North Korean Relations under the Koizumi Government," in *North Korea: The Politics of Regime Survival*, pp. 161–82.

48 Defense spending estimates from SIPRI's *Military Expenditure Database*; Japan and South Korean military expenditures converted from yen and won by using 1992 exchanges rates.

49 United Nations, *Treaty on the Nonproliferation of Nuclear Weapons*, United Nations, New York, http://disarmament.un.org/TreatyStatus.nsf (accessed on May 2, 2007); Chi Young Pak, *Korea and the United Nations* (Boston: Kluwer Law International, 2000), p. 134.

50 Center for Nonproliferation Studies, *IAEA–North Korea Nuclear Safeguards and Inspections 1990*, Monterey, CA, http://cns.miis.edu/research/korea/nuc/iaea90.htm (accessed on May 2, 2007).

51 United States Department of State, *Joint Declaration on the Denuclearization of the Korean Peninsula*, Washington, DC, 1992.

52 David Fischer, "The DPRK's Violation of Its NPT Safeguards Agreement with the IAEA," IAEA, www.iaea.org/NewsCenter/Focus/IaeaDprk/dprk.pdf (accessed on April 29, 2007).

53 United Nations, Department of Political Affairs, *Repertoire of the Practice of the Security Council, 1993–1995*, Chapter VIII, Advance Version, United Nations, www.un.org/Depts/dpa/repertoire (accessed May 5, 2007).

54 Joel Wit, Daniel Poneman and Robert Gallucci, *Going Critical: The First North Korean Nuclear Crisis* (Washington, DC: Brookings Institution Press, 2004).

55 International Atomic Energy Agency, *Information Circular*, Vienna, June 21, 1994, www.iaea.org/Publications/Documents/Infcircs/Others/inf447.shtml (accessed March 25, 2011).

56 Jimmy Carter, "Engaging North Korea," *The New York Times*, October 27, 2002.

57 *Agreed Framework Between the United States of America and the Democratic People's Republic of Korea*, Geneva, October 21, 1994.

58 Chuck Downs, *Over the Line: North Korea's Negotiating Strategy* (Washington, DC: American Enterprise Institute Press, 1999).

59 *Portions of Remarks by Senators McCain and Gramm, Just Returned from a Visit to South Korea, During Talk Show Interviews about the North Korean Crisis*, June 21, 1994, www.globalsecurity.org/wmd/library/news/dprk/1994/940621-dprk-usia. htm (accessed March 25, 2011).

60 Richard Cronin, *North Korea's Nuclear Weapons Program: U.S. Policy Options*, Congressional Research Service Report for Congress, Washington, DC, June 1994.

61 Anthony DiFilippo, *Japan's Nuclear Disarmament Policy and the U.S. Security Umbrella* (New York: Palgrave Macmillan, 2006); United Nations, *Status and Text of Treaties*, New York, http://disarmament.un.org/TreatyStatus.nsf (accessed May 2, 2007).

62 Larry Niksch, *North Korea's Nuclear Weapons Program*, Issue Brief, Congressional Research Service, The Library of Congress, Washington, DC, March 17, 2003, p. 6.

63 See, e.g., Bradley Martin, *Under the Loving Care of the Fatherly Leader: North Korea and the Kim Dynasty* (New York: Thomas Dunne Books, 2004), pp. 13 and 125.

64 Kim Il Sung, *For a Free and Peaceful New World*, Speech given to the Inter-Parliamentary Conference, Pyongyang, 1991.

65 Author meeting with the president of the Korean Association of Social Scientists, Pyongyang, January 6, 2009.

66 See KEDO, *The KEDO-DPRK Supply Agreement*, www.kedo.org (accessed March 25, 2011).

67 KEDO, *Agreement on Supply of Light-Water Reactor Project to the Democratic People's Republic of Korea Between the Korean Peninsula Energy Development Organization and the Government of the Democratic People's Republic of Korea*, New York, December 15, 1995.

68 United States General Accounting Office, Report to the Chairman, Committee on Energy and Natural Resources, US Senate, *Nuclear Nonproliferation: Difficulties in Accomplishing IAEA's Activities in North Korea* (Washington, DC: United States General Accounting Office, July 1998).

69 KEDO, *Korean Peninsula Energy Development Organization, Annual Report 2003*, New York, 2003, p. 5.

70 "There will be Nothing But Bad Results," *Korean Central News Agency*, December 9, 1996; "Invariable Hostile Policy Toward the DPRK," *Korean Central News Agency*, January 31, 1997.

71 "Papers Underscore Safeguarding Peace in Korea," *Korean Central News Agency*, June 25, 1997.

72 "LWR Project Starts," *Korean Central News Agency*, August 19, 1997.
73 " LWR Provision is U.S. Obligation, DPRK Foreign Ministry Spokesman," *Korean Central News Agency*, March 6, 1998.
74 Beginning in December 2004, KEDO extended the suspension of the light-water project for an additional year.
75 KEDO, *Korean Peninsula Energy Development Organization, Annual Report 2005*, New York, 2005, p. 6.
76 US Census Bureau, Foreign Trade Statistics, *Trade in Goods with North Korea*, www.census.gov/foreign-trade/balance/c5790.html#2000 (accessed May 11, 2007).
77 "U.S. Perfidious Behavior," *Korean Central News Agency*, March 30, 1998.
78 United States General Accounting Office, Report to the Chairman, Committee on International Relations, House of Representatives, *Nuclear Nonproliferation: Status of Heavy Oil Delivered to North Korea under the Agreed Framework* (Washington, DC: United States General Accounting Office, September 1999).
79 "U.S. Should Take Practical Steps as Soon as Possible," *Korean Central News Agency*, May 8, 1998. Also see, "LWR Project is not U.S. Present to DPRK: KCNA Commentary," *Korean Central News Agency*, July 18, 1998.
80 "Foreign Ministry Spokesman of DPRK–U.S. Talks," *Korean Central News Agency*, August 13, 1998.
81 KEDO, *Korean Peninsula Energy Development Organization, Annual Report 2001*, New York, 2001, pp. 12–13.
82 "Interview: William Perry," *Frontline*, February 26, 2003, www.pbs.org/wgbh/pages/frontline/shows/kim/interviews/perry.html (accessed March 25, 2011).
83 KEDO, *Korean Peninsula Energy Development Organization, Annual Report 2002*, New York, 2002, p. 12.
84 KEDO, *Korean Peninsula Energy Development Organization, Annual Report 2005*, New York, 2005, pp. 10–13.
85 "U.S., South Korea Warned Against Acting Rashly," *Korean Central News Agency*, August 24, 1998; "Prelude to Second Korean War," *Korean Central News Agency*, August 26, 1998; "Rodong Sinmun on 'Uji Focus Lens,'" *Korean Central News Agency*, August 29, 1998; "Ulchi-Fcus Lens," GlobalSecurity.org, www.globalsecurity.org/military/ops/ulchi-focus-lens.htm (accessed May 18, 2007).
86 DiFilippo, *The Challenges of the U.S.-Japan Military Arrangement: Competing Security Transitions in a Changing International Environment*, pp. 45–47,79. Pressured by Washington and Seoul, Tokyo announced in October 1998 that it was prepared to resume funding to KEDO. See, Voice of America, "Japan/North Korea/ KEDO," October 21, 1998, www.fas.org/news/dprk/1998/981021-dprk2.htm (accessed March 25, 2011).
87 "Serious Shortage of Electricity," *Korean Central News Agency*, February 2, 2000.
88 "U.S. Skepticism over DPRK–U.S. Agreed Framework," *Korean Central News Agency*, April 3, 2000.
89 "Spokesman for the DPRK Foreign Ministry on New Administration's Policy Toward the DPRK," *Korean Central News Agency*, February 22, 2001.
90 US Department of State, *Four-Party Talks on the Korean Peninsula, 1997–1998*, www.state.gov/www/regions/eap/korea_4party_talks_1997.html (accessed May 14, 2007).
91 Pak, *Korea and the United Nations*, p. 30.
92 DiFilippo, *The U.S.–Japan Military Arrangement: Competing Security Transitions in a Changing International Environment*.
93 Kim, "Kim Jong Il's Military-First Politics," pp. 59–74; Smith, *Hungry for Peace*, p. 79.
94 Data from various issues of the CIA's *The World Factbook*.

95 US Department of State, Bureau of East Asian and Pacific Affairs, *Background Note: North Korea*, April 2007, www.state.gov/r/pa/ei/bgn/2792.htm (accessed March 28, 2011).

96 Shi Yongming, "Relations at a Crossroad," *The Beijing Review*, vol. 50, no. 11, March 15, 2007, pp. 10–11.

97 Byung Chul Koh, "'Military-First Politics' and Building a 'Powerful and Prosperous Nation' in North Korea," The Nautilus Institute, *Policy Forum Online*, April 14, 2005, www.nautilus.org/fora/security/0532AKoh.html (accessed April 7, 2011).

98 According to NK News, *songun* appears 2,823 times in articles published by the *Korean Central News Agency* between April 2003 and May 2007, and 4,293 times between April 2003 and late February 2009, www.nk-news.net/index.php (accessed March 28, 2011).

99 Nicholas Eberstadt, *The End of North Korea* (Washington, DC: American Enterprise Institute, 1999). See also Nicholas Eberstadt, "The Persistence of North Korea," *Policy Review*, Hoover Institution, Stanford University, no. 127, October & November, 2004; Cumings, *North Korea: Another Country*, pp. 197–99; Bruce Cumings, "The North Korea Problem: Dealing with Irrationality," *Current History*, September 2009, pp. 284–90.

100 Charles Pritchard, *Failed Diplomacy: The Tragic Story of How North Korea Got the Bomb* (Washington, DC: The Brookings Institution, 2007).

101 US House of Representatives, Hearing Before the Subcommittee on East Asia and the Pacific, *U.S.–North Korea Relations after the Policy Review* (Washington, DC: US Government Printing Office, July 26, 2001).

102 *Nuclear Posture Review* [Excerpts], submitted to Congress on December 31, 2001, www.globalsecurity.org/wmd/library/policy/dod/npr.htm (accessed March 28, 2011).

103 Agreed Framework, www.kedo.org/pdfs/AgreedFramework.pdf (accessed March 28, 2011).

104 William Perry, *Review of the United States Policy Toward North Korea: Findings and Recommendations*, Washington, DC, October 12, 1999.

105 Office of the Secretary of Defense, *Proliferation: Threat and Response*, Washington, DC, January 2001.

106 Vice Admiral Lowell Jacoby, Defense Intelligence Agency, US Senate Select Committee on Intelligence, *Open Hearing: Current and Projected National Security Threats to the United States*, Washington, DC, February 11, 2003.

107 US Senate Select Committee on Intelligence, *SSCI Questions for the Record Regarding February 11, 2003 DCI [Director of Central Intelligence] Worldwide Threat Briefing*, Washington, DC, August 14, 2003; Anthony DiFilippo, "US Policy and the Nuclear Weapons Ambitions of the 'Axis of Evil' Countries," *New Political Science*, vol. 28, no. 1, March 2006, pp. 105–6.

108 George Tenet, Director of Central Intelligence, US Senate Select Committee on Intelligence, *Open Hearing: Current and Projected National Security Threats to the United States*, February 11, 2003.

109 Yoichi Funabashi, *The Peninsula Question: A Chronicle of the Second North Korean Nuclear Crisis* (Washington, DC: Brookings Institution Press, 2007), pp. 118–21.

110 US Department of State, Office of the Spokesman, Press Statement, *Report on the U.S. Visit to the Site Kumchang-ni* [sometimes written Kumchang-ri], *Democratic People's Republic of Korea*, Washington, DC, June 25, 1999.

111 "Conclusion of Non-aggression Treaty between DPRK and U.S. Called For," *Korean Central News Agency*, October 25, 2002; "DPRK Foreign Ministry Spokesman on Powell's Remarks," *Korean Central News Agency*, January 29, 2003.

112 Quoted in Funabashi, *The Peninsula Question*, p. 123.
113 "Keynote Speeches Made at Six-way Talks," *Korean Central News Agency*, August 29, 2003.
114 Hui Zhang, "Assessing North Korea's Uranium Enrichment Capabilities," *Bulletin of the Atomic Scientists*, June 18, 2009.
115 Kun Young Park, "Nuclear Politicking on the Korean Peninsula: A Highly Enriched Uranium Program Coming Out of the Pandora's Box," *Korea Journal*, Summer 2009, pp. 99–118.
116 For a discussion of the political problems associated with US intelligence-gathering efforts with respect to enemy states see James Lebovic, "Perception and Politics in Intelligence Assessment: U.S. Estimates of the Soviet and 'Rogue-State' Nuclear Threats," *International Studies Perspectives*, vol. 10, 2009, pp. 394–412.
117 Fox News, "Clinton: Nobody Knows Whether North Korea Had Uranium Program," February 20, 2009, www.foxnews.com/politics/first100days/2009/02/20/clinton-knows-north-korea-uranium-program (accessed March 28, 2011).
118 Ministry of Foreign Affairs, *Press Conference*, Tokyo, February 28, 2003; Ministry of Foreign Affairs, *Third Round of Six-Party Talks Concerning North Korean Nuclear Issues*, Tokyo, June 2004.
119 "KCNA Urges Japan to Honor Spirit of DPRK-Japan Pyongyang Declaration," *Korean Central News Agency*, March 22, 2003.
120 "Dangerous Preliminary War Aimed at Second Korean War Flailed," *Korean Central News Agency*, March 28, 2003.
121 "U.S. to Blame for Derailing the Process of Denuclearization on the Korean Peninsula," *Korean Central News Agency*, May 12, 2003.
122 "DPRK to React against U.S. Arms Buildup Plan by Its Effective Method," *Korean Central News Agency*, June 9, 2003; "U.S. and Japanese Military Nexus Slammed," *Korean Central News Agency*, June 9, 2003.
123 "DPRK's Determination to Strongly React to U.S. Hard-Line Measure Reiterated," *Korean Central News Agency*, June 18, 2003.
124 Scott Snyder, *China's Rise and the Two Koreas* (Boulder, CO: Lynne Rienner, 2009), pp. 121–25.
125 "DPRK FM on Its Stand to Suspend Its Participation in Six-Party Talks for Indefinite Period," *Korean Central News Agency*, February 10, 2005.
126 "Report on State Budget Delivered at the DPRK SPA [Supreme People's Assembly] Session," *Korean Central News Agency*, April 11, 2005.
127 US Department of State, Secretary Condoleezza Rice, *Briefing on the Agreement at the Six-Party Talks in Beijing*, Washington, DC, February 13, 2007.
128 US Department of State, Christopher Hill, *Evening Walkthrough with Reporters at the Six-Party Talks*, Beijing, February 13, 2007. For an argument that assistance is a better choice than sanctions in dealing with Pyongyang, see Ruediger Frank, "The Political Economy of Sanctions against North Korea," *Asian Perspective*, vol. 30, no. 3, 2006, pp. 5–36.
129 "U.S. Promises to Drop Financial Sanctions against N. Korea: Nuclear Envoy," *Yonhap News*, March 10, 2007.
130 The White House, *President Bush and Prime Minister Abe of Japan Participate in a Joint Press Availability*, Camp David, Maryland, April 27, 2007.
131 "U.S. Patience on N Korea not Unlimited: Gates," *The Hankyoreh*, June 2, 2007.
132 "U.N. Inspector Reports on North Korea Visit," *The New York Times*, March 14, 2007; "N. Korea Insists U.S. Unfreeze $25 M," *The Washington Post*, March 17, 2007.
133 "Spokesman for the DPRK Foreign Ministry on Issue of Remittance of De-Frozen Fund of DPRK," *Korean Central News Agency*, May 15, 2007.
134 The Japan Institute of International Affairs, *Resolving the North Korean Nuclear Problem: A Regional Approach and the Role of Japan*, JIIA Policy Report, Tokyo, July 2005.

135 Ministry of Foreign Affairs of the People's Republic of China, *Initial Actions for the Implementation of the Joint Statement*, Beijing, February 13, 2007, www.fmprc.gov.cn/eng/zxxx/t297463.htm (accessed March 28, 2011).

136 "Pyongyang Envoy Hits Tokyo for Withholding Energy Aid," *The Japan Times Online*, March 15, 2007.

137 Ministry of Foreign Affairs, *Press Conference, 2 March 2007*, Tokyo, March 2, 2007.

138 "Abe Denies Evidence of Coercion in Japan's WWII Sex Slavery," *Mainichi Daily News*, March 2, 2007.

139 Ministry of Foreign Affairs, *Statement by the Chief Cabinet Secretary Yohei Kono on the Result of the Study on the Issue of "Comfort Women,"* Tokyo, August 4, 1993.

140 Tessa Morris-Suzuki, "Japan's 'Comfort Women': It's Time for the Truth (in the Ordinary, Everyday Sense of the Word)," *Japan Focus*, March 8, 2007, www.japanfocus.org/products/topdf/2373 (March 9, 2007).

141 "Abe Says No Apology on Comfort Women," *Asahi Shimbun*, March 6, 2007; "Abe: No Apology over U.S. 'Comfort Women' Resolution," *Daily Yomiuri Online*, March 6, 2007; "Japan Refuses Denial of Role in World War II Sex Slavery," *The New York Times*, March 10, 2007.

142 "Japan Urged to Pay for Crimes Related to 'Comfort Women' for Imperial Japanese Army," *Korean Central News Agency*, March 7, 2007.

143 "Japan-North Korea Talks Cut Short," *BBC News*, International Version, March 8, 2007, http://news.bbc.co.uk/2/hi/asia-pacific/6429255.stm (accessed March 28, 2011).

144 "Abduction Issue May Cripple 6-Way Talks," *Asahi Shimbun*, March 22, 2007.

145 "Songun Politics Praised as Patriotic One," *Korean Central News Agency*, June 18, 2007.

146 "DPRK Foreign Ministry Spokesman Blasts U.S. Establishment of MD," *Korean Central News Agency*, June 15, 2007.

147 "KCNA Indicts Japan for Its Moves to Emerges [as] a Military Power," *Korean Central News Agency*, June 29, 2007.

148 "Foreign Ministry Spokesman on Solution to Issue of Frozen Funds," *Korean Central News Agency*, June 25, 2007.

149 "North Korea: U.S. Condemns Missile Tests," *The New York Times*, June 28, 2007.

150 "Abe Blasts North Korea for Ill-Time Sea of Japan Missile Launches," *The Japan Times Online*, June 29, 2007.

151 Author meeting with the President of the Korean Association of Social Scientists, Pyongyang, January 6, 2009.

3 Unlikely bedfellows

US–North Korea inducements in the rearming of Japan

This chapter shows that Japan's movement onto the path to become a "normal country," or *futsu kokka*, with high-level military readiness, the desire to participate in international security affairs unfettered by its constitution and the capability to impose economic sanctions, specifically on North Korea (and more recently on Iran[1]) has been driven by the confluence of three important factors. These factors are Washington's continuous prompting to get Tokyo more involved in military and international security affairs, the conservative-nationalist push in Japan to make it a normal country, and the military actions of the Democratic People's Republic of Korea (DPRK). Together, these factors have defined Japan's security interest in recent years.

It is true that many Japanese people remain committed to Japan's anti-militarist culture that emerged soon after the country's defeat in the Pacific War, despite the fact that a number of its norms have been undermined and its institutional bulwarks have been compromised by policymakers, as is evidenced in Tokyo's support for the 2003 US-led invasion of Iraq.[2] It is one thing to say that today this anti-militarist culture slows down the efforts of many policymakers in Japan to make it a normal country, although this argument sometimes blurs the distinction between public sentiment and policy.[3] However, it is quite another thing to say that Japan's anti-militarist culture has prevented it from moving decisively in the direction of becoming a normal country.[4] For well over a decade, rising nationalism and strengthened conservatism have been militating against the pacifist sentiments of the past.[5] Today, remnants of the Yoshida Doctrine, a nonmilitarist policy approach established during the early Cold War by Prime Minister Shigeru Yoshida that sopped up some key pacifist principles while emphasizing economic development and commitment to the security alliance with Washington, have not precluded Tokyo's steady successful push to strengthen Japan's military capabilities.[6]

The Japanese right: how the present connects to the past

Not only did Washington rather quickly become displeased with Japan's 1947 pacifist constitution and wanted Tokyo to increase the nation's defense budget so that it could support US security objectives. There also was covert US intervention in Japanese politics and society. Although keeping US troops in Okinawa was one of Washington's major security objectives for Northeast Asia, it also wanted very much for Japan to be a military-capable ally that would not turn to the left.

Recently declassified information published by the US State Department in 2006 indicates that during the period 1958 to 1968 Washington authorized four clandestine operations in Japan. Under the pretense that financial backing was coming from American businesses, beginning in 1958, the Central Intelligence Agency (CIA) provided money to some Japanese conservative politicians identified as supporting US policies. Very concerned that leftist politics in Japan would gain enough traction to interfere with US objectives, the CIA began providing funds to moderates in 1959 hoping to cause party fragmentation and to create a "responsible" opposition made up of pro-American Japanese politicians. More generally, for several years the US government earmarked funds for propaganda and related purposes in Japan, as much as $450,000 in 1964, with the expectation of having important parts of Japanese society shun leftist politics.[7] (For more details, see Chapter 5.)

Compared to recent years, Japanese socialists and communists were noticeably stronger during the Cold War. Working to counter the grip of the conservative and pro-American Liberal Democratic Party (LDP), which remained dominant from 1955 to 1993, the socialist and communist parties filled opposition roles in Japanese politics, with the former serving for years as the main opposition party. Staunch supporters of Article 9, Japan's war-renouncing constitutional clause, the socialists and communists served as the political guardians of Japanese pacifism. However, in the mid 1990s the left lost considerable ground, which meant that Japan no longer had an effective way to restrain the nationalism that lay close to the political surface.

The decline of the left also meant there was no political mechanism in place that could offset the steady push from Washington to get Japanese forces actively involved in international security affairs. When Washington asked for Japan's military participation during the first Gulf War in 1991 and Tokyo refused on constitutional grounds, Japanese nationalists experienced a political epiphany. Although still a minority position, that some Japanese nationalists were prominent statesmen was important. Thus, by the mid 1990s the nationalist campaign to get Japan on the path to become a normal country willing to participate in international military affairs was underway.

Growing pressure from Washington intended to get Japan to assume big power security responsibilities fit nicely with the emerging nationalist campaign to make it a normal country. Tokyo was becoming increasingly concerned with Pyongyang's security objectives, especially after the DPRK launched a Rodong missile into the Sea of Japan in May 1993. With the threat from China seen as a long-term problem, Tokyo came to see North Korea as Japan's immediate security concern in Northeast Asia.

Pyongyang's decision to launch the more advanced Taepodong-1 in late August 1998 that flew over Japanese territory rattled Tokyo and provided an opportunity to those in Japan who had been pushing hard for it to take up the responsibilities of a normal country. Complicating all of this was the continued simmering of the past abduction of Japanese nationals by DPRK agents and the failure of Tokyo and Pyongyang to hold normalization talks between 1992 and 2000. The emergence of the second DPRK nuclear crisis in 2002 came at a time in Japan when nationalists were solidifying their efforts to make Japan a normal country.

The LDP's inherent conservatism and strong penchant for supporting US policies not only attracted nationalists but also nationalist sympathizers, such as former Prime Minister Junichiro Koizumi. Prior to leaving office, Koizumi endorsed his chief cabinet secretary, nationalist Shinzo Abe, who became the country's next prime minister.

Several empirical indicators show unequivocally that Japan has moved significantly along the path to become a normal country in a relatively short time, a trek that has been galvanized since 2002 by the abduction issue. Well before this, Japan had initiated a process that resulted in the strengthening of its military relationship with the United States, which included the right to cooperate with Washington in security matters beyond Japanese geographical borders. Tokyo's commitment to the full development and deployment of a missile defense system is still another important indicator of its determination to make Japan a normal state. The same was true for Tokyo's interest in acquiring the F-22 Raptor, a very advanced fighter aircraft. Indeed, if it were not for the ban on the sale of the F-22 Raptor to foreign governments, Japan would be the proud owner of a number of these fighters. The announcement by US Defense Secretary Robert Gates in April 2009 that the United States planned to end the F-22 program was not exactly the news that Tokyo wanted to hear.[8] However, the F-35 Strike Force Fighter, which apparently will have to serve as a substitute for the F-22, will mesh well with Tokyo's determination to make Japan a normal country.

Additionally, in October 2004, the Koizumi-commissioned Council on Security and Defense Capabilities gave legitimacy to talk of Japan launching a preemptive strike while simultaneously increasing the vulnerability of Japan's *senshu boei* (exclusively oriented defense). In its final report the Council stated that "regarding the question of whether it is appropriate to possess offensive capabilities against enemy missile bases" the Japanese government must give careful consideration to this course of action after it weighs other important options.[9] The campaign to revise Article 9, the launching of several spy satellites, having one of the largest military budgets in the world, and upgrading the Defense Agency to the Ministry of Defense all attest to the fact that policymakers in Tokyo have been working hard to make Japan a normal country and to meet US expectations.

The decision in 2010 by the coalition government led by Prime Minister Yukio Hatoyama of the Democratic Party of Japan (DPJ) to end Japan's refueling operations in the Indian Ocean, which had been supporting US efforts in Afghanistan for a number of years, was not welcomed by the Obama administration. However, this decision, which had been encouraged by the Social Democratic Party, then the small socialist part of the coalition government, has had little to no impact on impeding Tokyo's long-term efforts to make Japan a normal country.

Creating the momentum for change

Whether the US occupation authority was responsible for imposing the pacifist constitutional clause on Japan or, as General Douglas MacArthur unequivocally indicated, Article 9 was the brainchild of Prime Minister Kijuro Shidehara,[10] Washington nonetheless quickly concluded that this was a mistake. Not too long after the 1951 US–Japan security treaty had been inked, the Eisenhower administration began what became an enduring US campaign to bring Japan back into the realist world where military power mattered.

Defeated in the Pacific War, Japan adopted an anti-military culture, signified by its policy commitment to *senshu boei*. For most Japanese, the immediate concern after the war was to rebuild the economy. Later, when the goals of economic rebuilding had been reached and surpassed, Tokyo was generally content with remaining a civilian power. Thus, most Japanese policymakers and people remained convinced that the principles of national pacifism had served the nation well.

However, calls for Japan to increase its military spending to reflect its strong economy were made repeatedly by many Washington policymakers and US analysts. Moreover, Japan was constantly said to be receiving a "free ride," protected by American military might, including having a place under the US nuclear umbrella. Like many in Washington, Japanese revisionists, generally nationalists who were a minority voice during the early postwar years, had become convinced that the pacifist constitution should never have happened. Following the departure of Prime Minister Shigeru Yoshida in late 1954, Prime Minister Ichiro Hatoyama began seeking constitutional revision, including Article 9.[11]

Controlled by the LDP during the Cold War, Tokyo viewed the ideologically different political systems in Northeast Asia – the Soviet Union, China and North Korea – as potential threats to Japan. When the Cold War ended, the political situation changed for Japan, although not all that much. Indeed, the Cold War did not really end in Northeast Asia. With the Soviet threat gone and with the perceived threat from Russia ratcheting downward, Tokyo trained its security sights on China and North Korea. That Tokyo had established diplomatic relations with Beijing in 1972 seemed to be a positive step, but one that over time never eliminated the talk of the China threat in Japan. Today, Tokyo sees Beijing's military modernization and big defense budgets as problematic and maintains, "there is concern how the military power of China will influence the regional state of affairs and the security of Japan."[12]

Washington's criticism of Japan's "checkbook diplomacy" during the 1991 Gulf War was not Tokyo's only problem. Long critical of the constitutional restraint placed on Japanese military initiatives, nationalist and conservative forces in Japan began to emphasize the abnormality of its role in international society. In June 1992, the Japanese government passed the International Peace Cooperation Law, which authorized very limited participation of the Self Defense Forces (SDF) in UN authorized peacekeeping operations. For too many in Tokyo, this law did not nearly go far enough.

Efforts that began in the second half of the 1990s to strengthen the US–Japan security alliance and that paid off by the end of the decade became a cause of great concern, especially for Beijing and Pyongyang.[13] Since the strengthened security alliance gave Japan regional responsibilities that it did not have in the past, both Pyongyang and Beijing worried that perhaps Japanese remilitarization was taking hold.[14] Moreover, beginning in 2000, the LDP initiated what became a sustained push to revise the constitution, particularly Article 9. Shortly after the terrorist attacks on the United States in September 2001, the Koizumi government rushed legislation through the Diet that authorized SDF assistance to US troops fighting the war on terrorism in Afghanistan, and then later won approval for sending the SDF to Iraq.

Tokyo was also becoming increasingly vocal about its long-held desire for Japan to become a permanent member of the UN Security Council.[15] Second only to the United States in financial contributions to the United Nations, Tokyo continued to stress its rationale for Japan to acquire a permanent seat on the Security Council, something that Washington has been willing to give only tepid support to. But Japan's UN financial contributions and a hefty budget for the country's Official Development Assistant program were not the only cards that Tokyo could now show in its bid to acquire a permanent seat on the Security Council. Having allowed the SDF to participate in missions in both Afghanistan and Iraq, Tokyo wanted very much to demonstrate to the international community that Japan now was indeed deserving of permanent membership in the Security Council.

Washington's influence

The protracted discussion in Japan about constitutional revision has not been welcomed by its neighbors, including the North Koreans, who harbor bad memories of the many atrocities committed by the Japanese military when it occupied the Korean Peninsula. In recent years, many in Washington have believed strongly that if the Japanese are going to be true partners in the bilateral security alliance, Article 9 must be revised.

Constant criticism by Washington centering on the need for Japan to spend more on defense has kept pressure on Tokyo to increase the country's military expenditures. For example, in a speech given in 2008 in Tokyo, US Ambassador to Japan, J. Thomas Schieffer stated, "The exception to increased spending on defense in Northeast Asia is Japan." Schieffer emphasized that Washington feels "that Japan should consider the benefits of increasing its own defense spending to make a greater, not lesser, contribution to its own security."[16] Although Japan's defense spending has declined slightly in the last few years, nonetheless since 1993 Japanese military expenditures have remained constant at 1 percent of gross domestic product. In 2007, Japan's military expenditures were the fifth highest in the world.[17]

Japan's decision to deploy its SDF to Iraq, albeit in noncombat capacity, openly contravened its oft-stated recognition of the United Nations as the legitimate arbiter of international conflicts. That the United Nations never sanctioned the US-led invasion of Iraq in 2003 points directly to Tokyo's aspiration to have Japan become recognized as a normal country. Pleasing Washington, Tokyo abandoned its historical commitment to the United Nations so that Japan could take another step in the direction of becoming a normal country.

Tokyo has been a strong supporter of Washington's counterproliferation campaign, which has become noticeably more aggressive since the 2001 terrorist attacks on the United States. While nuclear disarmament and nonprolifera- tion should be viewed as two sides of the same coin, enhanced focus on coun- terproliferation blatantly ignores the existing arsenals of the nuclear weapons states and their obligation to work toward the goal of eliminating their nuclear weapons, as specified in Article VI of the Nuclear Nonproliferation Treaty.

North Korea's launching a rocket without prior notification over Japanese territory in August 1998 became the ultimate catalyst for Tokyo to sign on to the US missile defense system (MDS). However, this event certainly should not be seen as the only inducement. For some time before this launch, Washington had been attempting to persuade Tokyo of the need for Japanese participation in a ballistic MDS. Even though some in Tokyo, and notably within the Defense Agency, believed that Japanese security required the intro- duction of a ballistic MDS, this was not, at first, the consensus position.[18] Thus, to discount North Korea's and even China's perceived threat to Japan from Tokyo's decision to move forward with MSD would be wrong; however, it would be equally wrong to minimize US pressure on Japanese officials, which began during the Reagan years.

Japan's desire to acquire an advanced fighter

One of the more interesting issues to appear recently is Tokyo's desire to acquire the US-made F-22 Raptor, a purchase that were it to have materia- lized would have certainly generated criticism that Japan is well on its way to abandoning *senshu boei*. Although in this case Washington played no direct part in pressuring Tokyo to purchase the F-22 Raptor, its unyielding exhortations for Japan to assume more military and security responsibilities cannot be disassociated from this issue.

The F-22 Raptor is a stealth fighter that flies at supersonic speed. Its design and performance capabilities have one principal objective: air superiority. Lockheed Martin Corporation, the prime contractor, describes the F-22 Raptor as having "enhanced offensive and defensive avionics and low observability or stealth."[19] It is an invasive, tactical aircraft with a price tag of about $150 million per plane. In February 2006, there was growing interest in Washington to sell the F-22 to some US allies, something that had been prohibited for several years to protect American military technology. At the top of the foreign-buyer list was Tokyo, which, according to an official in the Japanese Defense Agency, had contacted both the US Air Force and Lockheed Martin to express its interest in replacing Japan's aging F-4s. At the time, an official from Lockheed Martin pointed out that the plan to sell the F-22 to US allies was "at the three- or four-star level; it's not at the highest level yet, [which is to say] to the people who really count – but it's getting there."[20] The push to allow for the authorization of foreign sales of the F-22 showed some progress in June 2006, when the US House of Representatives voted by voice to end the ban on the sale of the aircraft to US allies.[21] However, Congressional conferees soon decided to retain the ban on selling the very technologically advanced F-22 to foreign governments.[22]

Japan nonetheless continued to show interest in purchasing this fighter. Unlike a few years before, by 2008 higher-level officials in Washington had been reviewing the possibility of selling the F-22 to US allies, and Japan remained at the top of the list of foreign buyers.[23] In June 2009, the Armed Services Committee passed an amendment to the 2010 defense budget that mandated the US Department of Defense to examine the possibility of selling the F-22 only to Japan.[24] Immediately critical, Pyongyang pointed out that Japan's continuing desire to purchase the F-22 proves that "the Japanese reactionaries seek to round off the capacity for mounting a surprise preemptive attack on other countries and secure a military guarantee for realizing their wild ambition for overseas expansion."[25]

After a vote by the US House of Representatives to discontinue funding for the F-22, a fighter strongly opposed by President Obama and Secretary of Defense Robert Gates, Tokyo recognized by July 2009 that its chances of being able to purchase F-22s were quite small. Rather than the F-22, the Obama administration supports the manufacture of another stealth fighter, the F-35. With the likelihood of purchasing the F-22 becoming increasingly bleak and still determined to acquire an advanced stealth fighter, Tokyo began considering the F-35 during the summer of 2009.[26] By the fall, Washington, apparently seeing no problem with selling the F-35 to Japan, told Tokyo that it had to pay ¥1 billion (approximately $11.3 million) for information on this advanced stealth fighter.[27]

Several factors shed light on why Japan first wanted the F-22 and subsequently the F-35. The overarching factor is the Japanese right's quest to make

Japan a normal country. Others are continuing the pressure by Washington on Tokyo to increase Japanese defense spending; strong US encouragement of Japan to assume more international security responsibilities; and the receptivity of the political right in Japan to this pressure and encouragement.

Still another factor that has persuaded Tokyo that Japan's security needs would be best served by acquiring these very sophisticated fighters has been its perception of threats from North Korea and China. This, however, immediately raises the question of why Tokyo remained interested in purchasing aircraft designed to establish air dominance and concomitant kill capacity if Japan intends to maintain *senshu boei* for the foreseeable future. Since 2004, Tokyo has on at least two occasions indicated that it would be permissible for Japan to launch a preemptive strike; the most recent occurred in the wake of North Korea's series of missiles tests undertaken in early July 2006.[28] The public expression of the permissibility of a preemptive strike shows the growing influence of Japanese conservatives and nationalists, and gives credence to the argument that some in Tokyo would like to revise Japan's decades-old defense policy. Short of this, since survey data shows that about two-thirds of the Japanese public still does not support the revision of Article 9,[29] Tokyo can simply continue doing what it has been doing for years, which is to rely on an expansive interpretation of Article 9. Although Tokyo officially interprets Article 9 of the constitution as limiting Japan "to the minimum necessary for self-defense,"[30] this is ostensibly at odds with the Japanese government's strong desire to purchase the invasive F-22 Raptor, a "multi-role fighter," as billed by the US Air Force, designed to establish "air dominance" and produce an "exponential leap in warfighting capabilities."[31] Much the same can be said of the stealth-equipped F-35 Joint Strike Fighter, which according to Lockheed Martin, the manufacturer, "provides quantum leaps in survivability and lethality."

The North Korean connection

Today, Tokyo sees North Korea, which has not been reluctant to demonstrate the results of its *songun* (military-first) policy, as Japan's biggest security concern.[32] While on the one hand, the DPRK is responding to the hard-line policy of the United States that Tokyo has supported, on the other hand, Pyongyang has not been short on provocation. Pyongyang's propensity to be provocative has typically occurred when it believes that Washington is ignoring North Korea.

Repeated official expressions of concern about the Chinese military threat notwithstanding, there is the sobering reality that upsetting the Sino-Japanese economic relationship would strike a severe blow to both Tokyo and Beijing. The magnitude of Sino-Japanese trade is staggering. For the ninth consecutive year in 2007, Sino-Japanese trade continued to break records, reaching more than $236 billion. In 2007, China's trade with Japan surpassed its trade with the United States, which had previously been Japan's most important trade partner.[33] Moreover, Japanese businesses continue to establish themselves in China, and Japan's direct investments there are currently substantial.[34] Indeed, these kinds of economic ties do not exist between Japan and North Korea.

Pyongyang asserted soon after it launched the Taepodong-1 in late summer 1998 that the three-stage artificial satellite, the *Kwangmyŏngsŏng-1*, had been successful and that the United States and Japan should not be critical of the DPRK, since both countries have launched satellites, but unlike North Korea, theirs was with the intention of conducting espionage.[35] While Pyongyang's definition of a successful launch pertained specifically to the DPRK's use "of 100 percent local technology and local effort," there were observable (successful) outcomes in Japan as well resulting from this event.

Because of the DPRK missile launch in 1998, not only did Tokyo announce its intention to join the United States in beginning work on missile defense, but it also decided to develop Japanese spy satellites. Japan's development of spy satellites would lessen its dependence on US intelligence but it could have adverse effects on American businesses producing satellite technology. In September 1999, Washington and Tokyo signed a formal agreement committing Japan to purchase parts needed to develop its first spy satellite.[36]

The Law Concerning the National Space Development Agency of Japan, enacted in 1969, stipulated that the launching of artificial rockets and satellites would be "exclusively for peaceful purposes."[37] In 1994, discussion emerged in Japan pertaining to the military use of space.[38] Circumventing the 1969 law, Tokyo launched two Japanese spy satellites in March 2003. Pyongyang's decision to launch the Taepodong-1 in August 1998 galvanized the existing momentum in Tokyo to make Japan a normal country, of which MDS and spy satellites are crucial components.

Exacerbating the effects of the 1998 DPRK rocket launch was that Pyongyang did not announce the event in advance. If Pyongyang truly believed that the launching of the Taepodong-1 would not be viewed as provocative and was done simply to bolster the nationalistic spirit of North Koreans, it would have made certain that other countries knew its intentions beforehand. However, there is reason to suspect that Pyongyang did intend the launch to be provocative. A few days after the launch, the DPRK Foreign Ministry indicated that whether this experience "will be used for a military purpose or not, entirely depends on forces hostile to us."[39]

Pyongyang's launching of several missiles in early July 2006 was consistent with its *modus operandi*. Similar to the rocket launched in 1998, Pyongyang again became troubled in July 2006 because the Bush administration had not been paying enough attention to resolving the DPRK nuclear crisis. After US satellites detected evidence of an imminent DPRK missile test, the DPRK responded that it was no longer "bound by any statement such as the Pyongyang Declaration."[40] Signed in September 2002 by Japanese Prime Minister Junichiro Koizumi and North Korean leader Kim Jong Il, the Pyongyang Declaration specified the DPRK's agreement to "maintain the moratorium on missile launching in and after 2003."

Pyongyang had initially declared a self-imposed moratorium on long-range missile tests in September 1999, provided discussions with Washington continued. Pyongyang reaffirmed its moratorium on long-range missile testing in the US–DPRK Joint Communiqué issued in October 2000.[41] However, the North Korean Foreign Ministry pointed out in March 2005 that because bilateral discussions between Pyongyang and Washington ended once the Bush administration came to power in 2001, the DPRK was "not bound to any international treaty or law as far as the missile issue is concerned."[42] A DPRK official at the United Nations in New York, Han Song-ryol, indicated in late June 2006, "We are aware of the U.S. concerns about our missile-test launch. So our position is that we should resolve the issue through [bilateral] negotiations,"[43] a proposal that Washington quickly rejected, given its commitment to the six-party talks involving the United States, North and South Korea, China, Japan and Russia.

Both Washington and Tokyo announced that if Pyongyang conducted a missile test they would take quick and punitive action. Still well before the missile launch, Washington and Tokyo initiated discussions on a resolution at the United Nations that would penalize North Korea, should it go ahead with missile testing. Meanwhile, Washington and Tokyo sent ships close to North Korea to detect the anticipated missile testing, and the Pentagon announced that it was dispatching Patriot missiles to Japan that could conceivably intercept North Korean missiles.[44]

The DPRK immediately claimed in early July 2006 after it launched missiles that it had not violated the Pyongyang Declaration. Since the Pyongyang Declaration indicated that Japan and the DPRK would be working to normalize bilateral relations, the North Korean Foreign Ministry stressed that the missile-test moratorium specified in the agreement was no longer binding. Stating that Tokyo had abandoned its commitment to the Pyongyang Declaration and that it has been following Washington's hostile policy toward the DPRK, the North Korean Foreign Ministry maintained that Japanese officials have steered bilateral relations back to where they were prior to the 2002 Koizumi-Kim summit. Pointing to the US imposition of financial sanctions on the DPRK in the wake of the Joint Statement that came out of the six-party talks in September 2005, and emphasizing that Washington had prevented its implementation by conducting military exercises aimed at North Korea, the foreign ministry maintained that there was no reason any longer to postpone missile testing. Serving to further justify its missile test, the DPRK Foreign Ministry rhetorically asked if either Washington or Tokyo had informed Pyongyang prior to the many missiles tests they have conducted near North Korea.[45]

The DPRK's chief negotiator for Japan–North Korean normalization talks, Song Il Ho, told Japanese reporters assembled in Pyongyang that Tokyo's failure to make amends for its imperial conquest of Korea forced Pyongyang's hand. Said Song, "It is acceptable for North Korea to impose sanctions against a Japan that has avoided making a final accounting of its past" and that Tokyo's protest of the DPRK missile launches would lead to "an even stronger physical response".[46]

The gist of the DPRK argument was that its July 2006 missile testing was justifiable, a position fully endorsed by its supporters outside of North Korea.[47] Pyongyang believed that even it if had announced the missile launches beforehand, the DPRK would still be strongly criticized, especially by Tokyo and Washington. Intended to grab Washington's attention, Pyongyang's decision to launch missiles and not to provide advance notification gave Japanese conservatives the political justification to push harder to make Japan a normal country, which would now include the creation of a sanctions regime aimed squarely at North Korea.

Reactions to Japan's consideration of preemptive strike

Seoul made clear that it viewed the talk in Tokyo pertaining to a "preemptive strike" and the "use of force" following the July 2006 missile tests by North Korea as a threat. Just days after the talk of a preemptive strike emerged, a spokesperson for Cheong Wa Dae (South Korea's executive office and residence of the president) issued a statement indicating that recalling Japan's past justification for invading Korea, which was to protect Japanese citizens living in the peninsula, its current "grave and threatening" remarks put regional peace and stability at risk. The South Korean statement went on to stress that while North Korea's missiles launches were provocative, Tokyo has used "this opportunity" to raise the issue of a "'preemptive strike' in an attempt to further intensify a crisis on the Korean Peninsula and to justify the militarization of Japan."[48]

Beijing saw Japanese officials' remarks pertaining to a possible preemptive strike against the DPRK in much the same way as Seoul. The Chinese Foreign Ministry pointed out that these remarks were "extremely irresponsible," since in addition to worsening tensions in Northeast Asia, they came at a time when the international community is working to establish diplomatic solutions to problems.[49] Moreover, at least some in Beijing contended that the DPRK missile launches provided Tokyo with a justification for bolstering Japan's military alliance with Washington.[50]

Pyongyang indicated that Japanese officials' discussion "of 'preemptive attack' on the DPRK will escalate the stand-off between the DPRK and Japan and coil up the tensions in Northeast Asia."[51] Like Beijing, Pyongyang expressed its concerns about Japan's white paper on defense, which called for a strengthening of the US–Japan military alliance.[52] Referring to Japan and the United States, Pyongyang emphasized "Their theory of preemptive attack on the DPRK is a move as dangerous as a declaration of war to reinvade Korea."[53]

Tokyo reacts to DPRK missiles tests

Tokyo lost no time amplifying the hostile intent of the missile tests conducted by the DPRK in July 2006. On the same day as the missile tests, Tokyo sent a letter of protest to Pyongyang, via the Japanese embassy in Beijing. Tokyo announced that the North Korean missile tests threatened Japanese security, regional peace and stability, and violated the Pyongyang Declaration.[54]

Just hours after the DPRK missile launches Prime Minister Koizumi was on the telephone with President Bush. Their telephone conversation noted that they had demonstrated the strength of the US–Japan security alliance as well as their influence in getting an emergency session of the UN Security Council called to discuss a resolution to address North Korea's missiles tests. With regard to the latter issue, the Bush–Koizumi telephone conversation stressed "the importance of delivering a unified strong message from the international community" to Pyongyang.[55]

Two days after the DPRK missile launches and after conferring with Washington and London, Tokyo presented to the UN Security Council a draft resolution that sought sanctions against North Korea. Endorsed also by Paris, Tokyo's draft resolution denounced the North Korean missile launches. Specifically, it contained language prohibiting any country from sending or acquiring missile products or technology related to the DPRK's missile or weapons of mass destruction (WMD) efforts and forbade all financial dealings associated with its missile and WMD programs.[56] However, despite Tokyo and Washington's efforts to get Beijing to go along with Japan's tough resolution, neither China – the DPRK's closet ally – nor Russia believed that employing a hard-line approach was the appropriate course of action.

Beijing stated that Tokyo's draft resolution was "an overreaction," while Moscow viewed it as "overloaded with emotions." Moderate South Korean President Roh Moo-hyun declared that Tokyo was creating too much of a "fuss" over the DPRK missile launches.[57] Calling the Japanese ambassador to South Korea to the foreign ministry's office in Seoul, the South Korean government articulated its position to Tokyo. Seoul emphasized that a gradual approach was the best way to deal with Pyongyang and, referring to Tokyo's resolution, "any unilateral move to pass an anti-North Korea resolution through the UNSC [United Nations Security Council] is not desirable."[58]

Beijing and Moscow at first preferred that the Security Council issue a less controversial Presidential Statement rather than a more demanding and punitive resolution. Indeed, Beijing felt that a Presidential Statement from the Security Council would send "strong messages" to Pyongyang. After China's bilateral efforts to gain North Korea's compliance to resolve the matter failed, Beijing and Moscow drafted a resolution that was less punitive than Japan's initial document and which, again unlike Tokyo's draft, did not seek to invoke Chapter VII, Article 42 of the UN Charter, which legitimates the use of armed force to gain compliance.[59] In the meantime, Han Song-ryol, a North Korean official at the United Nations in New York, articulated Pyongyang's solution. Han stressed that peaceful co-existence with the DPRK is a choice that Washington has to make and that the way to resume the stalled six-party talks is for Washington to end the financial sanctions that it had recently imposed on North Korea.[60] At the same time, DPRK Deputy Foreign Minister

Kim Hyong Jun stated while traveling in South Africa, "As soon as the United States lifts financial sanctions, we will readily participate in the next round of the six-party talks."[61]

Immediately after the DPRK missile tests, Tokyo invoked a previously enacted law that permitted the Japanese government to prohibit ships considered a security risk from entering Japan. The day after the missile tests, Tokyo banned the North Korean ship Mangyongbong-92, which regularly docked at Niigata, from entering Japan for six months. Having consistently and reasonably successfully lobbied the Japanese political right in the past, the Association of Families Kidnapped by North Korea emphasized that Tokyo should not remove the ban on DPRK ships until Pyongyang satisfactorily resolves the abduction issue.[62]

In mid July, the UN Security Council unanimously approved Resolution 1695, which condemned the DPRK for its missile launches and demanded that it put on hold its missile activities and reinstitute its moratorium on missile testing. Although the resolution did not rely on Chapter VII, Article 42 as Tokyo and Washington wanted, it did require that countries not send or obtain missile equipment, parts and technology relating to the DPRK's missile or WMD programs and that they not have financial dealings associated with these efforts.[63] Significantly, a survey conducted by the *Asahi Shimbun* showed that 85 percent of Japanese voters supported the adoption of the Security Council's resolution, at least partly because 77 percent of the respondents believed that DPRK missiles threaten Japan.[64]

Vice-Minister for Foreign Affairs Shintaro Ito, the Japanese representative in New York at the Security Council, praised the passage of Resolution 1695, which in effect was a compromise document reflecting Tokyo and Washington's hard-line interests, as well as Beijing and Moscow's conciliatory position. Ito stressed that the Council responded expeditiously to the DPRK's missile launches, which threatened Japan's and the region's security and emphasized that Tokyo planned to institute "those measures that are necessary to achieve the objectives set out in the resolution."[65] Japanese Foreign Minister Taro Aso pointed out after the adoption of Resolution 1695 that Tokyo "will continue to strictly implement export control measures and take appropriate steps necessary to control the transfer of financial resources, for the purpose of non-proliferation of missiles and weapons of mass destruction to North Korea."[66]

US Ambassador to the United Nations John Bolton also indicated his satisfaction with the approval of Resolution 1695 by the Security Council. Bolton maintained that by launching several missiles in early July, North Korea had violated, among other international agreements, the Joint Statement of the six-party talks held in Beijing in September 2005, which reaffirmed the Pyongyang Declaration between Japan and the DPRK and therefore the latter's commitment to a moratorium on missile tests. The Russian, French and British representatives at the Security Council meeting made clear their concern about the DPRK missile launches. The Chinese representative, Wang

Guangya, expressed his government's agreement with the resolution; however, he also stressed that it was important for all countries to exercise restraint, emphasizing that Beijing would not support any action that would create additional tension. Pak Gil Yon, the North Korean representative in New York, forthrightly rejected Resolution 1695, calling it an effort by some nations to wrongly use the Security Council for their political objectives and to force DPRK compliance.[67]

In Pyongyang, the DPRK Foreign Ministry described the adoption of the UN resolution as "a product of the U.S. hostile policy toward" North Korea, insisting that "It is brigandish logic to claim that missile launches conducted by the U.S. and Japan are legal while the training of missile launches conducted by the DPRK to defend itself is illegal."[68] Pyongyang later severely criticized US Secretary of State Condoleezza Rice for commenting that the DPRK should have provided advance notice to other countries of its intention to launch missiles and for stating that North Korea is capable of carrying out a nuclear strike. Pyongyang stressed that it authorized the missile launches only subsequent to it being sure that no harm or damage would result from its decision.[69]

Despite Pyongyang's efforts to deflect global criticism by attempting to justify the missile tests, international condemnation had spread quickly from New York to St. Petersburg. On the same day that the Security Council adopted Resolution 1695, the G8 began its annual meetings in St. Petersburg. The G8's summary statement underscored the members' collective endorsement of the Resolution 1695 and advised Pyongyang to resume its moratorium on missiles testing.[70]

Less than a week before the resignation of Prime Minister Koizumi in September 2006, who in the past had been reluctant to impose sanctions on the DPRK,[71] Tokyo took steps to stop the flow of financial resources to North Korea. Seeking as much attention as it could muster, five Japanese government organizations – the Ministry of Finance, the Ministry of Foreign Affairs, the Ministry of Economy, Trade and Industry, the National Police Agency and the Financial Services Agency – together announced the Koizumi Cabinet's decision to impose financial sanctions on North Korea. The cabinet's decision, which took effect immediately, prohibited Japanese institutions from having unauthorized financial dealings with 15 non-Japanese businesses and one individual said to have been supporting the DPRK's WMD or missile programs. Washington had named the individual (Jacob Steiger, a Swiss businessman) and 12 of the 15 companies, leaving Tokyo to add only three establishments.[72]

Tokyo was reasonably sure that the sanctions it imposed on North Korea would not encounter much political resistance at home. As will be shown in Chapter 6, the major opposition political parties in Japan rebuked Pyongyang's decision to launch missiles. Organized labor in Japan also denounced the DPRK missile launches. Rengo (Japanese Trade Union Confederation), Japan's largest labor organization with nearly seven million members, issued a statement that condemned Pyongyang's action, supported Tokyo's decision to suspend the entry of the Mangyongbong-92 into Japan and encouraged the government "to take resolute measures, including economic sanctions, in a firm manner."[73]

Tokyo knew as well that the Japanese public, which, egged on by the right, had become increasingly frustrated by the failure of Pyongyang to settle the abduction issue and would not oppose the economic sanctions that it directly imposed on North Korea in September 2006. A survey conducted by *Kyodo News* shortly after Tokyo temporarily banned the Mangyongbong-92 from entering Japan showed that over 80 percent of the respondents believed that Tokyo should impose stringent economic sanctions on the DPRK. A short time later, a *Mainichi Shimbun* survey indicated that 70 percent of the respondents wanted additional and severe sanctions to be imposed on North Korea.[74]

Pyongyang reacted harshly to Tokyo's imposition of new financial sanctions, maintaining that the decision to do so by the Koizumi cabinet "can not be construed otherwise than a politically motivated charade intended to please its American master, pursuant to Washington's hostile policy towards the DPRK." Stressing that Tokyo's provocative decision to impose new economic sanctions on the DPRK contravened the spirit of the Pyongyang Declaration and exacerbated bilateral tensions, Pyongyang promised to take steps to offset Japan's move.[75]

However much the DPRK despised the new sanctions, it was using the Pyongyang Declaration in two different ways. Pyongyang's major justification for the July 2006 missiles launches – that the DPRK's moratorium on missile testing no longer had to be maintained, since Tokyo was not working in good faith to normalize bilateral relations – was at variance with its charge that Japan was "trampling upon the spirit and requirements" of the Pyongyang Declaration.

This is not to say that Japanese policymakers have had a unified view of the Pyongyang Declaration. After the DPRK nuclear crisis emerged in 2002, some within the Ministry of Foreign Affairs still wanted to normalize relations with North Korea, since they believed that rapprochement, as called for in the Pyongyang Declaration, would be good for Japan and would considerably improve the security environment in Northeast Asia. But those in Tokyo who advocated a more conservative political track, which became dominant, were especially unenthusiastic about Japan normalizing relations with North Korea. These policymakers were of like mind with those officials in Washington who held that Japan must not normalize relations with North Korea, at least not until the United States declares a successful resolution to the DPRK nuclear crisis.

Security reaction To DPRK missile tests

Shortly after the DPRK missile tests in July 2006, Tokyo announced that it would send up its third satellite to monitor the DPRK's activities.[76] Tokyo launched the intelligence-gathering satellite, despite both US and Japanese experts calling the DPRK's long-range Taepodong-2 launch a complete failure.[77] Along with the United States hastening its missile defense activities in Japan subsequent to the DPRK missile tests, Tokyo stepped up it plans.

In late August 2006, the USS Shiloh arrived in Japan, an Aegis vessel with sophisticated missile-defense capabilities.[78] In late September, the United States had moved an advanced radar detection system from one of its bases in Aomori Prefecture in northern Japan to another military location in this prefecture so that it could better monitor North Korean missile activities.[79]

In late July, Washington and Tokyo jointly announced that US-owned Patriot Advanced Capability-3 (PAC-3) defense missiles would be deployed to Okinawa. The plan immediately met with resistance from the governor of Okinawa prefecture Keiichi Inamine and from the mayors of Okinawa City and Kadena Town, two of the three places that are home to the Kadena Air Base, a major US military facility in Japan where many of the PAC-3s would soon be heading. Later, when US forces began moving equipment for the PAC-3s to Kadena Air Base the mayor of Okinawa City, Mitsuko Tomon, filed an official protest with a regional office of Japan's Defense Facilities Administration Agency, remonstrating that local approval had not been granted for the PAC-3 deployment.[80] By the end of October 2006, US forces had placed a number of launchers for PAC-2s and PAC-3s at the Kadena Air base, only about 200 yards from the Kadena town building.[81]

Because of the DPRK missiles launches, Tokyo asked Washington in July 2006 to sell more PAC-3 missiles to Japan. Seeing Tokyo's request as reasonable, the Bush administration authorized the sale of 80 additional PAC-3s to Japan.[82] Although the PAC-2 missiles had previously been deployed in Japan, the Japanese government installed a more advanced PAC-3 system early in 2007 to improve the nation's security from DPRK missile launches.[83]

Pyongyang responded harshly to Tokyo's deployment of PAC-3s and to the recent change allowing the Japanese minister of defense rather than the prime minister decide when to launch missiles in an emergency. Pyongyang maintained that, in pursuing its objective to participate in international security initiatives with the United States, Japan's increased military capabilities have made it a "a significant force of war."[84]

Soon after Tokyo launched its third spy satellite in September 2006, it maintained this action was not meant to be provocative and that the satellite had purposes other than security.[85] However, Pyongyang suspected that the DPRK would be the primary target of the latest satellite and that it would therefore be undergoing even more scrutiny by Tokyo. Pyongyang claimed that the spy satellite would help Tokyo fulfill its goal of reinvading the Korean Peninsula. Pyongyang remarked that, notwithstanding its previous warning that it views Japan's launching of spy satellites as a major threat to the DPRK's national security, Tokyo went ahead with the launch anyway. Because the launching of this spy satellite occurred at the same time that Tokyo had been trying to revise its pacifist constitution, Pyongyang indicated that it is especially threatening to the DPRK and that it will take the necessary steps to defend itself.[86]

Pyongyang also used Japan's launching of a solar satellite affixed to a M-5 solid fuel rocket to rebuke Tokyo. Pyongyang charged that Japan's claim that the satellite launch is intended only as a science project is a pretext concealing Tokyo's real objective. Pyongyang maintained that, because the M-5 rocket, used for the seventh time, relied on solid fuel, what Japan learned from the launch would be applied to missile development, moving it closer to fulfilling the objective of becoming a military power.[87]

DPRK nuclear testing

Washington first suggested the possibility of a North Korean nuclear test in April 2005. Referring to pictures from US satellites, an official in Washington then stated, "We see things. But much of what we see is open to interpretation."[88] Sixteen months later, in August 2006, a high-ranking Bush administration official in the State Department told *ABC News*, "It is the view of the intelligence community that a [North Korean nuclear] test is a real possibility."[89]

Shortly after this, Kim Jong Il told Chinese and Russian officials in Pyongyang that North Korea was getting ready to conduct its first nuclear test.[90] Pyongyang also did not let pass unnoticed the fact that the United States performed its 23rd subcritical nuclear test in late August, calling it a violation of the Comprehensive Test Ban Treaty and a continuing effort by Washington to build small, yet powerful, nuclear weapons to carry out its policy of preemptive strike.[91]

In August 2006, the Bush administration relayed intelligence information from its satellite photographs to Japan, telling Tokyo that North Korea could be getting ready to conduct an underground nuclear test in the northeastern part of the country, which is a geographic quadrant close to Japan. However, Japan's two spy satellites could not corroborate the information Washington sent. Although Tokyo concluded that a DPRK nuclear test was not likely to take place any time soon, the possibility still existed that it could occur.[92] In South Korea, President Roh Moo-hyun stressed that Seoul has no information one way or the other about whether Pyongyang was preparing to carry out a nuclear test.[93] South Korea's top intelligence officer Kim Seung-kyu pointed out that, while a DPRK nuclear test was a possibility, the report by *ABC News* stating that US intelligence had identified cables visible at a site in northeast North Korea was not conclusive, since "the finding of cables there does not necessary [*sic*] mean that they are related to a nuclear test."[94]

In early September 2006 the Japanese right got a boost from former prime minister and defense chief Yasuhiro Nakasone. Known for his hawkish, nationalist views, the elder Nakasone is the founder and chairman of the Institute for International Policy Studies (IIPS), which in June 2005 released a proposal to revise the Japanese constitution, including Article 9, so that Japan could participate in "international cooperative frameworks."[95] Coinciding with the raised tensions in Tokyo stemming from the DPRK's missile launches in July 2006, the IIPS released a report in September, entitled *A Vision of Japan in the 21st Century*. Upon releasing this report Nakasone commented, "There are countries with nuclear weapons in Japan's vicinity. We are currently dependent on U.S. nuclear weapons, but it is not necessarily known whether the U.S. attitude will continue."[96] In addition to reiterating the need to revise Article 9 and that "Japan should find a way to exercise the right of collective self-defense," the 2006 IIPS report stressed several other important things. The report indicated that Japan should adopt a "proactive" security posture that is in accordance with the nation's alliance with the United States, "boost" its "defense capabilities," and noted that if Tokyo concludes there is a looming security threat to the nation "the use of force against enemy bases should not be ruled out" – thus a preemptive strike. While the IIPS report stated that Japan should remain a nonnuclear state and work to strengthen the nuclear nonproliferation regime, it also recommended – consistent with past comments made by Nakasone – that to be ready for future changes in the international arena Japan should undertake "a thorough study of the nuclear issue."[97]

In late September 2006, just days before the DPRK conducted its nuclear test, North Korea's representative at the United Nations, Choe Su Hon, told the General Assembly, "it is crystal clear" that the United States does not endorse the six-party talks nor want to see the denuclearization of the Korean Peninsula. Choe stressed that Washington has become increasingly hostile toward North Korea, including posing the threat of a preemptive nuclear strike against it, "thus driving the DPRK to inevitably possess nuclear deterrent after all." Determined not to leave the Japanese out of the picture, Choe stated that Japan should not be given a permanent seat on the UN Security Council, not only because of what it did during the Second World War, but also because for decades it "has been distorting its aggressive history instead of liquidating it."[98] In early October 2006, the North Korean Foreign Ministry announced, "the DPRK will in the future conduct a nuclear test," adding "under the condition where safety is firmly guaranteed."[99]

Pyongyang's announcement that it planned to perform a nuclear test caused the international community to sternly rebuke North Korea. Already a nonpermanent member of the Security Council until the end of 2006, Japan as scheduled took over as this body's head for the month of October, with Ambassador Kenzo Oshima serving as president. Right after the DPRK's announcement, the Security Council met. After the meeting, Security Council President Oshima emphasized that the members were unanimous in expressing "very strong concern" regarding the DPRK's stated intention, with all parties advising Pyongyang not to conduct a nuclear test. However, Oshima also pointed out that there were differing views among members about how to deal with the DPRK threat.[100] Both China and Russia did not support the Security Council adopting a tough position that would unnecessarily pressure Pyongyang.[101] Although the Chinese Ministry of Foreign Affairs responded immediately to Pyongyang's threat stating: "We hope that the DPRK must keep calm and restraint on the nuclear test issue," Beijing preferred to see the North Korean nuclear issue resolved through the six-party talks.[102]

Responding to a question on whether Tokyo would consider developing nuclear weapons if North Korea conducted a nuclear test, the foreign ministry's deputy press secretary Tomohiko Taniguchi indicated that Japan had invested a lot in keeping the country's commitment to the Three Nonnuclear Principles, which are not to produce, acquire or allow the entry of nuclear weapons into Japanese territory. Taniguchi emphasized that it would be a major decision for Tokyo to discard the Three Nonnuclear Principles, in large part because working to develop nuclear weapons would be the opposite of the policy that Japan has invested so much in for many years. Although Taniguchi stressed that Tokyo's security relationship with Washington guarantees Japan a place under the US nuclear umbrella, he also, as we will see later in this chapter, correctly noted, "I should not be surprised if the [nuclear weapons] debate is going to be intensified."[103]

Tokyo and Washington indicated that should Pyongyang go ahead with the nuclear test they would sanction North Korea, and would immediately begin working on a Security Council Resolution that relied on Chapter VII of the UN Charter, which authorizes economic sanctions and the use of military force.[104] However, because Tokyo and Washington wanted a quick response, and knowing that a Security Council resolution condemning Pyongyang's threat would be difficult to obtain, given resistance from Beijing and Moscow, they recognized that a Presidential Statement was a more likely outcome.[105] Immediately after the DPRK nuclear-test threat, Tokyo formulated a draft, which Oshima made available to the Security Council, which it intended to become a Presidential Statement.[106] In Washington a meeting with US National Security Advisor Stephen Hadley, Yuriko Koike, Special Advisor to the Prime Minister on national security, later indicated that she and her US counterpart wanted a Presidential Statement from the Security Council, and that they both agreed a North Korean nuclear test would be "absolutely unacceptable." Before the UN General Assembly Japanese diplomat Yoshiki Mine similarly stated that a North Korean nuclear test would be viewed as "totally unacceptable."[107] Showing Tokyo's strong interest in getting an expeditious response, Prime Minister Abe's Chief Cabinet Secretary Yasuhisa Shiozaki indicated the members of the Security Council "have likely been working for a press statement from the outset." However, the Abe government was not united on this matter, since others preferred a strong authoritative Presidential Statement from the UNSC.[108]

As it turned out, the Security Council did produce a Presidential Statement, which had originally been drafted by Japan.[109] Read to the Security Council on October 6, 2006 by Ambassador Oshima, the Presidential Statement emphasized that should Pyongyang make good on its threat to conduct a nuclear test, this "would bring universal condemnation by the international community." The Presidential Statement closed with a stern warning to

Pyongyang, stressing that if the DPRK conducts a nuclear test "the Security Council will act consistent with its responsibility under the Charter of the United Nations."[110] In Tokyo, Foreign Minister Aso lauded the Presidential Statement, which served as another example of the need for Tokyo to adopt a "proactive diplomacy" approach to security that Abe identified during his first speech to the Diet in September.[111] Aso's statement underscored the point that Japan reacted promptly to Pyongyang's announcement that it planned to conduct a nuclear test and that, because Oshima served as the president of the Security Council, it was able to cooperate with the other members to formulate the consensus that the DPRK threat was unacceptable.[112]

Nonetheless, Pyongyang made good on its threat and performed its first nuclear test in early October 2006.[113] There were differing statements concerning the magnitude of the North Korean test but most observers, with the exception of Moscow, identified it as relatively small. The US Geological Survey announced that a magnitude 4.2 (light) seismic disturbance had occurred on October 9, 235 miles Northeast of Pyongyang.[114]

Tokyo and Washington reacted with meteoric speed to Pyongyang's declaration that it had performed a nuclear test. During a press conference, Abe emphasized that, because of Pyongyang's announcement, the Japanese government "shall immediately embark on consideration of harsh measures," which included urging the UN Security Council to adopt a tough position to deal with North Korea. Thus, at the time Abe indicated that Tokyo would be working with the Security Council, in addition to "measures that Japan alone can take," to respond to the North Korean announcement. Abe promised during the press conference that his government would make use of the "best possible surveillance" to determine the radioactive fallout on Japan from the North Korean explosion to protect the Japanese people.[115] In Washington, President Bush labeled Pyongyang's announcement a "provocative act" that demands "immediate response,"[116] not too different from the language later used by Abe, who called it a "provocative action" that required "Japan adopt harsh measures."[117] During a telephone conversation, Bush and Abe concurred that the UN Security Council must employ "decisive action" against North Korea.[118]

Keeping Abe's promise, just hours after the North's nuclear test, Tokyo sent three sophisticated T-4 supersonic jets to monitor the air quality in nearby areas, including the Sea of Japan, the body of water that separates Japan from the Korean Peninsula. Tokyo later reported that the Air Self Defense Forces found no evidence of radioactivity from the North Korean explosion.[119]

Two days after the North Korean nuclear test, the Abe government announced that it was ready to apply sanctions, a decision, according Chief Cabinet Secretary Shiozaki, partly prompted by Pyongyang's disingenuous attitude toward the abduction issue. Song Il Ho, the North Korean official who had led Pyongyang's efforts to normalize relations with Japan, threatened that if Tokyo imposes sanctions on the DPRK "we will take strong countermeasures." Song further stated that Pyongyang would consider sanctions imposed by Japan "more serious in nature" than from anywhere else, since Tokyo has not made amends for Japanese past atrocities committed on the Korean Peninsula.[120] Pyongyang's threat notwithstanding, the Abe government decided to prohibit DPRK ships from coming to Japan, to end all imports from North Korea, and to prevent almost all North Koreans from entering Japan, all of which took effect within a matter of days.[121] The US State Department lauded Tokyo for independently imposing sanctions on North Korea because of its "reported nuclear test," indicating also that this decision makes clear to the DPRK that "its reckless behavior will only further increase its political and economic isolation."[122] Similar to the Abe government, Bush also stated then that the abduction of Megumi Yokota (one of the Japanese citizens previously kidnapped by North Korea) "speaks to the nature of the regime."[123]

A global consensus immediately formed condemning Pyongyang's announcement that it had performed a nuclear test, with even Beijing stating that the DPRK "outrageously conducted a nuclear test in defiance of unanimous opposition from the international community."[124] However, it was Washington and Tokyo that assumed the responsibly of making sure that North Korea would be quickly punished by the UN Security Council. Having gone through several revisions, the Security Council unanimously adopted the US resolution condemning North Korea five days after it announced that it had conducted a nuclear test, though at the time there was no official confirmation that the DPRK had performed such a test. Resolution 1718 stated that sanctions would be imposed according to the UN Charter's Chapter VII, Article 41,[125] which does not permit the use of military force. Different from Washington and Tokyo, neither Beijing nor Moscow wanted a resolution that could ultimately rely on the use of military force.[126] Among several other things, the resolution prohibited member governments from doing business with North Korea in areas that involved many military-related items, including those connected to the DPRK's WMD programs.

After the adoption of the resolution, Japan's Ambassador Oshima saw it as among the most significant judgments that the Security Council has made in some time.[127] US Ambassador John Bolton stressed that the DPRK's announcement that it had conducted a nuclear test "unquestionably poses one of the gravest threats to international peace and security that this Council has ever had to confront." Bolton also stated that the resolution would send an unambiguous message to Pyongyang "and other would be proliferators" that the international community will not tolerate the DPRK's efforts to develop WMD.[128] Having never seen the United States as a benevolent hegemon nor, accordingly, willing to be overtaken by American cultural hegemony,[129] Pyongyang later shot back, arguing that it was the United States that was responsible for "bringing nuclear threat and proliferation to the international community and eventually destroying the world nuclear disarmament system."[130]

China's Ambassador Wang Guangya explained to the Security Council after the adoption of the resolution that, although his government generally supported it, Beijing did not accept the provision calling for the inspection of cargo entering and leaving the DPRK. Like China, Russia's Ambassador Vitaly Churkin expressed his government's support for the resolution passed by the Security Council. Stating that unilaterally imposed sanctions do not help to resolve problems, Churkin also cautioned that they should not be kept in place for an indefinite period but removed once it is evident that the DPRK has complied with the resolution. Invited to the Security Council meeting, the DPRK representative, Ambassador Pak Gil Yon, emphasized before his abrupt departure, that his government did not accept the resolution and believed that it cannot be justified. Pak stressed that the Security Council has acted in a "gangster-like" manner, since it completely ignored the US threat to launch a pre-emptive nuclear attack on the DPRK. Attempting to rationalize his country's nuclear test but also maintaining the DPRK's continued desire to denuclearize the Korean Peninsula, Pak stated that it was Washington's hostile policy toward North Korea that forced Pyongyang's hand, causing it to conduct a nuclear test for self-defense.[131] A few days later DPRK delegate Kim Kwang Il made similar comments to the UN General Assembly.[132]

In Pyongyang, the foreign ministry made clear that it did not accept Security Council Resolution 1718, calling it "a declaration of war against the DPRK" and stating that it demonstrated the hostility of Washington's policy of wanting to destroy North Korean socialism. Maintaining that the nuclear test strengthened the self-defense capabilities of the DPRK, the foreign ministry also stated that it improved the security environment of the Korean Peninsula and of all of Northeast Asia, since it served to check the threat posed by US nuclear weapons to the region.[133]

Two days after the UN Security Council adopted Resolution 1718 Washington officially announced that it had acquired radioactive evidence verifying that the DPRK conducted a nuclear test.[134] Prime Minister Abe stated that the US announcement increases the chances that North Korea conducted a nuclear test, adding that, "In response, Japan will gather and analyze intelligence and determine for itself the legitimacy of the claim."[135] Later, Chief Cabinet Secretary Shiozaki announced that as a result of analyzing data from the United States and South Korea, "The Japanese government has come to the conclusion that it is highly likely that North Korea carried out a nuclear test."[136]

On the last day of the six-party talks held in December 2006, Tokyo announced Japan's intention to launch its fourth spy satellite in February 2007.[137] Not surprisingly, Pyongyang viewed this as still another indication of Tokyo's plans to bolster the country's military capabilities. The DPRK's *Rodong Sinmun* commented: "The full-dressed launching of spy satellites by Japan under the plausible cloak of 'scientific researches' goes to prove that its moves for turning itself into a military giant and staging reinvasion have reached a dangerous phase."[138]

According to US intelligence, the DPRK nuclear test used a plutonium device.[139] While Republicans were quick to blame the Clinton administration for the DPRK nuclear test and Democrats were equally expeditious in labeling the Bush administration's North Korean policy a failure, what was not discussed was a scenario that possibly led to Pyongyang's decision to conduct such a test.

Since the fall of 2002, when the Bush administration claimed that the North had been concealing a uranium-enrichment program to develop nuclear weapons, Pyongyang repeatedly maintained that Washington's hostile policy forced it to make decisions that it otherwise would not have made. Still, the nuclear test that Pyongyang authorized in October 2006 did not demonstrate that the DPRK had successfully harnessed the advanced technological know-how exhibited in the tests performed by other nuclear states.[140] It is certainly possible that Pyongyang began in earnest to develop plutonium-type nuclear devices *after* concluding that it could not deal in any other way with the Bush administration's hostile DPRK policy. Had the DPRK developed two or so nuclear weapons as several US observers have asserted before 2002, it is likely that North Korea would have been able to detonate a nuclear device beyond the sub-kiloton magnitude. In any case, it is reasonable to hypothesize that the absence of what Pyongyang perceived as a sustained and hostile US policy would have prevented it from conducting a nuclear test.

But the fact of the matter is that Pyongyang did conduct a nuclear test. Moreover, it maintained that a nuclear deterrent was indispensable to *songun* and the only way to counter Washington's hostile policy, which included the threat of a nuclear attack.[141] The DPRK's Sin Son Ho told the UN General Assembly's First Committee on Disarmament and International Security in October 2008, "Our choice to possess a nuclear deterrent is due to the deep-rooted US hostile policy and nuclear threats, which continue for more than half a century."[142] Pyongyang also linked *songun* to economic prosperity. Calling the DPRK's nuclear test a "success" and asserting that its scientific and technological achievements will create prosperity, Pyongyang paradoxically maintained, "Invincible arms are the most valuable wealth for national prosperity ... Many countries had gone to ruin because of their weak force of arms, but there is no country that has gone to ruin because of famine."[143]

Other sources of provocation

Like other countries, the DPRK's underground nuclear test was provocative and undermined the nuclear nonproliferation regime. Pyongyang's nuclear and missile testing coexisted with what it viewed as Washington's sustained hard-line policy, which won the support of liberals and conservatives.[144] Moreover, Tokyo's support of Washington's hard-line DPRK policy remained consistent with its continuing efforts to make Japan a normal country.

More so than in the Clinton administration, a number of officials in the Bush administration wanted to see the implosion of the DPRK, especially during the early years. That the DPRK did not implode was disturbing to these officials, perhaps even boosting their desire to sustain a provocative

North Korean policy,[145] which arguably led to the DPRK's first nuclear test. Survey data from a research company in South Korea found that 43 percent of the respondents there – the largest proportion ahead of even North Korea, which was selected by about 37 percent of those polled – believed that Washington was most responsible for the DPRK nuclear test.[146]

From Pyongyang's perspective, a major source of US provocation, which Tokyo supported, involved DPRK funds in the Banco Delta Asia (BDA) located in the Macau region of China. After a recess of more than a month, the six-party talks resumed on September 13, 2005 and lasted until September 19. The Joint Statement that came out of the fourth round of the six-party talks in September 2005 raised the promising prospect that a resolution to the DPRK nuclear crisis could be in the offing.

On September 15, thus in the midst of the six-party talks, using the authority of the US Patriot Act, the US Treasury Department released a statement identifying the BDA as posing "an unacceptable risk of a money laundering and other financial crimes." The Treasury Department's statement went on to maintain that, BDA's "special relationship with the DPRK has specifically facilitated the criminal activities of North Korean government agencies and front companies" and in this capacity, besides playing a major part in laundering counterfeit US currency, has been involved in the distribution of contraband tobacco and illegal drugs.[147] Then, on October 21, the US Treasury announced that it was imposing sanctions on eight North Korean businesses, "involved in WMD proliferation out of North Korea."[148] Several days later, Pyongyang responded by calling the Treasury Department's sanctions against the eight DPRK establishments part of a series of "carefully prearranged provocative" actions by Washington to pressure the DPRK to abandon its nuclear weapons program without any corresponding move by the United States.[149]

Whether true of not, the charges leveled against Pyongyang raise the important question of why they coincided with the first real sign of progress made in the six-party talks, especially since Washington had long accused North Korea of being involved in a host of illicit activities, including counterfeiting and drug trafficking. Whatever the reason for the sanction announcements, the effect was that the Bush administration's imposition of them on North Korea created additional distrust and animus in Pyongyang of the United States.

Just three days before the six-party talks took place in Beijing in November 2005, President Bush stated that Japan is a US ally "in dealing with a tyrant in North Korea."[150] Pyongyang immediately responded that such slander unambiguously contravenes the Joint Statement, which calls on the DPRK and the United States to respect each other's sovereignty and to peacefully coexist. Pyongyang further stated that Bush's comment and the imposition of financial sanctions gives the DPRK reason to question how serious Washington is about seeing the Joint Statement go into effect and caused it to distrust the genuineness of US negotiations in the upcoming six-party talks.[151]

Indeed, Bush's remark more than likely even had a hard time bolstering the position of those observers who still hold tenaciously to the notion that the United States is a benevolent hegemon whose unilateral leadership can resolve international security problems.[152]

Right after the conclusion of the six-party talks in November 2005, Vice Foreign Minister and head DPRK negotiator Kim Kye-gwan stated: "The financial sanctions are in violation of the joint statement we have adopted and are going to hinder the implementation of the commitment we have made." Kim also stressed that his delegation made clear during the six-party talks that the DPRK wanted them removed and that Washington had agreed to have bilateral discussions with Pyongyang so that they could settle this problem.[153]

In a considerably longer statement appearing in early December 2005, the North Korean Foreign Ministry stressed that it interpreted Washington's imposition of financial sanctions, even as the six-party talks were taking place, as an attempt to "bring down the DPRK's system." Denying the charges that brought about the Treasury Department's sanctions, Pyongyang indicated that it stressed at the six-party talks that the United States must remove the financial sanctions. According to the foreign ministry, although Washington agreed to hold bilateral talks with Pyongyang on this matter, it later refused to meet with the DPRK.[154] Then on December 13, the US Treasury Department announced that, because North Korea's funds deposited in BDA had been frozen, it may be looking for other banks to work with and requested that "financial institutions worldwide" limit or cease doing business with the DPRK.[155]

The Bush administration insisted that the financial sanctions it imposed on the DPRK were unrelated to the six-party talks.[156] This, however, is not how Pyongyang interpreted the financial sanctions, maintaining instead that they were directly connected to these multilateral discussions. Seeing the financial sanctions as an unjustifiable attempt to bring down the DPRK, Pyongyang argued that Washington insisted that the financial sanctions are not an issue to be negotiated and, given the increased hostility evident in US policy, it questioned the need for the six-party talks to continue.[157]

Refusing to participate in the six-party talks, Pyongyang repeatedly claimed that it had no part in dealing with counterfeit US currency and had not been involved in drug trafficking or in illicit cigarette activities. It maintained that all of these charges had been drummed up by the Bush administration's hardliners who wanted to impede the progress of the six-party talks.[158] During a conversation with Selig Harrison while he was in Pyongyang, Kim Kye-gwan commented that disagreement within the Bush administration between those who want to talk with North Korea and those who despise the DPRK had caused stagnancy in US policy. Referring to the six-party talks held in September 2005, Kim stated that at that time "your side was planning for sanctions. Cheney did this to prevent further dialogue that would lead to peaceful coexistence."[159]

The Bush administration repeatedly stated that it would not meet bilaterally with the DPRK. At the same time, Pyongyang was becoming equally determined to maintain its boycott of the six-party talks until the United States removed the financial sanctions. The Bush administration eventually found a way to justify talking bilaterally to the DPRK outside of the six-party talks. Calling it a "briefing" rather than a meeting, Treasury and State representatives, as well as members of the National Security Council, met with DPRK officials in New York in early March 2006. Treasury told the DPRK delegation that the financial sanctions and the six-party talks were separate issues. Daniel Glaser, the Treasury Department's Deputy Assistant Secretary for Terrorist Financing and Financial Crimes, informed the DPRK delegation that the sanctions stemming from the BDA were not directed at North Korea, but rather designed to protect the United States from financial abuse. Glaser told the DPRK delegation that the Treasury Department acted against BDA "because its facilitation of North Korean illicit financial activity presents an unacceptable risk to the U.S. financial system." Heading the DPRK delegation, Li Gun denied the charges by the United States and told the American officials that they had not presented any evidence of North Korea's involvement in illegal financial activities. Li emphasized that the DPRK could not return to the six-party talks as long as the financial sanctions remained in place.[160]

Pyongyang later indicated that the DPRK had suggested a way to resolve the dispute at the meeting between North Korean and US officials in New York. Pyongyang had proposed that North Korea be permitted to open an account with an American bank so that Washington could easily monitor its activities. Pyongyang pointed out that through consultations between the United States and the DPRK they could resolve the so-called counterfeiting problem. Pyongyang maintained that the failure of US officials to give a clear answer was indicative of Washington's disinterest in the suggestion.[161]

Soon after the DPRK conducted its nuclear test, Secretary of State Rice reiterated during an interview in Beijing the Bush administration's position that bilateral discussions with Pyongyang outside of the six-party talks are out of the question. Rice stated: "The North Koreans would like nothing better than to divide us so that they can negotiate with each separately and they don't have to have the collective power of the five parties."[162] However, as we will see in more detail in Chapter 4, the Bush administration soon adopted a noticeably more conciliatory policy toward the DPRK.

On October 31, 2006, China's Foreign Ministry announced that, because of discussions held in Beijing between Chinese, the US and DPRK officials, the six-party talks would "be held soon."[163] While Beijing clearly played an important role in bringing Washington and Pyongyang together, despite his instructions to the contrary, US Assistant Secretary of State for East Asian and Pacific Affairs Christopher Hill had a bilateral meeting with Kim Kye-gwan.[164]

Although Hill's comments made after the trilateral and bilateral meetings in Beijing affirmed that an agreement had been reached to resume the six-party talks, they were noticeably inconsistent. Hill began by stating, "the DPRK was especially concerned that we address the situation of the financial measures that has, in their view, held up the talks for about a year now." Later, when questioned about whether Pyongyang had demanded any conditions before returning to the talks, Hill stated: "They did not. They made very clear these were not conditions, but they wanted to hear that we would address the issue of the financial measures in the context of the talks, and I said we were prepared to create a mechanism, a working group, to address these financial issues."[165]

Pyongyang had earlier stated on more than one occasion that it would not return to the six-party talks until Washington removed the financial sanctions. However, now it had agreed to resume these multilateral talks even though the sanctions were still in place. Although the State Department had explicitly indicated that the financial sanctions and the six-party talks were separate issues, it was now not only willing to discuss the sanctions at these multi-lateral meetings, but Hill was also maintaining that the discussion of sanctions was not a condition for Pyongyang agreeing to return to the talks. This was at odds with what Pyongyang maintained the next day. The North Korean Foreign Ministry emphasized that Pyongyang had made the decision to rejoin the six-party talks based "on the premise that the financial sanctions will be discussed and settled between the DPRK and the U.S. within the framework of the six-party talks."[166]

Then, suddenly, Washington and Tokyo threw a one-two punch. A Treasury Department statement maintained in early November that its investigation of the BDA revealed that, "everything that has come to light confirms the illicit activity of the bank," which includes taking a payment from Pyongyang for not exercising proper thoroughness on DPRK accounts.[167] Although Japan had kept its distance from the DPRK's frozen financial assets deposited in the BDA, this changed right after the announcement was made that the six-party talks would resume soon. Citing "investigative sources," the conservative *The Yomiuri Shimbun* reported that it had been determined that DPRK funds in the BDA had been used to pay Japanese companies in 2002 for purchases of items that could be part of North Korea's WMD programs.[168] Claiming this was the first piece of evidence that established Pyongyang had used funds in the BDA to pay for its WMD programs, this newspaper article, along with the statement by the US Treasury Department, did nothing to ameliorate the diplomatic environment for the anticipated resumption of the six-party talks.

What is not clear was whether Washington and Tokyo had been carrying out separate investigations or whether the results of the US investigation were shared with Tokyo. Certainly the coincident appearance of the Treasury Department statement and the report in Japan's largest daily newspaper create the suspicion that Washington and Tokyo had shared information in the investigation of North Korea's connection to the BDA. A Treasury Department official reservedly stated that she "cannot discuss the particulars of the investigation, including who we may be working with, other than to note our work with the Macanese authorities."[169]

During a press conference in Beijing, Assistant Secretary of State Hill stressed that Pyongyang indicated it did not approve of the sanctions attached to UN Security Council Resolution 1718 but that this had not been part of the discussion that led to the anticipated resumption of the multilateral talks. Hill stated that he told the North Koreans they are bound to comply with Resolution 1718. Responding to a question during the press conference, Hill emphasized that Resolution 1718 would "go forward" and that the only way Pyongyang could change this was for it to satisfy the conditions of the resolution, that is, to abandon its nuclear weapons and supporting programs.[170]

In early November, two senior State Department officials visited Tokyo, followed by the arrival of Deputy Treasury Secretary Robert Kimmitt. After a meeting with Foreign Minister Aso, Kimmitt stated, "The agreement was that we would continue to live up to our responsibilities under UN Security Council resolutions 1695 and 1718 and we look forward to working bilaterally and with other members of the international community to live up to those very important resolutions."[171] Kimmitt's statement followed on the heels of Tokyo's announcement that it did not intend to eliminate Japan's sanctions on North Korea until it completely abandons its nuclear weapons efforts. Making clear that Tokyo wanted Pyongyang to comply with the September 2005 Joint Statement and with Security Council Resolution 1718, Chief Cabinet Secretary Shiozaki stated, "we will continue with the sanctions."[172]

Tokyo did more than maintain the existing sanctions. In mid November 2006, Japan imposed additional sanctions on North Korea, this time specifically focusing on luxury products that presumably would affect DPRK leadership. Consistent with UN Security Council Resolution 1718, Abe's Cabinet banned the export of 24 luxury items, including jewelry, watches, art, cars, motorcycles, audiovisual equipment, furs and alcoholic beverages.[173]

At about the same time, R. Nicholas Burns, the State Department's Undersecretary for Political Affairs, testified before the House International Relations Committee. Burns stressed that Washington does not now, nor will it, accept North Korea as a nuclear weapons state,[174] a position that at least briefly seemed to have changed somewhat two years later.[175] Regarding sanctions, which with diplomacy constituted the Bush administration's "dual-track" policy, Burns stressed that the United States has moved to quickly implement Security Council Resolution 1718 and has also developed a list of luxury items that cannot be exported to North Korea. By indicating that the United States "currently sends very few, if any, of these goods to the DPRK," what Burns was tacitly conveying to the committee was that the ban on luxury items to North Korea was merely symbolic. A little later US Secretary of Commerce Carlos Gutierrez stated, "While North Korea's people starve and suffer, there is simply no excuse for the regime to be splurging on cognac and cigars. We will ban the export of these and other luxury goods that are purchased for no other reason than to benefit North Korea's governing elite."[176] However, the United States had a zero balance of trade with North Korea in September 2006 on *all goods* – zero imports and zero exports. From January to September of 2006, US exports to North Korea totaled $3,000, all of which were for books, manuscripts and newspapers.[177]

Only hours after the Chinese Foreign Ministry announced the date for the resumption of the six-party talks in December 2006, a top Treasury Department official threw still another jab at Pyongyang. In a speech given in New York, Undersecretary for Terrorism and Financial Intelligence Stuart Levey used North Korea as an example of a country involved in the proliferation of weapons of mass destruction. Levey went on to state that it is necessary to more thoroughly scrutinize terrorists and states involved in weapons proliferation "and prohibit their access – and that of their support networks – to the financial system." Said Levey, it is important to "isolate them financially and commercially, and ensure that all of their activities, whether seemingly legitimate or illicit, are shut down."[178]

Reacting to the announcement that a breakthrough had been reached in Beijing, Foreign Minister Aso, similar to the Bush administration, stated, "Japan does not intend to accept North Korea's return to the six-party talks on the premise that it is a country that owns nuclear weapons."[179] But Aso's statement, which was much like those of other Japanese officials, was hardly realistic. It is nearly inconceivable to think that Pyongyang would have eliminated the DPRK's nuclear weapons prior to the six-party talks and certainly not before it resolved the nuclear issue with the United States.

Pyongyang reacted harshly to the comments coming out of Tokyo, harking back to a position it had taken a few years before of not wanting Japan to participate in the six-party talks. Calling Japanese officials "imbeciles" for their latest comments, Pyongyang emphasized that since Tokyo simply follows what Washington does, Japan's participation in the six-party talks is not necessary.[180]

Later, a meeting in Tokyo between Chief Cabinet Secretary Shiozaki and two senior State Department officials ended with the agreement that the United States and Japan would demand that Pyongyang abandon its nuclear weapons and related infrastructure during the six-party talks, and that the abduction issue be resolved. During a press conference afterwards, Shiozaki brushed aside Pyongyang's call for Japan not participate in the six-party talks and then made a statement that stood at odds with what had earlier been agreed to in meeting with US officials. Said Shiozaki: "It's impossible for Japan to allow North Korea to return to the talks as a nuclear power."[181]

Pyongyang maintained that Tokyo's insistence to connect the abduction issue to the six-party talks was an attempt to spoil these multilateral discussions. Pyongyang reasoned that Tokyo's real goal is to prolong the North Korean nuclear issue so that it can continue to justify Japanese remilitarization. Claiming that its missiles and nuclear weapons are only for the defense of the DPRK, Pyongyang accused Tokyo of conjuring up the image of a North Korean threat so that Japan can increase its commitment to missile defense.[182]

Shoichi Nakagawa, the LDP's chairman of the Policy Research Council, joined the chorus of Japanese officials that had something to say about restarting the six-party talks. Nakagawa declared that Japan would be against resuming the six-party talks unless Pyongyang made some concessionary move. Maintained Nakagawa stated: "It's fine if North Korea can bring some contribution to peace, but simply starting talks is not meaningful ... Talks shouldn't reopen without careful consideration."[183] For its part, Pyongyang was convinced that Tokyo did not want the six-party talks to take place and, if they did, to connect them to the unrelated abduction issue. Seeing no reason for Japan to participate in the six-party talks, Pyongyang charged that if Tokyo believes that the abduction issue needs to be settled, it should start by addressing the cruelty it subjected more than eight million Koreans to when it annexed the peninsula.[184]

While one would expect that a nuclear-armed North Korea would be of most concern to the Abe government, it was not. Invited as a guest speaker at a rally populated largely by conservative proponents of the abduction issue just days before the start of the six-party talks in December 2006, Abe made his position clear. "We can never compromise on the abduction issue. I swear that my administration will tackle this as its top priority."[185]

Then, after having received what it said was an unsatisfactory response from the Japanese Red Cross, Pyongyang decided that it wanted to try to put Tokyo in the hot seat. Two days before the resumption of the six party talks in December 2006, Pyongyang announced that Kim Thae Yong, a North Korean linguist, had been abducted by Japan in late 1991. Pyongyang indicated that Kim had sent a letter that bore a Hokkaido postmark in April 1992 to the DPRK Education Commission stating that he was being held against his will.[186] At first, the Japanese Foreign Ministry refused to discuss the allegation publicly; however, a spokesperson for the ministry later stated that "an abduction by Japan is absolutely unthinkable," and indicated that this allegation would not stop Tokyo from discussing the abduction of its citizens by North Korea during the upcoming six-party talks.[187]

In his remarks on the first day of the December 2006 six-party talks, Japan's top negotiator Kenichiro Sasae did just that. Stating that North Korea must fulfill its commitment to the September 2005 Joint Statement, Sasae also emphasized to the participants of the six-party talks "the importance of settling the abduction issue." A member of the Japanese delegation indicated that the DPRK's Kim Kye-gwan never referred to Sasae's statement.[188]

Tokyo with nuclear ambitions?

Comments made by Japanese statesmen regarding the possibility of Japan possessing nuclear weapons are hardly new. However, once Japan fully embraced the path to become a normal country, Japanese statesmen became less reluctant than they were in the past to express their views on this matter.[189] Pyongyang's nuclear weapons test created an opportunity for some in Tokyo to bring the discussion of Japan possessing nuclear weapons into the public arena with little serious risk of political or public backlash.

The DPRK nuclear test instantly set off the ominous prospect that a nuclear arms race could ensue in Northeast Asia. Speculation immediately emerged that some in Washington, including several within the Bush administration, wanted to see Japan acquire nuclear weapons and that they had been attempting to persuade Japanese statesman, who had raised this controversial matter in the past, such as former Prime Minister Yasuhiro Nakasone and DPJ chief Ichiro Ozawa, to broach the discussion.[190]

While Shinzo Abe had no qualms about expressing his support for revising the constitution and specifically his intention to have Article 9 amended during his tenure as prime minister,[191] he was quite careful in the wake of the DPRK nuclear test not to publicly propose that Japan should consider acquiring nuclear weapons. In fact, the day after the DPRK nuclear test, the new prime minister told a Diet Budget Committee that Tokyo would maintain the Three Nonnuclear Principles.[192]

Although some in Washington would not oppose Japan having nuclear weapons and some would even encourage this, they are a small minority. A nuclear-armed Japan would set off an arms race in Northeast Asia, prompting not only the DPRK but also China and perhaps even South Korea to check Tokyo's initiative. In attempting to dampen calls for Japan to consider acquiring nuclear weapons, Thomas Schieffer, the US Ambassador there, stated just a few days after the DPRK nuclear test, "The Japanese can feel a strong sense of comfort in knowing that the nuclear power of the United States has protected them for more than 50 years."[193]

Despite Schieffer's comments, the desire of some in Japan to begin a discussion of acquiring nuclear weapons, one that would flout the country's "nuclear taboo," made its way to the surface within days after the DPRK nuclear test. Significantly, two of the major figures advancing this position were leading members of the LDP.

Less than a week after the DPRK nuclear test, the LDP's Shoichi Nakagawa stated that, "There could be an argument that possession of nuclear weapons diminishes the likelihood of being attacked as we could fight back in such an event. There can be discussions, of course." At variance with Prime Minister Abe's remarks to the Diet just a few days earlier, Nakagawa stated in reference to the Three Nonnuclear Principles, "We need to have thorough discussions on whether there is a need to review them."[194] Three days later, Japanese Minister of Foreign Affairs Taro Aso, who appeared mindful of Abe's previous declaration – which was, "We'll stick to the three nonnuclear principles as Japan's national policy [and t]he government will never discuss [the possession of nuclear arms]" – also had something to say about this matter. Aso commented that, although Tokyo remains committed to these principles, "People may think we shouldn't even consider or exchange views [on Japan's acquisition of nuclear weapons] even if a neighboring country possesses such arms. But it's important to have discussions on the matter."[195]

The same day that Aso made his remarks he also had a joint press conference in Tokyo with US Secretary of State Rice, who was attempting to get some guarantee from Japan that it did not plan to acquire nuclear weapons. To do this, Rice stressed that the "United States has the will and capability to meet the full range – and I underscore full range – of its deterrent and security commitments to Japan." Recognizing that Rice's comment was meant to indicate that the Bush administration preferred that Japanese leaders did not talk publicly about nuclear weapons, Aso stated at the press conference that Tokyo is not considering the acquisition of nuclear weapons and that it is not necessary for Japan to possess nuclear arms.[196]

However, Aso later told a Diet committee that, although Japan is not abandoning the Three Nonnuclear Principles, he did not support "suppressing a debate over whether we should or should not possess nuclear weapons."[197] Rice, nonetheless, continued to take the remarks made by Aso at the joint press conference as an assurance that Tokyo had no plans to acquire nuclear weapons, stressing during an interview that, "Japan has said very clearly that it has no intention of going nuclear and relies on the U.S. nuclear umbrella."[198]

When Nakagawa traveled to Washington at the end of October 2006, he again brought up the subject of the need to discuss the possibility of Japan acquiring nuclear arms, likening its current situation to that faced by the United States during the 1962 Cuban Missile Crisis.[199] Returning to Japan, Nakagawa reiterated his belief that Japan should debate the issue of nuclear weapons. However, there was opposition to Nakagawa and Aso's position among some Japanese officials,[200] with the opposition parties demanding the foreign minister's resignation.[201]

The Bush administration's fear that a nuclear arms race – arguably of its own making, because of its botched DPRK policy – could unfold in Northeast Asia became evident not only by it reassuring Tokyo that Japan would remain protected by the US nuclear shield but also by it giving a similar commitment to Seoul. At about the same time that Rice emphasized that Japan would remain protected by the US nuclear umbrella, General Peter Grace and the chairman of South Korea's Joint Chiefs of Staff Lee Sang-hee decided that a "strong signal" should be sent to Pyongyang because of its recent nuclear test. This signal, said South Korean Rear Admiral Ahn Ki-seok, was that the "U.S. military agreed on a concrete guarantee of a nuclear umbrella provision."[202] However, talk in Tokyo about the need to debate the possibility of Japan possessing nuclear weapons troubled Seoul, which retains horrific memories of past Japanese militarism. Referring to the both Aso and Nakagawa's remarks, then South Korean Foreign Minister and Secretary-General elect of the United Nations Ban Ki-moon stressed while in Tokyo in early November 2006 that, "I don't think that remarks like these are desirable for the future of Japan."[203]

Evidence that political posturing had entered the controversy became apparent in early November 2006 when Ichiro Ozawa, then the head of the DPJ, confronted the prime minister on the comments made by Aso and Nakagawa during a debate in the House of Councillors. In 2002, Ozawa himself created a controversy when he talked publicly about the possibility of Japan producing nuclear weapons from its plutonium stockpile to offset China's growing military power. Responding to Ozawa, Abe stated that he has never maintained that Japan should openly discuss the question of possessing nuclear weapons but then, demonstrating his unwillingness to direct Aso and Nakagawa to end their comments about nukes, added, "if we cannot debate nuclear issues, then we cannot talk about nuclear deterrence under the Japan–U.S. alliance."[204]

A statement from the Cabinet Office just days after Abe's remarks to Ozawa repeated an assertion made more than once in the past: it is not unconstitutional for Japan to possess nuclear weapons for self defense, even though the government has no intention of doing this. Then, the newly appointed Minister of State for Defense Fumio Kyuma weighed in. Kyuma maintained that it was important for Japan to begin a discussion on the last of the Three Nonnuclear Principles that prohibits nuclear weapons from entering the country. Kyuma argued that before the limit on territorial waters changed in 1977 from three to 12 nautical miles, US vessels carrying nuclear weapons could legally travel relatively close to the Japanese shore. Since the law changed, US warships have had to remain much further out at sea.[205] Angering some in the opposition parties, Kyuma said, "We need to discuss, to clarify those things."[206] Perhaps trying to dispel fears in the international community, Abe later commented while attending the gathering of the Asia-Pacific Economic Cooperation in Hanoi, "my government, and the Liberal Democratic Party in its official meetings, will not debate possessing nuclear arms."[207]

There is an irony to this story. Not too long after the questioning of the nuclear taboo began, the Japanese Foreign Ministry was lauding the adoption of Japan's thirteenth consecutive resolution on nuclear disarmament by the UN General Assembly's First Committee in November 2006.[208] For sure, the Japanese public's antinuclear sentiment was not swayed by the discussion of Japan possibly possessing nuclear weapons. A poll conducted by the *Yomiuri Shimbun* in mid November 2006 indicated that 80 percent of the respondents felt that Japan should retain the Three Nonnuclear Principles.[209] Significantly, typically overlooked in cursory and conventional analyses of the Japanese public's aversion to their government possessing nuclear weapons is the strong and continuing efforts of civil society, specifically the doggedness of antinuclear weapons organizations in Japan, which serve to sustain public opposition to nuclear arms.[210] Historically problematic, however, is that Tokyo has pushed to adopt security policies that have often not been in concert with Japanese public opinion.[211]

Pyongyang never mentioned that its decision to conduct a nuclear test provided some in Tokyo the opportunity to begin a discussion on Japan possessing nuclear weapons. Instead, Pyongyang viewed this discussion as just another excuse for Japan to push harder for remilitarization.

Despite the 2005 Joint Statement issued in Beijing in which Washington stated – and not for the first time – that there were no US nuclear weapons in

South Korea, and Seoul's reaffirmation of this,[212] Pyongyang believed other-wise. Pyongyang averred a little more than a month after it conducted a nuclear test that Washington had more than 1,000 nuclear weapons in South Korea.[213] Similarly, Pyongyang was not about to believe that Tokyo did not have designs on developing nuclear weapons. Pyongyang maintained that Japan's Three Nonnuclear Principles deflected attention from Tokyo's main objective, which is "realizing nuclear weaponization under the patronage of the U.S." Most especially, Pyongyang was not about to ignore the remark pertaining to permitting US warships armed with nuclear weapons to come closer to Japan via its territorial waters.[214]

Tokyo's conflicting positions on intercepting missiles targeting the United States

Prime Minister Abe was well aware that constitutional revision in Japan would take some time. In the interim, Abe indicated that his government had its policy sights trained on reinterpreting the constitution, specifically as it related to missile defense.

In 2003, the Koizumi government issued a statement when it decided to permit the deployment of the Japan–US missile defense system that empha-sized that Japan would not attempt to intercept missiles on a trajectory for a third country, that is, the United States. Reaffirmed by the Koizumi govern-ment in January 2005, this statement was in line with the interpretation of the constitution, which does not permit Japan to participate in collective defense. Although Washington and Tokyo have consistently pledged to work together on missile defense,[215] many American officials were not pleased with Japan's decision not to have its defense system attempt to intercept missiles presumed to be heading for the United States.

Aware of what Washington wanted and reacting to the threat from North Korea said by many in Tokyo to exist, Abe authorized studying the possibility of Japan intercepting missiles passing over Japanese territory that may be heading for the United States. Chief Cabinet Secretary Shiozaki stressed in November 2006 that the Abe government's decision, "Whether to review the [2003] statement or not is up to the result of the discussions."[216] US Ambas-sador to Japan Schieffer commented that he looked forward to seeing Tokyo legally recognize the importance of intercepting missiles heading toward the United States. Less tactful, US Deputy Undersecretary of Defense for Asia-Pacific Affairs Richard Lawless stated that Tokyo's interpretation of the con-stitution does not reflect favorably on the US–Japan security alliance, adding that it is "crazy" Japan cannot not intercept a missile on a trajectory to the United States.[217]

In the spring of 2007, Abe established a panel to study collective defense,[218] something many Japanese were not comfortable with. Indeed, survey data showed that nearly two-thirds of Japanese respondents wanted to retain Japan's existing constitutional restriction on collective defense.[219]

Perceived threat and lingering opposition among the Japanese public

Pyongyang's decision to conduct a nuclear test played an important part in helping to push the Japanese public further away from what previously was a substantial popular sentiment to achieve rapprochement with North Korea and toward the belief that it is a security threat to Japan. While only a few years before most Japanese people wanted Tokyo to normalize relations with North Korea, the constant attention given to the unresolved abduction issue in Japan, coupled with the decisions by Pyongyang to launch missiles in July 2006 and to later conduct a nuclear test, took its toll on the public.

A *Yomiuri Shimbun* poll conducted soon after the DPRK nuclear test showed that over 80 percent of those surveyed thought that the threat to Japan from North Korea had increased due to the nuclear test.[220] An *Asahi Shimbun* poll similarly indicated that more than 80 percent of the respondents felt threatened by the DPRK because of its nuclear test. This same survey showed that 62 percent thought that sanctions should be imposed on North Korea for conducting a nuclear test, a sentiment consistent with the Abe government's position.[221] Thus, the heightened sense of threat among the Japanese public made it easier for nationalists and conservatives to continue their push to make Japan a normal country.

However, there was still substantial opposition among the Japanese people to the government's initiative to upgrade the Defense Agency to a ministry. For years, Japan's pacifist constitution along with continuing public wariness of the country's militarist past prevented the change of the Defense Agency to a ministry. A survey conducted by the *Yomiuri Shimbun* in September 1997 showed that 52 percent of Japanese respondents opposed changing the Defense Agency to a ministry and only 24 percent endorsed this.[222] Despite missile and nuclear testing by the DPRK in 2006, a large proportion of the Japanese public still did not endorse the change of the Defense Agency to the Defense Ministry. After both houses of the Diet approved legislation in December 2006 that was initially introduced in June, the Defense Agency officially became the Ministry of Defense in early January 2007.[223] A *Yomiuri Shimbun* survey conducted at the end of January 2007 showed that while 46 percent of the respondents endorsed the change, 39 percent did not.[224]

Notes

1 Ministry of Foreign Affairs, *Accompanying Measures Pursuant to United Nations Security Council Resolution 1929*, Tokyo, September 3, 2010.
2 Yukiko Miyagi, "Foreign Policy Making under Koizumi: Norms and Japan's Role in 2003 Iraq War," *Foreign Policy Analysis*, vol. 5, 2009, pp. 349–66; Christopher Hughes, *Japan's Remilitarization* (London: Routledge, 2009), pp. 99–138.
3 Yasuo Takao, *Is Japan Really Remilitarizing? The Politics of Norm Formation and Change* (Victoria: Monash University Press), 2008.
4 Andrew Oros, *Normalizing Japan: Politics, Identity, and the Evolution of Security Practice* (Stanford, CA: Stanford University Press, 2008); Thomas Berger,

Cultures of Antimilitarism: National Security in Japan and West Germany (Baltimore, MD: Johns Hopkins University Press, 1998).

5 Masao Kunihiro, "The Decline and Fall of Pacifism," *The Bulletin of the Atomic Scientists*, vol. 53, no. 1, January/February 1997, pp. 35–39.

6 Richard Samuels, *Securing Japan: Tokyo's Grand Strategy and the Future of East Asia* (Ithaca, NY: Cornell University Press, 2007).

7 Office of the Historian, Bureau of Public Affairs, US Department of State, *Foreign Relations of the United States, 1964–1968*, Volume XXIX, Part 2, Japan (Washington, DC: United States Government Printing Office, 2006).

8 "Gates Proposes Ending F-22 Fighter Jet," *Kyodo News*, April 7, 2009.

9 Council on Security and Defense Capabilities, *Japan's Vision for Future Security and Defense Capabilities*, Tokyo, October 2004.

10 Douglas MacArthur, *Reminiscences* (New York: MacGraw-Hill, 1964), pp. 302–03.

11 P. Allan Dionisopoulos, "Revisionist Tendencies in Post-occupation Japan," *The Western Political Quarterly*, vol. 10, no. 4 December 1957, pp. 793–801; Isao Sato, "Comment: Revisionism During the Forty Years of the Constitution of Japan," *Law and Contemporary Problems*, vol. 53, no. 1, Winter and Spring 1990, pp. 97–104; John Maki, "The Constitution of Japan: Pacifism, Popular Sovereignty, and Fundamental Human Rights," *Law and Contemporary Problems*, vol. 53, no. 1, Winter and Spring 1990, pp. 73–87.

12 Ministry of Defense, *Defense of Japan 2009* (Annual White Paper), Tokyo, 2009.

13 Anthony DiFilippo, "Opposing Positions in Japan's Security Policy: Toward a New Security Dynamic," *East Asia: An International Quarterly*, vol. 20, no.1, Spring 2002, pp. 107–35.

14 Anthony DiFilippo, *The U.S.–Japan Military Arrangement: Competing Security Transitions in a Changing International Environment* (Armonk, NY: M.E. Sharpe, 2002).

15 Ministry of Foreign Affairs, *Statement by H.E. Ms. Yuriko Kawaguchi, Minister of Foreign Affairs of Japan at the Fifty-Eighth Session of the General Assembly of the United Nations*, New York, September 23, 2003; Reinhard Drifte, *Japan's Quest for a Permanent Security Council Seat: A Matter of Pride or Justice?* (London: Macmillan, 2000); Ministry of Foreign Affairs, *Diplomatic Bluebook: 2006* (Ministry of Foreign Affairs, Tokyo, 2006), Chapter 3.

16 J. Thomas Schieffer, *The Price of Security in a Changing World*, Address to the Foreign Correspondents Club of Japan, Embassy of the United States, Tokyo, May 20, 2008.

17 Stockholm International Peace Research Institute (SIPRI), *The SIPRI Military Expenditure Data Base*, www.sipri.org/contents/milap/milex/mex_database1.html (accessed on April 5, 2011).

18 David Wright and Eryn MacDonald, "Japan and the Navy Theater-Wide Missile Defense System," Workshop Dealing with East Asian Regional Security Futures: Theater Missile Defense Implications, The United Nations University, Tokyo, June 24–25, 2000; Masahiro Akiyama, "A Discussion of the Current Security Issues in Japan: Security Guidelines, the Constitution, Legislative Reviews, and the Missile Threat," MIT Securities Studies Program, Seminar Series, March 15, 2000; Michael Swaine with Loren Runyon, "Ballistic Missiles and Missile Defense in Asia," National Bureau of Asian Research, vol. 13, no. 3, June 2002, pp. 58–63.

19 Lockheed Martin Corporation, *F-22 Raptor*, Marietta, GA, January 15, 2009, www.f22-raptor.com/about/index.html (accessed March 28, 2011).

20 "Air Force Plans to Sell F-22As to Allies," *Military.com*, www.military.com/features/0,15240,88282,00.html (accessed August 13, 2006).

21 "House Votes to Let Allies Buy Top U.S. Fighter," *The Washington Post*, July 1, 2006; "US Seeks to Lift Export Sales Ban on F-22A," *Jane's Defence Weekly*,

June 26, 2006; "Possible F-22A Sales Target S. Korea & Japan," *Asian Security Monitor*, July 1, 2006, http://mingi.typepad.com/blog/2006/07/us_may_lift_exp. html (accessed August 13, 2006).

22 "Appropriators Approve F-22A Multiyear, But not Foreign Sales," *Aerospace Daily and Defense Report*, September 27, 2006.

23 Christopher Bolkcom and Emma Chanlett-Avery, *Potential F-22 Raptor Export to Japan*, Congressional Research Service, CRS Report for Congress, Washington, DC, July 2, 2007; "F-22 Raptors to Japan?" *Defense Industry Daily*, October 26, 2008.

24 "U.S. Move May Allow F-22 Exports to Japan," *Daily Yomiuri Online*, June 21, 2009.

25 "Japanese Reactionaries Chided for Seeking to Purchase F-22," *Korean Central News Agency*, June 24, 2009.

26 "Japan Still Keen on F-22 Despite U.S. Obstacles," *The Japan Times Online*, August 1, 2009; "Japan Set to Consider Alternative to F-22s Following Move by U.S. House," *The Mainichi Daily News*, August 1, 2009.

27 "U.S. Asks Tokyo to Pay ¥1 Billion for F-35 Details," *The Japan Times Online*, October 4, 2009.

28 "Pre-emptive Strike Ability Said Necessary for Japan," *The Japan Times Online*, October 2, 2004; "First Strike Permitted if Attack Imminent: Abe Hitting Missile Bases Seen as Self-Defense," *The Japan Times Online*, July 11, 2006.

29 "Poll: 66% Want Article 9 to Stay as Is," *Asahi Shimbun*, May 5, 2008; The Maureen and Mike Mansfield Foundation, *Asahi Shimbun April 2009 Public Opinion Poll on the Constitution*, May 2009, www.mansfieldfdn.org/polls/2009/poll-09-11.htm (accessed on April 5, 2011).

30 Japan Ministry of Defense, *Defense Policy*, www.mod.go.jp/e/d_policy/dp01.html (accessed) December 13, 2008).

31 *Air Force Link*, www.google.com/url?sa=t&source=web&ct=res&cd=12&url=http%3A%2F%2Fwww.af.mil%2Ffactsheets%2Ffactsheet.asp%3FfsID%3D199&ei=k3dGSfiuF4-Etgfi3IyBCg&usg=AFQjCNErGGqLxWZNt0Uhx0UlZuAxbJOa0A&sig2=INL9jsTeuXxFXkOjYxowLg (accessed December 15, 2008).

32 Ministry of Defense, *Defense of Japan 2009* (Annual White Paper), Tokyo, 2009; Christopher Hughes, "'Super-sizing' the DPRK Threat: Japan's Evolving Military Posture and North Korea," *Asian Survey*, vol. 49, no. 2, March/April 2009, pp. 291–311.

33 Japan External Trade Organization (JETRO), "China Overtakes the US as Japan's Largest Trading Partner," Tokyo, February 28, 2008.

34 Keynote Address of Yasuo Hayashi, Chairman and CEO of JETRO, *Sustainable Development of Japan–China Economic Relations and Prospects for Business Alliance*, Symposium of Japan–China Business Alliance, Beijing, June 7, 2007.

35 "Successful Launch of First Satellite in DPRK," *Korean Central News Agency,* September 4, 1998; "Foreign Ministry Spokesman on Successful Launch of Artificial Satellite," *Korean Central News Agency,* September 4, 2004.

36 "Japan Agrees to Buy U.S. Parts for Spy Satellites," *Space.com*, September 29, 1999, www.space.com/news/japan_spy_990929_wg.html (accessed on April 5, 2011).

37 United Nations Office for Outer Space Affairs, *Law Concerning the National Space Development Agency of Japan*, Vienna, June 23, 1969.

38 Federation of American Scientists, "Information Gathering Satellites Imagery Intelligence," www.fas.org/spp/guide/japan/military/imint/#ref33 (accessed August 21, 2006).

39 "Successful Launch of First Satellite in DPRK," *Korean Central News Agency,* September 4, 1998; "Foreign Ministry Spokesman on Successful Launch of Artificial Satellite," *Korean Central News Agency,* September 4, 1998.

40 Quoted in "North Korea Disavows Its Moratorium on Testing of Long-Range Missiles," *The New York Times*, June 20, 2006.

41 *US–DPRK Joint Communiqué*, Washington, DC, October 12, 2000.

42 "Memorandum of DPRK Foreign Ministry," *Korean Central News Agency*, March 3, 2005.

43 "N. Korea's Next Step Draws Keen Attention," *Yonhap News*, June 23, 2006.

44 "U.S. Readies System for Missile Defense," *The Washington Post*, June 21, 2006; "U.S. to Arm Bases in Japan with Interceptor Missiles," *The Japan Times Online*, June 27, 2006; "Aegis Warship to Monitor North: MSDF Destroyer Exits RIMPAC [Rim of the Pacific Exercise] over ICBM-Test Crisis," *The Japan Times Online*, June 30, 2006.

45 "DPRK Foreign Ministry Spokesman on Its Missile Launches," *Korean Central News Agency*, July 6, 2006.

46 "N. Korea Warns of 'Stronger' Action," *Asahi Shimbun*, July 8, 2006.

47 Dermot Hudson, "Missile Launch Demonstrates that DPRK is Powerful Independent Country of Songun and Juche," *Red Banner of Songun*, August 2007, www.redbannerofsongun.org; Songun Politics Study Group, "Forward Taepodong DPRK!" July 6, 2006, accessed at www.songunpoliticsstudygroup.org (accessed on August 29, 2006).

48 Cheong Wa Dae, Office of the President, Republic of Korea, *Briefing on Statements by Key Cabinet Members of the Japanese Government*, Seoul, July 11, 2006.

49 "Japanese Remarks of a 'Preemptive Strike' against the DPRK Criticized," *Xinhua Online*, July 12, 2006.

50 Zhou Yongsheng, "Closing of an Era," *Beijing Review*, vol. 49, no. 34, August 24, 2006, pp. 10–11.

51 "Japanese Authorities' Theory of 'Preemptive Attack' on DPRK Assailed," *Korean Central News Agency*, July 26, 2006.

52 "Japanese Reactionaries' Wild Ambition for Comeback to Korea under Fire," *Korean Central News Agency*, August 14, 2006; "Japan's Defense White Paper Stresses Japan–U.S. Alliance, *People's Daily Online*, August 1, 2006; Japan Defense Agency, *Defense of Japan 2006 White Paper*, Tokyo, 2006, Chapter 4.

53 Quoted in "DPRK Demands Japan Pay for Past Colonial Crimes," *People's Daily Online*, August 15, 2006.

54 Ministry of Foreign Affairs, *Japan Protests against Launch of Missiles by North Korea*, Tokyo, July 5, 2006.

55 Ministry of Foreign Affairs, *Statement by the Press Secretary/Director-General for Press and Public Relations on the Marine Scientific Research by the Government of the Republic of Korea in the Waters Where Claim of the Exclusive Economic Zones (EEZ) Overlap between Japan an the ROK and the Territorial Sea Around Takeshima Islands*, Tokyo, July 7, 2006.

56 "Japan Proposes Sanctions on N. Korea," *The Washington Post*, July 7, 2006; "Koizumi Bush Want U.N. to Stand Tough," *Asahi Shimbun*, July 6, 2006.

57 "Divisions over N Korean Missiles Show Japan as an Odd Man Out," *Mainichi Daily News*, July 15, 2006; "Missile Tests Divide Seoul from Tokyo," *The New York Times*, July 11, 2006.

58 Quoted in "S. Korea Calls in Japanese Envoy for Talks on N. Korean Missile Issue," *Yonhap News*, July 10, 2006.

59 "China, Russia, Call for a Diplomatic Resolution over DPRK Crisis," *Xinhua Online*, July 8, 2006; "U.N. Demands End to North Korean Missile Program," *The New York Times*, July 15, 2006.

60 "NK Willing to Return to Dialogue if U.S. Lifts Punitive Measures: NK En [voy]," *Yonhap News*, July 8, 2006.

61 Li Li, "Launching Another Crisis," *The Beijing Review*, vol. 49, no. 29, July 20, 2006, pp. 10–11.

62 "Protestors Greet Man Gyong Bong-92," *Asahi Shimbun*, July 6, 2006; "Japan Bans Port Calls by N. Korean Ships for Six Months in Retaliation for Missiles," *Mainichi Daily News*, July 5, 2006.

63 United Nations Security Council, *Resolution 1695 (2006)*, New York, July 15, 2006.
64 "85% of Voters Approved U.N. Resolution Condemning North Korea," *Asahi Shimbun*, July 25, 2006.
65 Ministry of Foreign Affairs, *Statement by H.E. Mr. Shintaro Ito Vice-Minister for Foreign Affairs of Japan at the Meeting of the Security Council*, Tokyo, July 15, 2006.
66 Ministry of Foreign Affairs, *Statement by Mr. Taro Aso, Minister for Foreign Affairs, on the Adoption of the United Nations Security Council Resolution 1695 on the Launch of Missiles by North Korea*, Tokyo, July 16, 2006.
67 United Nations Department of Public Information, *Security Council Condemns Democratic People's Republic of Korea's Missile Launches*, New York, July 15, 2006.
68 "DPRK Foreign Ministry Refutes 'Resolution of UN Security Council,'" *Korean Central News Agency*, July 16, 2006.
69 "KCNA Blasts Rice's Outcry," *Korean Central News Agency*, July 24, 2006.
70 G8, St. Petersburg, Russia, 2006, *Chair's Summary*, St. Petersburg, July 17, 2006, http://en.g8russia.ru/docs/25.html (accessed March 28, 2011).
71 Yoichi Funabashi, *The Peninsula Question: A Chronicle of the Second North Korean Nuclear Crisis* (Washington, DC: Brookings Institution Press, 2007), pp. 61 and 72.
72 Ministry of Foreign Affairs, *Press Conference, 19 September*, Tokyo, September 19, 2006; "Tokyo Cuts North's Cash Supply," *The Japan Times Online*, September 20, 2006; "Japan to Impose Stricter Sanctions against North Korea," *Mainichi Daily News*, September 15, 2006.
73 Nobuaki Koga, "Koga Says! Statement on North Korea's Missile Launches," *Rengo Updates*, July 5, 2006, www. jtuc-rengo.org/index.html (accessed March 28, 2011).
74 "80% in Poll Favor Strong Reaction to North Korea's Missile Launches," *The Japan Times Online*, July 9, 2006; "Majority of Japanese Pollees Favor Further Punishment for North Korea," *Mainichi Shimbun*, July 24, 2006.
75 "KCNA Blasts Japan's Financial Sanctions against DPRK," *Korean Central News Agency*, September 23, 2006; "Japan's 'Financial Sanctions' against DPRK Assailed," *Korean Central News Agency*, September 25, 2006.
76 "Nuclear Weapons: Japan to Launch Spy Satellite after N Korea Missiles," *The New Zealand Herald*, July 20, 2006.
77 "North Korea's Taepodong-2 Launch an 'Utter Failure,' Defense Officials Say," *Asahi Shimbun*, September 1, 2006; "Japan Launches Intelligence-Gathering Satellite Amid Concerns over N. Korea," *Mainichi Daily News*, September 11, 2006.
78 "Deployment of USS Shiloh a Shield against N. Korean Missiles Strikes," *Asahi Shimbun*, August 30, 2006.
79 "U.S. Relocates X-Band Radar in Aomori to Watch North Korea," *The Japan Times Online*, September 29, 2006.
80 "Local Mayors Oppose PAC-3 Deployment in Okinawa," *Japan Press Weekly*, July 21, 2006; "Mayor Protests Missile Defense System," *The Japan Times Online*, October 3, 2006.
81 "U.S. Missile Defense Underway in Okinawa," *Asahi Shimbun*, October 27, 2006.
82 "U.S. Offers Japan 80 More Patriot Missiles," *The Japan Times Online*, August 25, 2006.
83 "PAC-3 Deployed at Iruma Air Base," *Daily Yomiuri Online*, March 31, 2007.
84 "Japan's Moves for Rapid Reaction Force Blasted," *Korean Central News Agency*, April 11, 2007.
85 "Latest Spy Satellite Goes into Space without a Hitch," *The Japan Times Online*, September 12, 2006.
86 "Rodong Sinmun Comments on Japan's Launch of Spy Satellite," *Korean Central News Agency*, September 26, 2006.

87 "Japan's Launch of Orbiting Solar Observatory under Fire," *Korean Central News Agency*, October 3, 2006.
88 "Signs Stir Concern North Korea Might Test Nuclear Bomb," *The Washington Post*, April 23, 2005.
89 "N. Korea Appears to be Preparing for a Nuclear Test," *ABC News International*, August 17, 2006, http://abcnews.go.com/International/story?id=2326083&page=1 (accessed March 28, 2011).
90 "Nuclear Saber Rattling," *The Korea Times*, September 12, 2006.
91 Department of Energy, National Nuclear Security Administration, "Unicorn Subcritical Experiment Conducted at NTS [Nevada Test Site]," National Nuclear Security Administration, Washington, D.C., August 30, 2006; "U.S. Sub-Critical Nuclear Test Assailed," *Korean Central News Agency*, September 13, 2006.
92 "Japan Sees No Signs of Imminent North Korean Nuclear Test," *Asahi Shimbun*, September 22, 2006.
93 "Roh Plays Down NK Nuclear Threat," *The Korea Times*, September 8, 2006.
94 "North Korea's Nuclear Test Always Possible," *The Korea Times*, August 28, 2006.
95 Institute for International Policy Studies, *IIPS Draft for Revising the Constitution*, Tokyo, June 2005, www.iips.org/kenpozenbun-e.pdf (accessed March 28, 2011).
96 "Nakasone Proposes Japan Consider Nuclear Weapons," *The Japan Times Online*, September 6, 2006.
97 Institute for International Policy Studies, *A Vision of Japan in the 21st Century*, Tokyo, September 5, 2005, www.iips.org/National%20Vision.pdf (accessed March 28, 2011).
98 "At UN Debate, DPR Korea Accuses United States of Encouraging Nuclear Tensions," *UN News Centre*, New York, September 26, 2006.
99 "DPRK Foreign Ministry Clarifies Stand on New Measure to Bolster War Deterrent," *Korean Central News Agency*, October 3, 2006.
100 "DPR Korea: Security Council Consults Amid Concerns over Nuclear Test Plans," *UN News Centre*, October 4, 2006.
101 "UNSC Given DPRK Draft/Japan's Statement Urges Sanctions for Nuclear Weapons Test," *Daily Yomiuri Online*, October 6, 2006.
102 "China Urges DPRK to Keep Calm, Restraint on Nuclear Test Issue," *Xinhua Online*, October 4, 2006.
103 Ministry of Foreign Affairs, *Press Conference by the Deputy Press Secretary*, Tokyo, October 6, 2006.
104 "Govt Eyes Tough Sanctions on DPRK/May Expand Ban on Port Calls, Seek UNSC Resolution if Pyongyang Tests Nuke," *Daily Yomiuri Online*, October 5, 2006; "Japan, U.S. to Seek Sanctions if North Korea Sets Off Nuke," *The Japan Times Online*, October 8, 2006.
105 "Japan, U.S. Seek UNSC Presidential Statement on North Korea Nuke Threat," *Asahi Shimbun*, October 4, 2006.
106 "Japan, U.S. to Cooperate on Nuke Issue," *The Japan Times Online*, October 5, 2006; "Japan, U.S. United on N. Korea," *Daily Yomiuri Online*, October 5, 2006.
107 United Nations General Assembly, First Committee, *Japan, Republic of Korea Urge Democratic People's Republic of Korea to Refrain from Nuclear Weapon Test, in First Committee Debate*, Press Briefing, New York, October 4, 2006.
108 "A Weaker U.N. Stand Eyed for N. Korea," *Asahi Shimbun*, October 6, 2006.
109 "UNSC Given DPRK Draft/Japan's Statement Urges Sanctions for Nuclear Weapons," *Daily Yomiuri Online*, October 6, 2006.
110 United Nations Security Council, *Statement by the President of the Security Council*, New York, October 6, 2006; United Nations, Department of Public Information, *In Presidential Statement, Security Council Urges Democratic People's Republic of Korea not to Carry Out Nuclear Test*, New York, October 6,

2006; "DPR Korea: Security Council Says Nuclear Test is Threat to Peace, Warns of Action," *UN News Centre*, October 6, 2006.

111 Prime Minister of Japan and His Cabinet, *Policy Speech by Prime Minister Shinzo Abe to the 165th Session of the Diet*, Tokyo, September 29, 2006.

112 Ministry of Foreign Affairs, *Statement by Mr. Taro Aso, Minister of Foreign Affairs, on the Statement by the President of the United Nations Security Council Following the Statement by North Korea Regarding a Nuclear Test*, Tokyo, October 7, 2006.

113 "DPRK Successfully Conducts Underground Nuclear Test," *Korean Central News Agency*, October 9, 2006.

114 US Geological Survey, *Magnitude 4.2 – North Korea*, October 9, 2006, http://earthquake.usgs.gov/eqcenter/recenteqsww/Quakes/ustqab.php (accessed on October 11, 2006).

115 Prime Minister and His Cabinet, *Press Conference by Prime Minister Shinzo Abe Following His Visit to the Republic of Korea*, Tokyo, October 9, 2006.

116 "North Korea's Claim is Met with Doubt and Anger," *The New York Times*, October 9, 2006.

117 Prime Minister of Japan and His Cabinet, *Message from Prime Minister: Tough Measures Taken against North Korea*, Tokyo, October 12, 2006.

118 "Abe, Bush Vow to Take 'Decisive Action' against North Korea," *Mainichi Daily News*, October 11, 2006.

119 "ASDF T-4 Jets Deployed to Check the Radioactivity Level of Nuke Test," *Kyodo News*, October 9, 2006; "Japan Says No Radioactive Material Found in Air," *Kyodo News*, October 11, 2006.

120 "N. Korea Warns of Countermeasures against New Sanctions by Japan," *Kyodo News*, October 12, 2006.

121 "Japan Bans North Korean Ships, Imports and Citizens," *The Japan Times Online*, October 12, 2006; "Tokyo Acts Speedily on Sanctions," *Asahi Shimbun*, October 13, 2006.

122 US Department of State, *Japan – Announcement of Additional North Korean Sanctions*, Washington, DC, October 11, 2006.

123 "Bush Raps N. Korea for Abductions, Refers to Japanese Abductee Yokota," *Kyodo News*, October 11, 2006.

124 Ministry of Foreign Affairs of the People's Republic of China, *Statement of the Ministry of Foreign Affairs of the People's Republic of China*, Beijing, October 9, 2006.

125 United Nations Security Council, *Resolution 1718 (2006)*, New York, October 14, 2006; *UN News Centre*, "Security Council Imposes Sanctions on DPR Korea after Its Claimed Nuclear Test," October 16, 2006.

126 "U.S. Hits Obstacle in Getting Vote on North Korea," *International Herald Tribune*, October 14, 2006.

127 United Nations Security Council, *Security Council Condemns Nuclear Test by Democratic People's Republic of Korea Unanimously Adopting Resolution 1718 (2006)*, New York, October 14, 2006.

128 US Department of State, Ambassador John Bolton, US Representative to the United Nations, *The Adoption of United Nations Security Council Resolution 1718*, United Nations Press Release, New York, October 14, 2006.

129 Cultural hegemony is virtually equivalent to soft power, which is discussed in Joseph Nye, *Soft Power: The Means to Success in World Politics* (New York: Public Affairs, 2004).

130 "U.S. under Fire for Paralyzing World Nuclear Disarmament System," *Korean Central News Agency*, October 25, 2006.

131 United Nations Security Council, *Security Council Condemns Nuclear Test by Democratic People's Republic of Korea Unanimously Adopting Resolution 1718 (2006)*.

132 United Nations General Assembly, First Committee, *Draft Resolution on International Arms Trade Treaty One of the Eight Texts Introduced in Disarmament Committee*, New York, October 18, 2006.

133 "DPRK Foreign Ministry Spokesman Totally Refutes UNSC 'Resolution,'" *Korean Central News Agency*, October 17, 2006.

134 Office of the Director of National Intelligence, Public Affairs Office, *Statement by the Office of the Director of National Intelligence on the North Korean Nuclear Test*, Washington, DC, October 16, 2006.

135 Quoted in "Abe: Test Claim Appears Valid," *Daily Yomiuri Online*, October 18, 2006.

136 "Tokyo a Bit Clearer on Nuke Blast," *The Japan Times Online*, October 28, 2006.

137 "Japan Launches Fourth Spy Satellite," *The Japan Times Online*, December 23, 2006.

138 "Japan's Dangerous Drive to Become a Military Giant Debunked," *Korean Central News Agency*, March 5, 2007.

139 "North Korean Fuel Identified as Plutonium," *The New York Times*, October 17, 2006.

140 Jungmin Kang and Peter Hayes, "Did North Korea Successfully Conduct a Nuclear Test? A Technical Analysis," *Japan Focus*, October 22, 2006, accessed at www.japanfocus.org (accessed March 29, 2011); Richard Garwin and Frank von Hippel, "A Technical Analysis of North Korea's Oct. 9 Nuclear Test," *Arms Control Today*, November 2006.

141 "DPRK Vows to Stick to 'Military-First' Policy," *Xinhua Online*, December 5, 2006.

142 United Nations General Assembly, First Committee, *Nuclear Weapons, Irrational Doctrines Justifying Their Use, Non-Proliferation Treaty Non-Compliance Block Nuclear Disarmament, Iran Tells First Committee*, New York, October 13, 2008.

143 "Rodong Sinmun Praises Songun as Great Banner of National Prosperity," *Korean Central News Agency*, November 27, 2006.

144 Jasper Becker, *Rogue Regime: Kim Jong Il and the Looming Threat of North Korea* (New York: Oxford University Press, 2005); Jasper Becker, "The Depths of Evil," *New Statesman*, September 4, 2006, pp. 32–33; Robert Kaplan, "When North Korea Falls," *The Atlantic Monthly*, October 2006, pp. 64–73; Gordon Chang, *Nuclear Showdown: North Korea Takes on the World* (New York: Random House, 2006); Jeffrey Richelson, *Spying on the Bomb: American Nuclear Intelligence from Nazi Germany to Iran and North Korea* (New York: W.W. Norton, 2006), pp. 503–44.

145 Leon Sigal, "Try Engagement for a Change," *Global Asia: A Journal of the East Asia Foundation*, vol. 1., no. 1, September 2006, pp. 50–57.

146 "U.S. Most Responsible for Nuclear Test: Poll," *The Korea Times*, October 15, 2006.

147 US Treasury Department, *Treasury Designates Banco Delta Asia as Primary Money Laundering Concern under USA Patriot Act*, Washington, DC, September 15, 2005.

148 US Department of Treasury, *Treasury Targets North Korean Entities for Supporting WMD Proliferation*, Washington, DC, October 21, 2005.

149 "Dialogue and Sanctions Can Never Go Together: Rodong Sinmun," *Korean Central News Agency*, November 2, 2005.

150 The White House, *President Participates in Roundtable with Young Leaders in Brazil*, Brasilia, Brazil, November 6, 2005.

151 "Spokesman for DPRK FM Refutes U.S. Chief Executive's Anti-DPRK Vituperation," *Korean Central News Agency*, November 8, 2005.

152 Charles Krauthammer, "The Unipolar Moment," *Foreign Affairs*, vol. 70, no. 1, 1990/91, pp. 23–33; Robert Kagan, "Benevolent Empire," *Foreign Policy*, Summer 1998, pp. 24–35.

153 "Kim Urges Simultaneous Actions for Ending Nuclear Issue," *Xinhua Online*, November 12, 2005.
154 "DPRK FM Spokesman Urges U.S. to Lift Financial Sanctions against It," *Korean Central News Agency*, December 2, 2006.
155 Selig Harrison, "North Korea's Embarrassment," *The Hankyoreh*, July 7, 2006.
156 Todd Bullock, "Sanctions on North Korean Companies Unrelated to Six-Party Talks," US Department of State, International Information Programs, Washington, DC, January 6, 2006.
157 "DPRK Foreign Ministry's Spokesman Urges U.S. to Lift Financial Sanctions Against DPRK," *Korean Central News Agency*, January 9, 2006.
158 "KNCA Blasts U.S. Gimmick to Evade Responsibility for Deadlocked Talks," *Korean Central News Agency*, February 11, 2006.
159 Selig Harrison, "North Korea: A Nuclear Threat," *Newsweek, International Edition*, October 16, 2006.
160 US Department of Treasury, *Treasury Officials Brief North Koreans on Actions to Stem DPRK Illicit Financial Activity*, New York, March 7, 2006; US Department of State, International Information Programs, *Treasury Briefs North Korea on U. S. Financial Systems Protections*, Washington, DC, March 7, 2006; "N. Korea Sets Terms for Return to Nuclear Talks," *The Washington Post*, March 9, 2006.
161 "KCNA Urges U.S. to Lift Financial Sanctions," *Korean Central News Agency*, March 25, 2006; "U.S. Urged to Accept DPRK's Proposal," *Korean Central News Agency*, March 28, 2006.
162 United States Department of State, *Interview on CNN with Zain Verjee*, Beijing, October 20, 2006.
163 Ministry of Foreign Affairs of the People's Republic of China, *Heads of Delegation to the Six-Party Talks from China, the DPRK, and the U.S. had an Informal Meeting in Beijing*, Beijing, October 31, 2006.
164 Mike Chinoy, *Meltdown: The Inside Story of the North Korean Nuclear Crisis* (New York: St. Martin's Press, 2008), pp. 306–07.
165 US Department of State, US Embassy, *Press Conference at the U.S. Embassy, Beijing, China*, Beijing, October 31, 2006.
166 "Spokesman for the DPRK Foreign Ministry on Resumption of Six-Party Talks," *Korean Central News Agency*, November 1, 2006.
167 "U.S. Takes Tough Line on Macau Bank Ties with N Korea," *Reuters*, November 2, 2006.
168 "Macau Bank Tied to DPRK WMD Projects/Funds Sent from Accounts to Japan in '02," *Daily Yomiuri Online*, November 4, 2006.
169 Author correspondence with a US Treasury Department official, November 6, 2006.
170 US Department of State, US Embassy, *Press Conference at the U.S. Embassy, Beijing, China*, Beijing, October 31, 2006.
171 "U.S., Japan Plot Actions on North Korea Sanctions," *Yahoo! News*, November 7, 2006, from a story reported by Agence France Presse.
172 "Japan to Continue Sanctions on N Korea Despite Nuclear Talks Offer," *Forbes. Com*, November 1, 2006.
173 "Japan to Ban Luxury Goods Export to N. Korea from Wed.," *Kyodo News*, November 14, 2006; "Ban on Luxury Item Exports to N. Korea Comes into Effect," *The Nikkei Weekly*, November 20, 2006.
174 R. Nicholas Burns, Undersecretary for Political Affairs, *Testimony to the House International Relations Committee, U.S. Policy Toward North Korea*, Washington, DC, November 16, 2006.
175 In 2008, a controversy emerged because Washington more than once identified North Korea as a nuclear weapons state. For Pyongyang's Reaction see, "U.S. Recognizes DPRK as a Nuclear Weapons State," *Korean Central News Agency*,

December 11, 2008; "Lively Response to U.S. Recognition of DPRK as a Nuclear Weapons State," *Korean Central News Agency*, December 17, 2008.

176 US Department of State, International Information Programs, *United States to Ban the Export of Luxury Goods to the United States*, Washington, DC, December 1, 2006.

177 US Census Bureau, *Foreign Trade Statistics*, www.census.gov/foreign-trade/www/index.html (accessed December 14, 2006); US Department of Commerce, International Trade Administration, http://trade.gov/index.asp (accessed December 14, 2006); "U.S.–N.K. Trade at Virtual Standstill," *The Hankyoreh*, December 6, 2006.

178 United States Department of the Treasury, *Prepared Remarks of Stuart Levey, Undersecretary for Terrorism and Financial Intelligence, Before the U.S.–MENA Private Sector Dialogue on Combating Money Laundering and Terrorist Financing*, New York, December 11, 2006; "US Wants to Block All of N. Korea's Financial Deals," *The Korea Times*, December 12, 2006.

179 "Japan Opposes North Korea's Return to Talks Unless It Gives Up Nuclear Weapons," *Mainichi Daily News*, October 31, 2006.

180 "Spokesman for DPRK Foreign Ministry on Japan's Attitude toward Resumption of Six-Party Talks," *Korean Central News Agency*, November 4, 2006.

181 "Japan, U.S. to Pressure North Korea to Abandon Nuclear Program," *Mainichi Daily News*, November 6, 2006.

182 "KCNA Slashes at Japan's Intention to Play Bad Role at Six-Party Talks," *Korean Central News Agency*, December 6, 2006.

183 "Japan to Oppose Nuclear Talks Unless N. Korea is willing to Compromise," *International Herald Tribune*, December 10, 2006.

184 "Japan's Attempt to Scuttle the Six-Party Talks," *Korean Central News Agency*, December 11, 2006.

185 "Japan Rightists Fan Fury over North Korean Abductions," *The New York Times*, December 17, 2006.

186 "KCNA Demands Thorough Probe into Case of Missing Korean Linguist," *Korean Central News Agency*, December 16, 2006.

187 "Pyongyang Urges Japan to Investigate North Korean's Disappearance," *Mainichi Daily News*, December 17, 2006; "Tokyo Denies North Kidnap Claim," *The Japan Times Online*, December 19, 2006.

188 "Japan Seeks Quick Action to Settle Nuke, Abduction at 6-Way Talks," *Kyodo News*, December 18, 2006.

189 Anthony DiFilippo, *Japan's Nuclear Disarmament Policy and the U.S. Security Umbrella* (New York: Palgrave Macmillan, 2006); Anthony DiFilippo, "Can Japan Craft an International Nuclear Disarmament Policy?" *Asian Survey*, vol. 40, no. 4, July/August 2000, pp. 571–98.

190 Eric Johnston, "North's Gambit May Weaken Japanese Taboo on Nuke Talk," *The Japan Times Online*, October 12, 2006.

191 "Abe Sets Schedule to Revise Constitution," *Asahi Shimbun*, November 2, 2006.

192 "Abe Sticks to Nonnuclear Principles," *Mainichi Daily News*, October 10, 2006.

193 "Japan Protected by U.S. Nuclear Umbrella: Schieffer," *Mainichi Daily News*, October 12, 2006.

194 "LDP Policy Chief Calls for Debate on Nuke Option," *The Japan Times Online*, October 16, 2006.

195 "Foreign Minister Aso Stresses Japan Should Keep Nuclear Options Open," *Mainichi Daily News*, October 18, 2006.

196 "Japan Tells Rice It Will Not Seek Nuclear Weapons," *The New York Times*, October 18, 2006.

197 "Aso Calls for Policy Debate to Renew Non-Nuclear Commitment," *Mainichi Daily News*, October 24, 2006.

198 "Japan Not to Go Nuclear: Rice," *Mainichi Daily News*, October 25, 2006.
199 "Nakagawa Raises Nukes on U.S. Visit," *Asahi Shimbun*, October 30, 2006.
200 "Nuclear Option Debate Still Splits Japanese Leadership," *Mainichi Daily News*, November 5, 2006; "LDP Official to Ask Aso, Nakagawa to Refrain from Nuke Weapon Talk," *Kyodo News*, November 5, 2006.
201 "Opposition Calls for Aso's Resignation over Comments on Nuclear Weapons," *Mainichi Daily News*, November 9, 2006.
202 "U.S. Agrees on Concrete Nuclear Umbrella for S. Korea," *Yonhap News*, October 19, 2006.
203 "South Korean Foreign Minister Discourages Nuclear Weapons Debate in Japan," *Mainichi Daily News*, November 6, 2006.
204 "Abe Says No to Nukes but Allows Discussion," *The Japan Times Online*, November 9, 2006; "Abe Plays Down Debate over Japan Possessing Nuclear Weapons," *Mainichi Daily News*, November 9, 2006.
205 In 2010, a Japanese Ministry of Foreign Affairs panel concluded that a secret pact had been made between Tokyo and Washington that permitted US ships carrying nuclear weapons to enter Japan's ports during the Cold War, which violated the third principle of no-entry of nuclear weapons. See "Secret Pacts Existed; Denials 'Dishonest,'" *The Japan Times Online*, March 10, 2010.
206 "Opposition Balks at Debate over Allowing U.S. Nuclear Weapons in Its Waters," *Mainichi Daily News*, November 19, 2006.
207 "Abe Pledges Japan Won't Debate Going Nuclear," *Mainichi Daily News*, November 20, 2006.
208 Ministry of Foreign Affairs, *Statement by the Press Secretary/Director-General for Press and Public Relations, Ministry of Foreign Affairs, on the Adoption of the Draft Resolution on Nuclear Disarmament by Japan to the First Committee of the United Nations General Assembly*, Tokyo, October 27, 2006; United Nations General Assembly, First Committee, *Renewed Determination Towards the Total Elimination of Nuclear Weapons*, New York, October 26, 2006.
209 "Poll: 80% Support Upholding Japan's Nonnuclear Principles," *Daily Yomiuri Online*, November 21, 2006.
210 See, for example, Llewelyn Hughes, "Why Japan Will Not go Nuclear (Yet): International and Domestic Constraints on the Nuclearization of Japan," *International Security*, vol. 31, no. 4, Spring 2007, pp. 67–96.
211 Anthony DiFilippo, "How Tokyo's Security Policies Discount Public Opinion: Toward a New Agenda," *Pacifica Review: Peace, Security & Global Change*, vol. 14, no. 1, February 2002, pp. 23–48.
212 "No US Nukes in South Korea: Roh," *The Korea Times*, December 8, 2006.
213 "U.S. Termed Chief Nuclear Criminal," *Korean Central News Agency*, November 13, 2006.
214 "Japanese Reactionaries' Moves for Nuclear War Denounced," *Korean Central News Agency*, December 6, 2006.
215 Ministry of Foreign Affairs, *Joint Statement: U.S.–Japan Security Consultative Committee*, Washington, DC, February 19, 2005; Ministry of Foreign Affairs, *Security Consultative Committee Document, U.S.–Japan Alliance: Transformation and Realignment for the Future*, Tokyo, October 29, 2005; Ministry of Foreign Affairs, *United States–Japan Roadmap for Realignment Implementation*, Tokyo, May 1, 2006.
216 "Missile Shield Policy May be Reviewed," *The Japan Times Online*, November 21, 2006; DiFilippo, *Japan's Nuclear Disarmament Policy and the U.S. Security Umbrella*, pp. 61–62.
217 "Collective Defense Ban Crazy: Lawless," *The Japan Times Online*, December 7, 2006.
218 "Abe to Establish Panel on Collective Defense," *Asahi Shimbun*, April 5, 2007; "Abe's Panel on Examining Collective Defense Kicks Off," *The Japan Times Online*, May 19, 2007.

219 "62% OK with Japan's Ban on Collective Defense," *The Japan Times Online*, May 14, 2007.
220 "Survey: 81% Say Threat from North Korea Stronger," *Daily Yomiuri Online*, October 17, 2006.
221 "Survey: 62% Support Sanctions against North Korea," *Asahi Shimbun*, October 11, 2006.
222 "Poll: Defense Ministry Sees Growing Support," *Daily Yomiuri Online*, January 26, 2007.
223 "Defense Agency Upgraded to Full-Scale Defense Ministry," *Mainichi Daily News*, January 9, 2007. "Defense Ministry Launched, Upgraded from Agency after Half Century," *Kyodo News*, January 9, 2007.
224 "Poll: Defense Ministry Sees Growing Support," *Daily Yomiuri Online*, January 26, 2007.

4   The Making of DPRK Policies
in Washington and Tokyo

This chapter analyzes the influence of political forces both in the United States and Japan, and shows how each country has fashioned its respective policy to deal with the Democratic People's Republic of Korea (DPRK). This chapter pays close attention to the abduction of Japanese nationals by North Korea and to Washington's identification of the DPRK as a state sponsor of terrorism. Both of these issues have an important connection to the relationship between the United States and Japan.

Creating a confrontational US team

Not too long after the Bush administration came to power in 2001, it very quickly honed in on the adversaries of the United States and began developing confrontational policies toward states that had just months before been highlighted in a major neoconservative policy work, *Rebuilding America's Defenses*, published by the Project for the New American Century (PNAC).[1] In 1997, the PNAC produced a *Statement of Principles* that summarized its views. Critical of the Clinton administration's "incoherent policies" and maintaining that the foreign and defense policies of the United States had gone "adrift," PNAC's objective was to generate enthusiasm for America's global leadership. PNAC made clear that to accomplish this objective, the United States had to reach back to the Reagan presidency and reestablish "military strength and moral clarity." Five individuals who would later hold top positions in the administration of George W. Bush, signed PNAC's *Statement of Principles* – Dick Cheney (Vice President), Donald Rumsfeld (Secretary of Defense), Paul Wolfowitz (Deputy Secretary of Defense), Lewis "Scooter" Libby (Cheney's chief-of-staff) and Elliot Abrams (National Security Council).[2] By the time PNAC published *Rebuilding America's Defenses*, archetypical hardliner – some say neoconservative – John Bolton had become one of its directors. During his first term in office, Bush appointed Bolton to the position of Undersecretary of State for Arms Control and International Security, later making him the US Permanent Representative to the United Nations. All of these men also had previously held posts in the Reagan administration. Although not a signatory of the PNAC's *Statement of*

Principles, Robert "first-strike" Joseph, who also held positions in the Bush administration, initially as the National Security Council's director of non-proliferation, was a clone of John Bolton.[3] Joseph filled Bolton's vacated post at the State Department when Bush appointed him US Permanent Representative to the United Nations.

Although an affirmed intention of PNAC's *Statement of Principles* was to create moral clarity, some of the people appointed to top positions in the Bush administration seemed quite unlikely to have been able to provide that. When he worked for the Reagan administration, Elliott Abrams pleaded guilty to two misdemeanors stemming from the Iran-Contra scandal, a move he made to keep himself from possibly serving time in jail; President George H.W. Bush later pardoned him.[4] In 2005, President George W. Bush approved Wolfowitz's moving from the Defense Department to head the World Bank. Wolfowitz was later forced to resign from this position because of the preferential treatment he afforded his girlfriend who was also employed there. In March 2007, Scooter Libby was convicted of four felony counts connected to the intentional leaking in 2003 of the identity of CIA official Valerie Plame, wife of former Ambassador Joseph Wilson and a critic of the Bush administration's justification for invading Iraq.

When Bush gave his State of the Union Address in January 2002, proclaiming that Iraq, North Korea and Iran were the states constituting an "axis of evil," Bolton maintained that this "gladdened my heart."[5] Relying on deeply flawed intelligence and policies fashioned by giving free interpretive reign to top officials with decidedly parochially conservative agendas, the United States invaded Iraq; it also maintained that Iran had long been concealing its efforts to develop nuclear weapons and that the DPRK had a clandestine uranium-enrichment program to produce nuclear weapons.[6]

The Bush administration's North Korean policy

Although Robert Joseph early on spearheaded the Bush administration policy review of North Korea,[7] it nonetheless came pretty much right out of PNAC's playbook. Like Iraq and Iran, PNAC's 2000 report noted, North Korea was on a fast track to produce nuclear weapons to deter the United States. Among other things, PNAC's report also indicated that the DPRK was one of a handful of countries "deeply hostile" to the United States and stressed that "we cannot allow North Korea, Iran, Iraq or similar states to undermine American leadership, intimidate American allies or threaten the American homeland itself."[8]

From the beginning of the Bush administration, a number of its officials had so much disdain for the 1994 Agreed Framework they wanted it dead.[9] In March 2002, Bolton noted that the Bush administration had taken its "first step toward eliminating the charade that the Agreed Framework was somehow still viable."[10] The Bush administration's ineffective confrontational approach toward North Korea[11] reached an initial boiling point when

US Assistant Secretary of State for East Asian and Pacific Affairs James Kelly traveled to Pyongyang in October 2002, and accused the DPRK of having a covert uranium-enrichment program to develop nuclear weapons. After this, both Washington and Pyongyang caused things to boil over – again and again, as we saw in Chapter 2. When Pyongyang announced its intention to pull out of the NPT in January 2003, it stressed that the nation's security was in jeopardy because of the United States' "vicious hostile policy toward the DPRK."[12]

Pyongyang wanted a formal security agreement with the United States. It thoroughly rejected the Bush administration's repeated demand, also echoed by Tokyo, that the DPRK first and unconditionally accept complete, verifiable and irreversible dismantlement (CVID). Pyongyang insisted that the DPRK was not a defeated country and that CVID was a unilateral attempt by the United States, to disarm the North. Instead, Pyongyang wanted "simultaneous action" or "action for action" and eventually proposed a "reward for freeze" as a first step in the dismantlement process.[13]

In May 2003 in Krakow, Poland, Bush declared his intention to launch the Proliferation Security Initiative (PSI), a multilateral undertaking intended to prevent shipments of weapons of mass destruction and related material from being delivered.[14] The PSI was John Bolton's brainchild, begot when he held the position of undersecretary of state for arms and international security. Bolton's successor, Robert Joseph, shared his enthusiasm and commitment to PSI.[15]

Critics, among them Beijing, charged that the PSI, whose members include Japan, was inconsistent with international law. Favoring diplomacy rather than interdiction, China indicated early on that, with respect to PSI, "some countries of the world have doubts over the legality and effectiveness of the measure."[16] Moreover, good evidence available to the public has not shown that the PSI has been successful, despite the claims of Bolton and Joseph.[17] A recent study analyzing the highly publicized issue of the DPRK being involved in transporting weapons of mass destruction and parts on government vessels concludes that there is a paucity of evidence to show that this is true.[18]

The PSI's harshest critic was Pyongyang, which was confident that the DPRK was an intended target. Reacting to the first PSI exercise, the Pacific Protector, held off the coast of Australia in mid September 2003, Pyongyang charged, "The U.S. is the world's biggest criminal state as regards the proliferation of weapons. However, it is painting itself a 'champion of international justice', making the far-fetched assertion that the DPRK poses a threat by proliferating weapons. This cannot but be a mockery of the international community."[19]

Even before Bush formally announced the PSI, which Cheney and Rumsfeld also supported, his administration had its interdiction eye primarily and closely trained on North Korea.[20] Just days before Pyongyang announced its intention to withdraw from the NPT it sharply criticized Washington for its part in interdicting the DPRK ship Sosan in route to Yemen with a cargo of scud missiles, the incident that occasioned PSI five months later. The DPRK also criticized Secretary of State Colin Powell at this time for his comments, which reportedly threatened that the United States will do this again if it believes a North Korean ship is involved in proliferation activities. Calling the interdiction an act of "piracy," Pyongyang lashed out at the Bush adminis- tration, demanding an apology from Washington and stressing that it is well known that the DPRK manufactures and sells missiles but that it is the United States that "tops the world's list in producing and selling the weapons of mass destruction."[21]

Marking the first anniversary of PSI in Krakow, Bolton maintained, "North Korea is one of the most extensive proliferators in the world." Demonstrating his subjectivist view of North Korea, one also held by others within the Bush administration, Bolton asserted, "we fear that if they develop sufficient quantities of weapons grade uranium or plutonium that they, based on their history, would be prepared to sell that or actually sell weapons to other rogue states or terrorists groups."[22]

This "fear" factor was the second prong in the two-pronged strategy that the hard-liners used to shape and direct Washington's DPRK policy until the Bush administration finally recognized that change was necessary. The other prong was the confrontational approach. Significantly, for several years the Bush administration's hard-line DPRK policy meshed well with the Japanese nationalist views that strongly influenced, and eventually dominated, Japan's policy toward North Korea. Not only did the US hardliners and neo- conservatives prefer regime change in North Korea, Japanese nationalists also wanted this. For example, in October 2002 Naoyuki Agawa, Minister for Public Affairs at the Japan Embassy in Washington, pointed out during a lecture sponsored by the Institute for Corean-American Studies, "we Japanese have some very healthy nationalist feelings."[23] A little over a year later, during a discussion sponsored by the Sasakawa Peace Foundation, Agawa added clarity to his previous comment. Referring to North Korea, Agawa stated, "I think ultimately, the solution is regime change."[24]

In early 2007, the Bush administration suddenly abandoned its hard-line confrontational DPRK policy, much to the chagrin of the hardliners in Washington and the nationalists in Japan. As we shall see below, the Bush administration replaced its hard-line, confrontation policy toward North Korea with a conciliatory approach.

The action plan that came out of the February 2007 six-party talks created a pervading sense of optimism that the resolution of the DPRK nuclear issue was a strong possibility, especially since Washington and Pyongyang were on track to settle the row pertaining to North Korea's funds that had been frozen in its accounts with Banco Delta Asia. Having lost much of their influence in the making of DPRK policy, US hardliners anxiously anticipated the failure of the nonconfrontational approach because of what they claimed was North Korea's unpredictability and Kim Jong Il's untrustworthiness.

Several months after his stint as US permanent representative to the United Nations expired, Bolton opined in the *Wall Street Journal* in late August 2007, "Despite encomiums about the virtue of diplomacy, little real progress has been made in eliminating Pyongyang's [nuclear weapons] program."[25] This stood in stark contrast to what Christopher Hill, who had replaced James Kelly as Assistant Secretary of State for East Asian and Pacific Affairs in 2005, told reporters on the same day before a US–DPRK meeting in Geneva: "As President Bush said yesterday, there has been progress toward the denuclearization of the D.P.R.K."[26] At the conclusion of the two-day, bilateral working group meeting held in Geneva in early September, more good news became public. North Korea had agreed to the disablement of its nuclear programs, as well as a complete declaration of them by the end of December 2007.[27] Both of these commitments were subsequently stipulated in the Joint Document that came out of the six-party talks held in late September 2007.[28] According to the DPRK Foreign Ministry, at the September working group meeting in Geneva, Washington also made commitments to remove North Korea from the State Department's list of countries that support terrorism and to lift the sanctions associated with the Trading with the Enemy Act.[29]

By December 2007, Hill expressed his satisfaction with the progress made in resolving the DPRK nuclear issue. Pyongyang had already shut down its plutonium-reprocessing facilities at Yongbyon, for which it received its initial shipment of heavy oil, allowed personnel from the IAEA to visit North Korea, and was now in the process of disabling its nuclear weapons capability. All of this, plus a complete list of the DPRK's nuclear programs, had been specified in the action plan that resulted from the six-party talks held in February 2007. When Hill visited Pyongyang in early December, he stressed that the second phase of the agreement was concluding and that "we need to make sure that it ends well."[30] Since the disablement process was proceeding smoothly at this time, a good ending for Hill now also meant "a good declaration" in which Pyongyang would provide a complete list of the DPRK's nuclear work, including its activities in uranium enrichment. During Hill's December visit to Pyongyang, he delivered a letter to the DPRK's Foreign Ministry from President Bush to Kim Jong Il. In the letter, Bush wrote of the need for Pyongyang to provide a "complete and accurate" declaration, and that the denuclearization of the Korean Peninsula would provide the condition for rapprochement with the United States.

US hardliners: on the offensive

The US hardliners' policy had failed, first because very little progress had been made in resolving the North Korean nuclear issue. Second, it failed because Pyongyang used it to justify the DPRK's willingness to build up and demonstrate *songun*.

However, the hardliners both inside and outside of the Bush administration refused to acknowledge that their DPRK policy strategy had been ineffective.

Very soon after the February 2007 six-party party talks, Elliot Abrams, Bush's neoconservative deputy national security adviser, immediately sent out emails expressing his strong disagreement with the plan that came out of these discussions. Abrams, like many other hardliners, was particularly troubled by the action plan's offer to remove the DPRK from the US State Department's list of countries sponsoring terrorism.[31] Some hardliners asked, "When exactly did Kim Jong Il become trustworthy." Initially, they compared the February action plan to what the Clinton administration achieved in the Agreed Framework.[32] Although this criticism then appeared valid, the February action plan was nonetheless a major step forward from the nadir reached when Pyongyang detonated a nuclear device just four months earlier. Other hardliners called the February action plan "a strategic blunder masquerading as a diplomatic triumph."[33]

In late September 2007, Israel attacked a Syrian facility that it concluded was a nuclear site. Hardliners claimed that North Korea, which in the past has sold missiles to Damascus, had supplied nuclear materials to Syria and that this proliferation proved that the Bush administration would be making a big mistake if it thought that Pyongyang could be trusted to abide by a nuclear deal. Making this matter worse was that a few days before the Israeli attack, a North Korean ship had docked in a Syrian port. Andrew Semmel, Acting Deputy Assistant Secretary of State for Nuclear Nonproliferation Policy and Negotiations, commented shortly after the incident that technical personnel from North Korea are in Syria and suggested that Damascus might have "secret suppliers" for its clandestine nuclear program.[34] A top official in the Bush administration who opposed the new conciliatory approach anonymously stated in reference to the Syrian incident that despite what may very well be an instance of DPRK nuclear proliferation, "we are shaking hands with the North Koreans because they have again told us they are going to disarm."[35]

At the time, Seoul did not buy the hard-liner's argument. South Korea's Foreign Minister Song Min-soon indicated, "If Syria received nuclear materials from North Korea, it must have a facility to store the nuclear material, but as far as I know, Syria does not have any facility."[36] The DPRK Foreign Ministry vehemently denied the allegation in September 2007, maintaining, "This is sheer misinformation" and insisted that the DPRK "would never allow nuclear transfer," especially since in October 2006 it "solemnly declared" it would not be involved in nuclear proliferation.[37]

The hardliners were doing what they could to obstruct the forward momentum evident in the six-party talks and to prevent improved relations between Washington and Pyongyang. After the Syrian incident, the DPRK did briefly postpone its participation in the six-party talks. However, the hardliners could not even claim credit for this ephemeral delay, since Pyongyang gave no explanation and some surmised that the interruption was for a reason other than the Syrian incident.[38]

Significantly, the hardliners' major objection to the removal of North Korea from the US State Department's list of countries that support terrorism crossed paths with the nationalist-created obsession in Japan with the abduction issue. By the fall of 2002, the abduction issue had become the nucleus of Tokyo's DPRK policy that with the media had steered the Japanese people to emotional frenzy. For both Tokyo and the US hardliners, removing the DPRK from the State Department's list without first resolving the abduction issue would be wrong.

The hardliners largely relied on the argument that the removal of North Korea from the State Department's terrorism list would strike a serious blow to the US–Japan relationship. They maintained that by the Bush administration no longer identifying the DPRK as a state sponsor of terrorism, which the abduction issue had helped to justify, this could weaken Tokyo's commitment to the US–Japan security alliance. Even as it was becoming increasingly plain that the United States was less and less interested in connecting the resolution of the abduction issue to the settlement of the DPRK nuclear problem, Bush still attempted to save face. Thus, during a joint press conference with Prime Minister Fukuda in November 2007, Bush again emphasized how touched he was previously when he met with the Sakie Yokota, mother of Megumi Yokota (see below). Megumi had become the symbol of the emotionalism associated to the Japanese abduction movement because DPRK agents kidnapped her when she was just a young teenager. Referring to Ms Yokota, Bush stressed: "I told her and I'm going to tell the Japanese people once again, ... we will not forget the Japanese abductees, nor their families."[39]

In November 2007, *The Wall Street Journal* editorialized that US Ambassador to Japan J. Thomas Schieffer had earlier informed the president that setting aside the abduction issue and de-listing the DPRK could damage the bilateral security relationship, and that "U.S. support for Japan's position also goes to the heart of American credibility as a security partner." Bolton was more direct: "The State Department's lust to remove North Korea from the terrorism list is having a profoundly negative impact on our treaty ally."[40]

The politicization of the abduction issue: Japan's North Korean policy

While President Bush preferred the collapse of the North Korean regime led by Kim Jong Il, who he said he detested, Junichiro Koizumi envisioned Japanese rapprochement with the DPRK during his time as prime minister, especially during his early years in office.[41] Koizumi's first visit to North Korea in September 2002 is incontrovertible evidence of this since the diplomatic achievement was the Pyongyang Declaration.[42] North Korea's survival after the demise of the Soviet Union left a rancid taste in the mouths of Japanese nationalists. Although Koizumi certainly sympathized with the nationalists, his conservatism was not as extreme as theirs. Like the nationalists, Koizumi wanted Japan to become a "normal country." However, unlike Koizumi, the nationalists were not enthusiastic about Japan normalizing relations with North Korea, especially since for them too many questions remained unanswered about the abduction issue. For several years before Koizumi became prime minister in the spring of 2001, many nationalists and those concerned about the abduction issue had been urging the government to press North Korea on the then suspected kidnappings of Japanese citizens.

Japanese nationalists believe strongly that the government should develop and maintain visibly tough policy positions toward China and North Korea and even, though to a much lesser extent, toward South Korea. With regard to North Korea, they have been especially vocal about the need for the Japanese government to take a hard-line position, especially until there is a satisfactory resolution to the abduction issue. In May 1991, during the third round of normalization talks between Japan and North Korea, Tokyo first brought up the abduction of Lee Un-hae, a Japanese language instructor in North Korea believed to be Yaeko Taguchi who had been kidnapped in the late 1970s. Pyongyang vehemently denied the accusation, maintaining that Japan was trying to undermine the normalization talks. Later, Pyongyang refused to discuss the case of Lee Un-hae, resulting in the postponement of normalization talks.[43]

In early 1997, North Korean agents who had defected to South Korea told the horrifying story of the kidnapping of Megumi Yokota. An early advocate of bringing public attention to the atrocities associated with the abduction issue was Diet member Shingo Nishimura. In February 1997, Nishimura, a fervent nationalist who later served as parliamentary vice-minister in the Defense Agency and who was forced to resign in 1999 because of his public statement that Japan should consider acquiring nuclear weapons, questioned Prime Minister Ryutaro Hashimoto about the kidnapping of Megumi Yokota during a committee meeting of the House of Representatives. Nishimura and other politicians then had a meeting with some members of the abductees' families. In May 1997, Japan's National Police Agency identified ten Japanese victims suspected of being abducted by North Korea.[44] The heightened public and media attention given to the abduction issue led to the creation of the National Association for the Rescue of Japanese Kidnapped by North Korea (NARKN). In April 1998, NARKN had its first conference and has since functioned as both a support and a political action group. The year before, the Association of the Families of Victims Kidnapped by North Korea (AFVKN) was formed, an organization that has had the same objectives as NARKN.[45]

The DPRK initially reacted harshly to accusations that it perpetrated the kidnappings and forthrightly denied culpability for them, blaming them instead on Seoul's Agency for National Security Planning (ANSP). Pyongyang stated the Japanese newspapers the *Sankei Shimbun* and the *Mainichi Shimbun* were "well-known hack papers" that had been bribed to run their stories about the abduction of Megumi. Pyongyang also maintained that these reports and those appearing in "other venal media" in Japan contradicted the principles of the *juche* idea that would never permit kidnapping. However, Pyongyang took its denial much too far, claiming that Megumi, who was just 13 when she was kidnapped in 1977, "was an agent of the 'ANSP.'"[46]

After having discontinued food aid to North Korea because of its launching of a Taepodong-1 rocket in August 1998 that flew over Japanese territory, Tokyo resumed shipments in March and October 2000. However, Japanese conservatives did not want Tokyo to do this until Pyongyang had demonstrated its willingness to cooperate in resolving the missile, nuclear and abduction issues.[47] By 2000, well-known nationalists, such as Tokyo's Governor Shintaro Ishihara, Shinzo Abe, Shingo Nishimura and Katsuei Hirasawa had succeeded in getting the abduction issue raised to the highest level in the Japanese government. After the tenth round of the Japan–DPRK normalization talks held in August 2000 ended with no movement being made on the abduction issue, Prime Minister Yoshiro Mori met with members of the abductees' families. At this meeting, which took place just a little more than a month before the start of the eleventh round of Japan–DPRK normalizations talks to be held in Beijing at the end of October 2000, Mori made an important commitment to members of the abductees' families, who by this time had become a significant lobbying force in Japan. Mori stated, "It would be unthinkable for the government to normalize relations while ignoring the alleged abduction cases."[48] With the help of the Japanese media, which has remained relentless in fashioning a conservative perspective on the kidnappings,[49] and the nationalists, who continued to push hard on this matter, Mori's pledge became the defining criterion in Japan's policy toward North Korea.

Because of Secretary of State Madeleine Albright's trip to Pyongyang in October 2000, from which then arose speculation that a visit there by President Clinton might be possible, it was evident that relations between the United States and the DPRK were closer than they had ever been in the past. Before the year was over, Washington told officials in Tokyo that the failure to resolve the abduction issue would not prevent the removal of the DPRK from the US State Department's list of countries sponsoring terrorism. Since at the time DPRK's inclusion on the list had nothing to do with the abduction issue, the Clinton administration saw no reason why the kidnappings should prevent North Korea's removal.[50] By 2001 in Japan, propelled by the society-wide emotionalism that had been inspired by the nationalists, NARKN, AFVKN and a cooperative media, the abduction issue was quickly becoming the major publicly supported security concern.

In February 2002, just weeks after Bush delivered his "axis of evil" diatribe, he traveled to Tokyo and met with Koizumi. The prime minister commented during a joint press conference with the president: "Japan, through cooperation and coordination with the United States, would like to work on normalization of relations with North Korea."[51] Although Koizumi's interest in normalizing Japan–North Korean relations stood in stark contrast to Bush and his administration's hard-line DPRK policy, the prime minister recognized that rapprochement would ultimately depend on a cooperative effort with the United States. At the same time, Koizumi wanted to make Bush aware of the importance to Japan of resolving the alleged abduction issue, especially since at the end of 2001 the North Korean Red Cross had informed Tokyo that it was discontinuing its efforts to look for the "missing persons" – a designation that Pyongyang had used since November 1997.[52] Lobbied by NARKN only a week before Bush's trip to Japan, Koizumi told the president during their meeting that the alleged kidnappings were acts of terrorism committed by North Korea against Japanese nationals and that he wanted Washington's assistance to resolve the dispute.[53]

Having zeroed in on the abduction issue, the Japanese hardliners were relentless. Katusei Hirasawa, Shingo Nishimura and Yuriko Koite – who later came to hold two cabinet positions including Minister of Defense for a brief time and, before this, was Prime Minister Abe's Special Advisor on National Security Affairs – were among the founding Diet members of an organization formed in March 2002, months before the September Koizumi-Kim summit in Pyongyang. This nationalist-inspired organization introduced several hard-line policy measures directed at North Korea, one of which was that Tokyo should remain obdurate on the abduction issue. Hirasawa was also instrumental in orchestrating the displeasure that surfaced in Japan when Koizumi returned from his September 2002 summit with Kim Jong Il, a task made easy given the relationship he and DPRK hard-liner Katusmi Sato, the director of the Modern Korea Institute, had with NARKN and the Diet group demanding a resolution to the abduction issue.[54]

In August 2002, the Bush administration had informed Tokyo that it believed Pyongyang was concealing a uranium-enrichment program to develop nuclear weapons. This was well before Assistant Secretary of State Kelly traveled to North Korea in early October to confront Pyongyang about this matter. Meeting with Bush in New York just a few days before Koizumi's historic trip to Pyongyang in mid September, there were still very discernible differences between what Washington and Tokyo wanted from Pyongyang. While the Bush administration was primarily concerned with the DPRK's nuclear weapons capability, Tokyo's major interest before the Koizumi-Kim summit was the resolution of the abduction issue, which ideally would lead to normal bilateral relations. Before Koizumi's trip to Pyongyang, Bush made clear to the prime minister that Japan should not be in a rush to improve its bilateral relations with Pyongyang.[55]

Kim's admission to Prime Minister Koizumi during their September 2002 summit in Pyongyang, that DPRK agents were responsible for the kidnappings, catapulted the abduction issue to the very top of Japan's priority list. It gave Japanese nationalists just the political advantage they needed to contend effectively with those policymakers who, strongly supported by the public, wanted Tokyo to normalize relations with Pyongyang. The nationalists went to work immediately using the abduction issue to promulgate and bolster their claims that North Korea was a serious security threat to Japan, something that was rather quickly embraced by the Japanese public. The abduction issue had a catalytic effect on Japanese policymaking by helping Tokyo to embrace with zeal missile defense and completely adopt a "normal country" posture (as defined in Chapter 3).

Prior to Kim's revelation to Koizumi, the abductees' families wanted Tokyo to do more. Immediately after Kim's admission, they were pointedly critical, with the mother of one kidnapping victim saying, "I want to ask the government and the Foreign Ministry what on earth they have been doing up until now." Even before Koizumi, who acknowledged that the government had made mistakes, had a chance to talk to the abductees' family members after he returned from his summit with Kim, Shinzo Abe, then the deputy cabinet secretary, had already met with them and expressed their sentiments to a very sympathetic public.[56]

Not too long after Koizumi returned from his one-day visit to Pyongyang in September 2002, it became evident that his top aides, Chief Cabinet Secretary Yasuo Fukuda and Deputy Chief Cabinet Secretary Shinzo Abe had noticeably different views on how to handle the abduction issue. Fukuda, then taking the diplomatic track that supported normalizing relations with the DPRK, argued that, as per the agreement with Pyongyang, the five abductees North Korea had allowed to visit Japan should be sent back. Abe, standing firmly behind the nationalist position, insisted they should remain in Japan. For the nationalists and the abductees' families and their supporters, the central government had for too long intentionally kept the abduction issue on the back burner. Pushing for the ascendancy of the hard-line, nationalist position within the administration, Hirasawa stated: "The biggest failure of Mr. Koizumi is that he does not have a clear policy on North Korea."[57] Because much of Japan had become preoccupied with the kidnappings, Koizumi went with the most politically popular choice, deciding that the abductees would not return to North Korea, a decision that put rapprochement out of reach.

Meanwhile, there was no end in sight for resolving the North Korean nuclear crisis. After Kelly's trip to Pyongyang, the Bush administration refused to have bilateral discussions with DPRK officials. The Bush administration maintained that, since the problem was regional, talks should be multilateral. In April 2003, China managed to arrange trilateral talks in Beijing. While Koizumi believed that the discussions would make very little progress without participation from Japan and South Korea, Japanese hard-liner Katsuei Hirasawa felt otherwise. Hirasawa indicated that it was good that neither Tokyo or Seoul would be participating in the Beijing talks, maintaining that, "The U.S. can now take a hard-line in dealing with Pyongyang, which I believe is the only way to get through this impasse."[58]

Hirasawa's hard-line predilection for dealing with North Korea and in particular his obsession with the abduction issue eventually cost him his job in the Koizumi administration. Along with other Diet members, Hirasawa traveled to Beijing in December 2003 to meet with DPRK officials about the abduction issue. However, several months later, in early April 2004, Hirasawa and Taku Yamasaki, a close associate of Prime Minister Koizumi, who had recently lost his bid to be reelected to the Diet, made an unauthorized trip to China to meet with DPRK officials. NARKN was immediately critical of the trip, believing that negotiations with North Korea on the abduction issue should be government to government and not done privately, a position that Koizumi took as well. In response to the criticism that ensued from unauthorized meeting with DPRK officials, Hirasawa quickly resigned from his position as parliamentary secretary in the Ministry of Internal Affairs and Communications. Although Hirasawa had been a stalwart figure in pushing for the resolution of the abduction issue, the criticism surrounding his unauthorized meeting with the DPRK also led him to resign from his leadership position in the Diet group dealing with the kidnappings.[59]

The abduction issue: Washington comes on board

In 2003, Japan began encouraging the Bush administration to connect Pyongyang's cooperation on the abduction issue to the removal of the DPRK from the State Department's list of countries sponsoring terrorism, even though at this time the kidnapping problem was not a reason why North Korea was on the list.[60] Succumbing to political pressure from the abductees' families, Prime Minister Koizumi appealed to the Bush administration to have the abduction issue included as a reason for North Korea remaining in the State Department's report on global terrorism. When Deputy Secretary of State Richard Armitage traveled to Japan in February 2004 members of the abductees' families also appealed to him to have the abduction issue specified in his department's report on global terrorism.[61] These appeals were not too difficult to satisfy. Besides the close relationship between Bush and Koizumi, the administration's hardliners were highly sympathetic to the abduction issue, especially since it fit well with their need to monitor human rights violations they viewed as rampant in North Korea.

Not only were Japan's appeals successful but they also helped synchronize the hard-line DPRK policies of Washington and Tokyo. When Minister of Environment Yuriko Koike visited Washington in April 2004, Armitage told her that the abduction issue would be cited in his department's upcoming 2003 report (published in April 2004) on global terrorism.[62]

Well before this, however, Bush had been sending strong signals to Koizumi that the United States felt exactly the same way about the abduction issue as Japan. While visiting Bush at his ranch in Texas in May 2003 Prime Minister Koizumi stated, "I wish to express my sincere appreciation to the President for his strong support on the abduction issue."[63] Summarizing the views Koizumi expressed during his meeting with Bush, the Ministry of Foreign Affairs stressed that the prime minister had made clear that normalized relations with North Korea could not take place without settling the abduction issue. According to the ministry, Koizumi further indicated that, as per the Pyongyang Declaration, the nuclear and missile issues must also be resolved before Japan and North Korea can normalize relations. Regarding Bush, the foreign ministry indicated that the president had stated that the abductions carried out by North Korea were abhorrent acts and that the United States fully supports Japan's efforts to have Pyongyang become completely accountable for all of the Japanese people kidnapped by the DPRK.[64]

Moreover, John Bolton, then under secretary of state for arms control and international security, had provided considerable insight into his and what became the Bush administration's sentiment on this matter, well before Armitage informed Koike that the abduction issue would be specified in the State Department's report on international terrorism. In February 2004, Bolton emphasized that the United States supports Japan bringing up the abduction issue in a bilateral meeting that is likely to occur during the course off the six-party talks scheduled for the end of the month. Bolton also stated, "North Korea remains on the U.S. list of state sponsors of terrorism and I can't think of any other way to describe the abduction of innocent civilians from Japan or any other country to North Korea as something other than acts of terrorism."[65]

Just days before the publication of the 2003 report on global terrorism in April 2004, Cofer Black, a longtime CIA official and at the time the State Department's Coordinator for Counterterrorism, testified before the House Subcommittee on Terrorism. Stating that the abduction issue is "one of the most important" reasons why North Korea has been identified as a country that sponsors terrorism, Black told the subcommittee that Pyongyang had to deal with the kidnappings if it intends to be removed from the State Department's list.[66] During a press briefing in Washington on the day that the State Department released its *Patterns of Global Terrorism, 2003*, Black was asked why the abduction issue, which was not a new problem, was now for the first time identified in the report. Black answered by saying, "The United States, the Department of State thought it was important; it was a key; and that's why we included it."[67]

The *Yomiuri Shimbun* editorialized that the inclusion of the abduction issue as a reason for North Korea remaining on the US list of states sponsoring terrorism in support of Japan shows that Washington is saying two things. North Korea must get rid of its nuclear weapons program, as the six-party talks have specified, and it must "resolve problems related to the abduction cases if it wants to see an improvement of its relations with the United States."[68]

Pyongyang indicated that the abduction issue had become a new topic that the United States has linked to terrorism. It stated that the abduction issue is between the DPRK and Japan, that the Pyongyang Declaration had already settled this matter and that it is none of Washington's business.[69]

By the spring of 2004, with the inclusion of the abduction issue in the State Department's 2003 report on international terrorism, Washington and Tokyo's DPRK policies had come into synergy. The Bush administration had previously persuaded the Koizumi government to assist in the global war on terrorism. For this Tokyo expected a *quid pro quo*, which it got when the Bush administration accepted Japan's appeals to include the abduction in the State Department's report on global terrorism.

Nine days after the DPRK's announcement in February 2005 that it had built nuclear weapons,[70] US and Japanese officials assembled in Washington for a meeting of the Security Consultative Committee. At this time, they issued a joint statement, which indicated their concern about the DPRK's missile program and stressed the need for Pyongyang to resolve the nuclear and the abduction issues. Regarding the kidnappings, the joint statement indicated, "The U.S. Secretary of State reaffirmed the United States' full support of Japan's position on the abduction issue."[71]

Tokyo's obsession with the abduction issue and its insistence to bring up the kidnappings at the six-party talks slowly but steadily caused Japan to become an outlier. Apart from the Bush administration, which increased its political support for the abduction issue, South Korea, Russia and China did not feel that the six-party talks was the proper venue for resolving this bilateral problem between Japan and North Korea.

On the opening day of the six-party talks in July 2005, the Russian, Chinese and South Korean delegations made similar comments indicating their positions that the abduction issue should not be addressed at these meetings. Alexander Alexeyev, Russia's chief delegate and Deputy Foreign Minister commented that bringing up the abduction issue "can only thwart the attainment of concrete results in talks that are aimed at the denuclear-ization of the Korean Peninsula."[72] A spokesman for the Chinese delegation indicated that these discussions were not where Tokyo and Pyongyang should try to settle the abduction issue, adding, "we hope Japan and the DPRK can appropriately reach a resolution through bilateral channels."[73] Chinese Deputy Foreign Minister and chief delegate to the six-party talks Wu Dawei stated that these discussions should be focused on denuclearizing the Korean Peninsula, and "The concerns of any of the six should be those of all parties."[74] Song Min-soon, Seoul's Deputy Foreign Minister and chief delegate to these discussions, commented that the objective of the talks was to make the Korean Peninsula a nuclear-weapons-free area and so: "It is not ideal for the parties concerned to distract from this target during the new round of the six-party talks."[75] Despite the fact that Tokyo's determination to bring up the kidnap-pings at the six-party talks caused most of the other participants to oppose Japan's approach to this matter,[76] it only needed Washington's support to continue its campaign to internationalize the abduction issue.

The second phase of the fourth round of the six-party talks created a ray of optimism, since there was a reduction in the contentiousness that had previously characterized these discussions. On the last day of the talks in September 2005, the six parties agreed to a joint statement that, in addition to reminding the participants that the shared objective of the discussions was to ensure the peaceful denuclearization of the Korean Peninsula, stipulated that the DPRK had agreed to abandon its nuclear weapons and all of its nuclear weapons programs.[77]

Tokyo's obsession with the abduction issue may have caused it to see what was not present. Tokyo indicated that the joint statement formally expressed as one of its objectives that Japan and North Korea would normalize bilateral relations only after there was a resolution of the abduction and other problematic issues.[78] Although the joint statement did talk about the need for Japan and the DPRK to take steps to normalize their bilateral relationship, there is no explicit mention of the abductions in the document.

Nonetheless, the synergy between the Bush administration and Tokyo continued on the abduction issue. In an unambiguous demonstration of the Bush administration's intention to politicize the abduction issue, the president met with Megumi Yokota's mother and brother in April 2006. After the meeting, Bush commented: "I have just had one of the most moving meetings since I've been the President here in the Oval Office." He concluded by stating that the United States "will strongly work for freedom ... so that moms will never again have to worry about an abducted daughter."[79] In a display of solidarity with Japan during a joint Bush–Koizumi press conference held in Washington in June 2006, the president deferred a question asked to him on North Korea to the prime minister, who stated that Tokyo would continue to "maintain close cooperation and coordination with the United States including the abduction issue."[80]

US Ambassador Thomas Schieffer's exposure to the political ambience in Japan created by the abduction issue began not long after his arrival there in April 2005 when he met with members of the abductees' families. Less than a year later, in March 2006, Schieffer met Megumi Yokota's parents in Niigata to tour the area where DPRK agents had kidnapped her decades before. Promising to inform President Bush of his tour of the abduction site, Schieffer commented on the immorality of the kidnapping and that it was a very sad story. He then stated, "we must see that it doesn't happen again, and that those who perpetrated this injustice are brought to justice." Shinzo Abe, at the time Koizumi's chief cabinet secretary, immediately recognized the importance of a visit by a top US official to the site of Megumi's kidnapping, stating that it "was significant for the resolution of the abduction issue because it signals both to Japan and the world that the United States has interests in the issue."[81]

When Shinzo Abe became prime minister in September 2006, Japanese nationalism received an immediate power surge. Abe's "beautiful country" paradigm, which he formally introduced three days after taking office in a policy speech to the Japanese Diet, addressed the need for his administration to work on several issues, including the abductions and security. Expressing the need for "proactive diplomacy," Abe gave a nationalistic call in this speech while also showing his government's commitment to build a "Japan–U.S. Alliance for Asia and the World," words that raised many eyebrows in Seoul, Beijing and in Pyongyang, most especially. Pyongyang's initial reaction to Abe's objective of making Japan a beautiful country was to state that his administration consisted of "pro-U.S. flunkeys under the masks of 'nationalists,'" adding that the Asian and the international community is on to Tokyo's remilitarization plan and its desire to use the abduction issue and the threat from the DPRK as a basis for reinvasion.[82]

Referring to the DPRK's July 2006 missile launches, Abe stated in his speech that this behavior reaffirmed that Japan is confronting a major security issue. He made clear the importance of maintaining an unalterable commitment to what by then had become a Japanese edict – that Japan could not normalize relations with North Korea without first resolving the abduction issue – and announced his intention to establish and chair the Headquarters on the Abduction Issue. Vowing to employ a policy strategy of "dialogue and pressure," Abe indicated that he would work to settle the abduction issue and that, with regard to the resolution of the DPRK missile and nuclear problems, his government would remain committed to the six-party talks and, in particular, be certain to closely coordinate Japanese and U.S. efforts.[83] On the same day that he gave his policy speech, Abe met with members of AFVKN[84] and in October the Headquarters on the Abduction Issue held its first official meeting, with the prime minister serving as chair of this organization and with his entire cabinet present.[85]

Abe was determined to toughen up Japan's North Korean policy. Pushing hard to internationalize the kidnappings, the Abe government required in the fall of 2006 that NHK (Japan Broadcasting Corporation), the nation's public broadcaster, designate more airtime in its short wave international programs to address the abduction issue.[86] Then in January 2007, without precedent in modern times, the prime announced "a new start of broadcasting of the government's messages directed towards the abductees."[87] During the next few months the Abe government continued to push hard via the media to publicize the abduction issue. Despite the controversy that ensued within the media because of the government ordering NHK to broadcast the abduction issue on the airwaves,[88] Abe renewed this directive in March 2007.[89] Immediately after the failure of the Japan–North Korean working group to lay the groundwork for normalization talks in March, the Abe administration announced the government's intention to air a television commercial dealing with the kidnappings, with a price tag of ¥105,000,000 (approximately $1,197,400), on more than 100 private stations in Japan.[90]

When the moderate Yasuo Fukuda became prime minister in late September 2007, he continued to support the sanctions that his predecessors Abe and Koizumi had imposed on North Korea after it conducted missile tests and detonated a nuclear device in 2006. However genuinely important the resolution of the abduction issue may be to Tokyo, what cannot be ignored is that the kidnappings have played a major part in moving Japan along the path to become a normal country. In this respect, Fukuda's DPRK policy did not depart significantly from those of his recent predecessors.[91] When Taro Aso became prime minister in September 2008, the nationalist agenda was reinvigorated, since he underscored the priority that the Japanese government had assigned to the abduction issue.

Turning point

Washington and Tokyo's North Korean policy remained largely consistent, and indeed became increasingly indistinguishable, from almost the onset of the DPRK nuclear crisis in October 2002 until late 2006. It was at this time that three things converged forcing the Bush administration to take a hard look at the DPRK nuclear issue. This hard look revealed to the Bush administration that resolving the DPRK nuclear issue would mean sacrificing what previously had been an unshakable commitment to the Japanese abduction issue.

First, the November 2006 midterm elections put the Democratic Party in control of both the House and the Senate. The Democrats had won largely because Americans recognized that, the rhetoric coming from the White House about improving conditions in Iraq notwithstanding, the United States had sacrificed far too much and for far too long in a war that increasingly appeared unwinnable. Led by Secretary of State Rice, who was now less influenced by neoconservative and extreme hard-line thinking, the Bush administration recognized that the president's high disapproval ratings and dwindling public support for the ongoing Iraq War would seriously jeopardized his legacy.

Second, the Bush administration had also failed to come up with workable policies that would noticeably assuage Washington's disagreements with Iran and North Korea, which along with Iraq were members of the axis of evil. A major foreign policy win with either Tehran or Pyongyang was therefore necessary to prevent the president from losing additional face.

Third, although early on the Bush administration had been populated by a number of uncompromising neoconservatives and hardliners, by the end of 2006 many of them had left their government jobs. For the Bush administration, pulling out of Iraq before democracy prevailed there would be an acknowledgement of defeat and would only bring the battle to the United States. Since the Bush administration had repeatedly stated: "Iran remained the most active state sponsor of terrorism," it held unwaveringly to the view that Tehran was not likely to be won over.[92] This only left North Korea as a possible success story.

In November 2006 and then again in January 2007, the State Department's Christopher Hill met with his DPRK counterpart Kim Kye-gwan in Berlin. During these meetings, the two supposedly worked out an agreement that would eventually remove the DPRK from the US State Department's list of countries sponsoring terrorism and end the application of the Trading with the Enemy Act on North Korea. Hill and Kim purportedly signed a memorandum of understanding in Berlin that mirrored the agreement reached in February 2007 during six-party talks held in Beijing.[93] In short, the Bush administration had abandoned its opposition to bilateral talks with Pyongyang, which along with its adoption of a more conciliatory policy soon led to progress in the six-party talks.[94]

Among other things, the phased agreement reached in February 2007 during the six-party talks called for the DPRK to shut down and eventually to disable its nuclear facilities at Yongbyon and for Pyongyang to provide a complete declaration of all of its nuclear activities. For doing this, and in accordance with the "action for action" plan established at the six-party talks that took place in September 2005, the DPRK would receive substantial energy, economic and humanitarian assistance from the United States, South Korea, Russia, China and Japan. The agreement also stated that during the initial phase, the United States would start the process of taking the DPRK off of the State Department's list of countries sponsoring terrorism and would begin taking steps that would end the legal connection of North Korea to the Trading with the Enemy Act.[95]

The problem the Bush administration was facing in 2007 was that it had completely changed its policy on the abduction issue, thus making it susceptible to criticisms from Tokyo and from US hardliners and neoconservatives. Given that the Bush administration had now trained its policy eye on the DPRK nuclear issue, it was willing to overlook Tokyo's decision to ignore its obligation to contribute financially to the DPRK disablement process until progress had been made on the abduction issue. The Bush administration had little choice but to do this, since it had been publicly maintaining for years that it fully supported Japan's position on the abduction issue and saying that they were unequivocally acts of terrorism.

Reiterating the US commitment made at the February 2007 six-party talks, the State Department's 2006 report on global terrorism published in April 2007 indicted that Washington would initiate the process of taking the DPRK off of the list of countries sponsoring terrorism.[96] As it had often done in the past, the State Department's 2007 report on international terrorism published in April 2008 indicated that North Korea is not believed to have been involved in any terrorist act since the late 1980s. The 2007 report next mentioned, as it also had done many times in the past, that the DPRK continues to provide a safe haven for members of the Japanese Red Army (who defected to North Korea after bringing a hijacked Japanese airliner there in 1971). Like the abduction issue, Washington had made it clear to Tokyo that, even though members of the Japanese Red Army continued to reside in North Korea, this matter needed to be worked out between the Japanese and North Korean governments and was therefore not going to prevent the DPRK from being removed from the US State Department's terrorism.[97] The 2007 report "reaffirmed" Washington's position "regarding the removal of the designation of the DPRK as a state sponsor of terrorism in parallel with the DPRK's actions on denuclearization and in accordance with the criteria set forth in U.S. law."[98]

In May 2008, US Ambassador to South Korea Alexander Vershbow stated that the abduction issue is not a "prerequisite" for removing the DPRK from the State Department's list of countries supporting terrorism, certainly not what Tokyo wanted to hear. Vershbow added that Washington is prepared to remove the DPRK from the list and to free it from the constraints stemming from the Trading with the Enemy Act "as soon as we have a complete and correct declaration."[99]

Tokyo was first directly told about the changed relationship between the abduction issue and the de-listing of the DPRK in April 2007 when Prime Minister Abe was Bush's guest at the presidential retreat in Camp David. There, Secretary of State Condoleezza Rice told Abe that the resolution of the abduction issue was not a precondition for the removal of the DPRK from the US list of countries sponsoring terrorism.[100]

With the Bush administration adopting a conciliatory policy, the United States and the DPRK eventually settled their long-standing dispute relating to the frozen DPRK funds deposited in the Banco Delta Asia. This, in turn, allowed them to begin making progress toward realizing the agreement reached at the six-party talks in February 2007.

Mixed reactions

Tokyo responded in different ways after Washington formally introduced its commitment at the February 2007 six-party talks to remove the DPRK from the State Department's list of countries sponsoring terrorism. Trying its best to separate a discussion about de-listing the DPRK from its actual removal, Tokyo was initially in denial. Immediately after the conclusion of the February 2007 six-party talks, both Prime Minister Abe and Chief Cabinet Secretary Yasuhisa Shiozaki made the point that the two are very different issues.[101] Tokyo just could not accept the fact that the Bush administration, which had been such a staunch and unwavering supporter of Japan in getting the abduction issue resolved, was suddenly willing to sacrifice this for the DPRK's denuclearization.

Soon Tokyo attempted to use its long-established friendly relationship with the United States to persuade the Bush administration not to remove the DPRK from the US terrorist list until there was a resolution of the abduction issue. During her trip to the United States in May 2007, Japanese official and DPRK hardliner Kyoko Nakayama asked a State Department official not to de-list North Korea until there was a satisfactory resolution to the kidnapping problem.[102] Several months later, once it became clear that the Bush administration was serious about removing the DPRK from the US terrorist list, Tokyo's position toughened. Nakayama, who served as Councilor of the Cabinet Secretariat for the abduction issue during the Koizumi administration and later was appointed by Abe in September 2006 as Special Advisor to the Prime Minister on the abduction issue,[103] a position she continued to hold after Fukuda became prime minister in September 2007, articulated Tokyo's perturbation with Washington. Nakayama commented in October 2007, "A country that does not free hostages is a terrorist state, pure and simple." Reflecting the chagrin of many conservative Japanese policymakers, she remarked: "If the U.S. moves while completely ignoring the abduction issue, you can expect that relations between Japan and the United States will not improve."[104] Chief Cabinet Secretary and Minister of State for the Abduction Issue Nobutaka Machimura publicly conveyed a similar message by stating that de-listing the DPRK "certainly would not have a good influence on the Japan–U.S. relationship."[105] As noted above, Bush had indicated in November when he met with Fukuda in Washington that the abduction issue would not be forgotten. However, neither he nor the prime minister publicly addressed the de-listing of North Korea. This matter had to be discussed privately, with Tokyo pressing Washington not to remove the DPRK from the State Department's list until there was a resolution to the kidnapping problem.[106]

In December, a US official maintained that he "was fairly confident" that the relationship between Washington and Tokyo would be strengthened during the coming year. Insisting, like Bush, that Washington would not forget about the abduction issue, the US official stressed that when the DPRK fulfills its obligation specified during the February 2007 six-party talks and is removed from the terrorist list, its relations with the United States will improve. As normalization efforts proceed, Washington will have "enhanced leverage" to convince Pyongyang to resolve the abduction issue.[107]

The Japanese people, who had become increasingly connected to the abduction issue since Kim Jong Il's admission of DPRK culpability in 2002, had noticeably changed their view of the United States by the fall of 2007. And Washington's plan to remove the DPRK from the US list of states sponsoring terrorism appeared to be a major reason for this change. A survey conducted by the government's Cabinet Office in October 2007 showed that the percentage of Japanese respondents who thought that the relationship between Japan and the United Sates was not in good shape increased sharply from the previous year – from about 12 percent to just over 20 percent.[108]

The members of the abductees' families were also uneasy about the prospect of North Korea being removed from the State Department's list of countries supporting terrorism. In November 2007, several members of the abductees' families visited Washington; their objective was to meet with Assistant Secretary of State for East Asian and Pacific Affairs Christopher Hill and to urge the US government not to de-list North Korea. Upon returning, the dismayed vice chairman of AFVKN commented: "We went to the United States as we felt we couldn't just sit back, but I have been made aware it is out of reach of the power we the families alone can exert."[109]

Although the disablement process was moving along at a pace reasonably satisfactory to Washington, Pyongyang nevertheless failed to meet the December 31 deadline. But what bothered the Bush administration was not so much that the disablement process had not been completed, since safety had to take precedence over expeditiousness, but that Pyongyang had failed to provide a declaration completely detailing its nuclear activities that was acceptable to Washington. The declaration that Pyongyang submitted in November did not include any mention of a uranium-enrichment program or any information about the DPRK's nuclear assistance to Syria.

Once Tokyo was certain that the Bush administration was willing to remove the DPRK from the US State Department's terrorism list, Tokyo had to play a different political hand. Tokyo understood that what it had done since this announcement was first made in early 2007 had not worked. Thus, after Pyongyang missed the December 31 deadline Tokyo, like Washington, was quick to point out that the DPRK had not lived up to its end of the bargain that it had made at the six-party talks.

Foreign Minister Masahiko Koumura stated in early January 2008 that Pyongyang had made the "political decision" not to submit "a complete and correct declaration," and so until it does nothing much will happen.[110] Expressing his dissatisfaction that the DPRK had not completed its declaration on time, the foreign ministry's chief of the Asian and Oceanian Affairs Bureau Kenichiro Sasae, standing next to Christopher Hill, insisted that Japan would work with the United States and the other four participants in the six-party talks to make progress on the nuclear issue. With North Korea in political arrears, Sasae used his time with Hill to restate Japan's position that satisfactory progress must be made on the abduction issue and that until such time the United States should not remove the DPRK from its terrorist list.[111]

Chief Cabinet Secretary Nobutaka Machimura stated that the lack of reference to North Korea in the president's January 2008 State of the Union address could perhaps be the result of "positive" diplomatic developments with Pyongyang. Machimura also repeated almost verbatim what Foreign Minister Kourmura had said just days before, which was that it was clear that the DPRK had not yet submitted a complete declaration and without one the denuclearization process could not proceed.[112]

Seeing little benefit in publicly pressing the Bush administration not to remove the DPRK from the US terrorist list until progress had been made on the abduction issue, Tokyo had decided to stand with Washington in calling for Pyongyang to give a complete accounting of its nuclear activities. Reflecting Tokyo's commitment to a hard-line policy and its inveterate skepticism, Vice Foreign Minister Shotaro Yachi commented in early January: "It's clear from last year's developments that [the North Koreans] will not easily make a complete and correct declaration, so I don't think it will take place all of a sudden just because we've entered the new year."[113]

This line of thinking was virtually identical to that held by US hardliners and neoconservatives, who consistently maintained that Pyongyang could not be trusted and that there should be no expectation that it will change anytime soon. Writing in *The Wall Street Journal* just a few days after Yachi made his remarks, John Bolton commented that Pyongyang's failure to fully disclose its nuclear programs "has again shown its true colors." Praising Fukuda's hard-line DPRK policy, Bolton, referring to the agreement reached at the February 2007 six-party talks, stated: "North Korea has dragged out its performance for nearly a year, has less and less incentive to make Mr. Bush look good, and has in sight the possibility of a resumed Clinton administration, or something even weaker."[114]

The DPRK Foreign Ministry announced in early January 2008 that, because the parties to the six-way talks had not lived up to their part of the bargain, it had no other recourse but "to adjust the tempo of disablement," which had previously been moving along rather quickly. Pyongyang insisted that shipments of heavy oil and related material and equipment were significantly behind schedule and this was not in keeping with the "action for action" agreement reached at the September 2005 six-party talks. Displeased that Washington had not yet crossed the DPRK off of its terrorist list and eliminated the restrictions stemming from the Trading with the Enemy Act, the North Korean Foreign Ministry stressed that it had made available to the United Sates information on its nuclear activities that was in its November report. Pyongyang maintained that it had responded cooperatively to US assertions about DPRK uranium-enrichment work by allowing Americans to inspect suspicious aluminum tubes, and provided them with samples when they visited North Korean military facilities. Besides allaying US concerns that the aluminum tubes had been used for enriching uranium, the foreign ministry also emphasized that it had reaffirmed in the October 2007 agreement that came out of the six-party talks that "it does not transfer nuclear weapons, technology and knowledge."[115]

What the DPRK Foreign Ministry did not say was that the inspection of the aluminum tubes by the United States ascertained traces of enriched uranium, though experts pointed out that minute particles of uranium could have easily come from other sources, such as Pakistan, as was found to be the case by the IAEA with Iran.[116] Although it did not inform the Japanese government until late spring 2008, the IAEA had also found something when its team visited DPRK nuclear and related facilities in July 2007: vacuum-pumping equipment made in Japan. Shipped without government approval from Japan to North Korea via Taiwan and apparently without the responsible Japanese company's knowledge, the Japanese daily the *Yomiuri Shimbun* connected the equipment to uranium-enrichment work conducted by the DPRK. There was, however, some doubt about the veracity of the newspaper's contention, since an individual closely connected to the IAEA later stated: "The agency has no information at the moment that could be linked to an enrichment program" in the DPRK.[117]

By March 2008, Pyongyang had grown annoyed that the Bush administration had been deferring the resolution of the nuclear issue and that it had not removed sanctions on the DPRK. Pyongyang maintained that Washington had been "persistently trying to cook up fictions" about a uranium-enrichment program and proliferation activities with Syria.[118]

Bilateral meetings between US and DPRK officials in Geneva in March and again in Singapore in April 2008 led to a compromise that promised to end the deadlock in the denuclearization process. Pyongyang agreed to acknowledge US concerns about both a DPRK uranium-enrichment program and proliferation activities with respect to Syria.[119] However, such acknowledgements were not admissions of guilt or complicity but simply an expression that the DPRK recognized Washington's concerns. Responding to the compromise reached in Singapore, the North Korean Foreign Ministry stated simply that the "agreement fully proved the effectiveness of the DPRK–U.S. talks."[120] In what represented an absolute about-face from the position the Bush administration held for years, the State Department's Hill pointed out, "We are trying to focus on the plutonium as we try to resolve our suspicions on uranium enrichment. That's where the bombs are. We don't have suspicions about plutonium; we have cold hard facts about plutonium."[121] Slow to be won over to Washington's new position, Tokyo at this time still wanted a full account of the DPRK's nuclear activities.

In late February 2008 during a meeting in Tokyo, Israeli Prime Minister Ehud Olmert told Fukuda that the site in Syria, which Israeli planes destroyed the previous September, was a nuclear facility being built with technical help from the DPRK. Officials in Japan's Ministry of Foreign Affairs in Tokyo were at odds over the interpretation of Olmert's statement. While one high-level official indicated that, though Olmert's statement was important and appeared "highly credible," still "we cannot confirm the facts," another stated that the prime minister "may have only presented the facts that were favorable for the Israeli side."[122]

Although Tokyo temporarily had shifted part of its public persona to the DPRK nuclear issue, the kidnappings remained the Japanese government's central concern. The fact that Washington and Pyongyang had found a way to circumvent the stalemate to the uranium-enrichment and Syrian-proliferation issues did not lessen Tokyo's resolve to settle the abduction problem. Very shortly after Washington and Pyongyang reached an agreement on what an acceptable declaration would look like, Chief Cabinet Secretary Nobutaka Machimura made an important announcement. In April 2008, Machimura stated that the government had decided to extend the sanctions for another six months on North Korea (for the third time), because it had not made progress in resolving the nuclear, missile and abduction issues and because it had not yet submitted an acceptable declaration of its nuclear activities.[123]

Irate after learning of Tokyo's decision to extend the sanctions again, Pyongyang accused the Fukuda government of following an "aggressive and reactionary policy," and drew a parallel between this and the "diplomacy of Abe." Pyongyang charged that what motivated the Fukuda government was the desire to bring DPRK-Japan relations to their nadir so that Tokyo could "hasten the military preparations for overseas aggression."[124]

The hard-liner offensive and Tokyo's support

Unlike Tokyo, Washington had been fully apprised by Israel even before it carried out the bombing in Syria. After having experienced months of progress in resolving the DPRK nuclear issue, the Bush administration suddenly decided in late April 2008 to don a hard-line suit – if only briefly – and risk infuriating Pyongyang by making public its claim that North Korea had assisted Syria in the construction of its nuclear facility. Vice President Cheney and the remaining hardliners in the Bush administration had not been pleased with the State Department's extension of a conciliatory hand to Pyongyang and were especially opposed to Washington's plan to remove the DPRK from the US terrorism list, which was increasingly appearing imminent. Outside of the administration, hardliners like Bolton continued to rant about the security dangers associated with making concessions to North Korea.[125] Prime Minister Fukuda indicated that he was "concerned" about the Bush administration's claim that North Korea had been helping Syria. Indicating that the Bush administration stood behind, although very briefly, its charge against DPRK, US Ambassador to Japan Schieffer stated after meeting with Chief Cabinet Secretary Nobutaka Machimura: "We believe that North Korea assisted Syria in the attempted development of a nuclear reactor that would have produced plutonium."[126]

However, US hardliners, whose public fulminations were briefly transformed into a policy aside welcomed by Japanese nationalists and some others in Tokyo, could not overcome the momentum that had been created by the Bush administration's adoption of a conciliatory North Korean policy. Pyongyang never responded to the revived claim that it had been assisting Syria to construct a nuclear reactor. Spurred by its belief that it would soon be removed from the US terrorist list, Pyongyang saw the hardliners' spring offensive as follows: it reasoned that too much progress had already been made in resolving the nuclear issue and bet that the their revival was only ephemeral.

Pyongyang made the correct bet. The hardliners' hopes were soon dashed. As quickly as this new claim about DPRK assistance to Syria surfaced is how quickly the Bush administration moved past it. There was, of course, the matter of evidence to deal with. Briefing Congress on the Syrian issue, two senior US intelligence officers admitted that the available evidence only provided "low confidence" that Damascus intended to develop a nuclear weapon.[127] Damascus eventually agreed to let the IAEA inspect the suspected site. Just days before the IAEA was set to leave for Syria in June 2008, its director-general Mohamed ElBaradei stated during an interview in Dubai, "We have no evidence that Syria has the human resources that would allow it to carry out a large nuclear program. We do not see Syria having nuclear fuel."[128]

By May 2008, Pyongyang had given the United States more than 18,000 pages of information pertaining to its plutonium-related nuclear production and indicated that it would destroy the cooling tower at the Yongbyon nuclear facility within a day after Washington took the DPRK off of its terrorist list.[129] Together, the commitment to destroy the cooling tower and the submission of papers on North Korean nuclear activities made the hardliners' objective, which was for the United States to return full bore to the earlier, largely uncompromising policy, even more unlikely than before.

Tokyo also continued trying to get the Bush administration to maintain the designation of the DPRK as a state sponsor of terrorism, at least until progress had been made on the abduction issue.[130] Tokyo was therefore very pleased that in early June two Republican members of the House Committee on Foreign Affairs sent a letter to Secretary of State Rice stating: "We urge you to make the abduction issue and other critical human rights concerns a key element in your ongoing negotiations with North Korea."[131]

Although by this time Rice had largely disassociated herself from the hardliners and the neoconservatives, the fact that she had been in their political grasp for so long precluded her from being completely unsusceptible to their influence. During a speech given in June at the Heritage Foundation, Rice made it clear that Pyongyang's submission of its nuclear declaration to China would occur in just days. Once this happened, she stated, the president would relate to Congress the administration's desire to remove the DPRK from the list of countries that sponsor terrorism and end the constraints stemming from the Trading with the Enemy Act. However, still feeling the need to assuage criticism from the far right, Rice stressed that not only was verification important to the administration but that it had to acquire more information on the DPRK's nuclear activities. In contrast to the State Department's chief DPRK negotiator, Christopher Hill, who only two months earlier spoke of "suspicions" about Pyongyang's uranium-enrichment activities, Rice stated during her speech that there is "additional information about North Korea's uranium enrichment capability."[132] This new information that Rice was referring to was the small amounts of highly enriched uranium that had been found on some of the DPRK's many thousands of pages that it had recently submitted to Washington in May.[133] However, this new evidence hardly represented a smoking gun that proved the DPRK had been maintaining a uranium-enrichment program to develop nuclear weapons. What she never even alluded to was that these traces could have easily come from equipment from another country, such Pakistan. Rice also emphasized during her speech that the Bush administration knows "that North Korea has had an active plutonium program for many years" and that it "has proliferated nuclear technology to Syria."

Still, Rice intended none of this to be especially vitriolic nor did Pyongyang perceive this as such. Pyongyang understood that because there continued to exist pressure from US hardliners and from Tokyo there were remnants of hostility in the Bush administration's DPRK policy but not enough – at least not at this juncture – to derail the cooperative diplomacy that had been developing some momentum.

Tokyo and Pyongyang: still trying?

A somewhat surprising development took place in mid June 2008. Tokyo and Pyongyang suddenly announced that they soon would be holding bilateral talks in Beijing, the first since September 2007. Japanese Foreign Minister Koumura stressed prior to the two-day meetings that Japan – following the template agreed to at the six-party talks in February 2007 – would employ an "action for action" approach in dealing with Pyongyang during the bilateral discussions.

During the first day of the talks the foreign ministry's Director-General of the Asian and Oceanian Affairs Bureau, Akitaka Saiki, wasted no time restating Japan's position on the abduction issue.[134] Encouraged by the generally auspicious mood that had come to characterize the denuclearization process, and wanting Washington to take notice of the DPRK's good will, hoping that this would expedite its removal from the US terrorism list, Song Il Ho, North Korea's official in charge of normalization discussions with Japan, indicated that his country would reinvestigate the abduction issue. This was good news for Tokyo, since from the time of the first Koizumi-Kim summit in September 2002, the DPRK had up to this point repeatedly maintained that the abduction issue had been resolved. Song also agreed to hand over the surviving members of the Japanese Red Army who had taken refuge in North Korea. Maintaining that Pyongyang "has made a small step, so we will make a small step too," Koumura announced that the Japanese government would remove a few of the sanctions that it imposed on the DPRK after the North Korean missile and nuclear tests in 2006.[135]

This, however, did not sit very well with the abductees' family members. Dissatisfied with the Japanese government, which announced that a "certain degree of progress" had been made to resolve the abduction issue, the chairman of AFVKN stated: "We've heard the word 'reinvestigation' three or four times and it's turned out that there were no" additional abductees. AFVKN was also not impressed by Pyongyang's stated willingness to hand over the surviving members of the Japanese Red Army, who Tokyo believes may have had a hand in the kidnappings.[136]

Fearing damage could be done to the six-party talks, which had not reconvened because Pyongyang had not submitted its nuclear declaration, Kim Sook, South Korea's chief delegate to these multilateral discussions, suggested in June 2008 that Tokyo needed to do more than just remove a few sanctions that it imposed on the DPRK. Kim stated that "Now is the time for Japan to start participating over energy and economic assistance."[137] However, Tokyo was not about to heed Seoul's advice. Now predisposed to be tougher on the DPRK than the United States, it took Tokyo several more months – until November 2008, when the verification problem emerged as central to the six-party talks – before it decided not to press the uranium-enrichment and Syrian issues.[138]

Rice and Hill continued to present to Japan the Bush administration's relatively newly articulated position that the abduction issue is not only very important to the Japanese government and people but also to the United States, promising that Washington would not relent in its effort to resolve it.[139] However, Tokyo insisted that more needed to be done to get North Korea's compliance. Foreign Minister Koumura stated that keeping the DPRK on the US terrorism list would provide Tokyo with a "bargaining chip," giving it additional "leverage." Tokyo also wanted Pyongyang to submit a complete declaration, rather than one that did not include an account of its nuclear weapons or explanations relating to the US allegations of its uranium-enrichment and proliferation activities with Syria. Koumura maintained that by not de-listing the DPRK "we can play this card further on the nuclear issue, as well as at the Japan–North Korea talks, especially on the abduction issue."[140] Unable to convince Washington to play this card, Koumura indicated that Tokyo wanted a special investigative body to be established that would monitor the extent of the DPRK's reinvestigation of the abduction issue. Appearing to renege on an early promise made by Tokyo, Koumura maintained that "As long as there is no progress in this respect there will be no partial lifting" of the sanctions that Japan had previously imposed on North Korea.[141]

Pyongyang immediately picked up on Japan's latest move. In June 2008, Pyongyang maintained that "ultra-rightist organizations" in Japan and erstwhile Prime Minister Abe had expressed vehement opposition to the proposed limited removal of sanctions on the DPRK. Suspecting the worse, Pyongyang asserted that Japanese nationalists are driven by their determination of not allowing DPRK–Japanese rapprochement to take place, something that would make it easier for them to accomplish "their highest partisan goal," which is to militarize Japan.[142]

North Korea's de-listing: phase I

Although Prime Minister Fukuda stated in late June 2008 that "no differences in opinions at all" exist between the United States and Japan with regard to Washington's North Korean policy,[143] this was hardly the case. At about this same time, the Bush administration informed Foreign Minister Koumura that the process of taking the DPRK off of the US terrorism list would begin as soon as Pyongyang submitted its long-overdue nuclear declaration.

Knowing that much of the Japanese public and, most especially, ardent nationalists and abductees' family members would not take kindly to the news of Washington beginning the process of de-listing North Korea, Tokyo designed a new strategy to deal with the abduction issue. Tokyo's new strategy was to use the month and a half it would take from when President Bush notified Congress of his intention to de-list North Korea until the process was completed to pressure Pyongyang to resolve the abduction issue. With this new plan in mind, a senior official from the Japanese Foreign Ministry commented: "This summer will be a very hot summer."[144]

Only two days after the Bush administration informed Tokyo of its intent to de-list North Korea, the DPRK submitted its nuclear declaration to China. Immediately after this, Bush announced that he had removed the restrictions on North Korea associated with the Trading with the Enemy Act and that he was notifying Congress of his intention to remove the DPRK from the US terrorism list, a process that would take 45 days to complete.[145] As promised, the next day the DPRK blew up its nuclear cooling tower at Yongbyon, which Pyongyang said afterwards was "a step taken out of goodwill" to demonstrate it is serious about denuclearization, and maintained that it had "more than 80 percent" completed the disablement of its nuclear facilities.[146]

One day before Bush announced the de-listing of North Korea, he had a telephone conversation with Fukuda in which he reassured the prime minister that the United States would not forget about the abduction issue and it would continue to press the DPRK to resolve this matter.[147] When President Bush announced that his administration would begin the process of de-listing the DPRK he stated: "The United States will never forget the abduction of Japanese citizens by the North Koreans. We will continue to closely cooperate and coordinate with Japan and press North Korea to swiftly resolve the abduction issue."[148] However, according to a researcher in the DPRK Foreign Ministry working on Japanese issues, he "never heard of this request" from the United States.[149]

Armed with the Bush administration's expressed commitment not to abandon the abduction issue, Tokyo took its determination to resolve the kidnappings to the G-8 Foreign Ministers' Meeting held in Kyoto in June 2008. In the wake of Bush's de-listing announcement, the chair of the meeting, Japanese Foreign Minister Koumura, stressed in his statement the importance of North Korea moving quickly to bring about an "early resolution of the abduction issue." During the press conference after the G-8 Meeting, Secretary Rice indicated that the Bush administration has made it clear to North Korea that the abduction issue is not only important to Japan. Stressing that it "is a serious human rights issue," Rice stated that the Bush administration expects this issue to be settled because it "is of great concern" to the United States.[150]

The fact of the matter is that Bush's announced de-listing of North Korea had literally represented a very significant departure from its previous, seemingly unwavering, resolve to settle the abduction issue. Prior to 2007 the kidnappings were not only considered acts of terrorism by the Bush administration but because of this they helped justify the DPRK's inclusion on the US terrorism list. There was, therefore, a glaring difference between Tokyo's continued willingness to insist that the abductions perpetrated by North Korea were unprecedented acts of state sponsored terrorism, and the Bush administration's new position that no longer officially equated the kidnappings with terrorism.

Tokyo attempted to minimize the Bush administration's announcement that it was in the process of de-listing the DPRK. An official in the Japanese Ministry of Foreign Affairs stressed that the de-listing and particularly the removal of the DPRK from the restrictions stemming from the Trading with the Enemy Act were more symbolic than substantive.[151] However, the announced de-listing openly troubled others, some of whom were disturbed by the failure of the DPRK to provide, along with the submission of its declaration, any details pertaining to its nuclear weapons that Tokyo very much wanted. Chief Cabinet Secretary Nobutaka Machimura emphatically indicated that Japan, which would be a very substantial contributor of energy and economic assistance to North Korea, would continue to withhold both until satisfactory progress is made on the abduction issue, stating in no uncertain terms: "North Korea needs Japanese capital and technology." There was also sharp criticism of Washington. Expressing his discontent with Washington, a former Japanese prime minister stated that the Bush administration "has given priority to its relationship with North Korea over the Japan-U.S. alliance."[152]

Family members of the abductees and individuals representing their interests were also not pleased with Washington's decision to begin the de-listing process. For this, they blamed both the Japanese and the US governments. Showing his criticism of the Japanese government, an official of AFVKN stressed, "The move toward de-listing must have been known earlier [to Tokyo]. A sense of distrust is growing among the family members." Sakai Yokota, the mother of the young abductee Megumi, also expressed frustration with the Japanese government: "For such a long while, a state has been unable to save its citizens. What, I wonder, is the real nature of all this?"[153] AFVKN believed that the Japanese government could have done more to elicit cooperation from Washington not to de-list the DPRK, but that this did not happen because the Japanese government has routinely followed the United States.[154] Suggesting that the powers that be had not done enough to oppose the de-listing, COMJAN (the Investigation Commission on Missing Japanese Probably Related to North Korea), which was formed in January 2003,[155] maintained that the government of Japan is divided into two main factions on the abduction issue, those who wanted to maintain the *status quo* and the moderates. According to COMJAN, the moderates, who had aligned with the Prime Minister Fukuda, did not totally object to Washington's changed DPRK policy.[156]

Revealing her dissatisfaction with Washington and its decision to de-list North Korea, Ms. Yokota stated: "It was a bit too soon. I'm really disappointed." Stressing that Washington's decision to remove North Korea from its list will significantly reduce the effects of sanctions, the chairman of AFVKN pointed out: "The United States said it would consult with Japan before deciding on de-listing but that was not the case. For all the best efforts we have made, I'm left with empty feelings."[157] AFVKN expressed feelings of abandonment by the United States and, suspicious of Washington's objectives, questioned whether the Bush administration was sincere with regard to its comments that it will continue to support Japan's efforts to resolve the abduction issue.[158]

Then there was the Japanese public, which generally was neither happy with the de-listing by Washington nor the way the central government handled the matter. A survey conducted by the *Mainichi Shimbun* in July 2008 showed that a plurality of 47 percent of respondents felt that Washington's de-listing of North Korea would make it more difficult to settle the abduction issue. An *Asahi Shimbun* poll conducted at about the same time showed that 76 percent of Japanese respondents did not have a positive view of Pyongyang's nuclear declaration. This survey also showed that 71 percent of the respondents did not look favorably on the Bush administration's decision to begin the process of de-listing the DPRK, and that 81 percent believed that North Korea's removal from the list would have either a negative (51 percent) or negligible (30 percent) effect on resolving the abduction issue.[159] However, the Japanese public directed most of its discontent at Tokyo, which maintained in still another anomalous manner that the DPRK's recently submitted declaration would help resolve the North Korean nuclear issue. In stark contrast to this explanation, two-thirds of the respondents in the *Mainichi Shimbun* survey stated that they were against the position taken by the unpopular Fukuda government.

Tokyo was not successful in its attempt to achieve progress on the abduction issue at the six-party talks that took place in July 2008. Some Japanese officials expected Pyongyang to "show a more proactive attitude" with regard to the abduction issue. Pyongyang's refusal to deal with the reinvestigation issue suggests that its agreement to do so was intended to keep the Bush administration happy so that the president would go ahead with the announcement to remove the DPRK from the US terrorist list.

Tokyo decided to play down its inability to persuade Pyongyang to address the reinvestigation, stressing that at the six-party talks Japan's Akitaka Saiki met with Kim Kye-gwan rather than Song Il Ho, the North Korean official in charge of Japanese–DPRK normalization discussions. This diplomatic mismatch, plus the fact that none of the officials in the DPRK delegation at the six-party talks specialized in Japanese relations, gave Tokyo the opportunity to suggest that little progress should have been expected.[160] An official in the Ministry of Foreign Affairs, as well as AFVKN, reasoned that Japan's failure to achieve any success on the abduction issue at the July six-party talks was due to the inability of Kim Kye-gwan, charged exclusively with negotiating the nuclear problem, to be able to deal authoritatively with the kidnappings.[161]

As much as Tokyo disliked hearing Bush's announcement that he was beginning the process of de-listing the DPRK, this paled in comparison to the public reaction by far-right conservatives in the United States. John Bolton declared that the administration's decision was "shameful," and that "This represents the final collapse of Bush's foreign policy." Conservative Republican, Representative Edward Royce, stated that only more "North Korean skullduggery" discovered during the short time it takes for the process to be completed would prevent it from not being removed from the terrorism list. Republican Representative Ileana Ros-Lehtinen, one of the two authors of the letter requesting that the abduction issue remain a major component of the Bush administration's negotiations with Pyongyang, sent to Secretary Rice in early June, expressed her "profound disappointment" with the decision to de-list North Korea.[162] So disturbed was Ros-Lehtinen that she co-sponsored a bill, which was introduced to the House Committee on Foreign Affairs the same day that Bush announced the beginning of the DPRK de-listing process, designed to interfere with the removal of the DPRK from the State Department's terrorism list.[163]

North Korea's de-listing: phase II, the hardliners' last stand

By August 2008, North Korea had disabled much of its nuclear capabilities, though the road to this point had been far from smooth. Pyongyang expected that the DPRK would be de-listed in mid August, not very long after it submitted its nuclear declaration to Beijing in June. Pyongyang was cautiously optimistic that, because of the Bush administration's relatively new DPRK policy, Washington had become more interested in settling the nuclear row than catering to Tokyo on the abduction issue. The remaining hardliners in the Bush administration, influenced by those who had already left their government positions, were determined to show that the conciliatory approach to North Korea was wrong.

In July, the Bush administration very suddenly gave responsibility for verifying the disablement of North Korea's nuclear capabilities to a group of hardliners, instead of leaving this matter in the hands of Christopher Hill or Sung Kim, the US Special Envoy for the six-party talks.[164] Just days before her traveling to Beijing to discuss the North Korean verification issue as part of the six-party talks, Patricia McNerney, an official in the US State Department's Bureau of International Security and Nonproliferation, revealed her predisposition to side with the hardliners. McNerney, a senior advisor to her former boss at the State Department, the outspoken John Bolton, stated that he "has been critical of this [the U.S.-North Korean] agreement." McNerney went on to point out that Bolton, "I think he's rightly, is sceptical of North Korean intentions."[165]

Opposed by Hill, the Bush administration's hard-line verification plan called for "full access to all materials" at DPRK sites that could have at anytime been associated with nuclear work and "full access to any site, facility or location," that Washington believed had been connected to nuclear activities, including military facilities. The verification protocol that the United States wanted was comprehensive and intrusive and included the gathering and removal of samples.[166]

When the mid-August deadline passed and the DPRK still had not been removed from the US State Department's list of countries sponsoring terrorism, Pyongyang took immediate action. Pyongyang maintained that despite its submission of an "accurate and complete declaration" as required by agreement reached during the six-party talks, the United States "has not honored its commitment to write the DPRK off the list of state sponsors of terrorism."[167] Because of this, Pyongyang announced its decision to reverse the disablement process at Yongbyon, first by ending it and then by restoring its nuclear facilities. Although acknowledging the importance of verification, Pyongyang insisted that unilateral verification was never part of the deal to remove the DPRK from the US list of states sponsoring terrorism. It stressed that nowhere is there either a written or verbal agreement between the United States and North Korea or within the context of the six-party talks for the DPRK to yield to a "special inspection" before being de-listed. What was agreed to, Pyongyang said, was the creation of monitoring and verification procedures that would be used to ensure the denuclearization of the Korean Peninsula, not a verification protocol that applied unilaterally to the DPRK. Pyongyang maintained that the inspection protocol demanded by the United States violated the sovereignty of the DPRK, which therefore put it at odds with the *juche* idea.[168]

As specified in the Joint Statement of September 2005, the ultimate goal of the six-party talks is "the verifiable denuclearization of the Korean Peninsula." Thus, not only would it have to be substantiated that the DPRK had gotten completely out of the nuclear-weapons-making business but the United States would also need to verify that none of its nuclear weapons remained in South Korea.

In mid September 2008, the Bush administration changed its position. Hill indicated that the United States was ready to be flexible with North Korea on the verification issue.[169] In early October, Hill was in Pyongyang ironing out a compromise on verification.[170] At a special briefing held on Saturday, October 11, 2008, the State Department announced that Secretary Rice had signed the documents that officially removed he DPRK from its list of state sponsors of terrorism.[171]

While Pyongyang had previously declared that it "does not care whether it continues remaining on the list of 'those countries which are disobedient to the U.S.,'" this really was not indicative of its true feelings. Pyongyang long wanted the DPRK removed from the US State Department's list of countries sponsoring terrorism. Pyongyang viewed de-listing and the elimination of the constraints stemming from the Trading with the Enemy Act as important steps in the direction of integrating the DPRK into the international community and as helping its efforts to invigorate the economy. In January 2009, when asked about the relationship of Pyongyang's plan to energize the economy and the removal of the DPRK from the list of states sponsoring terrorism and the end to the restrictions associated with the Trading with the Enemy Act, a prominent North Korean remarked, "I cannot say it has nothing at all to do with that."[172] Sounding very pleased that this was now all behind North Korea, Pyongyang commented: "We welcome the U.S. which has honored its commitment to de-list the DPRK as a state sponsor of terrorism in the wake of ending the application of the Trading with the Enemy Act." Pyongyang was also pleased that it had reached an agreement with Washington on "a fair verification procedure" and announced that it restarted the disablement work at the Yongbyon nuclear facilities.[173]

On the day that the de-listing took place, the State Department made public a document specifying what it said had been agreed to in Pyongyang in early October. The agreement, which the State Department maintained "had been codified in a joint document between the United States and North Korea," contained five verification standards. First, all of the countries involved in the six-party talks could take part in the verification work. Second, the IAEA would play an important part in the verification activities. Third, inspectors would be granted access to all of the nuclear facilities that the DPRK declared and, with "mutual consent," they would be permitted access to undeclared locations. Fourth, scientific techniques, "including sampling and forensic activities" would be permitted. Fifth, the verification protocol that Washington and Pyongyang had agreed to covers plutonium, uranium and proliferation activities; moreover, previous monitoring agreements reached during the six-party talks remained applicable to proliferation and uranium activities.[174]

An ongoing saga

The Japanese government felt umbrage that it received almost no advanced notice of the DPRK's de-listing.[175] Moreover, when the de-listing announcement was made by the Bush administration, Japanese Finance Minister Shoichi Nakagawa, who was in Washington, stated that it was "extremely regrettable" that North Korea had been taken off the US terrorism list and that the "abductions amount to terrorist acts."[176]

In late July, even before the de-listing, AFVKN emphasized that the Bush administration's official announcement that it plans to remove the DPRK from its list of states sponsoring terrorism is "damaging U.S.–Japan relations."[177] Reacting to the official de-listing of North Korea, this same individual said that it was "betrayal" by Washington, while Megumi's mother, Sakie Yokota, insisted that North Korea is still "a terrorism-assisting country."[178] Like Tokyo, AFVKN maintains that North Korea "is still a terrorist state," even though "America no longer believes this."[179]

Newly elected Prime Minister Taro Aso expressed his displeasure with the de-listing, and emphasized to Japanese legislators that he had told Washington he wanted the abduction issue resolved. Foreign Minister Hirofumi Nakasone stated that Japan considers "resolving the abduction issue as being most important" and that its policy "remains unchanged."[180] After the de-listing of North Korea by the Bush administration, Aso called his cabinet officers together for a plenary session of the government's Headquarters for the Abduction Issue, only the second such meeting since former Prime Minister Shinzo Abe established the organization in 2006.[181]

Soon after the US State Department removed the DPRK from its list of countries sponsoring terrorism, survey data showed that the percentage of Japanese who felt that US–Japan relations were in good or very good shape had declined to 34 percent, down from 39 percent in 2007. Nearly four-fifths (77 percent) of the Japanese respondents to a survey conducted in 2008 felt that the United States and Japan were not working well together in dealing with North Korea.[182]

The de-listing of the DPRK also troubled US hardliners. The hardliners neither wanted the DPRK removed from Washington's terrorism list nor did they stop viewing North Korea as a terrorist state. However, the Bush administration did not want to risk jeopardizing the six-party talks or have to deal with a second DPRK nuclear test during its remaining time in office.

This easing up on the DPRK with respect to verification by the Bush administration meant keeping Paula DeSutter, the Assistant Secretary of State for Verification, Compliance, and Implementation in the dark about the specifics of the agreement Hill had reached in Pyongyang until the day before the de-listing. Sutter, whose erstwhile boss was John Bolton, defended him during the State Department's special briefing on this matter, saying, "John is the epitome of a skeptical policymaker, and that's appropriate."[183]

For a short time, Pyongyang was happy with the verification deal it reached with Hill in early October 2008, calling it a "fair verification procedure." However, things began to quickly heat up again. Having indicated, on the day of the DPRK's removal from the list of states sponsoring terrorism, that sampling by international inspectors had been part of the agreement reached between North Korea and the United States during the early October meeting in Pyongyang, the Bush administration continued to press this matter. Paula DeSutter, who pointed out that she had contacted Hill and that he agreed to let a representative from her office attend the next meeting of the six-party talks, stated: "sampling is a very normal part of many arms control agreements."[184]

Pyongyang had a very different take on this matter. Pyongyang claimed that there was much "misinformation" circulating about the verification issue that both blames the DPRK for slowing down the denuclearization process and that is attempting to get it to succumb to an agreement at the six-party talks that requires the "collection of samples." Pyongyang insisted that its written agreement with the Bush administration in October included only information relating to the Yongbyon nuclear complex. According to Pyongyang, the verification protocol permitted visits to the Yongbyon nuclear complex, interviews with technicians working there and the review of documents connected to the facilities there. Pyongyang stressed that additional demands, specifically the "international standard" (i.e., sampling), would amount to a "house search" and violate the sovereignty of the DPRK. Because its receipt of compensation from the other participants in the six-party talks was behind schedule, Pyongyang indicated in November 2008 that it had significantly slowed down the disablement process and that should delays continue it would make the necessary adjustments.[185] Pyongyang later stated that the written verification agreement between the DPRK and the United States "includes no paragraph referring to the collection of samples." Pyongyang based its objection to sampling on the argument that since the United States and the DPRK were still technically at war, going beyond what had been agreed to in writing would violate the sovereignty of the DPRK. Pyongyang also stressed that calls for a verification protocol at the upcoming six-party talks to include taking samples would ignore the existence of the agreement that the DPRK and the United States had already reached in October.[186]

The discrepancy between the United States and the DPRK was not over whether the October agreement on verification included language about the collection of samples. The written verification agreement did not mention taking samples. DeSutter herself made this quite clear when she stated: "It is unfortunate for them [the North Koreans] that they are stuck on a word. If you don't have the word 'sampling' in the primary document, you can probably do something that is all right from a verification prospective [*sic*] so long as a secondary document is also equally binding."[187] What DeSutter and others therefore wanted was a secondary document – which would be drafted at the upcoming six-party talks – that would specifically authorize the collection of samples.

Because of the DPRK's position on the sampling issue, the six-party talks meetings held in December 2008 ended with no verification protocol. At these talks, Pyongyang refused to give more than it had formally committed to in the written verification agreement it reached in October with United States. In short, Pyongyang held tenaciously to the position that taking samples would infringe on the DPRK's sovereignty. Hill, on the other hand, blamed North Korea, asserting in Beijing after the conclusion of the six-party talks that the DPRK "was not ready to reach a verification protocol with all the standards that are required."[188] When he arrived in Washington, Hill stated, "I'm disappointed that the North Koreans weren't prepared to deal on the issues they knew they were supposed to deal on."[189]

What Hill did not say was that he was the one that left Pyongyang in early October with a written agreement that did not specify that the collection of samples would be part of the verification agreement. Hill also did not say that the details of his agreement were shared with only some officials in the Bush administration – and not, as we have seen, with DeSutter until just before the de-listing of North Korea. The division within the Bush administration between those, including Hill and Secretary Rice, who wanted to make progress on the denuclearization process with the DPRK and those, such as DeSutter, who were highly sympathetic to the hardliners' position, which endorsed the "Libyan model" of unilateral disarmament à la Bolton and Robert Joseph,[190] eventually played out to the latter group's advantage.

Media reports about the impasse stressed that Pyongyang was once again up to its old tricks of trying to get as much as it could from the other parties to the six-way talks and at the same time finagling to keep its nuclear weapons. However, Pyongyang told a completely different story, basing its refusal to accept the verification protocol that Washington and its allies wanted on other reasons.

First, Washington would be pressing hard to permit thorough inspection of any location, including military sites, something that Pyongyang did not want to happen again, as it did in early 1990s. Pyongyang's position was that because normal diplomatic relations between the United States and the DPRK did not exist, and since the two countries were still technically at war, it could not accept any course of action that would expose its military sites to inspection. Second, Pyongyang objected to the scouring of North Korean territory, as was done in Iraq. Third, Pyongyang opposed US demands to take samples. Pyongyang argued that the taking of samples, which would require sophisticated equipment and IAEA involvement, did not apply to the DPRK. Pyongyang maintained that, because it had formally withdrawn from the NPT, international verification standards would infringe upon the DPRK's sovereignty and were therefore unacceptable. Fourth, while Pyongyang did agree, as discussed above, to a compromise plan that involved the inspection of the Yongbyon facilities and interviews there, it insisted that the stipulation in the six-party talks' joint statement of September 2005 requiring "verifiable denuclearization of the Korean Peninsula" remained paramount. Pyongyang's position was that at the then-current disablement phase, verification is limited. At the final denuclearization phase, not only must it be verified that the DPRK has disarmed but it must also be verified that the United States has no nuclear weapons in South Korea. Pyongyang maintained that in dealing with the United States "giving one concession ultimately means giving ten concessions."[191]

Right after the conclusion of the December six-party talks, the State Department announced the suspension of heavy fuel deliveries to North Korea until such time that Pyongyang agreed to an acceptable verification protocol.[192] Faced with criticism from the hardliners that the Bush administration was not tough enough on North Korea and showing her frustration that considerably more had not been accomplished, Secretary of State Rice commented shortly after the failed six-party talks held in December: "I mean, who trusts the North Koreans? You'd have to be an idiot to trust the North Koreans."[193]

The apotheosis of gamesmanship: enter the Obama administration

Established in November 2008 and led by well-know nationalist Shintaro Ishihara, the governor of Tokyo, the 46-member Assembled Governors for the Return of Victims of Abduction by North Korea decided in January 2009 to put pressure on then President-elect Barack Obama. Deeply troubled by the Bush administration's removal of North Korea from the US State Department's list of countries sponsoring terrorism, several of the governors called Washington's policy "incoherent." Pointing out that President Bush had turned his back on Japan and the kidnapping victims, Ishihara stated that the "Lack of [U.S.] devotion and concern on the [abduction] issue has become a barrier" to settling the problem. The governors planned to send a letter to Obama requesting that the United States recognize Japan's "dialogue and pressure" strategy toward North Korea, suggesting that this was the best way to get Pyongyang to return the abductees.[194] However, once in office the Obama administration decided against taking any immediate action whatsoever on North Korea. This delay set the stage for an interesting display of political gamesmanship by Pyongyang, Washington, Tokyo and to a lesser extent Seoul.

Pyongyang was cautiously optimistic about the new Obama administration. One prominent North Korean remarked that he "hopes Obama is honest."[195]

Another perfunctorily commented, "we don't care whether a Democrat or a Republican becomes president," but he also stated that if "Obama wants dialogue, we will respond accordingly."[196]

For a short time, it looked as if the Obama administration would be willing to embrace coexistence with the DPRK. During her speech in February 2009 at the Asia Society in New York City, Secretary of State Hillary Clinton made clear that the Obama administration recognized the importance of restarting the six-party talks, adding the caveat that "it is incumbent upon North Korea to avoid any provocative action." Clinton also stated in her speech that if Pyongyang is ready to verifiably abandon its "nuclear weapons program, the Obama administration will be willing to normalize bilateral relations, replace the peninsula's longstanding armistice agreements with a permanent peace treaty, and assist in meeting the energy and other economic needs of the North Korean people."[197]

This appeared to fit reasonably well with Pyongyang's position, though it could easily be taken to establish the precondition that the DPRK must first verify that it has completely forsaken its nuclear weapons activities. In early January 2009, one prominent North Korean pointed out that the DPRK wants "peace and normalized relations with the United States" and that Pyongyang "welcomes a high-level official from the United States."[198] The vice president of the (North) Korean Association of Social Scientists pointed out that although unilateral disarmament is "unacceptable" to Pyongyang, "if the DPRK has trustful, normal relations with the United States then his country has no need to possess nuclear weapons." In a relatively critical tone, he stated that the United States has spread the rumor that the DPRK will never give up its nuclear weapons only so that it can maintain American troops in South Korea and Japan.[199]

As it turned out, Pyongyang was too anxious. Fueling Pyongyang's anxiety was that, given its heightened expectations about the new Obama administration, it perceived that the DPRK was being ignored and that Secretary Clinton was establishing the precondition that the North first verifiably abandon its nuclear weapons programs. Pyongyang had developed the pattern in the recent past of triggering a *songun*-demonstration event when it believed that the United States was not paying close enough attention to the DPRK. The difference now was that Pyongyang did not give Washington much time to act. Less than two weeks after Obama's inauguration, South Korean and US intelligence announced that North Korea was getting ready to test what was said to be a long-range missile.[200]

Selecting Japan as the first stop on her first overseas trip as Secretary of State, Clinton arrived in Tokyo in mid February 2009 and admonished that "The possible missile launch that North Korea is talking about would be very unhelpful in moving our relationship forward."[201] Later, she met with members of the abductees' families. However, prior to meeting with members of the abductees' families, Clinton had rekindled the rhetoric used during the last few months of the Bush administration in her speech at the Asia Society by stating: "I will assure our allies in Japan that we have not forgotten the families of the Japanese citizens abducted to North Korea." During her meeting with the family members in Japan, Clinton spoke of the need to "pressure" the DPRK to resolve the abduction issue. According to Shigeo Iizuka, chairman of NARKN, Clinton "said that isolated talks, just between the U.S. and North Korea, or between Japan and North Korea, would not work, because North Korea is a cruel country whose methods she cannot comprehend."[202] This display of tell-them-what-they-want-to-hear rhetoric harks back to the Bush administration during the time when the abduction issue was just as important to Washington as it was to Tokyo.

Aware that spy satellites were watching, Pyongyang referred dismissively to reports that the DPRK was getting ready to launch a long-range missile. Pyongyang maintained that these reports were not based on facts and that the DPRK had the sovereign right to engage in "space development." Pyongyang felt compelled to ratchet up the political noise by stating: "One will come to know later what will be launched in the DPRK."[203]

Still on her maiden overseas trip as Secretary of State, Clinton got Pyongyang's attention in Seoul by talking about potentially serious problems associated with succession in the DPRK. Just how succession would transpire in the DPRK has been a topic of interest to observers, both before and after Kim Jong Il was supposedly incapacitated for time by a stroke in August 2008.[204] When Kim Jong Il was not seen in public for awhile there was a proliferation of interest in the subject of succession in the DPRK, that is, before it became reasonably clear that his youngest son, Kim Jong Un, would likely become the next North Korean leader. Saying what Pyongyang did not want to hear, Clinton remarked: "If there is a succession, even if it's a peaceful succession that creates more uncertainty, and it may also encourage behaviors that are even more provocative, as a way to consolidate power within the society."[205] Then Clinton dropped the second shoe – the one that made it almost certain that Pyongyang would not concede to international calls that it not proceed with the launch. With regard to a meeting with Kim Jong Il, Secretary Clinton stated emphatically in Seoul: "I have no intention or plan. It is not something we are even contemplating."[206] Just a few days later, Pyongyang played its card by officially announcing that the "preparations for launching [the] experimental communications satellite *Kwangmyŏngsŏng-2* by means of a delivery rocket Unha-2 are now making brisk headway."[207]

Unlike the *Kwangmyŏngsŏng-1* satellite (commonly referred to as the Taepodong-1, launched in August 1998), this time Pyongyang provided advanced notice to international bodies - the International Civil Aviation Organization and the International Maritime Organization. In mid March, Pyongyang told at least one of these organizations that the launch would take place between April 4 and April 8, 2009.[208] Pyongyang announced that it had recently become a party to the 1967 Treaty on Principles Governing the Activities of States in the Exploration and Use of Outer Space, Including the Moon and Other Celestial Bodies.[209] This treaty states: "Outer space, including the moon and other celestial bodies, shall be free for exploration and use by all States without discrimination of any kind, on a basis of equality and in accordance with international law, and there shall be free access to all areas of celestial bodies."[210] However, Washington and Tokyo insisted that any ballistic launch by the DPRK would be a violation of UN Security Council Resolution 1718 created in the wake of North Korea's nuclear test in the fall of 2006.

By the second half of March 2009, the situation reached the point where a DPRK launch was inevitable. Quite different from its outreach to Iran in March when the president extended a conciliatory hand to Tehran, the Obama administration had decided to put the impasse pertaining to the DPRK nuclear issue on the back burner. In all likelihood, a Clinton trip or one made by a special envoy to the DPRK would have forestalled the quickly evolving imbroglio, as would a goodwill gesture from Pyongyang inviting the Secretary of State to visit the North.

Instead, neither Washington nor Pyongyang would blink first. Rather than employing amicable dialogue of any kind, both sides showed inexorable resolve to their respective positions, which caused a spike in animosity and military threats and readiness. Pyongyang declared: "The UNSC's discussion on the DPRK's projected satellite launch for peaceful purposes itself, to say nothing of its adoption of any document containing even a single word critical of the launch whether in the form of a 'presidential statement' or a 'press statement,' will be regarded as a blatant hostile act against the DPRK."[211] With support from Seoul and continuous urging from Tokyo, the Obama administration decided to show its willingness to be tough on North Korea. Secretary of State Clinton announced on the last day of March: "We had said repeatedly that their missile launch violates UN Security Council Resolution 1718, and there will be consequences certainly in the United Nations Security Council if they proceed with the launch."[212] About two weeks earlier, Japanese Prime Minister Taro Aso had stated that even a satellite launch "will be a blatant breach of U.N. Security Council Resolution 1718", vowing, "Japan must lodge a stern protest through the United Nations and resolutely demand it be called off."[213]

Beijing repeatedly called for all parties to show restraint, certainly not wanting the DPRK to proceed with the launch. Also fearing an escalation of tension, Moscow urged Pyongyang to cancel the launch. While Seoul's conservative government, led by President Lee Myung-bak, worked hard to coordinate its position with the concerns of the United States and Japan, Washington and Tokyo most especially exchanged threats with the DPRK. Pyongyang had been particularly angered by Seoul's conservative policies that emerged since Lee took office, maintaining that his government had "fully denied" the June 2000 and October 2007 declarations that had previously created a foundation for improved North–South relations.[214] The liberal position in South Korea, which was that the Lee government had abandoned the atmosphere of détente that had previously existed between the two Koreas, was virtually identical to Pyongyang's.[215]

The seemingly impending DPRK launch caused tensions to rise. Stoking these tensions was talk by Washington of possibly shooting down a North Korean missile and the joint US–South Korean military exercises scheduled for March 2009, which precipitated Pyongyang's announcement that it could not assure the safety of the South's civilian airliners flying in DPRK airspace during the maneuvers.[216] Pyongyang later warned, "Shooting our satellite for peaceful purposes will precisely mean a war."[217] Soon there were threats that Japan was considering using its anti-ballistic missile equipment to shoot down a DPRK rocket, and a warning from Pyongyang that it would attack US spy planes observing the North's launch site.

Warnings and threats continued, including the Japanese government's announcement that it would prolong sanctions on North Korea if it goes ahead with the launch. Determined to ensure that neither the United States nor Japan try to intercept the DPRK launch, Pyongyang ordered out for patrol an unspecified number a MiG-23 fighters in early April 2009.[218] Although Pyongyang sternly warned Washington, Seoul and Tokyo not to try to interfere with the launch, it was especially critical of Japan, whose Diet had just passed a resolution condemning the imminent DPRK launch.[219] Pyongyang stated: "only Japan is making much ado as if something serious had happened, finding fault with even the DPRK's above-said advance notice and terming the launch of 'Kwangmyŏngsŏng-2,' the DPRK's experimental communications satellite for peaceful purposes, a 'hostile act.'"[220] Just before the DPRK launch, the United States, Japan and South Korea had assembled a war-like display of military readiness to monitor the event - battleships, fighter planes and anti-ballistic missile and radar-tracking equipment.[221]

Once the launch occurred on April 5, the DPRK declared that it had succeeded in putting into orbit a communications satellite. However, Washington, Tokyo and Seoul insisted that the launch was a failure. Incensed, Tokyo immediately labeled the launch a "grave provocation from the viewpoint of security."[222]

For a few days before the launch, Tokyo had been leading the charge to have the UN Security Council pass a new resolution that would slap additional sanctions on the DPRK, pulling and eager and inexperienced Obama administration in its wake. They wanted this, despite the existing evidence showing that the sanctions stemming from UN Security Council Resolution 1718, passed after Pyongyang detonated a nuclear device in October 2006, did not adversely affected the DPRK's trade with China and South Korea, the two countries the North trades the most with.[223] Recognizing that a new Security Council resolution was very unlikely, Washington and Tokyo began to set their sights before the launch on strengthening the sanctions that were already imposed by the Security Council on the DPRK. Once the launch occurred, Japanese Ambassador to the United Nations, Yukio Takasu, formally requested that the UN Security Council "convene an urgent meeting" to deal with the North Korean launch.[224]

Because Beijing and Moscow continued to oppose a UN Security Council resolution, and because Washington recognized the impossible task of passing one, talk eventually shifted to a legally non-binding Presidential Statement. Opposition from Beijing and Moscow notwithstanding, the persistent lobbying efforts of Washington and Tokyo paid off: the Security Council issued an especially strong Presidential Statement on April 13, 2009. The Presidential Statement indicated that the Security Council "condemns" the DPRK for the launch, which it noted was in "contravention" of resolution 1718 passed in October 2006, and stressed that it would make the necessary adjustments to enforce the sanctions of this resolution by April 30.[225]

The day after the presidential statement was issued, Japan's Minister for Foreign Affairs Hirofumi Nakasone stated: "This is an exceptionally strongly worded statement, of high significance for the security not only of Japan, which was exposed to the most serious danger posed by the missile launch, but also of the northeast Asia region as a whole."[226]

The Obama administration provided a unique interpretation of international law, which does not consider a presidential statement legally binding. Washington's Permanent Representative to the United Nations Susan Rice indicated: "the United States views presidential statements, broadly speaking, as binding." Later, US State Department spokesperson Robert Wood reiterated the Obama's administration's position by maintaining that it "has the weight of international law, whether it be a statement or a resolution."[227]

Reacting to the "brigandish" presidential statement, Pyongyang vowed to no longer participate in the six-party talks nor be obligated by any agreements associated with them. Most problematic was that Pyongyang stated that it would "boost its nuclear deterrent for self-defence in every way" and would rebuild its nuclear facilities at Yongbyon "to their original state," comments that gave grist to the mill of those who said that the DPRK would never give up its nuclear arms. Maintaining that the Security Council's condemnation of its satellite launch violated the sovereignty of the DPRK, Pyongyang stressed that it "will defend the peace and security on the Korean Peninsula with the might of Songun in a responsible manner."[228] Pyongyang also made IAEA inspectors and US monitors at the Yongbyon nuclear complex leave the DPRK. As we shall see in Chapter 7, it was around this time that Pyongyang appears to have fully committed the DPRK to uranium enrichment and a light-water reactor project.

On the same day as the DPRK launch, AFVKN, NARKN, the Parliamentarian League for Early Repatriation of Japanese Citizens Kidnapped by North Korea and other supporters of rescuing the abductees urged the Japanese government to take a hard-line approach toward the DPRK.[229] Even before the Security Council's unanimous endorsement of the presidential statement, Tokyo had unilaterally imposed sanctions on the North. Extending the existing sanctions to one year from the previous six-month period used on four previous occasions, again partly because of the failure to resolve the abduction issue, Tokyo this time also added new restrictions. Created specifically because of the April launch, the new restrictions more closely monitor both the movement of money transported by travelers going from Japan to the DPRK and electronic capital transmissions to the North.[230] Reacting to the sanctions, a representative of the abductees' family members said "given [Pyongyang's] insincere response to the abduction issue and the launch of a missile, [the sanctions] are still not enough."[231]

Soon there emerged differences about whether the launch was a satellite, as Pyongyang repeatedly said, or a missile. Tokyo decided that the DPRK projectile was a missile, making its conclusion consistent with its earlier position that a launch by the North represents a provocative act that threatens regional security.[232] However, Seoul drew a very different conclusion on the DPRK launch. Although South Korea fully supported the Security Council's Presidential Statement, Defense Minster Lee Sang-hee stated that the DPRK launch "followed the trajectory of a satellite."[233]

For sure, Pyongyang could have postponed the launch until it had established better relations with Washington. Pyongyang almost immediately linked the launch to *songun*, an unambiguous sign that the hardliners had marginalized the moderates. Pyongyang proclaimed: "The DPRK's successful satellite launch is the shinning fruition of the Songun revolutionary leadership provided by Kim Jong Il by directing his utmost efforts to boosting the nation's political and military potentials and developing the science and technology despite the worse trial and adversity."[234]

Knowing that Beijing and Moscow would not support a resolution, Washington did not have to move as aggressively as it did to try to convince the Security Council to pass another resolution intended to punish North Korea. Like it did first with Iran and subsequently with Cuba, and to a limited extent with Venezuela and Nicaragua, the Obama administration could have amicably reached out directly to North Korea.

The Obama administration's continuing commitment to the six-party talks is just what Tokyo wanted. In the past, Tokyo had learned the hard way when Washington and Pyongyang had bilateral discussions that excluded Japan's interests, these talks eventually led to the removal of the DPRK from the State Department's list of countries sponsoring terrorism. For sure, Tokyo would have preferred seeing North Korea placed back on the list. However, what Tokyo got from the Obama administration was a promise two weeks after the DPRK rocket launch in April that bilateral talks between the United States and North Korea were not on the cards, at least not right away.[235]

Not long after the DPRK rocket launch, Mohamed ElBaradei, the director general of the IAEA, commented that the North Korean nuclear issue has been beleaguered by "mismanagement" for a number of years. ElBaradei went on to say that the result has been that "we have ended up with North Korea just having moved from a processing capacity into a country with nuclear weapons."[236] Fully supported by Tokyo, decisions made by the Obama administration during the first 100 days, and those made by Pyongyang's, contributed to this mismanagement. Making all of this worse was the DPRK's second nuclear test in May 2009.

Notes

1 A Report of the Project for the New American Century, *Rebuilding America's Defenses: Strategy, Forces and Resources for a New Century*, Washington, DC, September 2000.
2 Project for the New American Century, *Statement of Principles*, Washington, DC, June 3, 1997.
3 Tom Barry, "Meet Bolton's Replacement: Robert 'First Strike' Joseph," *Counterpunch*, June 15, 2005.
4 David Corn, "Elliot Abrams is Back!" *The Nation*, June 14, 2001; Tom Barry, "Bush's New Freedom Fighter, Elliott Abrams: The Neocon's Neocon," *Common Dreams.org*, February 9, 2005, www.commondreams.org/views05/0209-22.htm (accessed on April 5, 2011).
5 John Bolton, *Surrender is Not an Option: Defending America at the United Nations and Abroad* (New York: Threshold Editions, 2007), p. 76.
6 Anthony DiFilippo, "U.S. Policy and the Nuclear Weapons Ambitions of the 'Axis of Evil' Countries," *New Political Science*, vol. 28, no. 1, March 2006, pp. 101–23. During an interview former director-general of the International Atomic Energy Agency Mohamed ElBaradei said: "The Bush administration was saying in 2005 that Iran had an ongoing nuclear program, and we were accused of losing credibility by John Bolton and company when we said we did not see concrete proof of an ongoing program. But we were exonerated, if you like, and our conclusion was validated by the NIE [National Intelligence Estimate] report in 2007, which said that Iran had [done] some weaponization studies but was not developing weapons, and that they stopped it in 2003." See "Interview: Mohamed ElBaradei," *Foreign Policy*, January 26, 2010, www.foreignpolicy.com/articles/2010/01/22/interview_mohamed_elbaradei?page=0,1 (accessed on April 5, 2011).
7 "Late March, 2001: U.S. Issues 'Impossible' Demands to North Korea," *History Commons*, www.historycommons.org/context.jsp?item=alate0301impossiblenk# alate0301impossiblenk (accessed March 29, 2011).
8 A Report of the Project for the New American Century, *Rebuilding America's Defenses: Strategy, Forces and Resources for a New Century*, pp. 4, 51–52 and 75.
9 Robert Carlin and John Weeks, "Negotiating with North Korea: 1992–2007," Center for International Security and Cooperation, Stanford University, January 2008, p. 11.
10 Bolton, *Surrender is Not an Option*, p. 104.
11 C. Kenneth Quinones, "Dealing with Pyongyang: In Search of a More Effective Strategy," *International Journal of Korean Unification*, vol. 14, no. 1, 2005, pp. 1–30.
12 "Statement of DPRK Government on Its Withdrawal from the NPT," *Korean Central News Agency*, January 10, 2003.
13 "DPRK's Stand on Six-party Talks Clarified," *Korean Central News Agency*, August 13, 2003; "DPRK Foreign Ministry Spokesman on Meeting of Working Group of Six-way Talks," *Korean Central News Agency*, April 29, 2004; "KCNA on Working Group Meeting of Six-party Talks," *Korean Central News Agency*, May 10, 2004; "KCNA Urges U.S. to Accept DPRK's Proposal," *Korean Central News Agency*, May 21, 2004.
14 The White House, Office of the Press Secretary, *Remarks by the President to the People of Poland*, Krakow, Poland, May 31, 2003, www.whitehouse.gov/news/releases/2003/05/20030531-33.htmlon (accessed November 29, 2007).
15 Eben Kaplan, "The Proliferation Security Initiative," *Backgrounder*, Council on Foreign Relations, October 19, 2006.
16 Ministry of Foreign Affairs, People's Republic of China, *Foreign Ministry Spokesman Kong Quan's Press Conference*, Beijing, September 3, 2003, accessed at http://ipc.fmprc.gov.cn/eng/fyrth/t25626.htm on December 2, 2007.

17 Mark Valencia, "The Proliferation Security Initiative: A Glass Half Full," *Arms Control Today*, June 2007.

18 Hazel Smith, "North Korean Shipping: A Potential for WMD Proliferation?" East-West Center, *Asia Pacific Issues*, no. 87, February 2009.

19 "KCNA Assails U.S.-led Multinational Naval Blockade Exercises," *Korean Central News Agency*, September 16, 2003.

20 Bolton, *Surrender is Not an Option*, pp. 117–29.

21 "U.S. Urged to Apologize and Compensate for Its Piracy against DPRK Ship," *Korean Central News Agency*, January 7, 2003.

22 US Department of State, *Press Conference on the Proliferation Security Initiative*, Krakow, Poland, May 31, 2004 www.state.gov/t/us/rm/33556.htm (accessed November 29, 2007).

23 Naoyuki Agawa, *Japan's Role for Peace and Security in East Asia: Issues and Prospects*, Institute for Corean-American Studies Fall Symposium, Washington, DC, October 11, 2002, www.icasinc.org/2002/2002f/2002fnya.html (accessed March 29, 2011).

24 Seminar at the Sasakawa Peace Foundation, *Promoting Dialogue between the U.S. and Asia – Six-Party Talks What Does North Korea Really Want?* Washington, DC, November 19, 2003, www.spfusa.org/program/avs/2003/nov1903.pdf (accessed March 29, 2011).

25 John Bolton, "Pyongyang's Upper Hand," *The Wall Street Journal*, August 31, 2007.

26 US Department of State, *Press Briefing at U.S.-D.P.R.K. Bilateral Working Group Meeting*, Geneva, August 31, 2007, www.state.gov/p/eap/rls/rm/2007/91664.htm (accessed on December 9, 2007).

27 US Department of State, *North Korea to Disable Nuclear Programs by End of 2007*, Geneva, September 2, 2007, www.state.gov/p/eap/rls/rm/2007/91688.htm (accessed on December 9, 2007).

28 Full Text of Joint Document of the Second Session of the Sixth Round, Six-Party Talks, *Second-Phase Actions for the Implementation of the Joint Statement*, Beijing, October 3, 2007, http://news.xinhuanet.com/english/2007–10/03/content_6829017.htm (accessed on October 3, 2007).

29 "Foreign Ministry Spokesman on Recent DPRK–U.S. Talks," *Korean Central News Agency*, September 3, 2007.

30 US Department of State, *Remarks Upon Arrival in Pyongyang, North Korea*, Pyongyang, December 3, 2007 www.state.gov/p/eap/rls/rm/2007/96129.htm (accessed on December 3, 2007).

31 "Conservatives Assail North Korea Accord," *The Washington Post*, February 15, 2007.

32 Editors, "Agreeing to the Same Framework," *National Review Online*, February 14, 2007, http://article.nationalreview.com/?q=ZjliMGZmYzdjYzEwNGY1YzBh NDBlZTY2MmZiMmIyMGI= (accessed March 29, 2011).

33 Christopher Griffin and Nicholas Eberstadt, "Déjà Vu: Repeating Past Mistakes with North Korea," *San Diego Union Tribune*, February 25, 2007.

34 "U.S. Official Says that Syria May have Nuclear Ties," *The New York Times*, September 15, 2007; "Israel, U.S. Share Data on Suspected Nuclear Site," *The Washington Post*, September 21, 2007.

35 "The Right Confronts Rice over North Korean Policy," *The New York Times*, October 25, 2005.

36 "N. Korea Dismisses Suspicions over Nuclear Link to Syria," *Yonhap News Agency*, September 18, 2007.

37 "Rumor about 'Secret Nuclear Cooperation' between DPRK and Syria Dismissed," *Korean Central News Agency*, September 18, 2007.

38 "N. Korea Nuclear Talks," *Yonhap News Agency*, September 19, 2007.

39 The White House, *President Bush and Prime Minister Yasuo Fukuda in Joint Press Statements*, Washington, DC, November 16, 2007, www.whitehouse.gov/news/releases/2007/11/20071116–18.html (accessed on December 11, 2007).

40 "Pyongyang Fallout," *The Wall Street Journal*, November 16, 2007; John Bolton, "Bush's North Korea Meltdown," *The Wall Street Journal*, October 31, 2007.

41 Anthony DiFilippo, "Kojireta kankei no nichicho kokko seijohka," *Kitachosen o Meguru Hokutoh Ajia no Kokusai Kankei to Nihon*, henshuusha Yoichi Hirama, Yone Sugita (Tokyo: Akashi Shoten, 2003), pp. 66–84; "The Troubled Relationship: What Normalized Relations Would do for Japan and North Korea," in *Japan and Northeast Asian International Relations Involving North Korea*, eds. Yoichi Hirama and Yone Sugita (Tokyo: Akashi Shoten, 2003), pp. 66–84; Yoichi Funabashi, *The Peninsula Question; A Chronicle of the Second North Korean Nuclear Crisis* (Washington, DC: Brookings Institution Press, 2007), pp. 64–66 and 71–72.

42 Ministry of Foreign Affairs, *Japan–DPRK Pyongyang Declaration*, Pyongyang, September 17, 2002, www.mofa.go.jp/region/asia-paci/n_korea/pmv0209/pyongyang.html (accessed on December 17, 2007).

43 Government of Japan, Headquarters for the Abduction Issue, *The Abduction of Japanese Citizens by North Korea*, Tokyo, June 2007, http://202.232.58.50/foreign/abduction/cases.html#why (accessed on December 19, 2007); Ministry of Foreign Affairs, *Outline and Background of the Abduction Cases of Japanese Nationals by North Korea*, Tokyo, April 2002, www.mofa.go.jp/region/asia-paci/n_korea/abduct.html (accessed on December 19, 2007).

44 "Chronology of Japan-N. Korea Events Related to Abductions," *Kyodo News*, November 14, 2004.

45 Eric Johnston, "The North Korea Abduction Issue and Its Effect on Japanese Domestic Politics," Japan Policy Research Institute, JPRI Working Paper 101, June 2004; Anthony DiFilippo, *The Challenges of the U.S.–Japan Military Arrangement: Competing Security Transitions in a Changing International Environment* (Armonk, NY: M.E. Sharpe, 2002), pp. 112–13; Haruki Wada, "Re-Examining Alleged Abduction of Japanese," from *Sekai*, January and February 2001, www.kimsoft.com/2001/wada.htm (accessed December 18, 2007); National Association for the Rescue of Japanese Kidnapped by North Korea, www.sukuukai.jp/narkn/about.html (accessed December 18, 2007); Shigeru Yokota Father of the Abducted Megumi Yokota, Japan, http://64.233.169.104/search?q=cache:b0r3D8HfYQAJ:www.nkhumanrights.or.kr/bbs/board2/files/235_testimony-yokota(e22).doc+Shigeru+Yokota+Father+of+the+Abducted+Megumi&hl=en&ct=clnk&cd=2&gl=us (accessed December 18, 2007).

46 "Japanese Papers used by South Korea in Anti-DPRK Campaign," *Korean Central News Agency*, February 11, 1997.

47 Mark Manyin, *North Korea–Japan Relations: The Normalization Talks and the Compensation/Reparations Issue*, Congressional Research Service, Washington, DC, June 13, 2001.

48 "Mori Promises to Deal with the Alleged Abduction by N. Korea," *Kyodo News*, September 18, 2000.

49 "Public Opinion, Conservative Media Alter Policy on North Korea," *The Japan Times Online*, November 19, 2007.

50 Charles Pritchard, *Failed Diplomacy: The Tragic Story of How North Korea Got the Bomb* (Washington, DC: The Brookings Institution, 2007), p. 86.

51 Office of the Press Secretary, The White House, *President Bush, Prime Minister Koizumi Hold Press Conference*, Tokyo, February 18, 2002.

52 "Communiqué between Korean, Japanese Ruling Parties," *Korean Central News Agency*, November 14, 1997.

53 "Bush Arrives in Tokyo, Keeps Hard Line on 'Axis,'" *The Japan Times Online*, February 18, 2002; "Kin Thank Koizumi for Raising Abduction Issue," *The*

Japan Times Online, February 19, 2002; LDP, *Normalization of Diplomatic Relations between Japan and North Korea Depends on Resolution of the Abduction Issue*, Tokyo, March 12, 2002, www.jimin.jp/jimin/english/news/news00.html (accessed March 28, 2010).

54 Yoneyuki Sugita, "An Active Japanese Foreign Policy Impeded by a Frustrated Public in a Post-Cold War Era," *International Journal of Korean Unification Studies*, vol. 14, no. 2, 2005, pp. 171–94.

55 Anthony DiFilippo, "Security Trials, Nuclear Tribulations, and Rapprochement in Japan-North Korean Relations," *The Journal of Pacific Asia*, vol. 11, 2004, pp. 7–31; "Analysis: Japan, U.S. Differ on N. Korea," *Asahi Shimbun*, September 14, 2002.

56 "Relatives of Japanese Abductees Criticize Government's Response," *The New York Times*, September 19, 2002.

57 "Koizumi Hit over Wishy-Washy North Korea Policy," *The Japan Times Online*, September 6, 2003.

58 "U.S. Meeting with North Korea on Nuclear Dev. Program," *Voice of America*, April 22, 2003, www.voanews.com/english/archive/2003–4/a-2003-04-22-12-U-S. cfm (accessed on December 18, 2007).

59 "Hirasawa Exits Post over Secret Talks with Pyongyang," *The Japan Times Online*, April 3, 2004; "Group Slams Two LDP Officials for Secret Meeting with North Korean," *The Japan Times Online*, April 5, 2004; "Lawmakers Hirasawa to Resign from Post Dealing with Abductions," *Kyodo News*, April 6, 2004.

60 Mark Manyin, *Japan–North Korea Relations: Selected Issues*, Congressional Research Service, Washington, DC, November 26, 2003.

61 "Abduction Issue Key to N. Korea Removal from Terror List: U.S.," *Japan Economic Newswire*, April 1, 2004.

62 US Department of State, *Patterns of Global Terrorism, 2003*, Washington, DC, April 29, 2004; "U.S. Mentions Abduction for the 1st Time in Terrorism Report," *Kyodo News*, May 3, 2004; "Armitage Confirms Inclusion of Abduction Issue in U.S. Terror Report," *Kyodo News*, April 26, 2004.

63 The White House, Office of the Press Secretary, *President Bush Meets with Japanese Prime Minister Koizumi*, Crawford, TX, May 23, 2003.

64 Ministry of Foreign Affairs, *Overview of Japan–US Summit Meeting*, Tokyo, May 26, 2003.

65 US Department of State, John Bolton, Under Secretary for Arms Control and International Security, *International Security Issues, Arms Control Matters, and Nonproliferation*, Press Conference at US Embassy, Beijing, February 16, 2004.

66 "Abduction Issue Key to N. Korea Removal from Terror List: U.S." *Kyodo News*, April 5, 2004.

67 US Department of State, *Ambassador J. Cofer Black, Coordinator, Office of the Coordinator for Counterterrorism*, Foreign Press Center Briefing, Washington, DC, April 29, 2004.

68 "U.S. Report Gives Japan Leverage on Abductions," *The Daily Yomiuri*, May 1, 2004, as reported in *Kyodo News*, May 1, 2004.

69 "U.S. Accusations Against DPRK over 'Issue of Terrorism' Denounced," *Korean Central News Agency*, May 3, 2004.

70 "DPRK FM on Its Stand to Suspend Its Participation in Six-Party Talks for Indefinite Period," *Korean Central News Agency*, February 10, 2005.

71 US Department of States, *U.S.–Japan Joint Statement on North Korea*, Washington, DC, February 19, 2005.

72 "Russia Urges Japan not to Place the Abduction Issue on Agenda of North Korean Nuclear Talks," *RIA* (Russia News and Information Agency) *Novosti*, July 26, 2005, http://en.rian.ru/russia/20050726/40976802.html (accessed March 29, 2011).

73 "China Wants Japan, N Korea to Resolve Abduction Issue Bilaterally," *Kyodo News*, July 26, 2005.

74 "Six-Party Talks to Resume after 3-Week Recess," *People's Daily Online*, August 7, 2005.

75 Embassy of the People's Republic of China in Australia, *Fourth Round of the Six-Party Talks Begins in Beijing*, July 26, 2005, http://au.china-embassy.org/eng/xw/t204936.htm (accessed March 29, 2011).

76 Kuniko Ashizawa, "Tokyo's Quandary, Beijing's Moment in the Six-Party Talks: A Regional Multilateral Approach to Resolve the DPRK's Nuclear Problem," *Pacific Affairs*, vol. 79, no. 3, Fall 2006, pp. 411–32.

77 US Department of State, *Joint Statement of the Fourth Round of the Six-Party Talks*, Beijing, September 19, 2005, www.state.gov/r/pa/prs/ps/2005/53490.htm (accessed on January 15, 2008).

78 Government of Japan, Headquarters for the Abduction Issue, *The Abduction of Japanese Citizens to North Korea*, Tokyo, October 12, 2007 (updated), www.kantei.go.jp/foreign/abduction/index.html (accessed March 29, 2011).

79 The White House, Office of the Press Secretary, *President Meets with North Korean Defectors and Family Members of Japanese Abducted by North Korea*, Washington, DC, April 28, 2006.

80 The White House, Office of the Press Secretary, *President Bush and Japanese Prime Minister Koizumi Participate in a Joint Press Availability*, Washington, DC, June 29, 2006.

81 "U.S. Ambassador Visits Megumi Yokota's Abduction," *The Mainichi Daily News*, March 16, 2006; "U.S. Envoy Visits Kidnap Site," *International Herald Tribune*, March 16, 2006; "Schieffer Visits Site of Yokota Abduction," *Asahi Shimbun*, March 17, 2006; "Schieffer Visits Site of Yokota's 1977 Abduction," *The Japan Times Online*, March 17, 2006.

82 "KNCA Blasts Pro-U.S. Japanese Charlatans' Shameless Anti-DPRK Moves," *Korean Central News Agency*, October 30, 2005.

83 Prime Minister of Japan and His Cabinet, *Policy Speech by Prime Minister Shinzo Abe to the 165th Session of the Diet*, Tokyo, September 29, 2006.

84 Prime Minister of Japan and His Cabinet, *Prime Minster Meets with Representatives of the Association of the Families of Victims Kidnapped by North Korea (AFVKN)*, Tokyo, September 29, 2006.

85 Prime Minister of Japan and His Cabinet, *1st Meeting of the Headquarters on the Abduction Issue*, Tokyo, October 16, 2006.

86 "Minister Orders NHK to Focus on Abductions," *The Japan Time Online*, November 11, 2006; "Japan Rightists Fan Fury over North Korea Abductions," *The New York Times*, December 17, 2006.

87 Prime Minister of Japan and His Cabinet, *Policy Speech by Prime Minister Shinzo Abe to the 166th Session of the Diet*, Tokyo, January 26, 2007.

88 "Broadcasters Concerned over Government Interference in NHK," *Nikkei Weekly*, November 13, 2006.

89 "Gov't to Order NHK to Focus on Abduction Issue in Radio Programs," *Japan Economic Newswire*, March 14, 2007.

90 "Japan to Air TV Spots on N Korea," *Agence France Presse*, March 9, 2007.

91 Prime Minister of Japan and His Cabinet, *Policy Speech by Prime Minister Yasuo Fukuda to the 169th Session of the Diet*, Tokyo, January 18, 2008.

92 US Department of State, *Country Reports on Terrorism 2005*, Washington, DC, April 28, 2006.

93 Larry Niksch, *North Korea: Terrorism List Removal?* Congressional Research Service, Washington, DC, December 11, 2007; "Washington, Pyongyang Signed Nuclear Memorandum Last Month," *Asahi Shimbun*, February 8, 2007; "Hill Denies Signing Alleged Memorandum with DPRK," *Xinhua Online*, February 8, 2007.

94 Gilbert Rozman, "The North Korean Nuclear Crisis and U.S. Security in Northeast Asia," *Asian Survey*, vol. 47, no. 4, July/August 2007, pp. 601–21.
95 Ministry of Foreign Affairs of the People's Republic of China, *Initial Actions for the Implementation of the Joint Statement*, Beijing, February 13, 2007, www.fmprc.gov.cn/eng/topics/fifth/t297463.htm (accessed March 29, 2011).
96 US Department of State, *Country Reports on Terrorism 2006*, Washington, DC, April 30, 2007. Washington originally designated the DPRK a state sponsor of terrorism in 1983. After the bombing of a Korean Air Lines fight in 1988, President Reagan redesignated the DPRK as a state sponsor of terrorism. See Anthony DiFilippo, "North Korea as a State Sponsor of Terrorism: Views from Tokyo and Pyongyang," *International Journal of Korean Unification Studies*, vol. 17, no. 1, 2008, pp. 1–40.
97 "U.S. Delinks JAL Hijackers, North Korea Terror Status," *The Japan Times Online*, November 23, 2007.
98 US Department of State, *Country Reports on Terrorism 2007*, Washington, DC, April 30, 2008.
99 "Abduction not an Issue for Terror List Removal: Vershbow," *Yonhap News Agency*, May 14, 2008.
100 "Rice Downplays Link between N. Korea Abductions and Terror Status Issues," *Jiji Press*, May 12, 2007; "Abductions No Bar to U.S. Delisting of North," *Asahi Shimbun*, May 14, 2007.
101 "N. Korea Stays on U.S. Terrorist List Until Abduction Issue Solved: Japan," *Kyodo News*, February 14, 2007.
102 "Nakayama Urges U.S. not to Remove N. Korea from Terrorist List," *Kyodo News*, May 31, 2007.
103 "Abe's Point Woman on the Abductees Firm," *The Japan Times Online*, December 22, 2006.
104 "Japan Warns US over North Korea," *Agence France Press*, Tokyo, October 25, 2007.
105 "N. Korea Removal from Blacklist May Hurt Japan–U.S. Ties: Machimura," *Kyodo News*, November 12, 2007.
106 "Japan–US Alliance Struggling: Media," *Agence France Presse*, November 18, 2007.
107 "Delisting North Korea not to Hurt Ties with Japan: U.S. Official," *Kyodo News*, December 14, 2007; "Focus: U.S. Diplomacy with N. Korea to Test Ties with Japan in 2008," *Kyodo News*, December 27, 2008.
108 "Record 20% of Japanese Say U.S.–Japan Relations not Good," *Asahi Shimbun*, December 3, 2007; "U.S. Policy Toward Pyongyang Looks to Test Japan Relations," *The Japan Times Online*, January 1, 2008.
109 "Abductees' Families Leave for Washington," *NHK Online*, November 11, 2007; "Abductees' Kin to Urge U.S. not to Remove N. Korea from Terror List," *Kyodo News*, November 11, 2007; "'Abductees' Kin Return to Japan, Express Disappointment," *Kyodo News*, November 18, 2008.
110 Ministry of Foreign Affairs, *Press Conference by Minster of Foreign Affairs Masahiko Koumura*, Tokyo, January 8, 2008.
111 "Japan, U.S. Step Up Call for N. Korea for Full Nuclear Declaration," *Kyodo News*, January 8, 2008.
112 "Japan Remains Calm over Bush not Mentioning N. Korea in Speech," *Japan Economic Newswire*, January 29, 2009; "Japan Reiterates Its Call on North Korea to Fulfill Nuclear Commitments," *Kyodo News*, January 29, 2008.
113 "Japan, U.S. Step Up Call for N. Korea for Full Nuclear Declaration," *Kyodo News*, January 8, 2008.
114 John Bolton, "North Korea's True Colors," *The Wall Street Journal*, January 11, 2008.
115 "DPRK Foreign Ministry Spokesman on Issue of Implementation of October 3 Agreement," *Korean Central News Agency*, January 4, 2008.

116 "Uranium Traces Found on N. Korean Tubes," *The Washington Post*, December 21, 2007.

117 "Japan-Made Pumps 'used at N-Facilities in N. Korea'," *Daily Yomiuri Online*, June 12, 2008; "IAEA Found Japanese-Made Pump in N. Korean Nuclear Facility," *Kyodo News*, June 12, 2008.

118 "DPRK Foreign Ministry Spokesman Blasts U.S. Delaying Tactics in Solution of Nuclear Issue," *Korean Central News Agency*, March 28, 2008.

119 Previously the US position was that the DPRK must submit a "complete and correct" declaration, which includes "clarification of any proliferation activities" and which also had to "address concerns related to any uranium enrichment programs and activities." *Statement of Christopher Hill, Assistant Secretary of State, Bureau of East Asian and Pacific Affairs, Before the Senate Foreign Relations Committee, Status of the Six-Party Talks for the Denuclearization of the Korean Peninsula*, Washington, DC, February 6, 2008.

120 "Spokesman for the DPRK Foreign Ministry on DPRK-U.S. Talk," *Korean Central News Agency*, April 9, 2008.

121 "U.S. Nuclear Envoy Indicates Early N. Korea Removal from Terror List," *Kyodo News*, March 19, 2008; "U.S. Ready to Ease Sanctions on N. Korea," *The Washington Post*, April 11, 2008.

122 "Syria Got N. Korea Help for N-Facility," *Asahi Shimbun*, March 31, 2008.

123 "Cabinet Extends North Sanctions," *The Japan Times Online*, April 12, 2008; "Intl Pressure Needed on N. Korea/As Sanctions aren't Working, Japan Should Enlist Support of Concerned Nations," *Daily Yomiuri Online*, April 15, 2008.

124 "Japanese Reactionaries' Extension of Sanctions against DPRK under Fire," *Korean Central News Agency*, April 19, 2008.

125 John Bolton, "Bush's North Korea Capitulation," *The Wall Street Journal*, April 15, 2008.

126 "Japan Concerned about N. Korea Aid to Syria's Nuclear Program," *Kyodo News*, April 25, 2008.

127 "U.S. Sees N. Korean Links to Reactor," *The New York Times*, April 24, 2008; "Bush Administration Releases Images to Bolster Its Claims about Syrian Reactor," *The New York Times*, April 25, 2008.

128 "IAEA Says Syria Lacks Skills for Nuclear Facility," *Reuters UK*, June 17, 2008.

129 "N. Korea Agrees to Blow Up Tower at Its Nuclear Facility," *The Washington Post*, May 2, 2008; "N. Korea Hands over Plutonium Documents to U.S.," *Kyodo News*, May 8, 2008; "North Korea Turns over Nuclear Weapons Papers to U.S., But Full Account of Nuclear Past Elusive," *The Mainichi Daily News*, May 9, 2008.

130 "Abduction Issue on Agenda for N. Korea-U.S. Talks," *Yonhap News Agency*, May 27, 2008; "N.K. Nuclear Talks at Crucial Juncture this Week: Source," *Yonhap News Agency*, June 8, 2008.

131 "U.S. Lawmakers Pressure Rice to Push Abductions with North Korea," *The Japan Times Online*, June 8, 2008.

132 US Department of State, Condoleezza Rice, *U.S. Policy Toward Asia*, Address at the Heritage Foundation, Washington, DC, June 18, 2008; US Department of State, Condoleezza Rice, *Interview with the Wall Street Journal Editorial Board*, New York, June 19, 2008.

133 "New Data Found on North Korea's Nuclear Capacity," *The Washington Post*, June 21, 2008.

134 "Tokyo Plans 'Action for Action' Policy over Pyongyang's Abductions," *The Japan Times Online*, June 11, 2008; "Japan Repeats Demand on N. Korea Abduction Cases on 1st Day of Talks," *Kyodo News*, June 11, 2008.

135 "Pyongyang to Reopen Abduction Probe," *The Japan Times Online*, June 14, 2008; "New Abductee Probe Set/North Korean Move Prompts Govt to Lift Some Sanctions," *The Daily Yomiuri Online*, June 14, 2008.

136 "Kin Express Disappointment with 'Progress' on Abduction Issue," *Kyodo News*, June 14, 2008.
137 "Japan Urged to Provide N. Korea with Energy Aid," *Yonhap News Agency*, June 8, 2008.
138 "Japan Ready to Drop Some Demands for 6-party Document," *Kyodo News*, November 4, 2008.
139 "U.S. Assures Japan Abductions Still on Its Mind in N. Korea Delisting," *Kyodo News*, June 19, 2008; "U.S. Still to Press N. Korea on Abduction Issue after Delisting: Rice," *Kyodo News*, June 24, 2008.
140 "Keep North on List: Komura," *The Japan Times Online*, June 21, 2008; "Komura Hints 6-Way Talks May Move Forward before Full N. Korea Account," *Kyodo News*, June 20, 2008.
141 "'No Lifting of Sanctions' without Probe Check," *The Daily Yomiuri Online*, June 23, 2008.
142 "KCNA Blasts Japanese Political Charlatans," *Korean Central News Agency*, June 23, 2008.
143 "Fukuda Would Welcome N. Korea Declaration for Resolving Nuke Issue," *Kyodo News*, June 24, 2008.
144 "U.S. Notifies Tokyo of Plan to Delist North Korea," *The Japan Times Online*, June 25, 2008.
145 The White House, Office of the Press Secretary, *President Bush Discuses North Korea*, Washington, DC, June 26, 2008.
146 "DPRK Foreign Ministry Spokesman on Implementation of Agreement Adopted by Six-Party Talks," *Korean Central News Agency*, July 4, 2008.
147 "U.S. Delisting N. Korea will not Change Stance on Abductions: Machimura," *Kyodo News*, June 26, 2008.
148 The White House, Office of the Press Secretary, *President Bush Discuses North Korea*, Washington, DC, June 26, 2008.
149 Author meeting with a researcher dealing with Japanese issues in the DPRK Foreign Ministry, Pyongyang, January 8, 2009.
150 Ministry of Foreign Affairs, *G8 Foreign Ministers' Meeting, Chairman's Statement*, and *Joint Press Conference by the G8 Foreign Ministers*, Kyoto, June 26–27, 2008, www. mofa.go.jp/policy/economy/summit/f_kyoto08/index.html (accessed April 5, 2011).
151 Author interview with official from Japan's Ministry of Foreign Affairs, Tokyo, July 18, 2008.
152 "U.S. Stance on DPRK Limits Japan's Choices," *Daily Yomiuri Online*, June 28, 2008; also see Linus Hagström, "Normalizing Japan: Supporter, Nuisance, or Wielder of Power in the North Korean Nuclear Talks," *Asian Survey*, vol. 49, no. 5, September/October 2009, pp. 831–51, for a discussion of Japan as a normal country and an economic power.
153 "U.S. Move to Delist N. Korea Irks Kin of Abducted Japanese," *Kyodo News*, June 27, 2008.
154 Author interview with official from AFVKN, Tokyo, July 14, 2008.
155 COMJAN, www.chosa-kai.jp/indexeng.htm (accessed March 30, 2011).
156 Author interview with a representative from COMJAN, Tokyo, July 14, 2008.
157 "U.S. Move to Delist N. Korea Irks Kin of Abducted Japanese," *Kyodo News*, June 27, 2008.
158 Author interview with official from AFVKN, Tokyo, July 14, 2008.
159 "47 Percent Say Move to Take N. Korea off Terror List Hinders Solution to Abduction Issue," *The Mainichi Daily News*, July 17, 2008; *Asahi Shimbun* survey data from the Maureen and Mike Mansfield Foundation, www.mansfieldfdn.org/polls/2008/poll-08-25.htm (April 5, 2011).
160 "Abduction Issue Stalls at 6-Way Talks in Beijing," *The Japan Times Online*, July 14, 2008.

161 Author interview with official from Japan's Ministry of Foreign Affairs, Tokyo, July 18, 2008 and author interview with a representative from AFVKN, Tokyo, July 14, 2008.

162 "Bush's Fellow Republicans Criticize President for Removing N Korea from US Terror Blacklist," *The International Herald Tribune*, June 26, 2008.

163 The Library of Congress, *H.R. 6420 To Toll the Congressional Notification Period for Removing North Korea from the State Sponsors of Terrorism list*, Washington, DC, June 26, 2008, http://thomas.loc.gov/cgi-bin/bdquery/z?d110:h6420 (accessed on April 5, 2011).

164 "U.S. Hardliners Verifying N. Korea's Nuclear Disarmament: Sources," *Yonhap News Agency*, July 20, 2008.

165 "U.S. State Department Representative Speaks on Nuclear Weapons," broadcasted on ABC Local Radio, Australia, July 1, 2008, www.abc.net.au/pm/content/2008/s2291334.htm (accessed March 30, 2011).

166 "Far-Reaching U.S. Plan Impaired N. Korean Deal," *The Washington Post*, September 26, 2008.

167 "KCNA Slams U.S. Provocative Act to Scuttle Denuclearization Process of Korean Peninsula," *Korean Central News Agency*, August 18, 2008.

168 "Foreign Ministry's Spokesman on DPRK's Decision to Suspend Activities to Disable Nuclear Facilities," *Korean Central News Agency*, August 26, 2008; "Foreign Ministry Spokesman Blasts U.S. for Putting on Hold Effectuation of Its Measure," *Korean Central News Agency*, September 19, 2008; "N. Korea Starts Reassembling Nuclear Facility: Sources," *Kyodo News*, September 3, 2008.

169 "U.S. 'Flexible' on N. Korea N-report Verification," *Daily Yomiuri Online*, September 12, 2008.

170 "Hill Visits Pyongyang for Showdown in Nuclear Talks," *Yonhap News Agency*, October 1, 2008.

171 US Department of State, *On the Record Briefing: Special Envoy for the Six-party Talks Ambassador Sung Kim, Assistant Secretary of State for Public Affairs Sean McCormack, Assistant Secretary of State for Verification, Compliance, and Implementation Paula Sutter, and Acting Assistant Secretary of State for International Security and Nonproliferation Patricia McNerney on North Korea*, Washington, DC, October 11, 2008.

172 Author meeting with the Vice President of the Korean Association of Social Scientists and former government official, Pyongyang, January 6, 2006.

173 "Foreign Ministry Spokesman on DPRK's Will to Cooperate in Verification of Objects of Nuclear Disarmament." *Korean Central News Agency*, October 12, 2008.

174 US Department of State, *U.S.–North Korea Understandings on Verification*, Washington, DC, October 11, 2008.

175 "De-listing of North Korea Catches Japan Unawares," *Asahi Shimbun*, October 13, 2008.

176 "U.S. Drops North Korea from Terrorism List," *The Washington Post*, October 12, 2008.

177 Author interview with AFVKN official, Tokyo, July 14, 2008.

178 "Abductees' Families Angered by U.S. Move," *The Japan Times Online*, October 13, 2008; "U.S. Move on N. Korea Assailed in Japan," *The Washington Post*, October 13, 2008.

179 Author interview with official of AFVKN, Tokyo, July 14, 2008.

180 "Aso Expresses 'Dissatisfaction' over De-listing of N. Korea," *Kyodo News*, October 14, 2008.

181 Government of Japan, Headquarters for the Abduction Issue, *Newsletter (No. 3) from the Headquarters for the Abduction Issue*, Tokyo, October 17, 2008.

182 "34% of Japanese Think Japan–U.S. Ties are Good," *Daily Yomiuri Online*, December 18, 2008.

183 US Department of State, *On the Record Briefing: Special Envoy for the Six-party Talks Ambassador Sung Kim, Assistant Secretary of State for Public Affairs Sean McCormack, Assistant Secretary of State for Verification, Compliance, and Implementation Paula Sutter, and Acting Assistant Secretary of State for International Security and Nonproliferation Patricia McNerney on North Korea*, Washington, DC, October 11, 2008.

184 "Sampling Core Part of Verification Deal with N. Korea: U.S. Official," *Yonhap News Agency*, November 26, 2008.

185 "Foreign Ministry Spokesman Holds Some Forces Accountable for Delayed Implementation of Agreement," *Korean Central News Agency*, November 12, 2008.

186 "KCNA Dismisses Misinformation about Verification Issue," *Korean Central News Agency*, November 24, 2008.

187 "Sampling Core Part of Verification Deal with N. Korea: U.S. Official," November 26, 2008, *Yonhap News Agency*.

188 "N. Korea Doesn't Agree to Written Pact," *The Washington Post*, December 12, 2008.

189 "U.S. Says No More Fuel to N. Korea Till Verification Deal," *Kyodo News*, December 12, 2009.

190 Funabashi, *The Peninsula Question*, pp. 354–55.

191 Author meeting with vice president of the Korean Association of Social Scientists and former government official, Pyongyang, January 6, 2009.

192 US Department of State, *State Department Press Briefing*, December 12, 2008.

193 "Rice Says Only an 'Idiot' Would Trust N. Korea," *Yonhap News Agency*, December 20, 2008.

194 "Ishihara Urges Obama to Act on Abductees," *The Japan Times Online*, January 14, 2009.

195 Author morning meeting with the President of the Korean Association of Social Scientists, Pyongyang, January 6, 2009.

196 Author afternoon meeting with Vice President of the Korean Association of Social Scientists and former DPRK government official, Pyongyang, January 6, 2009.

197 US Department of State, Office of the Spokesman, *Remarks: Secretary of State Hillary Rodham Clinton at the Asia Society*, New York, February 13, 2009.

198 Author evening meeting with a prominent North Korean, Pyongyang, January 5, 2009.

199 Author afternoon meeting with Vice President of the Korean Association of Social Scientists and former DPRK government official, Pyongyang, January 6, 2009.

200 "North Korean Seen Preparing for a Missile Launch," *Yonhap News Agency*, February 2, 2009.

201 "Clinton Warns N. Korea on Missiles," *The New York Times*, February 16, 2009.

202 "Clinton Meets Abductees' Relatives, Pledges to Help Find Resolution," *The Japan Times Online*, February 18, 2009.

203 "KCNA on DPRK's Right to Space Development," *Korean Central News Agency*, February 16, 2009.

204 Ken Gause, "Can the North Korean Regime Survive Kim Jong Il?" *The Korean Journal of Defense Analysis*, vol. 20, no. 2, June 2008, pp. 93–111; Paul Stares and Joel Wit, *Preparing for Sudden Change in North Korea*, Council Special Report No. 42 (New York: Council on Foreign Relations, January 2009).

205 "Clinton Downplays N. Korean Succession Issue," *The Korea Times*, February 20, 2009.

206 "Clinton Says U.S. not 'Even Contemplating' Meeting with North Korean Leader," *Yonhap News Agency*, February 20, 2009.

207 "Preparations for Launch of Experimental Communications Satellite in Full Gear," *Korean Central News*, February 24, 2009.

208 "N. Korea Tells International Agency Launching Satellite Next Month," *Kyodo News*, March 12, 2009.

209 "KCNA Report on DPRK's Accession to International Space Treaty and Convention," *Korean Central News Agency*, March 12, 2009.

210 The Multilaterals, *Project Treaty on Principles Governing the Activities of States in the Exploration and Use of Outer Space, Including the Moon and Other Celestial Bodies (October 1967)*, The Fletcher School of Law and Diplomacy, Tufts University.

211 "DPRK's Stand on Satellite Launch for Peaceful Purposes Re-clarified," *Korean Central News Agency*, March 26, 2009.

212 US Department of State, Hillary Rodham Clinton, *Press Availability Following International Conference on Afghanistan*, The Hague, March 31, 2009.

213 "Japan Urges N. Korea to Cancel Satellite," *Kyodo News*, March 13, 2009.

214 Author meeting with the Director of the DPRK Institute for Disarmament and Peace, Pyongyang, January 9, 2009.

215 Kim Ji Soek, "Yi Myung Bal Dae Tong Ryong Nam Buk Kwan Kye Puleora" ("President Lee, Salvage the Relationship between North and South Korea"), *The Hankyoreh*, August 4, 2009.

216 "U.S. and S. Korean Puppets Warned not to Act Rashly," *Korean Central News Agency*, March 5, 2009.

217 "Lee Myung Bak Group and U.S. and Japanese Aggressors Urged to Act with Discretion," *Korean Central News Agency*, March 9, 2009.

218 "N. Korea Deploys Fighter Jets to Guard Rocket Launch: Officials," *Yonhap News Agency*, April 2, 2009.

219 "Diet Passes Resolution Demanding N. Korea Halt Launch," *The Japan Times Online*, April 1, 2009.

220 "KPA [Korean People's Army] General Staff Warns against Any Interception of Satellite," *Korean Central News Agency*, April 2, 2009.

221 "Vast Network to Track N. Korean Launch," *Asahi Shimbun*, April 4, 2009.

222 "North Korea Fires Rocket over Tohoku," *The Japan Times Online*, April 5, 2009.

223 Marcus Noland, "The (Non) Impact of U.N. Sanctions on North Korea," *Asia Policy*, no. 7, January 2009, pp. 61–88.

224 "Security Council to Hold Meeting on N. Korea Rocket Launch Sun." *Kyodo News*, April 5, 2009.

225 United Nations Security Council, *Statement by the President of the Security Council*, New York, April 13, 2009; UN News Service, "Security Council Condemns DPR Korea's Recent Launch," New York, April 13, 2009.

226 Ministry of Foreign Affairs, *Statement by Mr. Hirofumi Nakasone, Minister for Foreign Affairs, on the Issuance of a Statement by the President of the United Nations Security Council regarding the Missile Launch by North Korea*, Tokyo, April 14, 2009.

227 US Department of State, *Remarks on the Presidential Statement Concerning North Korea*, New York City, April 13, 2009; US Department of State, *Daily Press Briefing*, Washington, DC, April 14, 2009.

228 "DPRK Foreign Ministry Vehemently Refutes UNSC's 'Presidential Statement,'" *Korean Central News Agency*, April 14, 2009.

229 "Abductees' Kin Seek Tougher Sanctions against N. Korea after Launch," *Kyodo News*, April 5, 2009; "Abductee Groups Seek Strong Response Following North Korea Missile Launch," *The Mainichi Daily News*, April, 6, 2009.

230 Government of Japan, *Newsletter (No. 5) from the Headquarters for the Abduction Issue*, Tokyo, April 15, 2009.

231 "Sanctions Still Insufficient, Says Leader of Abductee Kin Group," *Kyodo News*, April 10, 2009.

232 "It's Official: N. Korea Fired a 'Missile'," *Asahi Shimbun*, April 11, 2009.
233 "South Korea Says North Korean Rocket Followed a 'Satellite' Trajectory," *Yonhap News Agency*, April 14, 2009.
234 "Rodong Sinmun on Successful Satellite Launch," *Korean Central News Agency*, April 7, 2009.
235 "U.S. Not to Hold Direct Talks with N. Korea for the Time Being," *Kyodo News*, April 19, 2009.
236 "IAEA Chief Calls N. Korea Nuclear Standoff Lesson in 'Mismanagement,'" *Kyodo News*, April 20, 2009.

5 Caught in the crossfire

North Korean loyalists in Japan

From the time that the first Koreans came to Japan more than 100 years ago until today, the Japanese have treated them as less than equal. Having this ethnocentric perspective many years ago helped make Tokyo's annexation of the Korean Peninsula easier to justify. Concomitant to the creation of the two Koreas after the Second World War, *zainichi* Koreans (long-term residents of Japan) developed divergent political allegiances. Many *zainichi* Koreans supported the South Korean government, while many others believed that the communist North best reflected their interests and concerns.

Japan and South Korea eventually established diplomatic relations in December 1965. However, Cold War politics kept Japan and the Democratic People's Republic of Korea (DPRK) on opposite sides of the political fence, thus putting the prospect of a normalized relationship far out of reach. Still opposed to complete assimilation in Japanese society, *zainichi chōsenjin* identify themselves as overseas or Korean nationals of the DPRK. Because of their financial and political support of the DPRK, Pyongyang has monitored the treatment of *zainichi chōsenjin* in Japan.

A brief history

The Japanese colonization of the Korean Peninsula between 1910 and 1945 created enduring problems for *zainichi* Koreans, some of whom had actually migrated to Japan in the late 1800s. During the colonial period, Koreans came to Japan for one of two reasons. Because the Japanese had appropriated so much of the land on the peninsula, some Koreans migrated to Japan seeking a better life. Later, some Koreans were forced to come to Japan to satisfy the demand there for cheap labor created by the Japanese involvement in the Second World War. Female Koreans were also brought to Japan. Some female Koreans in Japan were industrial laborers. Most *juugun ianfu* (enslaved prostitutes) or comfort women, who were mainly Korean females, satisfied the sexual desires of Japanese troops in other countries during Japan's imperialist crusade. However, some of the comfort women served male Korean workers in Japan while others satisfied the sexual desires of the Japanese military in the homeland, including Okinawa. Tokyo maintained a forced assimilation policy for *zainichi* Koreans, requiring them to become Japanese citizens and select Japanese names. After the Second World War, the Japanese government designated Koreans living in Japan as foreigners, which meant they lost their citizenship rights, including the right to vote, though they were still considered Japanese nationals. Immediately after the Occupation ended in April 1952, the Japanese government abrogated the Japanese nationality for Koreans.[1] Although the Japanese government did allow *zainichi* to submit application material for citizenship, relatively few did this during the 1950s.[2]

When the Second World War ended, there were approximately 2.4 million Koreans living in Japan. Because many returned to southern parts of Korea in 1946 with the help of Choryon (the League of Koreans), their numbers were significantly reduced to between 600,000 and 700,000 by the year's end.[3] According to the General Association of Korean Residents in Japan, commonly known as *Chongryon*[4] in Korean and *Chosen Soren* in Japanese, and the current association representing those *zainichi* Koreans supporting the DPRK, by 1946 approximately 1.3 million had left Japan to take up residence in Korea. However, Chongryon insists that by 1947, because the political conditions in the South had deteriorated so badly owing to the occupying US military government, some who had left returned to Japan, and that the 620,000 or so *zainichi* had no choice but to remain in Japan.[5]

Established on October 15, 1945, Choryon was the first political organization in Japan having as its objectives the well being of Koreans, the advancement of the Korean Peninsula and the return of *zainichi* Koreans to Korea. Growing steadily closer to the Japanese Communist Party, which then advocated the principles of socialist revolution, Tokyo and the US Occupation authorities became increasingly concerned about Choryon. Troubled also by Choryon's open public support for the communist DPRK, which had been established in September 1948, a month after the creation of the Republic of Korea, the Japanese government, with the support of the Occupation authorities, passed the Organization Control Law in April 1949 to deal with domestic dissension that roused public unrest. About five months later, Japanese and US Occupation authorities abruptly ended Choryon. Claiming that Choryon was an "undemocratic and terrorist organization," approximately 500 Japanese police without prior notice arrived at Choryon's headquarters in Tokyo on September 8, 1949 and issued the order for it to cease to exist.[6]

The division of Korea into two nations simultaneously bifurcated Koreans in Japan, some supporting the North and others the South. Established on October 3, 1946, Mindan (Korean Residents Union in Japan) emphasized that it maintained a "completely different" political perspective than Choryon, which it saw as "offensive."[7] Although there were a number of political sources that contributed to the emergence of Mindan, two organizations were especially important – Kensei (Youth Alliance Promoting the Foundation of Chosun) and Kendou (Alliance of New Chosun Construction). Seeking an alternative to Choryon, Kensei wanted "a public organization not biased by ideology." However, Mindan's endorsement by South Korea almost immediately after its creation in 1948 does not seem to meet this objective, since for several years after its inception the Republic of Korea was led by the US-approved and strongly anti-communist autocrat Syngman Rhee.[8]

Following the breakup of Choryon, *zainichi* Koreans that pledged their allegiance to the DPRK established Minjon (United Democratic Front of Koreans in Japan) on January 9, 1951, about seven months after the start of the Korean War in 1950. Many of the former members of Choryon by this time had joined the Japanese Communist Party, which had committed itself to sustained confrontation against both American and Japanese capitalism. Within Minjon, there were ongoing disputes between those who sided with the international position adopted by the Japanese Communist Party, which sought to promote the socialist revolution globally, and those whose focus was on dealing specifically with the problems stemming from Rhee's autocratic rule in South Korea and on issues pertaining to the DPRK. Although both factions within Minjon saw intervention in Japanese politics as important, their internal differences were significant, especially after the internationalists, who remained closely tied to the Japanese Communist Party, became the dominant force within the organization. The DPRK's announcement in early 1955 that it wanted to normalize relations with Japan forced the Japanese Communist Party to rethink its position toward its Korean membership. For the Japanese Communist Party, these Koreans could easily become an impediment in its struggle against the Japanese government. For those members of Minjon who remained focused on Korean-related issues, the political gulf within the organization had become far too wide to tolerate. For them, "self help" was no longer feasible, causing them to dissolve Minjon on May 24, 1955; the next day, former members of Minjon established Chongryon.[9]

Because North Korean leader Kim Il Sung believed that prior organizations representing Koreans in Japan were flawed, in that they did not have an "independent action platform" that allowed for the proper management of the affairs of the *zainichi* or that served them as true DPRK citizens, he provided them with "*juche*-oriented guidance." Kim's guiding criteria were to protect the ethnic and democratic rights of the *zainichi*, while expecting that they provide economic assistance to the DPRK for its development and political support for the reunification of Korea. Admonishing them to avoid the past mistakes of Choryon and Minjon, Kim made explicit that Korean nationals living in Japan should not meddle in the internal affairs of Japanese politics. Thus, based on the *juche* idea of independence or self-reliance, Chongryon was created with a different political mandate than those adopted by its predecessor organizations, Choryon and Minjon.[10]

In 1955, there were 577,882 *zainichi* Koreans in Japan; of these, approximately 250,000 were Chongryon Koreans, that is, *zainichi chōsenjin*.[11] At this time, the *zainichi* Koreans as a whole were particularly opposed to the Japanese government's revision of the 1952 Alien Registration Law. The revision of this law in April 1955 required the fingerprinting of all foreigners over 16 years of age staying in Japan for more than 90 days. Having been established just days after this revision, Chongryon had a serious problem to contend with: what it believed to be the increased political suppression of *zainichi* Koreans. Because Koreans were the largest ethnic minority group in Japan, Chongryon viewed the 1947 Alien Registration Ordinance, the creation of the 1951 Immigration Control Ordinance, and the 1952 Alien Registration Law as being detrimental to the *zainichi* and evidence that the Japanese government had concluded that they were likely to be criminals. The fingerprinting requirement appended to the Alien Registration Law in 1955 strengthened Chongryon's belief that the Japanese government had the unequivocal intention to suppress *zainichi* Koreans.[12] After years of opposition by *zainichi* Koreans and a memorandum signed by Tokyo and Seoul, the Japanese government amended the Alien Registration Law in 1992 to exempt (beginning in January 1993) permanent foreign residents and special foreign residents from the fingerprint requirement.[13]

Chongryon's principle of not interfering in Japanese politics and Mindan's relatively acceptable political posture notwithstanding, the Japanese government was not at all pleased that so many *zainichi* Koreans were in Japan in 1955. It was especially not pleased that, since the creation of the two Koreas, so many *zainichi* Koreans supported the communist DPRK. Though the vast majority of *zainichi* or their ancestors had mainly come from the southern regions of Korea, their poor treatment and inferior social status in Japan, along with the influence of the Japanese Communist Party, caused many of them to identify and accept the working class ideology promulgated by the DPRK.[14]

In 1955, some prominent Japanese leaders, including government officials, began to consider seriously the idea of returning thousands of *zainichi* Koreans to North Korea. Masutaro Inoue, an erstwhile top official in the Japanese Ministry of Foreign Affairs, aggressively promoted the repatriation idea. Inoue strongly encouraged the repatriation of Koreans for both economic and political reasons, maintaining that their return to North Korea would relieve the Japanese government of the burden of making social welfare payments to the *zainichi* Koreans who were "very violent," "in dark ignorance," and "indigent and vaguely communist." Between 1959 and 1961, almost 75,000 *zainichi* Koreans left Japan for the DPRK; by 1984, more than 93,000 had relocated to North Korea. A few years before the repatriation began in 1959, Tokyo secretly contacted Pyongyang with the intention of convincing it to accept the plan. Initially hesitant, Pyongyang eventually endorsed the repatriation effort, as did Chongryon, both believing that the mass exodus of Koreans to North Korea would benefit the Korean emigrants and the DPRK. Seoul, however, had decisively rejected the repatriation plan. The Japanese government, then headed by Prime Minister Nobusuke Kishi of the Liberal Democratic Party (LDP), wanted to normalize relations with South Korea. Tokyo worried that if Syngman Rhee, who had not indicated any interest in accepting large numbers of Koreans from Japan, demanded that the entire *zainichi* population pledge allegiance to South Korea, Japan would be forever stuck with them. In Japan, Mindan went to work immediately to stop the repatriation of *zainichi* Koreans to the DPRK, claiming without its efforts many more would have been subjected to the "living hell" of life in the North. Despite the objections of Seoul and Mindan, Tokyo had the singular desire of getting as many Koreans as it could out of Japan. Working closely with the Japanese Red Cross, Tokyo managed to convince the International Red Cross that *zainichi* Koreans had been apprised of their political and social welfare rights and were making fully informed decisions to relocate to the DPRK. Despite its claim, the Japanese government fell far short of giving the *zainichi* Korean community a full accounting of its rights and, at the same time, provided an overly sanguine picture of their condition in Japan to the International Red Cross, which wanted to ensure that the repatriation was justifiable and aboveboard.[15]

In short, the repatriation plan that Tokyo engineered and implemented was self-serving, having only the nationalistic interests of Japan in mind – a xenophobic scheme targeting *zainichi* Koreans that far exceeded the Japanese dislike for other foreigners. The plan was neither a genuine attempt to help *zainichi* Koreans nor one that empathized with their conditions in Japan. Tokyo's plan pushed to the fore the wider chauvinistic sentiment existing amongst the Japanese people of the *zainichi* Koreans, whose legacy in Japan had been marred by discriminatory treatment.[16] The tens of thousands of *zainichi* Koreans who relocated to the DPRK were therefore truly émigrés, encouraged by Tokyo to leave Japan for political reasons that corresponded with the interests and concerns of the Japanese government.

By contrast, although Chongryon's role in spearheading the repatriation of *zainichi* Koreans to the DPRK was also political, its objective was to help them. Chongryon believed that the exodus of *zainichi* from Japan would end their oppressive and discriminatory treatment while also helping to strengthen the DPRK. That the *zainichi* Koreans who left Japan beginning in the late 1950s did not find the "workers' paradise" that they believed the DPRK to be and that some had found their stay in the North very unpleasant[17] was not because Chongryon had designed a duplicitous scheme against them. Thus, while Tokyo and Chongryon had been very much involved in the repatriation effort, they had disparate political objectives.

What was Washington's role in the repatriation? Toward the end of the planning stage in 1958 and in 1959 when the repatriation began, Washington implemented covert programs designed to influence Japanese politics – just the opposite of what Chongryon had committed to do. Although it is likely that Washington was not fully cognizant of the repatriation plan at the outset, it was by at least 1959 and did nothing to stop the relocation efforts. US Ambassador to Japan Douglas MacArthur II commented in 1959 that he could not be critical of the Japanese people's desire to rid the country of *zainichi*, since "the Koreans left in Japan are a poor lot including many Communists and many criminals."[18]

Fearing the ascendancy of the left in Japan, the Central Intelligence Agency (CIA) provided some funds and electoral advice to a small number of pro-US, conservative politicians in Japan just before the May 1958 elections of the powerful lower house. When the elections were over, the US-leaning LDP won a majority of the national vote. Although this program continued for several years, the CIA began providing funds to the Japan Socialist Party (JSP) in 1960. Because the JSP endorsed the idea of "unarmed neutrality" at the same time that some members strongly supported the international diffusion of Japan's pacifist constitution, Washington did not see the party's political objectives, as they then existed, as congruent with those of the United States in East Asia. Washington wanted the JSP to become a "responsible" opposition party more inclined to support US objectives.[19]

Thus, once Washington learned of the repatriation plan it is not at all surprising that it largely ignored it. Putting pressure on Tokyo to stop the repatriation would have been a reversal of the view Washington had developed of the *zainichi* Koreans during the occupation, particularly those who threw their political support behind the DPRK. Most importantly, given the Japanese people's lowly view of *zainichi* Koreans, such a move could have also caused the ruling LDP to loose some support among the electorate, something that Washington certainly did not want to happen.

Chongryon continued to promote and organize the relocation of *zainichi* Koreans to the DPRK well into the 1990s, indicating in 1997 that by this time about 100,000 had returned to their "socialist fatherland to lead a happy life there," a claim that obviously ignored the very serious humanitarian crises that beset North Korea in the mid 1990s. Chongryon also points with pride to the fact that it has helped thousands of *zainichi* Koreans visit the DPRK over the years. For its part, Pyongyang enacted the Nationality Law in October 1963. This law afforded Pyongyang the justification to assume legal and political protection of Chongryon Koreans and effectively made them overseas nationals or citizens of the DPRK.[20]

A troubled prelude to the abduction revelation

Before Kim Jong Il's admission of DPRK culpability for the abduction of Japanese citizens, Chongryon and Chongryon Koreans were experiencing new kinds of serious problems in Japan. For many years after it began, Chongryon was generally recognized as more politically effective than Mindan. By the end of the 1990s, however, Chongryon acknowledged that it had a serious problem and that to rectify it the association had to undergo a "paradigm shift." During a Chongryon meeting held in Tokyo in September 1999, First Vice Chairman So Man Sul stated: "As a result of putting emphasis only on politico-ideology rather than on the daily life of Koreans here, our activity is losing support from within." So indicated that out of the 660,000 or so *zainichi* Koreans then in Japan, the number who had maintained their North Korean nationality was likely to be less than 160,000. According to So, approximately 10,000 *zainichi* Koreans a year had been abandoning their (North and South) Korean nationality and were attempting to become

Japanese citizens. To deal with this loss of support, So stressed that it was important for Chongryon to develop a "citizen-oriented" strategy consisting of five key points. Two especially noteworthy points indicated by Chongryon at this time were that the association would work to improve its external image and to develop better relations with its Japanese neighbors.

However, Chongryon's member affiliation problem did not emanate simply from the internal dynamics and shifting tides within Japanese society during the 1990s. These factors also do not alone account for why Chongryon wanted to initiate community-centered gatherings and "refrain from holding centripetal, politically charged activities." Nor do they explain why Chongryon called for the amelioration of its external image and for it to work harder to extend the hand of friendship to the Japanese people.[21]

To some extent, Pyongyang's activities explain why Chongryon recognized that it needed to implement a drastic change in strategy by the late 1990s. The first DPRK nuclear crisis during the early 1990s and Pyongyang's 1993 launch of a Rodong 1 missile worsened Chongryon's image in Japan. Thus, these events intensified the discriminatory treatment of Chongryon Koreans, making them, including Korean children, more susceptible to overt acts of hostility from some Japanese.[22] As discussed in Chapter 2, Pyongyang decided in late August 1998 to launch a Taepondong-1 rocket, which infuriated Tokyo and the Japanese people since the it flew over Japanese territory. Again, the reaction in Japan, both by the government and some Japanese people, created additional problems for Chongryon Koreans.[23]

That Chongryon was not totally responsible for its declining support amongst the *zainichi* during the 1990s cannot be reasonably separated from Pyongyang's *songun* activities. Rather than face political repercussions in Japan, some *zainichi* Koreans decided to distance themselves from Chongryon, while others opted for naturalization.

During 2001, major political changes took place in both the United States and Japan that certainly did nothing to improve Chongryon's status. These changes played a big part in putting off normalization talks between Japan and North Korea. Tokyo and Pyongyang held normalization talks in August 2000 and again October. However, the twelfth round of talks did not occur until the end of October 2002 – a full two years later.[24] The Bush administration came to power in January 2001 and not long after this adopted a much tougher policy toward the DPRK than had been used by the Clinton White House. In April 2001, Junichiro Koizumi, who largely embraced US security policies, became prime minister. While himself not a nationalist, Koizumi often identified with their position. Japanese nationalists were becoming increasingly influential and consistently depicted Kim Jong Il's regime as corrupt, unpredictable and prone to provocation. None of this was helpful to Chongryon.

Chongryon's first direct experience with stepped-up Japanese scrutiny and pressure came in late November 2001 when the police in Tokyo raided its headquarters. The raid of Chongryon's headquarters, the first since the association was established in the 1950s, occurred after Kang Yong Gwan, the association's former chief financial official for 40 years, was arrested for embezzlement. While imprisoned, Kang's attorneys made more than 20 unsuccessful appeals for bail. In his second trial held in October 2005, Kang received a six-year prison sentence, the same as in his first trial. Prosecutors maintained that Kang, using a fictitious name, was responsible for having approximately ¥830 million (about $7 million in 2007 dollars) placed in the Chogin-Tokyo Credit Corporation, one of several Korean credit unions that eventually went bankrupt. Suspicions ran high in Tokyo that the funds eventually found their way to North Korea. Chongryon maintains that Kang's first trial revealed that Chogin-Tokyo Corporation both opened and managed the account and that Kang knew nothing about it. Chongryon called the police raid of its headquarters an example of "political suppression" and hundreds of Chongryon Koreans protested the police action. After the Tokyo High Court upheld Kang's conviction in 2005, more than 300 Chongryon Koreans protested, calling it an "unfair judgment." The police raid also got Pyongyang's full attention, which stated: "This was an unprecedented political crackdown upon Chongryon aimed to destroy it." Pyongyang maintained that many banks in Japan, including some affiliated with Mindan, have experienced bankruptcy because of the Japanese economic crisis and that Tokyo "groundlessly" linked Chongryon to the problems at the Korean bank. Pyongyang indicated that by doing harm to Chongryon, "the Japanese authorities wantonly infringed upon the dignity and sovereignty of the DPRK. They will have to pay for this crime." In Japan too there was an understanding that the raid of Chongryon's headquarters would damage Tokyo's relations with North Korea. LDP official Taku Yamasaki commented that Chongryon "had been functioning as a constant diplomatic channel to North Korea until now, but this function will be significantly hampered."[25]

From bad to worse: the abduction issue

Relations between Japan and North Korea have almost steadily deteriorated since Kim Jong Il admitted to Prime Minister Koizumi in Pyongyang in September 2002 that DPRK agents abducted a number of Japanese nationals many years ago. In Japan, Chongryon and Chongryon Koreans have had to contend with the untoward consequences of this worsened relationship, which has been aggravated by problems between the United States and the DPRK.

The Japanese government has long considered Chongryon a subversive organization that constantly needs to be monitored. However, in the wake of Kim's admission about the abductions, Chongryon and Chongryon Koreans immediately had to face a new reality. Chongryon Koreans, said one Korean restaurateur, "never thought North Korea would do such a thing, it should never have been allowed to happen."[26] Some *zainichi* Koreans, who had earlier believed that the DPRK was a political victim of US and Japanese policies, indicated after Kim's disclosure about the abductions that they could no longer sympathize with Pyongyang.[27] Still, both Chongryon and Chongryon Koreans believed that the Japanese reaction to the abduction issue was insensitive and cruel. One Chongryon official in Osaka put it this way: "We understand very well the feelings of those Japanese families whose loved ones were abducted. But [the] Japanese don't ask themselves why we are separated from our families in North Korea. They don't study modern history, so they don't feel anything for the thousands of Koreans who were forcibly taken to Japan under Japanese rule."[28] A Korean human rights activist in Japan similarly remarked: "Korean residents can sympathize with the Japanese people about the abduction issue but the Japanese people forget about war time problems."[29]

Kim's admission to Koizumi proved to be a watershed in some Chongryon schools in Japan. Before Kim's admission to Koizumi, Chongryon schools displayed portraits of the Great Leader, Kim Il Sung, and the Dear Leader, Kim Jong Il, in all classrooms. After Kim's admission, said a Chongryon administrative assistant in a school located in Kobe, "they were taken down. Now, their portraits are only in the teachers' room. And the studies of Kim Jong Il's childhood were removed from the curriculum."[30]

The revelation about the DPRK's involvement in the abductions ignited a massive bashing of North Korea by the Japanese media, which quickly and adversely affected Chongryon and Chongryon Koreans. Chongryon maintains that soon after Kim's admission Japanese officials began "politically exaggerating" the abduction issue "and stirred up anti-Korean sentiments among Japanese people through the mass-media."[31] This kind of media coverage perhaps helps to explain why some Japanese reacted violently toward Chongryon-related schools and associations. One teacher who had taught at the Chongryon high school in Yokohama, which because of the number of threats it received had to have a policeperson guard the facility, stated: "There's anti-Korean feeling everywhere these days, the students feel anxious and uneasy."[32] A human rights organization for Koreans in Japan emphasized that soon after Kim's admission about the abductions over 400 harassment instances by Japanese against Koreans took place in Japan, many of which were directed at children. Because of the malicious slitting of a young Korean schoolgirl's uniform, the *chima-chogori* could no longer be worn by Chongryon Korean girls.[33] Chongryon's data indicates that there were 51 reported assaults and abusive language instances directed at Korean schoolchildren during the period September 2002 to December 2003. During this time, Chongryon schools received 186 telephone threats and letters, and 114 defamatory email messages. Moreover, subsequent harassment of Chongryon and Chongryon Koreans continued to occur in Japan.[34]

Kim's acknowledgement about the abductions also put Chongryon immediately under suspicion. Less than a month after Koizumi returned from his first trip to Pyongyang the Japanese government went to work attempting to implicate Chongryon in the abduction issue. In early November 2002, a top official in Japan's Public Security Investigation Agency told a Diet committee that his agency was beginning to carefully examine Chongryon and was considering the use of the Anti-Subversive Activities Act because of the association's reputed "involvement" in the past abductions of Japanese nationals.[35]

On September 1, 2003, the eightieth anniversary of the Great Kanto Earthquake, the natural disaster that spurred mass hysteria in Japan and that led to the horrific and brutal death of thousands of Koreans by Japanese police and military forces, as well as by civilian mobs,[36] Chongryon issued an important political statement. Entitled "Never forget the bitter history," Chongryon's statement indicated that the political right and the media have been developing a decidedly extremist, nationalistic environment in Japan that is deluding the Japanese public, and that "bears a close resemblance to the situation before and after the massacre.[37]

With relations between Japan and the DPRK worse than they had ever been, several political parties in Japan, as we will see in Chapter 6, endorsed a bill in 2004 that would prohibit the North Korean ferry, the Mangyongbong-92, from docking at Niigata's port. Besides giving Chongryon Koreans the opportunity to visit their homeland, the Mangyongbong-92 regularly provided them with affordable transportation from Japan to the DPRK. Calling it a "hostile policy," Chongryon Koreans in Tokyo, Osaka and Nagoya protested the bill in late March 2004, in what amounted to an unsuccessful effort to prevent the legislation from being taken up and subsequently passed by the Diet. Not too long after their protest, Chongryon Koreans submitted an appeal to Prime Minister Koizumi urging the normalization of Japan–North Korean relations. Their appeal also stressed: "We Korean residents in Japan are deeply concerned about the bill to ban the entry of ships of a specific country to Japanese ports, which is against the spirit of the Pyongyang Declaration, aggravates bilateral relations between the DPRK and Japan and infringes upon the human rights of Koreans in Japan."[38]

While Chongryon was angered by the impact of the port ban on the *zainichi chōsenjin*, Tokyo justified it as a way, when combined with the revision to the Foreign Exchange and Foreign Trade Control Law, to help stem the movement of money to North Korea.[39] Although the actual amount of legal and illegal money going from Japan to North Korea can never be known for certain, it appears to have decreased sharply in recent years. During the 1970s and 1980s, large amounts of money from Pachinko Parlors, of which about 30 percent are owned by *zainichi chōsenjin*, supposedly moved illegally through Japanese ports to the DPRK. During the bubble economy of the late 1980s and 1990s, an estimated ¥60 billion (approximately $416 million, for example, in 1990) in legal and illegal money went annually from Japan to North Korea. By 2006, money going from Japan to North Korea is said to have declined precipitously, to an estimated high of ¥6 billion (about $52 million). Accusations have also been made that the Mangyongbong-92, which was built in 1992, had been used for illegal purposes.[40] In January 2003, the Tokyo Metropolitan Police informed the media that the Mangyongbong-92 had likely been involved in criminal activities, including providing a DPRK agent in Japan with instructions for spying. Although Chongryon consistently denied all illicit allegations relating to the ship, Prime Minister Koizumi indicated at the time that the Mangyongbong-92 should be monitored "lest it be used for crime."[41]

Despite the fact that the 2002 Pyongyang Declaration stated: "Both sides decided that they would sincerely discuss the issue of the status of the Korean residents in Japan,"[42] not only had this not occurred many months later, but by 2004 the DPRK felt compelled to express to the United Nations the conditions confronting Chongryon Koreans. In late March 2004, Pyongyang took its grievance pertaining to the Japanese treatment of Chongryon Koreans to the United Nations Commission on Human Rights. In its statement to the Commission, Pyongyang maintained that the "Japanese ultra-rightwing gangsters, who have been inspired by the systematic discrimination of their government against Korean residents, have gone as far as to attack the Korean institutions and make publicly violent assaults and threats toward even young schoolchildren."[43]

Prime Minister Koizumi was a consummate politician. While on the one hand he made clear publicly that Chongryon Koreans' use of the Mangyongbong-92 required monitoring, on the other hand, he also felt that it was necessary to show good will toward them. When Chongryon held its twentieth congress in Tokyo in May 2004, Koizumi sent a congratulatory statement – the first ever by a Japanese prime minister – to Chongryon, which the association gratefully acknowledged.[44] However, there is a bigger political story here that shows that Koizumi's intentions were hardly above reproach. Although Koizumi embraced several nationalist policies, such as the abduction issue, he also wanted to normalize Japan–North Korean relations while he was prime minister. Significantly, Koizumi's congratulatory statement to Chongryon, which won political points with DPRK officials, came just a few days after he took his second one-day visit to Pyongyang on May 22, 2004.

For Chongryon, things continued to get worse. Police raids on several Chongryon-affiliated organizations in October 2005 based on the suspicion of violating the Pharmaceutical Affairs Law rankled Chongryon. Surmising that the police had tipped the media beforehand, Chongryon denounced the raids as unjust and criticized the Japanese media for providing misleading information to the public on Chongryon and the DPRK, as it had been doing with the abduction issue.[45]

When Shinzo Abe, a prominent nationalist and advocate of a hard-line DPRK policy, became prime minister in September 2006, Chongryon's situation went from bad to critical. As the leading public figure in Japan calling for the resolution of the abduction issue, Abe left no doubt about his view of Chongryon. In June 2007 Prime Minister Abe alleged: "It is obvious that Chongryon's members were involved in the abduction and committed other crimes. The group is under surveillance."[46] This is not the first time that Abe accused Chongryon Koreans of nefarious activities. In 2005, while he was a top official in the LDP, Abe appeared on an NHK (Japan Broadcasting

Company) television news show and claimed that two prominent Chongryon Koreans were spies working for North Korea.[47]

It did not take long for Chongryon and Chongryon Koreans to develop a deep-seated disdain for the Abe government, which they saw as the most repressive since after the Second World War. Outside of Japan, some likened the Abe government's horrendous treatment of Koreans in Japan to what occurred after the Great Kanto Earthquake in September 1923,[48] an analogy Chongryon also used in wake of Kim Jong Il's admission about the abductions.[49] Given the horrid meaning associated with the Great Kanto Earthquake for Koreans in Japan, the use of this analogy after September 2002 reflected the perception of those who strongly believed that the Japanese government, and especially the Abe administration, had become determined to employ a markedly more aggressive political campaign against Chongryon and Chongryon Koreans.

A historical digression will be helpful here. The Great Kanto Earthquake was a seismic catastrophe that devastated Tokyo, Yokohama and other nearby areas and caused the death of more than 130,000 people. Rumors spread shortly after the massive earthquake, which may have been as high as 8.4 on the Richter scale, that Koreans in Japan were exploiting the chaos. Some Japanese accused Koreans of adding to the quake's destructiveness and human devastation by setting fires and poisoning water. This resulted in a brutal retaliation by the Japanese – some who supposedly exclaimed, "Wipe out Koreans"[50] – and the killing of some 6,000 Koreans who had come to Japan because of the repressive policies associated with Tokyo's colonization of the Korean Peninsula.[51]

According to *The People's Korea*, an English-language online news page published in one of Chongryon's buildings in Tokyo, the Abe government began its assault on Chongryon Koreas at the end of 2006. In January 2007, the director of Japan's National Police Agency, which is under the auspices of the Cabinet Office, maintained that to facilitate an end to the abduction issue, his organization would do all that it could to "expose Koreans' criminal acts." Accordingly, Chongryon-related organizations were searched for suspected violations of pharmaceutical, tax and accounting laws, and many uninvited Japanese police showed up at a Korean primary school.[52] Among other things, as will be shown in more detail below, in April 2007, the Japanese police raided Chongryon's offices in Tokyo, including its headquarters, because of suspicions connected to the abduction issue.[53]

In March 2007, Chongryon appeared before the UN Human Rights Council in Geneva. Concerned about recent arrests, police raids and other discriminatory practices targeting Chongryon and Chongryon Koreans, a statement issued by a Chongryon chapter stressed the "unfair crackdown based on [the Japanese government's] hostile policy toward North Korea," which "violates the International Convention on the Elimination of All Forms of Racial Discrimination."[54]

By summer 2007, Chongyron had become incensed because Abe labeled it a criminal organization and because of the media's failure to scrutinize allegations and political discrimination directed at Chongryon Koreans.[55] Coming to the defense of its nationals living abroad, the DPRK stepped up its complaints of Japan, regularly maintaining that Tokyo was suppressing Chongryon and Chongryon Koreans.[56] After the six-party talks (between the United States, China, Japan, Russia and North and South Korea) were held in July 2007, Vice Foreign Minister Kim Kye-gwan made clear that Pyongyang was deeply troubled by Tokyo's current treatment of Chongryon. Kim stated in Beijing before returning to the North Korean capital that he had told Kenichiro Sasae, the Director General of the Asian and Oceanian Affairs Bureau in Japan's Ministry of Foreign Affairs, that additional pressure on Chongryon, which then was in the midst of having its headquarters confiscated by the Japanese government, will lead to "disaster, so be careful."[57] Increasingly angered by what it called Japan's "crackdown" of Chongryon and Chongryon Koreans throughout the country, Pyongyang maintained that Tokyo's behavior "is a grave provocation against the DPRK," and warned of "a more serious political crisis" than what already exists, including putting the six-party talks at risk.[58]

In July 2007, the DPRK attempted to convince the UN's General Committee that the General Assembly should officially deal with "contemporary forms of xenophobia" that Chongryon Koreas are experiencing in Japan. The DPRK's UN representative told the General Committee that for the last 12 months Tokyo was guilty of "inhumane acts" and that its discriminatory treatment of Chongryon Koreans had crossed into a "reckless and hideous phase" of human rights violations. Comparing the current treatment of Koreans in Japan to the Great Kanto Earthquake, the DPRK representative maintained that currently Chongryon Koreans have been facing a "terror-ridden atmosphere." In addition to the police raids and searches of schools, homes and offices belonging to Chongryon and Chongryon Koreans, the DPRK representative told the General Committee of "evil-minded" telephone calls and email messages to Chongryon Koreans, including threats, such as "We will strike you with Molotov cocktails," as well as, "We will kill you all, go back to Korea." Despite the deliberateness of the DPRK delegate, the General Committee, which also listened to the Japanese representative maintain that North Korea had provided "groundless allegations" against Japan, decided not to add Pyongyang's concerns about the treatment of Chongryon's Koreans to the agenda of the General Assembly. The General Committee agreed with the Japanese representative that the North Korean request did not meet the criterion that an issue must be "of an important and urgent character" before it can be placed on the UN General Assembly's agenda. The General Committee recommended that the DPRK take the matter to the UN General Assembly's Third Committee – the Social, Humanitarian and Cultural Committee.[59]

Pyongyang did just that. In October 2007, the DPRK representative argued before the Third Committee that Tokyo had cracked down on Chongryon Koreans and deployed "hundreds of heavily armed police and armoured vehicles on the General Association of Korean Residents in Japan." Defending Tokyo's actions, the Japanese representative stated that the DPRK's accusations "were groundless and unacceptable," maintaining that the actions his government had taken "had been within the law, and those who had engaged in criminal activities had to be duly punished." Displeased with these remarks, the DPRK representative stated: "the action taken against Koreans in Japan was premeditated, systematic and a political effort by Japanese authorities to stamp out a Korean organization and its activities." He further indicated that Japan has been completely ignoring the crimes that it had committed in the past. After reiterating that Japan had acted against Chongryon because crimes had been committed, the Japanese representative stated: "there was also a matter of money owed to the Government by the Korean organization." The Japanese representative also stated, "that human rights violations, such as the ongoing abduction issue, had not been solved" and pointed out that Pyongyang should not use the past to justify the DPRK's human rights abuses.[60]

For its part, Pyongyang's actions have not helped the political plight of Chongryon Koreans. The series of missile tests the DPRK conducted in July 2006 followed a few months later by its detonation of an underground nuclear device piled more unneeded problems on Chongryon's back and on those of Chongryon Koreans.

Other than empathetically insisting that it was not involved in any way with the missiles launched by the DPRK in 2006, Chongryon officially maintains that "we say nothing" else. However, some within Chongryon believe that Tokyo has purposefully overreacted to the nuclear test and most especially to the DPRK's missile launches. These Chongryon representatives stress that many other countries have tested missiles but Japan has only reacted excessively to those launched by the DPRK. For them, Japan has used the missile launches to justify its hostile policies toward the DPRK. Some Chongryon Koreans privately maintain that the Bush administration's threats to attack the DPRK justified Pyongyang's development of a nuclear deterrence.[61]

In the wake of the DPRK's first nuclear test, Chongryon's Director of International Affairs, So Chong-on commented: "The atmosphere in Japan is now the worse," while a statement issued by the association stressed: "Koreans who have nothing to do with the nuclear test have become the victim."[62] However, Chongryon's tacit endorsement of the DPRK's first nuclear test did not help matters. Published by Chongryon's newspaper *Choson Sinbo*, *The People's Korea* reprinted the official *Korean Central News Agency's* article stating that the DPRK's nuclear test contributed to the stability of the Korean Peninsula and to Northeast Asia.[63]

The missile and nuclear testing conducted by the DPRK in 2006 immediately and very decisively drew increased attention to the importance that Japanese nationalists had been placing on the abduction issue, and provided political fodder that helped further raise suspicions about Chongryon's activities. Given the lack of normal bilateral relations between Japan and the DPRK, Pyongyang, unlike Tokyo, continued to view Chongryon as serving an important purpose.[64] However, according to Chongryon, Pyongyang does not apprise it of DPRK political matters. For example, denying any connection whatsoever to the abduction issue, Chongryon stresses that it and Chongryon Koreans were just as shocked as the Japanese people to learn of Kim's admission that North Korean agents were responsible for the kidnappings.[65]

It has been stated that Pyongyang has never officially announced or attempted to explain Chongryon's connection to or exonerate it from the abduction issue.[66] Although one could question the veracity of Pyongyang's statements, it has indicated that Chongryon played no part in the abductions of Japanese nationals. Angered by the Abe administration's treatment of Chongryon and Chongryon Koreans, the *Korean Central News Agency* (KCNA) indicated in July 2007 that the Japanese prime minister's accusations pertaining to Chongryon's involvement in the kidnappings were irresponsible. Specifically, KCNA reported:

> Abe at a press conference called on June 12 [2007] blustered that "it was becoming evident that Chongryon was involved in abduction and other crimes" and "it became a target of investigation under the law on the prevention of subversive activities." These reckless remarks revealed the intention of the prime minister to build up public opinion for inciting enmity and national chauvinism towards Chongryon and the Koreans in Japan and spearhead the brutal political terrorism intended to stamp out Chongryon.[67]

Obstacles to the political assimilation of Chongryon Koreans

While *zainichi* Koreans have been categorically subjected to many forms of discrimination over the years in Japanese society, Chongryon Koreans have had to contend with the additional issue that Japan and the DPRK have retained the political animus stemming from the ideological divide created at the onset of the Cold War. For this reason, Chongryon maintains that it and its members have been the victims of political retribution by the Japanese government, a problem that has also been manifested in the everyday contacts Chongryon Koreans have had with some Japanese people.

Chongryon maintains that it currently has somewhere between 150,000 and 200,000 members and supporters in Japan. Chongryon stresses that not all of its supporters are members, since admission of membership can lead to problems for Chongryon Koreans.[68] Today's *zainichi* Koreans are increasingly third and fourth generation residents. Almost all *zainichi* Koreans make use of either Chongryon or Mindan at some point in their lives and many get involved with both organizations because of the support services they provide.[69] However, some *zainichi* prefer affiliating with Mindan, believing that, because of the discrimination leveled at Chongryon Koreans, they will encounter fewer problems and business impediments.

Although not recognized as meeting the educational standards established by the Japanese government, today there are between 10,000 and 15,000 Korean students in Chongryon schools. Some of these students come from families that support Mindan.[70] The lack of accreditation by the Japanese government of Chongryon schools portends potential employment problems for graduates.

Chongryon Koreans generally retain their *chōsen* identity, the term that pertains to the pre-1948 undivided Korea. For them, the Japanese government uses the designation *chōsen-seki*, while referring to those *zainichi* who have adopted a South Korean identity as *kankoku-seki*. *Chōsen-seki* often face discrimination in employment and housing.[71] *Chōsen-seki* also must contend with business-related problems in Japan.

Unlike Chongryon, Mindan has advocated voting rights for the *zainichi* Koreans. Beginning in 1994, Mindan began an assertive campaign to get local voting rights. In 1998, the Local Suffrage Investment Law for Permanent Foreign Residents was introduced to the Diet. Blocked by Japanese conservatives, this legislation has still not been enacted, though Mindan continues to push hard for its ratification by the Diet.[72] In contrast, although there is not unanimity within Chongryon on the matter of voting rights, most within the organization believe that there are too many other political, social and economic problems facing *zainichi* Koreans that must be resolved before mounting a campaign to acquire suffrage. Moreover, Chongryon stresses that because the *zainichi* Koreans and specifically Chongryon Koreans are minorities, finding a politician that would fairly represent them would be exceedingly difficult in Japan today.[73]

Regularly facing discrimination, something that is pervasively inherent in Japanese society and politics for Chongryon Koreans, today they must live with the reality that as permanent residents they are marginal people in a country that is not their true political home. While most Chongryon Koreans recognize that they will continue to live in Japan and not repatriate to the DPRK, they nonetheless identify North Korea as their real home.[74] Today, according to a Chongryon official, Chongryon Koreans see themselves as "foreigners in Japan."[75]

In jeopardy: Chongryon's headquarters

In 2003, Chongryon directly experienced the devastating consequences of nationalist politics in Japan. Because Japanese–North Korean relations had never been normalized, Chongryon had long been recognized as Pyongyang's *de facto* embassy in Japan. In 1972, Tokyo Metropolitan Governor Ryokichi Minobe formally exempted all Chongryon buildings under his jurisdiction from property taxes, a policy that eventually took hold in other areas of Japan. For several years after the nationalist Shintaro Ishihara was elected Tokyo Metropolitan Governor in 1999, Chongryon still held its tax-exempt status. However, this changed less than a year after Kim Jong Il owned up to the abductions in September 2002. In 2003, Ishihara's Tokyo Metropolitan

Government handed Chongryon a tax bill of ¥42 million (approximately $358,000). Taking the cue from Ishihara, soon other localities in Japan decided to revoke Chongryon's tax-exempt status. Because Chongryon was not able to pay its taxes, the Tokyo Metropolitan Government officially took control of three of its properties, including its ten-story headquarters in the Chiyoda Ward, until April 2007 when it paid its back taxes. Although a Chongryon-connected organization initiated legal proceedings in 2004, arguing that the levying of taxes on its properties, something that had not been done before, was "discriminatory treatment that has no legitimate reason," the Tokyo District Court disagreed. Ruling in July 2007, the court maintained that the Tokyo Metropolitan Government had the right to change Chongryon's tax status.[76]

Soon after the court's ruling, Pyongyang lashed out at the Abe government and at Ishihara. Pyongyang charged that the Tokyo District Court's ruling "was made against the background of a series of politically motivated repressive actions spearheaded by the Abe government." Pyongyang was especially critical of Governor Ishihara, maintaining that he "is showing extra zeal in this repressive campaign over the issue of the hall in collusion with the Abe group."[77]

By 2007, Chongryon was in a serious financial bind, but now its problems were much bigger than unpaid taxes. In November 2005, the Japanese government's Resolution and Collection Corporation (RCC) announced that it would be filing a suit demanding that Chongryon repay ¥62.7 billion (approximately $531 million) it had borrowed from North Korean-linked credit unions that went bankrupt beginning in the late 1990s.[78] Chongryon, which acknowledged its debt responsibility in the amount specified, maintains that initially it had good business negotiations with the RCC. However, says Chongryon, by late 2005 politics began to drive the RCC, which abruptly ended negotiations. RCC's announcement that it would be suing Chongryon came less than a month after Prime Minister Koizumi appointed Abe to the position of chief cabinet secretary. Once this occurred, Chongryon maintains, its relationship with the RCC changed from good to bad.[79]

Unable to raise the funds to pay off its loan-debt to the RCC, Chongryon reasoned in April 2007 that the sale of its headquarters would help resolve its financial problems. Although the pressures stemming from being in arrears with the Japanese government was bad enough, Chongryon had another serious issue to deal with. The Japanese police raid of three its offices in April 2007, and the home of a woman because of suspicions that information could be acquired relating to the abduction issue, "outraged" Chongryon. Insisting that the police raids were a "political crackdown" by Abe, who was then prime minister, and his government, Chongryon issued a statement that identified what it believed were Tokyo's motives. Chongryon's statement maintained: "The raids are an act of planned political oppression against Chongryon by Japanese authorities that try to use the abduction issue politically ahead of Prime Minister Abe's visit to the United States."[80]

Believing that the Abe government had targeted Chongryon,[81] the association's leadership thought that selling their headquarters was the best decision they could then make. It was at this time that Chongryon's problems became multifaceted, simultaneously becoming an intriguing story that involved a former Japanese spy, charges of fraud, arrests and re-arrests.

Shigetake Ogata, the erstwhile director of Japan's Public Security Intelligence Agency who used to be in charge of monitoring Chongryon's activities, struck a deal with Koken Tsuchiya, Chongryon's lawyer. Ogata, who then headed the investment firm Harvest, had arranged to buy Chongryon's headquarters. Brokered by former real estate executive Tadao Mitsui, the deal to sell Chongryon's headquarters was set for ¥3.5 billion (approximately $30.6 million). The deal permitted Chongryon to rent the building for ¥350 million (about $3 million) per year, with the option to reacquire the property five years later for ¥3.85 billion. In June 2007, Ogata indicated that time was running out to conclude the sale, since the Tokyo District Court would soon be making its decision on the RCC lawsuit. Ogata stressed that "Chongryon will be ousted from the head office if it loses the lawsuit and the court seizes the property to put up for auction later, and that would hamper its role of supporting Korean residents in Japan." Although on paper the property was transferred to Ogata's firm in late May, the transaction did not involve money. Ogata maintained that when news of the impending sale of Chongryon's headquarters hit the media, investors lost interest. In the meantime, the prosecutor's office in Tokyo had been looking askance at the deal. Believing that it was a fraudulent deal designed to keep Chongryon's headquarters from being seized by the RCC, in mid June Japanese authorities raided Ogata's home and office, as well as Tsuchiya's office. At about this time, Tsuchiya indicated that he had rescinded the property transaction.[82]

Because ownership of the headquarters passed from Ogata's Harvest back to Chongryon, Ishihara's Tokyo Metropolitan Government levied taxes on the property beginning in mid June. Unable to come up with the ¥75 million (approximately $654 thousand) in property taxes, the Tokyo Metropolitan Government took control (although just for awhile) of Chongryon's headquarters in August 2007.[83] However, the threat of its headquarters being confiscated by Japanese authorities is something that Chongryon had become used to. In June 2007, the Tokyo District Court ordered Chongryon to pay more than ¥62 billion to the RCC for past loans tied to the failed credit unions, a ruling that at the time appeared would soon permit the property to be confiscated and subject to public sale. Convinced that it could not win an appeal, Chongryon did not file for one. This, however, did not stop a Chongryon official from commenting: "We are angry. It's a politically motivated action designed to put down Chongryon."[84] As we will see below, a later ruling by the Tokyo District Court worked to Chongryon's advantage, at least temporarily.

At the end of June 2007, Ogata, Mitsui and former banker Koji Kawae were arrested for fraudulently attempting to take ownership of Chongryon's headquarters. Although the prosecutor's office had first believed that Chongryon had been involved in a scam with Ogata and his associates to save its headquarters, Japanese authorities later acknowledged that the association had done nothing wrong. Ogata and Mitsui were subsequently arrested a second time, this time for taking ¥480 million (about $4.1 million) from Chongryon in April for incidental costs related to the failed property sale. The prosecutor's office alleged that since Ogata and his associates knew they would not be able to come up with the money to complete the sale, they were conspiring to swindle Chongryon out of the ¥480 million. However, Chongryon saw this very differently, maintaining: "we have no perception that we have been cheated." In a written statement to the Tokyo District Public Prosecutor's Office, Tsuchiya, Chongryon's lawyer, indicated that the association would not be filing charges against Ogata. Indeed, Tsuchiya stressed: "From the beginning, Chongryon never said that it was deceived by Ogata."[85]

Although it is certainly possible that Ogata and his associates were trying to defraud Chongryon, how they were going to pull off taking possession of the association's headquarters without paying for it remains a mystery. Chongryon is confident that, despite Ogata's monitoring of the association in the past, he is a good person that arranged a deal with Tsuchiya that would have benefited the association. Chongryon believes that the Abe government wanted to make an example out of Ogata: anyone who tries to help Chongryon will face consequences similar to those that he has had to contend with.[86]

In June 2008, the Tokyo District Court gave Kawae a 24-month suspended sentence. A little over a year later, in July 2009, the Tokyo District Court gave Ogata and Mitsui 34-month and 36-month suspended sentences, respectively. Still maintaining his innocence, Ogata planned to appeal the sentence to the Tokyo High Court.[87]

Tokyo's aggressive handling of this issue is not consistent with the behavior of Japanese authorities, who have never attempted to help Chongryon in the past. Chongryon neither asked for nor appreciated this kind of assistance from the Japanese government. Although there remain a number of ambiguities and unanswered questions connected to this issue, it is clear that by Tokyo coming to Chongryon's defense and protecting it from the fraud allegedly perpetrated by Ogata and his associates, its headquarters were put in jeopardy.

Recently, Chongryon received what arguably amounts to a stay from the Japanese legal system. Following the Tokyo District Court's ruling in June 2007 that Chongryon had to repay the full amount of the ¥62 billion-plus loan that the RCC had assumed the responsibility to recoup, this public organization attempted to confiscate Chongryon's headquarters and its land. However, the RCC ran into an unexpected legal roadblock. Because Chongryon did not technically own the building – the real owner is *Chosen Chuokaikan Kanrikai* – RCC did not have the legal right to confiscate it. The RCC then sued, hoping to get the authorization to confiscate the headquarters and its land. In a separate action, the RCC sued to have the ownership of the property changed to Chongryon. In November 2008, the Tokyo District

Court ruled that the RCC could not take possession of Chongryon's head-quarters and property. The judge argued that confiscation of the headquarters and its land would be illegal, even if Chongryon were the owner, since this "is against the spirit of the property registration system, which precisely reflects property ownership and any changes." Happy with the outcome, a Chongryon representative stated: "The ruling is what we expected. The RCC's demand to seize properties from an entity with no debt to the RCC ignores reality and related laws." Displeased with the judge's decision, the RCC indicated that it would file an appeal. Apart from the possibility of an appeal being granted, Chongryon has more to worry about. The Tokyo District Court's future ruling on the RCC lawsuit, that is demanding the ownership of the head-quarters and its property be changed from *Chosen Chuokaikan Kanrikai* to Chongryon, could be problematic.[88]

New leaders, same policies and outcomes

After Shinzo Abe announced his resignation in September 2007, the possibi-lity arose that Japan's policies toward North Korea could change, especially with regard to the abduction issue that has created problems for Chongryon Koreans. However, Yasuo Fukuda's moderate government immediately put the spotlight on the abduction issue.

Continuing efforts begun during past administrations, newly appointed Minister for Foreign Affairs Masahiko Koumura told the UN General Assembly in September 2007: "It is essential that the international community send a strong message calling for the earliest resolution of the abduction issue." Although Koumura stressed that resolving the "unfortunate past" with respect to North Korea was also necessary, his concern was clearly on the abduction issue, which he emphasized remains "a serious challenge to human dignity."[89] Prime Minister Fukuda's first policy speech to the Diet in early October echoed his foreign minister's remarks. Calling the kidnappings a "ser-ious human rights issue," Fukuda told the Diet that his government would use "maximum efforts to realize the earliest return of all of the abductees," as well as resolve the past "and normalize relations with North Korea."[90] Fukuda, sounding much like his predecessor Abe, later told the abductees' families that if he could he would normalize relations with North Korea but that the resolution of the "abduction issue is the first step to that end."[91]

The determination of successive Japanese administrations to prioritize the kidnappings is perhaps best indicated by the retention of Kyoko Nakayama as a key strategist dealing with the abduction issue during the Koizumi, Abe and Fukuda administrations, as discussed in Chapter 4. Nakayama, a state-sperson known for her hard-line policy toward North Korea, supported the nationalist position: normalized relations with the DPRK will not occur until there is a resolution to the abduction issue that suits Japan.[92]

In April 2007, the Abe government extended for six months the sanctions it imposed on North Korea after Pyongyang detonated a nuclear device the previous October. These sanctions included prohibiting North Koreans from traveling to Japan and a ban on North Korean ships from entering the country, including the Mangyongbong-92. Pyongyang responded to the extension by maintaining that the Mangyongbong-92 had been permitted to enter Japan because of a previous agreement made between the DPRK and Japanese Red Cross agencies. It further stressed that, contrary to the charges made by Japanese reactionaries claiming that the vessel had been used to support illicit activities, such as the illegal transfer of money and spies, the ship had the purely "humanitarian purpose" of letting Chongryon Koreans visit their homeland. Tokyo, argued Pyongyang, had both a moral and legal responsibility to allow the Mangyongbong-92 passage to and from Japan.[93]

In September 2007, immediately after the conclusion of the second round of working group discussions between Japan and North Korea, which failed to make any headway on the abduction issue, the Abe cabinet again agreed to extend the sanctions imposed on the DPRK for an additional six months. Reacting to the plan to extend the sanctions, Nam Sung U, a top Chongryon official, stated: "It's unreasonable [for Tokyo] to have sanctions that violate the human rights [of North Korean nationals, i.e., *zainichi chōsenjin*] over only the one obstacle of the abduction issue."[94]

However, the official approval of extending these sanctions on North Korea did not come until Fukuda became prime minister. Just before cabinet approval, Fukuda's chief cabinet secretary Nobutaka Machimura announced that, because there has been no discernible progress made on the abduction issue: "We are not in a situation in which we can stop or ease the sanctions." Later, when Fukuda's cabinet officially approved the sanctions, Machimura stated that they "should be continued because there was no concrete progress on the abduction issue and also taking into consideration the situation regarding North Korea's nuclear program." However, the Fukuda administration, like the Abe government, had zeroed in on the abduction issue, since Pyongyang had announced a little before Machimura's comment that it would disable its nuclear facility at Yongbyon.[95]

Chongryon responded immediately to the Fukuda cabinet's authorization to extend the sanctions. Approximately 4,000 people, including Chongryon's chairman So Man Sul, gathered in Tokyo to protest the cabinet's decision to continue the sanctions on North Korea.[96] For its part, Pyongyang stressed that by extending the sanctions Tokyo is demonstrating that it is not interested in normalizing relations with the DPRK, and that it is attempting to prevent the six-party talks from bringing a peaceful resolution to the North Korea nuclear issue. Pyongyang also maintained that Tokyo's objective is to remilitarize Japan and ultimately to possess nuclear weapons, all of which shows that the Fukuda government "is trying to repeat what the preceding Cabinet did, crying over the abduction issue."[97]

Pyongyang had still another bone to pick with Tokyo pertaining to the continuation of the sanctions in October 2007. Having in the past lashed out against the NHK, Japan's public broadcasting organization, for disseminating government lies and propaganda, Pyongyang charged that the broadcaster was at it once again, this time relying on false reports from "riff-raffs, who deserted their homeland." Pyongyang charged that a NHK broadcast had falsely maintained that two North Korean vessels, the Mangyongbong-92 and the Samjiyon, had been used to support illicit activities. Based on information supplied by the defectors from the DPRK, the NHK broadcast claimed that *zainichi chōsenjin* had been both transporting funds to the DPRK, which Tokyo had clamped down on shortly after the North Korean nuclear issue emerged, and participating in other wrongful activities.[98] Criticizing Japan's determination to retain its policy on the abduction issue and its decision to continue "the embargo on DPRK-flagged ships," an obvious problem for Chongryon Koreans, Pyongyang maintained that the Fukuda government appears unable "to make a switchover in its foreign policy as it is under the strong pressure of ultra-right conservative forces at home."[99]

In November 2007, a number of Koreans met in Yamaguchi at a national meeting that dealt with Korean history in Japan and humans rights issues. Among the attendees was Ko Tok U, a top official in Chongryon. Part of the discussion at the meeting focused on Japan's failure to address its responsibilities for its past treatment of Koreans while continuing to violate the human rights of *zainichi* and to suppress Chongryon. At about this same time, a seminar in Tokyo focused on the Japanese government's repressive treatment of Chongryon and its disregard of the human rights of the *zainichi chōsenjin*.[100]

When Prime Minister Fukuda reshuffled his cabinet in August 2008, he promoted Nakayama to the position of Minister of State for Social Affairs and Gender Equality, Public Records Management and National Archives, the Abduction Issue.[101] Much to the chagrin of members of the abductees' families, who viewed Nakayama as a competent and staunch advocate of their cause, Taro Aso moved Nakayama back to her former post of Special Adviser to the Prime Minister for the Abduction Issue immediately after he became prime minister in September 2008. Not pleased with her removal from the ministerial position, members of the abductees' families worried that Aso would not be giving the abduction issue the attention that they believed it deserved. However, Chief Cabinet Secretary Takeo Kawamura, technically the Japanese government's point man on the abduction issue and who met with the abductees' family members during his second week in his new position, made clear that Nakayama would be playing an important role in the Aso government. During a September press conference Kawamura stated: "By having a special adviser, I think it will become clear how we are thinking about the [abduction] issue. I want to do my utmost to resolve this issue by closely cooperating with Ms. Nakayama."[102]

Given Prime Minister Aso's strong nationalist roots, it certainly came as no surprise to Chongryon and Chongryon Koreans that his government retained a strong commitment to the abduction issue. Moreover, the retention of the hard-line Kyoko Nakayama as special adviser to the prime minister, who angered Pyongyang in 2007 when she spoke out strongly against removing North Korea from the US terrorism list because she maintained that the kidnapping of Japanese nationals is state-sponsored terrorism,[103] meant that suspicions still ran high that Chongryon was somehow involved in the abductions. Under Aso's leadership, Pyongyang continued to complain about the Japanese government's suppression of Chongryon and Chongryon Koreans. Referring to the "Japanese reactionaries," Pyongyang charged in December 2008: "Their brutal crackdown upon Chongryon and the Koreans in Japan is something unprecedented since the end of the Second World War."[104]

In April 2009, Chongryon praised the DPRK's launch of the *Kwang-myŏngsŏng-2*, which Pyongyang had repeatedly stated was a communications satellite.[105] After the launch, far right-wing groups in Japan staged protests at Chongryon's headquarters in Tokyo for three days. From vans equipped with ear-piercing loudspeakers, protesters called out from morning to night, "Chongryon, disband itself" and "Koreans, get out of Japan." Other protesters displayed the placard that read: "Japan goes nuclear." Inside Chongryon's headquarters the staff received threatening telephone calls. Another group of protesters associated with Mindan also came to Chongryon's headquarters. Yelling "North Korea, dismantle nukes" and "North Korea, settle the issue of abduction," these protesters had with them what they said was a written statement singed by the president of Mindan protesting the DPRK launch. A number of vans with loudspeakers operated by individuals holding far right political positions went to the Chongryon building in Fukuoka Prefecture and blared pejorative remarks.[106]

Prior to the April launch, Mindan sent Chongryon a written appeal urging it to notify Pyongyang not to proceed with the launch. Chongryon denied Mindan's request, which stated: "Though we are the same race, it is absolutely impossible for us to understand [North Korea's position]. We've been angered [by its position]."[107]

The DPRK's second underground nuclear test in May 2009 did not help to improve relations between Chongryon and Mindan. At the same time, the DPRK's second nuclear test potentially exposed the Chongryon to the heightened wrath of far-right groups in Japan. This time, however, Japanese authorities were prepared to deal with the onslaught of protesters that would come to Chongryon's headquarters in Tokyo and its other buildings in Japan. Having had past experiences in dealing with protesters at Chongryon's properties, including the right-wing groups that showed up the association's headquarters when the DPRK conducted its first underground nuclear test in 2006,[108] the National Police Agency notified police departments throughout Japan warning them to be ready for protesters at Chongryon offices. Stationed at the headquarters of Chongryon in Tokyo were three anti-riot police vehicles; at the same time, vehicular restrictions at the building's entrance were being enforced. However, on the day the DPRK conducted its second nuclear test, the majority of Chongryon's staff did come to the headquarters. Because May 25, 2009, the day the DPRK performed its second nuclear test, marked the fifty-fourth anniversary of the founding of Chongryon, most of the staff did not report to work since they were commemorating the establishment of the association. As for word from Pyongyang, a Chongryon representative indicated that he had "not heard anything" from officials there.[109]

More than two months after the DPRK's second underground nuclear test a visible and very well-equipped police presence remained stationed at Chongryon's headquarters in Tokyo. When asked about this, a Chongryon official – intimating the dual purpose of the police presence – stated that they are always there "protecting and watching."[110]

However prepared the police were to protect Chongryon buildings, they were unable to afford this protection to one of its schools. In early December 2009, a number of members of *Zainichi Tokken o Yurusanai Shimin no Kai* (Citizen's Group against Privileges for *zainichi*), more commonly known as *Zaitokukai*, which is an ultra-right nationalist group, appeared at the front gate of a Chongryon primary school in Kyoto. Using a microphone and frightening the young children in the school with their derogatory comments, the *Zaitokukai* protestors blared out "you children of spies" and "bounce Korean schools out of Japan." The *Zaitokukai* protestors screamed that the school was "affiliated with Chongryon, which abducted the Japanese." The police eventually stopped the use of the microphone by the protesters; however, the authorities did not stop the protest, which had been precipitated by the school's use of a public area adjacent to it. Since the school did not have a field, it had been using the public space for sports and assembly activities. Strongly objecting to this, the *Zaitokukai* protesters stridently demanded that the school "go back to the paradise on earth, North Korea" and "go to the massive Kim Il Sung Square then put up the goal net and play football there."[111]

Pyongyang's second nuclear test also caused Tokyo to expand its sanctions regime. The expanded sanctions regime included a total ban on Japanese exports to the DPRK beginning in June 2009, something Chongryon maintains infringes upon the human rights of Chongryon Koreans. Chongryon responded to the export ban by calling it "The worse case of bullying Korean residents in Japan!" Chongryon notes that basic goods, such as soccer shoes, towels, food and medical books attempted to be mailed to the DPRK by elderly Korean women in their seventies and eighties living in Japan have been rejected at local post offices or later returned to them by the customs office. Moreover, because of the export ban, customs officials have returned newspapers, magazines and other printed material that some people in Japan have tried to mail to the DPRK. Strongly opposed to the strengthened sanctions regime, Chongryon stated: "No problem can be solved by pressure or sanctions. Let's call for Japan to turn away from its pressure-only policy to improve DPRK–Japan relations through dialogue!"[112]

The coming to power of the Democratic Party of Japan (DPJ) in 2009 showed that Prime Minister Yukio Hatoyama's new government had been strongly influenced by nationalist views – and thus public sentiment – on the kidnappings. In February 2010, discussions began in the Diet on a bill designed to waive tuition for students attending public high schools in Japan, something that, in its successful bid to wrest power from the LDP, the DPJ had promised before the August elections. Intended to encourage more young people to complete their high school education, the new bill also gives between ¥120,000 to ¥240,000 (approximately $1,285 to $2,570) per year for tuition subsidies to students attending private high schools and other institutions certified by the Japanese government. However, the Hatoyama government wanted to exclude giving the tuition funds to students attending Chongryon-affiliated high schools. Holding the same position as far right groups in Japan, Prime Minister Hatoyama's Minister of State for the Abduction Issue, Hiroshi Nakai, expressed his disapproval of providing funds to *chosen gakkou* (Chongryon-affiliated schools), stating: "This is about the people of a country that our government has imposed sanctions on due to the abductions." Attempting to justify his government's position, Prime Minister Hatoyama maintained: "The problem is how we should deal with the issue as we cannot examine the teaching content at these schools in the absence of diplomatic ties with North Korea. It is not related to the abduction issue."[113]

That the Minister of State for the Abduction Issue spearheaded the Hatoyama government's position says a lot about the connection between the kidnappings and the unwillingness to include pro-North Korean high schools, which are officially classified as vocational schools, in the tuition-waiver plan. Moreover, at a press conference in Tokyo in early March 2010, Chongryon Koreans pointed out that the Ministry of Education, Culture, Sports, Science and Technology had "made it clear that the plan would cover not only ordinary Japanese schools, but also vocational schools all over the country."[114] Thus, something had changed.

Less than two weeks after the press conference given by Chongyron Koreans, the Hatoyama government announced that it would not include *chosen gakkou* in the free-tuition plan. However, to allay criticisms on a very controversial matter – punishing Chongyron Korean high school students and their families – the Hatoyama government stated that an assessment committee within the Ministry of Education, which had not yet been formed, would make the final decision.[115]

No sooner had the Hatoyama government made this announcement than it changed its position somewhat. A report issued in mid March by the UN Committee on the Elimination of Racial Discrimination indicated its concern with discriminatory educational practices in Japan. Specifically, the Committee stressed its concern with respect to "the approach of some politicians suggesting the exclusion of North Korean schools from current proposals for legislative change in the State party to make high school education tuition free of charge in public and private high schools, technical colleges and various institutions with comparable high school curricula."[116] To offset the concern of the Committee on the Elimination of Racial Discrimination, and perhaps even the opposition coming from some political parties in Japan, including coalition parties (see Chapter 6), the Hatoyama government's new plan allowed for the eligibility of pro-Pyongyang high schools. However, to qualify for the tuition waiver each school would have to have its curriculum reviewed by the Ministry of Education's assessment body.[117]

Nonetheless, Minister of State for the Abduction Issue Nakai continued to make clear his strong opposition to provide tuition subsidies to students attending pro-Pyongyang high schools. Claiming that students attending pro-Pyongyang schools are brainwashed to accept North Korea's *juche* idea, Nakai told members of the abductees' families at the end of April 2010 that were the Japanese government to include *chosen gakkou* high schools in the tuition waiver program the money would be sent to Kim Jong Il.[118]

Conclusion

Today, the treatment of Chongryon Koreans and Chongryon is a consequence of Japan's imperial annexation of the Korean Peninsula. Similar to its predecessor organizations, Chongryon has had a bumpy political ride in Japan. The very poor relationship between Tokyo and Pyongyang, when combined with the longstanding mutual distrust between Japanese authorities and Chongryon, has helped to sustain a political environment that is not amenable to reconciling differences. This is especially true since September 2002, when Kim Jong Il told Prime Minister Koizumi that some rogue DPRK agents were responsible for abducting Japanese nationals decades ago. Pyongyang's *songun*-based decisions have exacerbated problems for Chongryon and Chongryon Koreans.

Tokyo still insists that Chongryon, which currently has about 10,000 employees, must be monitored to prevent North Korea from doing harm to Japan. Chongryon, just like any large organization, is likely to have had its share of individuals who have not followed society's laws. However, the question arises as to whether this justifies labeling Chongryon a miscreant association whose many thousands of members and supporters are malefactors always ready to break the law to help Pyongyang. Fueled by the unresolved abduction issue and the nonexistence of normal diplomatic relations between Japan and North Korea, Tokyo's politically driven suspicions of Chongryon, when combined with policies that have not markedly reduced the discriminatory treatment experienced by Chongryon Koreans, have created a confrontational environment that almost always pits government against Chongryon.

Notes

1 Yasunori Fukuoka, *Lives of Young Koreans in Japan*, trans. by Tom Gill (Melbourne: Trans Pacific Press, 2000), pp. 3–5, 11; Yasunori Fukuoka, "Koreans in Japan: Past and Present," *Saitama University Review*, vol. 31, no. 1, 1996; Sonia Ryang, *North Koreans in Japan: Language, Ideology, and Identity* (Boulder, CO: Westview Press, 1997), p. 6; Chunghee Sarah Soh, "The Korean 'Comfort Women' Tragedy

as Structural Violence," in *Rethinking Historical Injustice and Reconciliation in Northeast Asia: The Korean Experience*, eds. Gi-Wook Shin, Soon-Won Park, and Daqing Yang (New York: Routledge, 2007), pp. 17–35, esp. p. 24; George Hicks, *The Comfort Women: Japan's Brutal Regime of Enforced Prostitution in the Second World War* (New York: Norton & Company, 1994), pp. 108–09; Yoshimi Yoshiaki, *Comfort Women: Sexual Slavery in the Japanese Military During World War II*, trans. by Suzanne O'Brien (New York: Columbia University Press, 2000), esp. p. 91; Jin Saeng So, "The Self-Identities of *Zainichi* Koreans," The College of William & Mary, spring 2000, www.wm.edu/so/monitor/spring2000/paper1.htm (accessed on August 29, 2007).

2 Chikako Kashiwaaki, "The Politics of Legal Status: The Equation of Nationality with Ethnonational Identity," in *Koreans in Japan: Critical Voices from the Margin*, ed. Sonia Ryang (London: Routledge, 2000), pp. 13–31, esp. p. 26.

3 Ryang, *North Koreans in Japan*, p. 80; Tessa Morris-Suzuki, "Japan's Hidden Role in the 'Return' of Zainichi Koreans to North Korea," *ZNet*, February 7, 2005.

4 There are two English-language spellings of the General Association of Korean Residents in Japan: Chongryon and Chongryun. Throughout this work, the former spelling will be used, unless citing a source that uses that latter spelling.

5 "Facts About Chongryun," *The People's Korea*, August 6, 1997, www1.korea-np.co.jp/pk/003rd_issue/chongryun/contents.htm (accessed on April 7, 2011).

6 Author interview with Chongryon official, Tokyo, July 26, 2007; Ryang, *North Koreans in Japan*, pp. 79–82; *Community Democracy & Performance*, 1984, http://junana.com/CDP/corpus/QUOTES60.html (accessed August 17, 2007).

7 *Mindan News*, issue 2500, April 28, 2005, www.mindan.org/eng/newspaper/read_artcl.php?newsid=89 (accessed August 31, 2007).

8 Mindan, *History of Mindan*, www.mindan.org/eng/about/history.php (accessed September 2, 2007).

9 Author interview with Chongryon official, Tokyo, July 26, 2007; Ryang, *North Koreans in Japan*, pp. 89–90; "Formation of Chongryun," *The People's Korea*, 1997.

10 Author interview with Chongryon official, Tokyo, July 26, 2007; "Formation of Chongryun," *The People's Korea*, 1997.

11 Author interview with Chongryon official, Tokyo, July 26, 2007.

12 "Facts About Chongryun," *The People's Korea*, August 6, 1997, www1.korea-np.co.jp/pk/003rd_issue/chongryun/contents.htm (accessed on April 7, 2011).

13 Ministry of Foreign Affairs, *Fourth Periodic Report by the Government of Japan under Article 40 Paragraph 1(b) of the International Covenant on Civil and Political Rights*, Tokyo, 1996.

14 Fukuoka, *Lives of Young Koreans*, pp. 21–22.

15 Morris-Suzuki, "Japan's Hidden Role in the 'Return' of Zainichi Koreans to North Korea," *ZNet*, February 7, 2005; Tessa Morris-Suzuki, "The Forgotten Victims of the North Korean Crisis," *Policy Forum Online*, Nautilus Institute, March 13, 2007, www.nautilus.org/fora/security/07022MorrisSuzuki.html#sect2 (accessed on May 23, 2007); Tessa Morris-Suzuki, "The Forgotten Victims of the North Korean Crisis," *Japan Focus*, March 15, 2007, http://japnfocus.org/products/topdf/2382 (accessed on August 31, 2007); Mindan, "Struggle against 'Repatriation to the North,'" www.mindan.org/eng/about/history.phpon (accessed September 23, 2007).

16 John Lie, *Zainichi (Koreans in Japan): Diasporic Nationalism and Postcolonial Identity* (Berkeley: University of California Press, 2008), pp. 32–48.

17 Tessa Morris-Suzuki, *Exodus to North Korea: Shadows from Japan's Cold War* (Lanham, MD: Rowman & Littlefield, 2007), pp. 231–45.

18 Quoted in Morris-Suzuki, "The Forgotten Victims of the North Korean Crisis," *Policy Forum Online*, Nautilus Institute, March 13, 2007; Morris-Suzuki, "The Forgotten Victims of the North Korean Crisis," *Japan Focus*, March 15, 2007.

19 Office of the Historian, Bureau of Public Affairs, US Department of State, *Foreign Relations of the United States, 1964–1968, Volume XXIX, Part 2, Japan* (Washington, DC: United States Government Printing Office, 2006), p. 1; Anthony DiFilippo, *Cracks in the Alliance: Science, Technology and the Evolution of U.S.–Japan Relations* (Aldershot: Ashgate, 1997), pp. 212, 236.
20 "Facts About Chongryun," *The People's Korea*, 1997.
21 "Chongryun Eyes for Citizen-Centered Body – Paradigm Shift Urged," *The People's Korea*, 1999.
22 Gavan McCormack, "Difficult Neighbors: Japan and North Korea," in *Rethinking Historical Injustice and Reconciliation in Northeast Asia: The Korean Experience*, pp. 154–72, esp. p. 157.
23 Song Hesuk, "Target of Scapegoating: Why does Discrimination towards Koreans Persist in Japan?" The Association of Korean Human Rights in Japan, Tokyo, 2003.
24 Myonwoo Lee, "Japanese–North Korean Relations: Going in Circles," in *North Korea and Northeast Asia*, eds. Samuel Kim and Tai Hwan Lee (Lanham, MD: Rowman & Littlefield Publishers, 2002), pp. 91–92
25 "Gov't Defends Police Raid of Chongryun Head Office," *Kyodo News*, November 30, 2001; "Raid Exposes North Korean Support Network in Japan," *The New York Times*, December 1, 2001; "End to Japan's Political Suppression of Chongryon Demanded," *Korean Central News Agency*, December 12, 2001; "Japanese Authorities' Suppression of Chongryon under Fire," *Korean Central News Agency*, December 18, 2001; "Principles of Criminal Suits Denied," *The People's Korea*, October 15, 2005.
26 "Identity Crisis for Japan's Koreans," *BBC News*, World Edition, November 25, 2002.
27 Author interview with representatives from the Association of Korean Human Rights in Japan, Tokyo, July 24, 2007.
28 Quoted in Eric Johnston, "Pyongyang's Abductions Spell Fallout for Chongryun," *The Japan Times Online*, November 20, 2002.
29 Author interview with leaders of The Association of Korean Human Rights in Japan, Tokyo, July 24, 2007.
30 "Young 'Zainichi' Koreans Look Beyond Chongryon Ideology," *The Japan Times Online*, December 16, 2008.
31 The General Association of Korean Residents in Japan (Chongryon), *The Japanese Government's Human Rights Violation of Korean Residents in Japan*, Tokyo, March 1, 2008.
32 "Identity Crisis for Japan's Koreans," *BBC News*, World Edition, November 25, 2002.
33 Song, "Target of Scapegoating: Why does Discrimination towards Koreans Persist in Japan?" The Association of Korean Human Rights in Japan, Tokyo, 2003.
34 The General Association of Korean Residents in Japan (Chongryon), *The Japanese Government's Human Rights Violation of Korean Residents in Japan*, Tokyo, March 1, 2008.
35 "Chongryun Protests against Japanese Investigation Official's Remarks on Possible Application of Anti-Subversive Activities Law," *The People's Korea*, November 16, 2006.
36 Sonia Ryang, "The Tongue that Divided Life and Death: The 1923 Tokyo Earthquake and the Massacre of Koreans," *Japan Focus*, September 3, 2007.
37 "Koreans Demand Japan Apologize for 1923 Massacre of Korean," *The People's Korea*, September 13, 2003.
38 "Koreans in Japan Raise Voices against N. Korea-Targeted Bill to Bar Port Calls," *The People's Korea*, April 10, 2004.
39 "Japan's Ruling Party to Introduce Bill to Ban Entry of N. Korean Ships," *The People's Korea*, March 13, 2004.

40 Eric Johnston, "North's Sinister Acts Here May Find Warier Public in Nuke Test's Wake," *The Japan Times Online*, October 21, 2006; Eric Johnston, "The North Korea Abduction Issue and Its Effect on Japanese Domestic Politics," Japan Policy Research Institute, JPRI Working Paper No. 101, June 2004.

41 Bertil Lintner, "North Korea: It's Hard to Help Kim Jong Il," *Far Eastern Economic Review*, March 27, 2003.

42 Ministry of Foreign Affairs, *Japan-DPRK Pyongyang Declaration*, Pyongyang, September 17, 2002.

43 *Statement by the Delegation of the Democratic People's Republic*, UN Commission on Human Rights, Geneva, March 22, 2004, reproduced in "DPRK Urges Japan to Stop Racial Discrimination against Korean [*sic*]," *The People's Korea*, April 10, 2004.

44 "Chongryun Holds 20th Congress," *The People's Korea*, June 12, 2004.

45 "An Abnormal and Unfair Investigation," *The People's Korea*, October 10, 2005.

46 "Chongryun Never Gets Out from under a Cloud," *The Japan Times Online*, July 10, 2007.

47 "Chongryun Demands Abe Apologize for Labeling Officials Spies," *Kyodo News*, January 18, 2005.

48 "Abe Group's Suppression of Koreans in Japan Accused," *Korean Central News Agency*, July 28, 2007; "Japan's Evermore Pronounced Actions to Exterminate Other Nation Denounced," *Korean Central News Agency*, July 26, 2007; "More Rally Held to Denounce Japan's Outrage," *Korean Central News Agency*, July 13, 2007.

49 "Chongryun Appeals Against Harassment by Japanese," *The People's Korea*, October 25, 2003.

50 "Testimony by Survivor of Great Kanto Earthquake," *The People's Korea*, December 1, 1999.

51 Yoshiaki Ishiguro, "A Japanese National Crime: The Korean Massacre after the Kanto Earthquake of 1923," *Korea Journal*, vol. 38, no. 4, Winter 1998, pp. 331–54; Mai Denawa, "Behind the Accounts of the Great Kanto Earthquake of 1923," Dana and Vera Reynolds Collection, Brown University, Fall 2005, http://dl.lib. brown.edu/kanto/denewa.html (accessed August 31, 2007); Ryouko Hatari, Yuiko Imai and Ewa Wantanabe, "The Wild Rumor: Understanding the Anti-Korean Riots of 1923," *Compass Online*, 1996–97, www.tsujiru.net/compass/compass_1996/reg/hatari_imai_watanabe.htm (accessed August 31, 2007).

52 "Abe Gov't Strengthens Political Suppression of Koreans, Applies Laws Strictly only to Chongryun and Korean Residents," *The People Korea*, March 16, 2007, www.korea-np.co.jp/pk (accessed April 7, 2011); Legal Team for Undue Investigations against Chongryon and Koreans in Japan, Shigeru Tokoi (representative), "On Undue Compulsory Investigations against the General Association of Korean Residents in Japan (Chongryon) by the Japanese Government," unpublished paper, Tokyo, 2007.

53 "Japan Police Raid N. Korea-linked Group over Kidnap," *Reuters*, April 25, 2007.

54 "Chongryun to Tell U.N. about Japan Crackdown," *The Japan Times Online*, March 16, 2007.

55 "Abe's Remarks Assailed by Chongryon," *Korean Central News Agency*, June 27, 2007.

56 For example, see "DPRK Foreign Ministry Spokesman Blasts Anti-Chongryon Campaign in Japan," *Korean Central News Agency*, July 1, 2007.

57 "N. Korea Warns Japan for Resorting Only to Pressure," *Kyodo News*, July 21, 2007.

58 "DPRK Government Will Strive for Peace," *Korean Central News Agency*, August 5, 2005; "N. Korea Warns Japan's Anti-Chongryun Moves May Stall 6-Way Talks," *Kyodo News*, August 5, 2007.

59 United Nations, Department of Public Information, Sixty-First General Assembly, General Committee, *General Committee Recommends Against Inclusion of New Agenda Item on 'Contemporary Forms of Xenophobia,* New York, July 20, 2007.
60 United Nations, Department of Public Information, Sixty-Second General Assembly, Third Committee, *More Vital than Ever to Move Away from Selectivity and Partial Approaches to Human Rights Issues, Third Committee Told,* New York, October 31, 2007.
61 Author interviews with Chongryon representatives, Tokyo, July 26, 2007 and with representatives from the Association of Korean Human Rights in Japan, Tokyo, July 24, 2007.
62 "Nuke Test Sparks Backlash against North Korean Community in Japan," *Mainichi Daily News,* October 25, 2006.
63 See "DPRK Successfully Conducts Underground Nuclear Test," *The People's Korea,* October 9, 2006.
64 "Japan's Suppression of Chongryon under Fire," *Korean Central News Agency,* August 7, 2007.
65 Author interview with a Chongryon official, Tokyo, July 26, 2007.
66 Sonia Ryang, "Visible and Vulnerable: The Predicament of Koreans in Japan," in *Diaspora without Homeland: Being Korean in Japan,* eds. Sonia Ryang and John Lie (Berkeley: University of California Press, 2009), pp. 62–63.
67 "KCNA Blasts Japan's Suppression of Chongryon," *Korean Central News Agency,* July 10, 2007.
68 Author interview with Chongryon official, Tokyo, July 26, 2007.
69 So, "The Self-Identities of *Zainichi* Koreans."
70 Author interview with representatives from the Association of Korean Human Rights in Japan, Tokyo, July 24, 2007; "Young 'Zainichi' Koreans Look Beyond Chongryon Ideology," *The Japan Times Online,* December 16, 2008.
71 See U-ja Yang, "Highlighting Multiple Discrimination: Survey Report by *Zainichi* Korean Women on Ourselves," *Voices from Japan,* no. 18, Winter 2007, pp. 41–44; Jong-In Kim, "In the Course of Mounting Tension between North Korea and Japan: Difficulties for *Zainichi* Korean Women to Live in Japan," *Voices from Japan,* no. 18, Winter 2007, pp. 44–46.
72 Mindan, "Demanding the Rights as Local Citizens," www.mindan.org/eng/major/reference.php (accessed September 23, 2007).
73 Author interview with Chongryon official, Tokyo, July 26, 2007.
74 Sonia Ryang, "The North Korean Homeland of Koreans in Japan," in *Koreans in Japan: Critical Voices from the Margin,* ed. Sonia Ryang, pp. 32–54.
75 Author interview with Chongryon official, Tokyo, July 26, 2007.
76 "Court Rules Chongryun Property not Tax-Exempt," *The Japan Times Online,* July 21, 2007; "Putting Chongryon under the Microscope," *Daily Yomiuri Online,* July 5, 2007.
77 "Tokyo's District Court's Unjust Decision Protested," *Korean Central News Agency,* July 20, 2007.
78 "RCC to Sue Chongryun for 62.8 Billion Yen," *The Japan Times Online,* November 23, 2005.
79 Author interview with Chongryon representative, Tokyo, July 23, 2007.
80 "Japan's Raid on Pro-Pyongyang Group," *BBC News,* April 25, 2007; "Japan Police Raid N. Korea-Linked Group over Kidnap," *Reuters,* April 25, 2007.
81 Anthony DiFilippo, "Targeting Chongryun?" *Policy Forum Online,* Nautilus Institute, October 11, 2007, www.nautilus.org/fora/security/07076DiFilippo.html (accessed on October 11, 2007).
82 "Chongryun Tokyo HQ Sale Seems Set to Fail," *The Japan Times Online,* June 14, 2007; "HQ Sale Broke No Laws, Chongryun Lawyer Says," *The Japan Times Online,* June 15, 2007; "Chongryun's No. 2 Man Quizzed about HQ Deal," *The*

Japan Times Online, June 22, 2007; "Chongryon Deal 'Hinged on 700 Mil. Yen Premium,'" *Daily Yomiuri Online*, July 1, 2007.

83 "Chongryon HQ Seized over Tax Arrears," *The Japan Times Online*, August 11, 2007.

84 "Chongryun HQ Effectively Seized to Pay Off RCC," *The Japan Times Online*, June 27, 2007.

85 "Ex-Security Chief Held in Deal with Chongryon," *Asahi Shimbun*, June 29, 2007; "Ex-Intelligence Chief Rearrested for Fraud," *Asahi Shimbun*, July 19, 2007; "Editorial: Chongryon Scandal," *Asahi Shimbun*, July 20, 2007; "Chongryon won't File Complaint against Ogata," *Daily Yomiuri Online*, July 16, 2007.

86 Author interview with Chongryon representative, Tokyo, July 26, 2007.

87 "Chongryon Swindler Gets Suspended Term," *The Japan Times Online*, July 17, 2009.

88 "Court Dismisses RCC's Attempt to Seize Chongryon Properties," *Daily Yomiuri Online*, November 19, 2008; "Registration Spotlighted," *Daily Yomiuri Online*, November 19, 2008.

89 Ministry of Foreign Affairs, *Address by H.E. Mr. Masahiko Koumura Minster for Foreign Affairs of Japan at the 62nd Session of the General Assembly of the United Nations*, New York, September 28, 2007; "No New North Korea Policy, Komura Tells U.N. Assembly," *The Japan Times Online*, September 30, 2007.

90 Speeches and Statements by Prime Minister, *Policy Speech by Prime Minister Yasuo Fukuda to the 168th Session of the Diet*, Tokyo, October 1, 2007.

91 "Fukuda to Tackle Abductions as 1st Step to Restoring N. Korea Ties," *Kyodo News*, October 27, 2007.

92 Government of Japan, Headquarters for the Abduction Issue, *The Abduction of Japanese Citizens by North Korea*, Tokyo, April 1, 2008, www.kantei.go.jp/foreign/abduction/efforts.html#negotiations (accessed March 30, 2011).

93 "It is Legal and Moral Obligation of Japan to Protect Rights of Korean," *Korean Central News Agency*, June 6, 2007.

94 "Govt to Extend N. Korea Sanctions," *Daily Yomiuri Online*, September 8, 2007.

95 "Sanctions on North Korea to be Extended Six Months," *The Japan Times Online*, October 1, 2007; "Cabinet Oks North Korea Sanctions Extension," *The Japan Times Online*, October 10, 2007.

96 "Chongryon Stages Rally, Protests Japan's Sanctions against N. Korea," *Kyodo News*, October 10, 2007.

97 "Japan's Extension of Sanctions against DPRK Flailed," *Korean Central News Agency*, October 24, 2007.

98 "North Korea: It's Hard to Help Kim Jong Il," *Asia Pacific Media Services Limited*, March 27, 2003; "KCNA Discloses Sordid Nature of Japan's NHK," *Korean Central News Agency*, October 20, 2007.

99 "KCNA Urges Japan to Make Political Decision," *Korean Central News Agency*, November 10, 2007.

100 "Meeting for Koreans' Human Rights Held," *Korean Central News Agency*, November 9, 2007; Chongryon, "Koreans in Japan's History, Human Rights Week," November 12, 2007, accessed on Chongryon's website at www.chongryon.com, translated from Korean by Google; "Japanese Authorities' Suppression of Chongryon under Fire," *Korean Central News Agency*, November 15, 2007.

101 "Fukuda Overhauls Cabinet – LDP Executive Shakeup Also Elevates Aso to Party No. 2," *Daily Yomiuri Online*, August 2, 2008.

102 "Nakayama to be Reappointed Special Gov't Adviser on Abduction Issue," *Kyodo News*, September 25, 2008; "Kyoko Nakayama Appointed as Special Gov't Adviser on Abduction Issue," *Kyodo News*, September 29, 2008.

103 "KCNA Urges Japan to Swim with Trend of Times," *Korean Central News Agency*, November 6, 2007.

104 "Japanese Reactionaries Urged to Drop Their Hostile Policy Toward DPRK," *Korean Central News Agency*, December 9, 2008.

105 "DPRK's Satellite Launch Hailed by Chongryon," *Korean Central News Agency*, April 12, 2009.
106 "Japanese Reactionaries' Desperate Moves Against DPRK and Chongryon Flayed," *Korean Central News Agency*, April 11, 2009.
107 "Resident Korean Groups Disagree," *Daily Yomiuri Online*, April 4, 2009.
108 "Nuke Test Draws Protesters to Chongryon Office," *The Japan Times Online*, October 2006.
109 "Japan Raps N. Korea's Nuke Test, Requests UNSC Meeting," *Kyodo News*, May 25, 2009.
110 Author meeting with the director of Chongryon's International Affairs and Reunification Bureau, Tokyo, July 31, 2009.
111 See http://nobasestorieskorea.blogspot.com/2009/12/text-fwd-korean-father-residing-in.html (accessed March 30, 2011); a video of the *Zaitokukai* protest can be viewed at http://d.hatena.ne.jp/video/youtube/2szx-WWR0rw (accessed March 30, 2011).
112 The General Association of Korean Residents in Japan (Chongryon), *Let's Say No to the Infringement of Human Rights by Japanese Authorities! Facts About Unjustified Regulation Force under the Total Ban on Exports*, Tokyo, n.d.
113 "Hatoyama Denies Abduction Link to Excluding Pro-Pyongyang Schools," *Kyodo News*, February 25, 2010; "Pro-Pyongyang Korean Schools Unlikely to be Tuition-free: Hatoyama," *Kyodo News*, February 25, 2010; "Kids in Pro-North High Schools Fret Tuition Waiver Snub," *The Japan Times Online*, March 10, 2010.
114 *'Tuition-free Plan' and North Korea-affiliated High Schools*, Press Conference, The Foreign Correspondents Club of Japan, Tokyo, March 3, 2010.
115 "North Korean Schools to be Excluded from New Free Tuition System," *Mainichi Daily News*, March 13, 2010.
116 Committee on the Elimination of Racial Discrimination, Seventy-sixth Session, *Concluding Observations of the Committee on the Elimination of Racial Discrimination: Japan*, Geneva, March 16, 2010, www2.ohchr.org/english/bodies/cerd (accessed March 30, 2011).
117 "North Schools to Get Tuition Break," *The Japan Times Online*, March 30, 2010.
118 "At North-linked Schools, Kids get Brainwashed, Nakai Asserts," *The Japan Times Online*, April 27, 2010.

6 Politics, partisanship, and the stalemate in Japan–North Korea relations

Since the end of the Cold War, Japan and North Korea have made sporadic attempts, all to no avail, to establish normal bilateral relations. In recent years, some of the disagreements between Japan and North Korea have been identified as multilateral problems, making the prospect of rapprochement even more difficult. This chapter examines the circumstances, political and partisan, related to the failure of Japan and North Korea to improve bilateral diplomatic relations.

Rock bottom: Japan–North Korea relations

While Pyongyang insists that Japan must make reparations for its past imperialistic exploits, Tokyo maintains that the major problem preventing normalized relations with the DPRK is the abduction issue. This problem, quite often says the Japanese government, is its priority.[1] The failure of Japanese politicians and policymakers to embrace the abduction issue would resonate poorly with the electorate. Now fully embedded in Japanese culture, the abduction issue can be understood as a national victimization mentality.

Despite some – particularly past – interest in Tokyo and Pyongyang for Japan and North Korea to establish normal bilateral ties,[2] Japanese–North Korean relations are currently at a nadir. Since February 2006, when normalization talks between Japan and the DPRK failed, political relations between Tokyo and Pyongyang have been characterized by progressive paralysis. During the six-party talks between the United States, China, Russia, Japan and North and South Korea held in December 2006, officials from Japan and the DPRK had no bilateral contact. Tokyo and Pyongyang had therefore ignored their commitments to the 2005 Joint Statement of the six-party talks and to the Pyongyang Declaration to normalize relations.

Bilateral discussions between Tokyo and Pyongyang held in June and August 2008 briefly produced a glimmer of optimism – but ultimately did not improve bilateral relations. Most promising was the August meeting held in Shenyang, China, which included specific promises: from the DPRK, to begin another reinvestigation of the abduction issue and from Tokyo, as a first step, to undertake a partial lifting of sanctions that Japan had imposed on the

DPRK in the wake of its missile and nuclear testing in 2006. When Prime Minister Yasuo Fukuda resigned in September 2008, Pyongyang maintained that it immediately notified Tokyo that its position with regard to the August agreement, which laid the groundwork for rapprochement, was "invariable" but that it wanted to wait "to see the attitude of the new prime minister."[3] Following his overwhelming election as president of the ruling Liberal Democratic Party (LDP), the nationalist Taro Aso became prime minister of Japan on September 24, 2008. Five days later, Aso's new government announced that it planned to extend by an additional six months the sanctions that previously had been imposed on the DPRK. Although newly appointed Foreign Minister Hirofumi Nakasone maintained that Tokyo would stand behind its part of the bargain and partially lift sanctions on the DPRK once a new reinvestigation was underway,[4] Pyongyang interpreted this as a continuation of Tokyo's hostile policy evident, not so much in Fukuda's government but rather most especially in that of his predecessor, nationalist Shinzo Abe. Pyongyang maintained that Tokyo has consistently failed to work with the DPRK to resolve the abduction issue. Citing two examples, Pyongyang indicated that Tokyo refused to send the abductees that were permitted to visit Japan back to the DPRK as it said it would and, rather than partially lifting sanctions, it extended them.[5]

Problems in Japan–North Korean relations

It is far too easy to conclude that North Korea, which has often been characterized by the right as an irredeemably roguish state,[6] has been the sole cause of the recent upsurge in tensions between Tokyo and Pyongyang. Tokyo also has added to the extant problems between Japan and the DPRK.

Pyongyang's behavior and core issues relating to North Korea

A significant amount of international attention has been given to Pyongyang's decisions to conduct missile and nuclear tests, frequently said to have taken place in defiance of international norms. Indeed, even before the DPRK conducted its first nuclear test in 2006, there were scholarly projections attempting to identify the harmful economic consequences that such a "provocative" act would have on the Northeast Asian region.[7] By launching missiles, which entailed brushing aside its commitment to the Pyongyang Declaration not to engage in this activity, by withdrawing from the Nuclear Nonproliferation Treaty and by conducting nuclear tests, Pyongyang has contributed to the chorus of those predisposed to label the DPRK a rogue state.

Thus, it did not come as too much of a surprise that the international community, pushed along by unmitigated determination coming from Washington and Tokyo, quickly responded with condemnation to the DPRK's missile and nuclear testing in 2006[8] and to its subsequent activities in these areas.

Pyongyang's continuing efforts to develop *songun* corresponds with the Japanese public's perceived threat from North Korea. Japan's Cabinet Office survey conducted in October 2002 showed that about 49 percent of the respondents worried about the DPRK's efforts to build nuclear weapons, and that approximately 43 percent had concerns about its development of missiles. By 2004, these percentages had risen to about 56 percent for each issue. Missile and nuclear testing by the DPRK in 2006 made a bad situation even worse. In the fall of 2006, almost 80 percent of the respondents to the Cabinet Office survey indicated that they were concerned about the DPRK's nuclear program and approximately 72 percent said the same about its missiles.[9] Still at very high levels, the 2007 Cabinet Office's survey showed that Japanese concerned about DPRK missiles had fallen to 58 percent from the previous year, while those worrying about the North Korean nuclear issue had declined slightly to 75.1 percent.[10]

The unresolved abduction issue with North Korea, as surveys by Japan's Cabinet Office have shown for several years, has remained the single most important policy concern of the Japanese people – thus the now unwavering political attention to this issue in Japan. In 2000, two years before the nuclear crisis emerged in October 2002, more than two-thirds of the respondents in a survey conducted by the Japanese government's Cabinet Office said that they were concerned about the abduction issue. In 2006, almost 87 percent of the respondents in the Cabinet Office survey expressed concern about the abduction issue. By 2007, those concerned with the abduction issue, still noticeably more than worried about the nuclear and missile problems, increased to nearly 89 percent – a *cause celebre* for Japan's nationalists.

From Tokyo's perspective, Pyongyang's explanation of its abduction of Japanese citizens has been unsatisfactory. Although Pyongyang gave Tokyo the trial records from 1998 and 1999 of two DPRK agents responsible for the abductions, the Japanese government does not accept the DPRK's claim that the culpable individuals have been punished and has demanded their extradition to Japan.[11] Pyongyang maintains two of the agents that perpetrated the abductions have been "treated by law, they were executed."[12] This, however, has not satisfied Tokyo; Japan simply doubts Pyongyang's veracity and refuses to accept the DPRK's repeated claim that the abduction issue has been settled.

In April 2005, Tokyo added the sixteenth abduction victim to its list and another in November 2006, bringing the total to 17.[13] Pyongyang responded that the DPRK agent who Tokyo identified as the abductor does not exist and that Kyoko Matsumoto, the alleged abductee, "has not entered our country."[14]

Pyongyang has claimed responsibility for abducting 13 Japanese citizens. Of these, Pyongyang has returned five to Japan and, it says, eight abductees have died. Pyongyang maintains that the remaining four persons Tokyo says were abducted were never in the DPRK.[15] Song Il Ho, the official in the North Korean Ministry of Foreign Affairs who has been responsible for dealing with Japanese relations, has indicated that Pyongyang has already conducted "several investigations." Making the point that what Tokyo wants, to resolve the abduction issue, is just not possible, Song stated, "Japan's demand is that the DPRK should revive the dead and return them."[16]

Members of the abductees' families believe that the kidnapping victims that Pyongyang has said have died are still alive in North Korea. Tokyo also believes this. A top official in the Japanese government's Headquarters for the Abduction Issue said, "We want to believe they are alive," adding that there is "no conclusive evidence to prove they are dead."[17] Tokyo has rejected the documentation that North Korea sent to Japan about the abductees and contends that Pyongyang's "explanations are unnatural and ambiguous." Tokyo also maintains that the physical remains of Megumi Yokota and Kaoru Matsuki that it received from the DPRK "belong to other individuals,"[18] to which Pyongyang responded by stating that the Japanese government, succumbing to "ultra-right forces," has rejected the "sincere attitude towards its dialogue partner for its political plots and hostile acts against the DPRK."[19]

In December 2004, Tokyo announced that the cremated remains North Korea had sent to Japan did not belong to Megumi Yokota. The Japanese government made this announcement based on the DNA analysis conducted by Tomio Yoshii, a junior-level geneticist then at Teikyo University in Tokyo. Yoshii had no prior experience working with cremated remains and acknowledged that the testing method he used was not conclusive. Creating concern among some observers was that Japan's National Research Institute of Police Science, unlike Yoshii, was not able to perform DNA analysis on Megumi's ashes. Creating more controversy was that not too long after the Japanese government's announcement, Yoshii stated in an interview with *Nature*, the British weekly international science journal, that the results of his DNA analysis could have been contaminated. Calling Pyongyang's treatment of the matter "deplorable, the Japanese Ministry of Foreign Affairs said that previously the DPRK had sent the remains of a kidnapping victim to Japan and then subsequently revealed that the specimens had come from an individual other than the person it had originally indicated."[20] Moreover, Tokyo maintains that Yoshii had been "misquoted" in the interview with *Nature*.[21]

In June 2006, during an interview in North Korea with Kim Young-nam, a South Korean who freely took up residence in the DPRK and who later married and fathered a daughter, Eun-gyeong, with Megumi, stated that his wife had long been afflicted by depression and that she had committed suicide in 1994. Kim acknowledged during the interview that in 2004 North Korea had given a visiting Japanese mission Megumi's cremated remains. Kim, who Tokyo announced after conducting DNA analysis as the likely father of Eun-gyeong and Yokota's husband,[22] called the Japanese accusations that Megumi was still alive and that the ashes were not hers "insulting" and a "human rights abuse," adding "why would we claim the living as dead."[23]

The Japanese government believes that Pyongyang needs to do considerably more to resolve the abduction issue. Tokyo maintains, "if North Korea is serious, it can make quick progress."[24]

Japan's actions

Pyongyang continues to stress the atrocities committed by Japanese military forces when they occupied Korea for decades, and Japan's failure to compensate the DPRK for its many past crimes.[25] On many occasions, Pyongyang has also expressed opposition to what it perceives as Tokyo's toughed DPRK policy, and articulated concerns about Japan's continuing efforts to increase its military responsibilities and capabilities. Like Beijing and even Seoul, Pyongyang thus worries about Japanese remilitarization. Connected to this, as discussed in Chapter 3, is that Pyongyang has constantly emphasized the security threat it believes the DPRK faces from the strengthening US–Japan military alliance.[26]

Because Japan has not settled the history problem with the DPRK, Pyongyang has frequently referred to Japan as a "criminal state." In 2007, when Abe was trying hard to promote legislation that would change Japan's pacifist constitution, Pyongyang linked its designation of Japan as a "criminal state" to the current aggressive military objectives of Washington and Japanese reactionaries.[27] Since Abe resigned from the prime minister's position in September 2007, the revisionist push to rewrite Article 9, the war-renouncing constitutional clause, has subsided. However, Japanese nationalists and their conservative sympathizers still want to revise the constitution,[28] especially Article 9.

Pyongyang has also tied its designation of Japan as a "criminal state" to Tokyo's aggressive efforts in the United Nations to call attention to alleged and arguably politically motivated charges of human rights abuses in the DPRK,[29] which for the Japanese government includes the abduction issue.[30] In the past, Tokyo has drafted and sponsored a resolution annually submitted to the Third Committee of the United Nations General Assembly.[31] In November 2008, Pyongyang called Tokyo's decision to sponsor the resolution on human rights in the DPRK, which the General Assembly passed by a vote of 95 to 24, with 62 abstentions and 11 countries not voting, a "disgraceful act." Pyongyang maintained that the resolution "was the culmination of politicization and double standards," maintaining that Japan "was a criminal state" that "almost daily" violated the rights of Koreans and the General Association of Korean Residents in Japan (Chongryon).[32] After adding the countries that voted no to the General Assembly's resolution to those that abstained and to those that did not vote, Pyongyang reasoned that this explains why nations saw it as "fabricated by Japan and the EU [European Union]." Pyongyang charged that the resolution had been "Peppered with lies and fabrications," and that it had been propelled by "a political motive to tarnish the image of the DPRK in the international arena."[33]

Once again in 2009, Japan was one of the main sponsors of the UN Third Committee's draft resolution on human rights in North Korea. Pyongyang responded to the draft resolution much like it had in the past. Pyongyang said that the 2009 resolution was a "political plot hatched by hostile forces" that, with the US playing a main role, "instigated the EU, Japan and its other followers to fake up again a brigandish document defiling the system in the DPRK and infringing upon its sovereignty on the basis of all sorts of lies and fabrications."[34]

In New York, the DPRK's representative to the United Nations called the 2009 draft resolution a "political conspiracy" led by the United States. He stressed that the European Union "had devised an anti-Democratic People's Republic of Korea resolution with Japan – the criminal State [–] against humanity." The DPRK representative argued that this resolution had been annually presented since 2003 when Washington became embroiled with his country over the nuclear issue. Calling the draft resolution "the height of hypocrisy and arrogance," the DPRK representative stressed that the human rights record of the United States includes killing civilians, an apparent reference to US wars in Iraq and Afghanistan, while Japan was responsible for "crimes against humanity." The Japanese representative to the United Nations told the Third Committee that the draft resolution needed to be adopted, which it was, for the benefit of the people in the DPRK, including Japanese citizens who had been abducted there.[35]

In September 2006, Pyongyang made clear its strong disapproval of Japan's elevation of the Defense Agency to a ministry, which had been spearheaded by the LDP and supported by the New Komeito Party, the junior member in the ruling coalition, and eventually by the country's then largest opposition party, the Democratic Party of Japan (DPJ). Reacting to Tokyo's efforts to upgrade the Defense Agency to a ministry, Pyongyang maintained that this has been part of the "plan to turn Japan into a military power," something that is especially threatening to the DPRK, since the "Japanese reactionaries designated the Korean Peninsula as their primary target of overseas aggression."[36]

Neither the Japanese Communist Party (JCP) nor the Social Democratic Party (SDP), both small opposition parties, supported what proved to be a successful LDP push to have Japan's Defense Agency elevated to a ministry.[37] Similar to Pyongyang, the JCP charged, "The upgrading of the DA [Defense Agency] to a ministry has nothing to do with Japan's self-defense but is a step to allow Japan to wage wars abroad together with U.S. forces." Concerned that the Japanese government was undermining the nation's pacifist principles, JCP's chairman, Kazuo Shii, stated: "This bill goes against the Constitution by remaking the SDF [Self Defense Forces] into forces to be dispatched abroad."[38]

Pyongyang maintained that militarists in Japan have a plan for a preemptive attack on the DPRK they want to implement. By adding this "is why the ruling quarters of the land of Japs upgraded the Defence Agency to a ministry before the abolition of the 'pacifist constitution' and, on this basis, are trying to put greater spurs to scrap it," Pyongyang also showed that during this period of very bad relations it is not reluctant to use an ethnic epithet.[39]

In June 2006, the Japanese government passed a law that affords it the legal right to impose financial sanctions on North Korea for human rights violations and for the past abduction of Japanese citizens if the DPRK fails to take steps to rectify these matters. The North Korean human rights law requires that the Japanese government take full responsibility for the resolution of the abduction issue and that it increase international awareness of this problem.[40]

While Tokyo insisted that Pyongyang had not done nearly enough to resolve the abduction issue, Seoul saw it differently. About a month before the enactment of the North Korean human rights law, South Korea's Unification Minister Lee Jong-seok stressed that Tokyo has "underestimated" Pyongyang's attempts to resolve the abduction issue.[41] Not long after the enactment of the law an official in South Korea's embassy in Tokyo stated that Japan is making "too much fuss over the abduction" issue.[42] Seoul's perspective was an interesting contrast to Japan's, that is, before the conservative Lee Myung-bak became prime minister in early 2008, given that it believes in the past the North abducted approximately 500 South Koreans.[43] Indeed, Seoul's reaction to the suspected kidnapping of South Koreans by the DPRK before Lee took office – to accept them, albeit reluctantly, as an unfortunate part of the past – contrasts sharply with Tokyo's, which has increasingly yielded to the get-tough approach long preferred by a few political groups in Japan and conservative politicians determined to promote Japanese nationalism.[44]

The passage of the North Korean human rights law in 2006 was a legislative compromise that resulted from a draft proposed by the DPJ, and another introduced by the two members of Japan's coalition government at that time, the LDP and New Komeito.[45] While the JCP and the SDP maintained that the abduction issue remains a major unresolved problem, they nonetheless opposed the North Korean human rights law in a special committee in the Diet's lower house. The JCP argued that human rights violations in the DPRK and the abduction issue are not the same, but that the new law treats them as if they are. The JCP also maintained that because the law supports individuals who defect from the DPRK, it is actually interfering in "the domestic affairs of North Korea," and that since the international community has not endorsed the bill it will ultimately impede the settlement of the abduction issue.[46]

The JCP was correct. Pyongyang viewed the passage of the North Korean human rights law, the third law directed at the DPRK, as a "serious political provocation" by Tokyo. Pyongyang maintained that the Japanese government's obsession with the already-resolved abduction issue demonstrates that it indiscreetly intends to push bilateral relations to their lowest point.[47]

As discussed in Chapter 3, Japan launched spy satellites not long after the DPRK performed missile and nuclear testing in 2006. Besides Tokyo's successful efforts to help get the United Nations Security Council (UNSC) to respond decisively and punitively to the DPRK's missile and nuclear tests in 2006, the Japanese government independently sanctioned North Korea. In June 2004, with support from the LDP, the New Komeito and the DPJ, the Japanese government enacted a law that allowed it to prohibit ships thought to be a security risk from entering Japanese ports.[48] As we saw in Chapter 3, because of the DPRK missile tests in July 2006, Tokyo immediately barred the North Korean vessel the Mangyongbong-92 from docking in Niigata's port for six months, and in September it placed financial sanctions on a number of companies and one individual thought to be associated with North Korea's missile or weapons of mass destruction programs. These financial sanctions had their legal basis in an amendment to the Foreign Exchange and Foreign Trade Control Law that the Diet approved in February 2004, and that had then been supported by the LDP, New Komeito, the DPJ, and also, to a limited extent, the SDP.

Japan's opposition parties issued statements expressing their strong opposition to Pyongyang's missile testing in July 2006. The DPJ recommended that the Japanese government "take prompt and decisive actions" against North Korea.[49] Urging Pyongyang not to launch missiles in late June and stressing that getting ready to do so is tantamount to "brinkmanship," the JCP called on Pyongyang immediately after it launched the missiles to "end such lawless acts."[50] The SDP expressed its agreement with the adoption of UNSC Resolution 1695, as did JCP.[51]

All of Japan's opposition political parties roundly condemned Pyongyang's 2006 nuclear test. The SDP immediately rebuked North Korea for conducting a nuclear test. Along with stressing that the DPRK nuclear test violated the Pyongyang Declaration, the SDP emphasized that it added to the instability of Northeast Asia,[52] just the opposite of the North Korean position. Viewing the DPRK nuclear test as a threat to Japan and to Northeast Asia, the DPJ praised the adoption of UNSC Resolution 1718. The DPJ additionally noted that it acted "in concert with the other political parties" in supporting a resolution, which both chambers of the Diet passed, that condemned the DPRK's nuclear test.[53] Stating that it "strongly protested against North Korea's nuclear test," the JCP also announced its support for the adoption of Security Council Resolution 1718.[54]

In 2004, Pyongyang strongly opposed the Diet's adoption of the amendment to the Foreign Exchange and Foreign Trade Control Law. Pyongyang called it "a wanton violation of international law and a serious infringement upon the sovereignty of the DPRK as it is aimed to strangle the DPRK economically and isolate and stifle it in line with the U.S. imperialists' hostile policy toward the DPRK." Pyongyang charged that the Japanese government pushed the amendment through the legislative process because it was attempting to curry favor with the public so that the approaching elections for seats in the House of Councillors would be favorable – that is, to the ruling coalition.[55] Expectedly, a little over two years later Pyongyang vehemently objected to the sanctions – stemming from newly enacted laws – Tokyo imposed on North Korea in the wake of the missile and nuclear tests in 2006.[56]

In late December 2006, Pyongyang maintained that the Japanese militarists undertook a very visible offensive during the year, offering a litany of "criminal acts" it deemed threatening to the DPRK, most especially its concern about Japan's increased involvement with the United States in a joint missile defense system.[57] In April 2009, about three days after the DPRK launched what it called a communications satellite that elicited a tough reaction from Tokyo and Washington in particular, Pyongyang maintained that Japan, "a war criminal state," had long been preparing to possess nuclear weapons and so talk on this subject was consistent with past and recent behavior. Somewhat colorfully, Pyongyang stressed: "Having technology and means necessary for manufacturing nuclear weapons, Japan can launch reinvasion any time aboard a nuclear war chariot."[58]

After the DPRK launch in April, both houses of the Japanese Diet passed a resolution condemning the North's decision. However, in the both the House of Representatives and the House of Councillors the JCP and the SDP did not endorse the resolution. While the JCP voted no to the resolution, the SDP abstained. Both parties maintained that there was no evidence showing the DPRK launch was a ballistic missile.[59]

Calling the DPRK launch "a clear violation of a resolution passed by the UN Security Council," the LDP maintained in its statement condemning Pyongyang's decision that this "cannot be tolerated," since it "threatens the peace and stability of Northeast Asia." The LDP also called on Tokyo to strengthen Japan's security capabilities, including the improvement of "the condition of its anti-ballistic missile system."[60] By contrast, the JCP pointed out that it "does not support the view that North Korea launched the rocket in violation of the relevant UNSC resolution and that North Korea should be sanctioned further even if it was aimed at putting a satellite into orbit. This view will be an obstacle to the diplomatic effort to force North Korea to give up its nuclear weapons programs."[61]

However, Pyongyang was not about to give up its nuclear weapons – not yet anyway. Immediately after Pyongyang's second nuclear test in May 2009, Prime Minister Aso stated his government's position, which was not too different from President Obama's.[62] Fully consistent with the LDP's statement,[63] Aso proclaimed that the DPRK's nuclear test "constitutes a grave threat to Japan's security as well as seriously undermines the peace and security of Northeast Asia and the international community."[64]

Again, the Japanese Diet passed resolutions. However, this time the resolutions passed by both houses of the Diet were unanimous. At first undecided about its position on the resolution before the House of Representatives, even the JCP went on to support it, as well as the subsequent resolution in the House of Councillors. The Diet's resolutions were paradoxical, since they ignored not only Japan's place under the US nuclear umbrella but somehow concluded, presumably by relying largely on the "speech" given by President Obama in Prague in April 2009, which included comments on the need to eliminate nuclear weapons,[65] that there is an international disarmament "movement" afoot. In other words, the Diet's resolutions speciously linked two very disparate things: words – which 17 months later rang hollow, especially to Japanese nuclear weapons abolitionists, when the United States conducted its twenty-fourth subcritical nuclear test in September 2010[66] – and actions. Similar to the resolution in the lower house, the House of Councillors' resolution stipulated "repeated nuclear tests [undertaken by the DPRK] are a grave challenge to the international nonproliferation regime" and for this reason "buck the increasing momentum toward the eradication of nuclear arms."[67]

Like Washington, Tokyo adopted a tough stand designed to punish the DPRK after its second nuclear test. Together, Washington and Tokyo spearheaded the drive to pass UNSC Resolution 1874, the international community's response to the DPRK's second nuclear test. Consistent with its efforts to become a normal country, the Aso cabinet also adopted new and tougher sanctions than those already in existence in the wake of the DPRK's second nuclear test.[68]

As discussed in Chapter 5, in its report issued in March 2010 the UN Committee on the Elimination of Racial Discrimination expressed concern about Tokyo's plan to exclude students attending pro-North Korean high schools in Japan from getting tuition waivers, thereby playing some part in getting the Hatoyama government to alter its position somewhat. In addition to Chongryon's vehement disapproval of the government's plan, there was also opposition from some Japanese political parties – the Hatoyama government's junior coalition party members. A recent spin-off of the LDP, the People's New Party and the SDP, which together with the ruling DPJ made up the Hatoyama coalition government, both opposed the plan to exclude pro-North Korean schools.[69] Unlike the DPJ, the SDP and the New People's Party felt that discriminating against students at pro-Pyongyang high schools would be wrong. The JCP also opposed the Hatoyama government's DPJ-driven push to exclude pro-North Korean schools. The JCP took issue with those members of Hatoyama's cabinet who argued that the unresolved kidnapping problem is reason enough to exclude pro-Pyongyang high schools. The JCP maintained, "Korean children living in Japan and learning at schools in Japan have nothing to do with the abduction issue. Retaliatory treatment against these children is out of the question."[70]

Pyongyang also saw the discrimination in the Hatoyama government's plan. Pyongyang charged that because many Koreans in Japanese schools are descendants of people who "were forcibly taken to Japan by the Japanese imperialists in the past" the Hatoyama government has a "moral obligation" to provide them with an education and not to exclude them from the tuition-waiver plan.[71]

The combination of very poor approval ratings and the ineffective handling of the Okinawa base issue – whereby Hatoyama initially promised that his government would reduce the burden on the Okinawan people, stemming from the presence of US military facilities on the island, but eventually yielded to Washington – cost the prime minister his job. In office only nine months, Hatoyama resigned in early June 2010. The DPJ's Naoto Kan became prime minister and reappointed Hiroshi Nakai as Minister of State for the Abduction Issue,[72] who continued to oppose having Chongryon-affiliated schools included in the program that would reimburse student tuitions.

In November 2010, immediately after North and South Korea traded salvos, in which two marines and two civilians on South Korea's Yeonpyeong Island were killed by DPRK artillery, the tuition-waiver plan suffered another setback. The government of DPJ Prime Minister Naoto Kan announced that "amid the tension on the Korean Peninsula, it is better to suspend the procedures" of whether to include pro-Pyongyang-affiliated schools in the tuition-waiver plan.[73] Pyongyang made clear that it supported Korean residents in Japan who protested the Kan government's decision.[74]

Out of the blue: the North Korean terrorism issue redux

Although Prime Minister Aso knew that the Obama administration, like the Bush White House, wanted to resolve the nuclear issue and denuclearize the Korean Peninsula, it quickly became clear that the new government in Washington was uncertain about how to deal with the DPRK.[75] Aso suggested right after North Korea conducted its second underground nuclear test that his government had been pressing the Obama administration to return the DPRK to the US list of states sponsoring terrorism[76] – code for the formal reinclusion of the abduction issue in the US's DPRK policy.

Less than two weeks after the DPRK's second nuclear test, the very conservative Aso government had persuaded the "liberal" Obama administration to consider redesignating North Korea a terrorist state. Referring to the re-listing of the DPRK, Secretary of State Hillary Clinton said during an interview in early June 2009: "There's a process for it" and that "Obviously we would want to see recent evidence of their support for international terrorism."[77]

However, this would have been difficult to do. For many years, the US State Department has indicated that North Korea is not known to have been involved in any terrorist activities since the late 1980s – and even this is in dispute.[78] Moreover, the US State Department's 2008 report on global terrorism points out that the removal of the DPRK from the list of countries sponsoring terrorism occurred in accordance with US law and included the "certification that the Government of North Korea had not provided any support for international terrorism during the preceding six-month period."[79] Pyongyang, therefore, would have had to radically change the behavior it had consistently exhibited for more than two decades.

Within hours of Secretary Clinton's remark, Chief Cabinet Secretary Takeo Kawamura commented: "The Japanese government feels [that Washington returning the DPRK to the US terrorism list is] necessary as we think the abduction [issue] is terrorism itself, and we'd like to closely monitor the developments." Director-General of the Asian and Oceanian Affairs Bureau and Japan's top representative to the six-party talks Akitaka Saiki also chimed in, stating that he wanted Washington to render "some political decision" and redesignate the DPRK as a state sponsor of terrorism.[80]

At the time when Secretary Clinton commented that the United States was considering re-listing the DPRK, the DPJ was still a few months away from its historic landslide victory in August 2009 that resulted in Yukio Hatoyama becoming prime minister in September. At the time president of the DPJ, Hatoyama's position on the abduction issue was consistent with that of the Aso government. Pleased that Secretary of State Clinton had spoken about the possibility of putting the DPRK back on the US terrorism list, Hatoyama remarked in June 2009: "Its seems only natural."[81] Indeed, well over a year before becoming prime minister, Hatoyama insisted that the DPRK should not be removed from the US terrorism list.[82]

No matter what the Japanese wanted, the Obama administration faced the reality that putting the DPRK back on the US list of countries sponsoring terrorism would have made the North Korean nuclear issue impossible to resolve. Pyongyang already maintains that Japan has nuclear weapons ambitions and that United States "is conniving at the development of nuclear weapons and access to them by the pro-U.S. forces and its allies, backing them and even cooperating with them, prompted by its double standards and biased stand."[83] Had the Obama administration placed the DPRK back on the US terrorism list, this would have immediately opened up old wounds and given Pyongyang additional motivation to develop nuclear weapons and resist denuclearization. As it turned out, in February 2010, President Obama stated in a letter he sent to House and Senate leaders: "the DPRK does not meet the statutory criteria to again be designated as a state sponsor of terrorism."[84] The Obama administration reaffirmed this in June 2010, despite repeated claims by Washington and Seoul that the DPRK had been responsible for sinking the South Korean warship, Cheonan, in March.[85]

In any case, unwavering attention to the abduction issue by Japanese policymakers remains very evident. A DPJ member of the House of Councillors, Shin-kun Haku, asked Prime Minister Hatoyama during a meeting in February 2010 what his administration was going to do about the abduction issue. Hatoyama stated: "Abduction is totally unforgivable. We would like to make every effort as a government to ensure that the abductees can return home safely as soon as possible." Hatoyama also emphasized that his administration would expand intelligence-collection activities relating to the abductions. Turning to Minister of State for the Abduction Issue Hiroshi Nakai, Haku stated that, despite the importance of the abduction issue, there have been no new developments. Nakai responded by telling Haku that after becoming Minister of State for the Abduction Issue he became aware that previously little information had been collected and investigative work done on the kidnappings. Nakai stated that the Hatoyama government's budget for the next fiscal year would roughly double the funding for these efforts. Said Nakai: "We are creating a system with the intention of focusing on thorough information-gathering and determining the fate of the abductees, and we are currently assembling human resources and proceeding with the preparations for this."[86]

The Hatoyama government made these decisions very quickly after it came to power. At its first meeting held in late October 2009, the members of redesigned Headquarters for the Abduction Issue decided "to increase the staff and budget for its activities, especially for building up the capacity for intelligence-gathering." Rather than consisting of the prime minister's entire cabinet as when it was established by former Prime Minister Abe, the "new" Headquarters is designed to be more efficient and adaptable. As such, it has only four members: the prime minister, the minister of state for the abduction issue, the chief cabinet secretary and the minister for foreign affairs.[87] Like its predecessors, the administration led by the DPJ's Naoto Kan has shown that it also has a strong and unremitting predilection to resolve the abduction issue to Japan's satisfaction.

Conflated problems

Further complicating the Japan–DPRK relationship is Tokyo's conflation of the nuclear, missile and abduction issues. In June 2003 Prime Minister Junichiro Koizumi declared in a joint press conference with South Korean President Roh Moo-hyun that Japan had adopted a policy approach of "dialogue and pressure" to deal with the North Korean nuclear crisis.[88] However, after Koizumi made his second trip to Pyongyang in May 2004, Tokyo began to adopt a noticeably tougher policy approach toward North Korea.[89] By mid 2004, now fully committed to making Japan a normal country, this strong preference to use pressure had spread to "various issues" involving North Korea.[90]

When the Japanese government passed the amendment to the Foreign Exchange and Foreign Trade Control Law in February 2004, Prime Minister Koizumi indicated that he did not have any immediate plans to sanction the DPRK and that he hoped "North Korea would show a sincere response so that the abduction issue and the nuclear issue would be resolved soon." At about the same time, Vice Foreign Minister Yukio Takeuchi pointed out that, if Pyongyang created more security problems in the region, Japan might impose sanctions on North Korea.[91] In May 2004, less than a month before the Japanese government passed the law permitting it to prohibit port calls by vessels considered a security risk to Japan, Shinzo Abe, then Secretary General of the LDP stated: "Unless the abduction issue is completely resolved, we have to enact this legislation during the current session."[92]

Prime Minister Koizumi's appointment of Shinzo Abe to the position of chief cabinet secretary in October 2005 greatly pleased ardent supporters of the abduction issue. Abe stressed that it was imperative that this matter be resolved, often saying before Japan and North Korea could establish normal bilateral relations. While Abe served as chief cabinet secretary, the Koizumi government scored important political victories in its work to internationalize the abduction issue. Apart from members of Megumi Yokota's family meeting with Bush at the White House in April 2006, her mother also testified before the House of Representatives' International Relations Committee, which promised to get the abduction issue on the agenda of the upcoming G-8 meeting to be held in July.[93] As we saw in Chapter 4, Prime Minister Abe's administration directed the public company, Japan Broadcasting Corporation (NHK), to increase its focus on the abduction issue. This caused some in Japan, including the DPJ and the JCP, to believe that the government had seriously compromised the freedom of the media.[94]

Japanese political parties, the abduction issue and reaction to the DPRK

Although publicly maintaining that the missile, nuclear and abduction issues all need to be settled, the LDP and DPJ have ostensibly taken the position, which corresponds with public sentiment, that normalized relations with North Korea cannot occur until there is a resolution of the abduction issue. However, in private LDP and DPJ policymakers explain that the nuclear, missile and abduction issues need to be resolved and only when pressed do they reveal their predisposition for settling the kidnapping problem.[95] Thus, policymakers understand that the missile and nuclear problems are potentially immediate threats to Japan and appear to use the abduction issue because it comports with public sentiment.

To resolve the abduction issue, the LDP, which acknowledges that the United States has a "huge impact" on Japan's efforts to normalize relations with North Korea,[96] believes that it needs good, objective information from Pyongyang and that currently there is "no path in that direction." This helps explain why the LDP has talked tough about how to deal with the abduction issue. After Tokyo said that DNA testing of the ashes of Megumi Yokota showed that they were not hers, the LDP concluded: "There is no alternative to sanctions."[97] Although Tokyo had passed laws permitting it to sanction the DPRK, it was initially reluctant to do this until the second half of 2006, notwithstanding minority opposition from the JCP and to a lesser extent from the SDP.

Not everyone in the LDP has felt the same way about how to deal with the DPRK. In January 2007, senior LDP Diet member Taku Yamasaki created somewhat of a stir when he visited Pyongyang without the consent of the Abe government in an effort to improve Japan-DPRK relations. A close ally of Junichiro Koizumi, Yamasaki, like the former prime minister, had held onto the hope of normalizing bilateral relations with North Korea. In contrast to hard-line critics who called his trip to the DPRK an act of "dual diplomacy," Yamasaki stressed the need for "dialogue" and "persuasion" with Pyongyang. Indicating his opposition to Yamasaki's trip, Abe remarked: "Japan is now putting pressure on North Korea to take a sincere step [to rein in] its nuclear weapons and missile development as well as [settle] its abduction [of Japanese nationals]. We want [Yamasaki] to realize this."[98]

New Komeito has maintained that the abduction issue is the most important bilateral problem between Japan and North Korea. For New Komeito, the resolution of the abduction issue, which it sees as a human rights problem, requires dialogue between Tokyo and Pyongyang. New Komeito, however, is not optimistic about having useful and productive dialogue with Pyongyang on the abduction issue, maintaining that because it has "broken promises" and created distrust, "nobody knows what is true." Like the LDP, New Komeito believes that Tokyo should be tough on North Korea and supports sanctions, reasoning that "maybe" they will work.[99]

Before becoming the dominant political party in Japan in August 2009, the DPJ had been critical that the LDP-controlled government initially ignored the abduction issue. However, once Kim Jong Il admitted the DPRK was responsible for the abductions, "this struck a cord with the Japanese people," and then with the government of Japan. Within the DPJ there is the belief that, in addition to bilateral work, part of which involves Pyongyang handing over to Japan those responsible for the kidnappings, there must be multi-lateral pressure placed on North Korea to deal with the human rights pro-blems there and to resolve the abduction issue.[100] In December 2004, four DPJ members of the House of Representatives called on the government to get tough with Pyongyang, with three seeing the need for the imposition of sanctions on North Korea and one recommending giving this strong consideration. React-ing to the results from the examination of Megumi Yokota's ashes, one DPJ representative stated: "We created legislation to make economic sanctions possible in just such an eventuality." Another DPJ member even questioned the benefit to Japan of normalizing relations with North Korea.[101]

Although the SDP eventually came to appreciate how important the abduction issue is to the Japanese people, in the past it had a very different position on the kidnappings. Japanese socialists had for some time supported the DPRK. Before Kim Jong Il's admission in 2002 of DPRK culpability, the SDP refused to accept North Korea's involvement in the kidnappings, saying in 1997 that the abduction issue is "a fiction devised by South Korean intel-ligence." Subsequent to Kim Jong Il's admission of DPRK involvement in the kidnappings, the SDP apologized for being remiss about the abduction issue, but to no avail.[102] It is likely that the SDP paid a big price for its past posi-tion on North Korea. Once Japan's largest opposition party, in the general elections held in November 2003, a little over a year after Kim's admission, the SDP won only six seats, down considerably from previous elections.

Although more recently the SDP has advocated somewhat of a conciliatory approach to deal with North Korea, it also faults Pyongyang for not provid-ing enough details about the kidnappings. The SDP sees the missile, nuclear and abductions issues as very important and wants the Japanese government to work harder to try to negotiate a resolution to these problems with Pyon-gyang. It further believes that the Japanese government needs to be more concerned than it has been with normalizing relations with North Korea. However, the SDP wants to know the situation of the abductees, specifically what they are doing in North Korea. The SDP believes that Pyongyang has not provided a "reasonable message" on either the abduction or the nor-malization issues, and maintains that while Kim apologized to Koizumi for the kidnappings, Pyongyang has not apologized to the Japanese people.[103]

The JCP also stresses that the missile, nuclear and abductions issues need to be resolved with North Korea. JCP maintains that Koizumi was sincere about improving bilateral relations when he twice visited Pyongyang and that some in the Japanese Ministry of Foreign Affairs want to resolve the problems with North Korea and establish normal diplomatic relations. After learning about Kim Jong Il's admission to Koizumi, the JCP stated that it protested "against the serious crime of abduction, an unpardonable act."[104] Although the JCP recognizes the importance of the abduction issue to the Japanese people, it also understands that the kidnapping problem is very difficult to resolve, since the families of the abductees want them back in Japan or proof, specifically DNA evidence, that they are dead. The JCP, which has good relations with Chongryon or *chosen soren*, acknowledges that it has no influence on Pyongyang.[105]

The bottom line is that policymaking in Japan with respect to the DPRK has been and remains focused largely on the abduction issue, something supported by all Japanese political parties. This made it easy for Prime Minister Abe and Foreign Minister Aso to tell the Diet in January 2007 that, even though Japan has concerns about North Korea's missiles and nuclear weapons, normalization of relations with the DPRK could not occur until there has been a resolution of the abduction issue.[106] However, despite the public prioritization of the abduction issue in Japan, rapprochement with the DPRK appears firstly to be depended upon Washington resolving the North Korean nuclear problem to its satisfaction.

"History" as a conflating factor

Pyongyang has connected history to a number of problems it currently has with Japan. By drawing heavily on the past when it explains some of Japan's present-day behavior, Pyongyang too often uses the deeply rooted history problem as a political expedient rather than exploring the most practical and least conflictive path to improving bilateral relations. Although it is true that Japan has not done nearly enough to settle its past crimes with North Korea, Pyongyang's repeated, highly politically charged focus on history draws attention away from solutions to current bilateral problems.

Pyongyang believes that to prevent history from repeating itself it must implement aggressive countervailing measures. For more than a decade, this has translated into an increase in the DPRK's dependence on *songun*, which has only worsened North Korea's relationship with Japan. Pyongyang's increasing reliance on *songun* plays directly into the hands of Japanese nationalists – as well as North Korean bashers in the United States – who cast the DPRK's military actions as provocative and in turn have pushed hard to strengthen Japan's military readiness and security relations with Washington.

The DPRK's representative to the United Nations General Assembly recently shed much light on how Japan's past relationship with the Korean people affects Pyongyang's current perspective of the country. In December 2006, after the United Nations General Assembly's Third Committee passed a resolution on human rights violations in the DPRK, the North Korean representative indicated to the body that his country "held a deep-seated grudge against Japan that had to be paid in blood." The DPRK representative stated that the source of this grudge is the horrific treatment by Japan of millions of Koreans and the confinement to sexual slavery of tens of thousands of Korean women and girls by Japanese forces. Referring to the evil intentions that both the United States and Japan harbor toward North Korea, the DPRK representative emphasized that Pyongyang has been working to acquire "full preparedness" – that is, the continued development of *songun* – to counteract these threats.[107]

Pyongyang typically compares the abduction issue to the violations of human rights Japan inflicted on the Korean people during the period when it annexed the peninsula for 35 years.[108] Pyongyang maintains: "Japan wants to look like a victim in order not to apologize and compensate the DPRK." An official in the DPRK Foreign Ministry remarked: "[Japan is] a criminal state [that] tries to look like a victim state."[109]

However, the past atrocities committed by Japan on the Korean Peninsula did not cause DPRK agents, whether authorized or not by Pyongyang, to abduct Japanese nationals during the 1970s and 1980s. It is one thing to say, as Pyongyang often does, that the failure to resolve the history problem stemming from the Japanese annexation of the Korean Peninsula is an unfortunate reality of Japan–DPRK relations. However, it is quite another thing for Pyongyang to appear dismissive and perfunctory about the abduction of Japanese nationals, since these were criminal acts perpetrated by DPRK agents. Indeed, it serves no practical purpose for Pyongyang to stress repeatedly that one set of crimes is so much more heinous than the other.

Pyongyang also commonly uses Japan's past colonization of the Korean Peninsula and the brutality displayed by Japanese forces to argue that Tokyo has a revanchist agenda. Observing that Japan has been steadily moving toward remilitarization, Pyongyang has often asserted that Tokyo has its sights set on the reinvasion of Korea and the reinstitution of the country's Greater East Asia Co-Prosperity Sphere.[110] (Formally introduced in August 1940, the Greater East Asia Co-Prosperity Sphere was an autarkically propelled propaganda campaign that rejected Western power – "Asia for Asians" and the "Asian community." Japan used the notion of the Greater East Asia Co-Prosperity Sphere to justify among its colonies its vicious attempt to sustain Japanese imperialism up until its defeat in the Pacific War.[111]) Although its militaristic past was incontrovertibly brutal, this historical reality did not create an enduring and undiluted predisposition for military aggression in Japan's policy-making psyche. As discussed in Chapter 3, partly fueled by Tokyo's contention of the DPRK's threatening behavior, Japan's quest to become a normal country also has as much to do with the significant pressure applied for decades by the United States,[112] as it does with the resurgence of Japanese nationalism.[113]

The territorial dispute that both South and North Korea today share in opposing Japan's claim to the Dokdo or Tok Islet (the Japanese call this islet Takeshima) in the Sea of Japan or the East Sea still occasionally raises

Pyongyang's ire.[114] At times, Pyongyang has been very vocal in its opposition to Japan's claim to the Tok Islet, which for decades has been controlled by South Korea. The Korean Social Democratic Party of North Korea and the Democratic Labor Party of South Korea produced a joint statement in August 2008, in which the two parties indicated that they "bitterly denounce Japan for its moves to grab Tok Islet.[115] Responding to the Japanese Defense Ministry's claim in its 2009 White Paper that Takeshima (Tok Islet) belongs to Japan,[116] Pyongyang stated that this unequivocally shows Japan's "hostile policy towards the DPRK and ambition for reinvasion have reached an extreme phase."[117]

With Seoul and Beijing, Pyongyang has also spoken out strongly against Koizumi's six visits during his tenure as prime minister to the *Yasukuni Jinja*, a shrine in Tokyo that commemorates those who died in past Japanese wars. For China and both Koreas, the shrine symbolizes Japan's militaristic past, since it memorializes over two million deceased Japanese soldiers, as well as 14 recognized war criminals. However, visits to the Yasukuni Shrine have not been limited to former Prime Minister Koizumi. Pyongyang recently railed about the 48 members of the Japanese Diet who visited the shrine. In August 2008, Pyongyang maintained that, evidenced by their ongoing efforts, "Japanese ultra-right forces" remain determined "to legalize and popularize visits to the Yasukuni Shrine."[118] In May 2009, Pyongyang showed its disdain for the visit to the shrine by 87 conservative members of the Japanese Diet and, along with Beijing and Seoul, made clear that it was very displeased with the gift that then Prime Minister Taro Aso sent there. Pyongyang asserted: "The real intention of the visit is to imbue the Japanese people with the idea that they should not forget those killed in the war for continental aggression but whet the sword for reinvasion of Asian countries by inheriting their soul."[119] In the fall of 2009, Pyongyang lashed out at the more than 50 Japanese "ultra-right conservative" politicians, then including former Prime Minister Taro Aso, for visiting the Yasukuni Shrine. Pyongyang charged that this "reckless behavior" is a "criminal action fraught with the scheme for militarism and overseas aggression."[120]

Again an issue that has also bothered Beijing and Seoul, Pyongyang has repeatedly criticized the revisionist campaign in Japan that it and others say sanction the rewriting of history appearing in the textbooks used in Japanese schools. Pyongyang has maintained that, even though "they distorted stark historical facts and embellished or deleted Japan's crimes," the Japanese government nonetheless approved these textbooks.[121] As discussed in Chapter 5, still another current problem that Pyongyang connects to history is Japan's treatment of Chongryon and Chongryon Korean.

Conclusion

The Japan–North Korean relationship is currently in dire straits, with rapprochement now seemingly contingent upon the resolution of the DPRK nuclear problem. However, the resolution of the DPRK nuclear issue is not up to Tokyo, which publicly prioritizes the abduction issue, but rather requires a pronouncement by Washington. With respect especially to the abduction issue, not only are Washington's and Tokyo's differences with Pyongyang not always identical, that is, they have diverse and irrepressible interests, but a second nuclear test by the DPRK in May 2009 instantly created a major barrier that impeded improvement in US–North Korea relations and therefore Japan–North Korea relations.

Any contact the Obama administration makes with Pyongyang will continue to be met with a large amount of resistance from US hardliners and their neoconservative allies, since they, much like the Japanese and even the South Korean right, believe that Pyongyang cannot be trusted. More problematic now, however, is that hardliners in the United States are not alone in believing that Pyongyang always has something very deleterious up its sleeve; in other words, it cannot be trusted.[122] The Obama administration, at least during its first two years, has accepted this view of the DPRK. In Singapore, Secretary of Defense Robert Gates stated that routinely the North Koreans "create a crisis and the rest of us pay a price to return to the status quo ante. As the expression goes in the United States, I am tired of buying the same horse twice."[123] The Obama administration's Special Representative for North Korea Policy, Steven Bosworth, also has subscribed, at least in the past, to this perspective, maintaining that "there will always be some uncertainty as to whether Pyongyang is cheating," since it "has lied or deceived incessantly."[124]

The 1994 Agreed Framework fell apart because, spurred by US hardliners and neoconservativs who both subscribed to a unilateral policy toward the DPRK, the Bush administration and Pyongyang blamed each other for breaching the accord. DPRK's missile and nuclear testing in 2006 demonstrated that hardliners in Pyongyang ultimately acquired the upper hand over those with a preference for negotiation,[125] something that became clear again when the North detonated its second nuclear device.

Pressed hard by those advocating a nationalist agenda in Tokyo and to some extent by the conservative Lee Myung-bak government in South Korea, the Obama administration has drawn far too much of its North Korean policy from the unilateralist well. Because Pyongyang believed that early on the new Obama administration was ignoring the DPRK, this fortified the position of North Korean hardliners, who succeeded in getting hasty decisions to be made that used *songun* to grab the attention of Washington, its allies and others. These missteps from Washington and Pyongyang caused the denuclearization process to regress.

That the main Japanese political parties, despite their other differences, all underscore the importance of settling the abduction issue, made Tokyo's decision, which it reached precisely because of this unresolved problem, not to provide assistance to the DPRK, as stipulated in the joint statement that came out of the February 2007 six-party talks, that much easier. Even statements released by the JCP and the SDP immediately after the February 2007 six-party talks stressed the importance of resolving the abduction issue.[126]

The resolution of the abduction issue, which will require Pyongyang's sincere commitment, and Tokyo's willingness to make amends to the DPRK for its past crimes, can lead to normal Japan–North Korea relations. However, how Washington deals with Pyongyang is crucial to any efforts connected to rapprochement between Japan and the DPRK. However, under present conditions, specifically, without very different thinking in Tokyo and Pyongyang, before Japan–DPRK relations noticeably improve, Washington must declare an end to the North Korean nuclear issue. The last chapter will discuss new ways for Tokyo, Pyongyang and Washington to approach the ongoing problems they continue to face.

Notes

1 Author interview with officials in the Government of Japan, Headquarters for the Abduction Issue, Tokyo, July 14, 2008.
2 Anthony DiFilippo, "Security Trials, Nuclear Tribulations and Rapprochement in Japan–North Korean Relations," *Journal of Pacific Asia*, vol. 11, spring 2004, pp. 7–31; Anthony DiFilippo, "Nuclear Deterrence and Animosity in Japan–North Korean Relations: Steps to Coexistence," *Pacific Focus*, vol. XXI, no. 1, Spring 2006, pp. 137–74.
3 Author meeting with an official from the DPRK Ministry of Foreign Affairs, Pyongyang, January 8, 2009.
4 "Aso Cabinet Vows to Strengthen Asia Ties, Resolve N. Korea Abductions," *Kyodo News*, September 28, 2008; "Japan to Extend Sanctions against N. Korea Again," *Jiji Press*, September 29, 2008.
5 "KCNA's Slams Japan's Dishonest Stance Towards Issue of Fulfillment of Its Commitments," *Korean Central News Agency*, October 22, 2008.
6 Jasper Becker, *Rogue Regime: Kim Jong Il and the Looming Threat of North Korea* (New York: Oxford University Press, 2005); Jasper Becker, "The Depths of Evil," *New Statesman*, September 4, 2006, pp. 32–33; Gordon Chang, *Nuclear Showdown: North Korea Takes on the World* (New York: Random House, 2006); Robert Kaplan, "When North Korea Falls," *The Atlantic Monthly*, October 2006, pp. 64–73; Kongdan Oh and Ralph Hassig, *North Korea Through the Looking Glass* (Washington, DC: Brookings Institution Press, 2000). For a different perspective, see Hazel Smith, *Hungry for Peace, International Security, Humanitarian Assistance, and Social Change in North Korea* (Washington, DC: United States Institute of Peace Press, 2005), pp. 25–44.
7 Marcus Noland, "The Economic Implications of a North Korean Nuclear Test," *Asia Policy*, no. 2, July 2006, pp. 25–39.
8 Anthony DiFilippo, "Hubris, Intransigence, and the North Korean Nuclear Crisis," *Japan Focus*, January 8, 2007.
9 "66% of Japanese Favor Links with North Korea," *The Japan Times Online*, December 22, 2002; The Maureen and Mike Mansfield Foundation, *Public Opinion Survey on Diplomacy by the Cabinet Office of Japan*, December 2004, www.mansfieldfdn.org/polls/poll-05-6.htm (accessed on February 10, 2007); The Maureen and Mike Mansfield Foundation, *Public Opinion Survey on Diplomacy by the Cabinet Office of Japan*, December 2006, www.mansfieldfdn.org/polls/2006/poll-06-17.htm (accessed February 10, 2007).
10 Cabinet Office of Japan, Tokyo, 2007.
11 Government of Japan, Headquarters for the Abduction Issue, *For the Return of All of the Abductees: Points of Contention with the North Korean Position*, Tokyo,

July 2008; Ministry of Foreign Affairs, *Abductions of Japanese Citizens by North Korea*, Tokyo, 2008.

12 Author meeting with an official from the DPRK Ministry of Foreign Affairs, Pyongyang, January 8, 2009; "North Korea Executed Alleged Abduction Suspect – South Korean Daily," *Chosun Ilbo*, December 27, 2004.

13 Ministry of Foreign Affairs, *Abductions of Japanese Citizens by North Korea*, Tokyo, 2008; NARKN (National Association for the Rescue of Japanese Kidnapped by North Korea), www.sukuukai.jp/narkn/about.html (accessed January 16, 2007).

14 "North Denies Latest Abduction Entry," *The Japan Times Online*, November 25, 2006.

15 Government of Japan, Headquarters for the Abduction Issue, *For the Return of All of the Abductees: Points of Contention with the North Korean Position*, Tokyo, July 2008.

16 Interview with Song Il Ho, Chief Negotiator of DPRK–Japan Talks, "Pyongyang will not Yield an Inch in Demanding Japan's Liquidation of Past," *The People's Korea*, March 10, 2006.

17 Author interview with officials in the Government of Japan, Headquarters of the Abduction Issue, Tokyo, July 14, 2008.

18 Government of Japan, Headquarters for the Abduction Issue, *For the Return of All of the Abductees: Points of Contention with the North Korean Position*, Tokyo, July 2008.

19 "Foreign Ministry Spokesman on Japan's Anti-DPRK Campaign," *Korean Central News Agency*, December 31, 2004.

20 David Cyranoski, "DNA Burning Issue as Japan and Korea Clash over Kidnaps," *Nature*, vol. 433, February 3, 2005, p. 445. David Cyranoski, "Job Switch Stymies Japan's Abduction Probe," *Nature*, vol. 434, April 7, 2005, p. 685.

21 Author interview with official from the Cabinet Secretariat Office, Policy Planning Division, Headquarters for the Abduction Issue, Tokyo, July 24, 2009.

22 "Media Resources, Japan Brief," Foreign Press Center Japan, April 13, 2006, http://fpcj.jp/old/e/mres/japanbrief/jb_622.html (accessed on April 9, 2011).

23 "Kim Young-nam Says His Japanese Wife Megumi Killed Herself," *The Hankyoreh*, June 30, 2006; "Son in NK Denies Abduction," *The Korea Times*, June 30, 2006.

24 Author interview with officials in the Government of Japan, Headquarters of the Abduction Issue, Tokyo, July 14, 2008.

25 "Japan Urged to Redress Its Past Crimes," *Korean Central News Agency*, January 16, 2007.

26 "U.S. and Japan Accused of Their Moves for a New War," *Korean Central News Agency*, January 16, 2006.

27 "KCNA Blasts Japan's Moves for Constitutional Revision," *Korean Central News Agency*, May 25, 2007.

28 "Diet Should Start Review of Constitution ASAP," *Daily Yomiuri Online*, May 3, 2009.

29 Tim Beal, *North Korea: The Struggle Against American Power* (London: Pluto Press, 2005), pp. 129–66.

30 Ministry of Foreign Affairs, *The Adoption at the Third Committee, United Nations General Assembly, of the Resolution of the Situation of Human Rights in the Democratic People's Republic of Korea*, Tokyo, November 22, 2008.

31 Ministry of Foreign Affairs, *Statement by the Press Secretary/Director-General for Press and Public Relations, Ministry of Foreign Affairs, on the Adoption at the Third Committee, United Nations General Assembly, of the Resolution on the "Situation of Human Rights in the Democratic People's Republic of Korea,"* November 18, 2006.

32 United Nations General Assembly, Department of Public Information, *Third Committee Draft Resolutions Address Human Rights Situations in Myanmar, Democratic People's Republic of Korea, Iran*, New York, November 21, 2008.

33 "Anti-DPRK 'Resolution on Human Rights' Rebutted," *Korean Central News Agency*, December 1, 2008.

34 "DPRK Slams UN 'Human Rights Resolution,'" *Korean Central News Agency*, November 20, 2009.

35 United Nations General Assembly, Department of Public Information, *General Assembly will Adopt Declaration, Strategy to Counter World Drug Problem under Terms of Draft Resolution Approved by Third Committee*, New York, November 19, 2009.

36 "Japan's Attempt at Military Overseas Expansion Flayed," *Korean Central News Agency*, September 16, 2006.

37 "Lower House Oks Defense Ministry Bill," *The Japan Times Online*, December 1, 2006.

38 JCP, "Upgrading Defense Agency to Ministry Level to Fight Wars Abroad," *Japan Press Weekly*, October 26, 2006, www.japan-press.co.jp/2006/2501/military.html (accessed March 30, 2011); JCP, "JCP will Strive for Scrapping of Unconstitutional Defense Ministry Bill in Upper House: Shii," *Japan Press Weekly*, December 1, 2006, www.japan-press.co.jp/2006/2506/sdf3.html (accessed March 30, 2011).

39 "Upgrading Japan Defence Agency to Ministry Termed Move for Overseas Invasion," *Korean Central News Agency*, December 22, 2006; "Rodong Sinmun Lambastes Japan for Upgrading Defence Agency to Ministry," *Korean Central News Agency*, January 14, 2007.

40 "Diet Enacts N. Korea Sanctions Law," *Kyodo News*, June 16, 2006; "Diet Passes North Sanctions Bill," *The Japan Times Online*, June 17, 2006.

41 "N.K.'s Efforts on Japanese Abduction Issue 'Downplayed': Minister," *Yonhap News Agency*, May 3, 2006.

42 Author interview with South Korean official at Seoul's embassy in Tokyo, July 26, 2006.

43 "Abductions Now a Trilateral Issue/But Seoul Worried Pressing Too Hard Might Hinder Inter-Korean Ties," *Daily Yomiuri Online*, April 12, 2006; "'Yokota's Husband' Gets to Briefly See Kin," *The Japan Times Online*, June 29, 2006.

44 Yoneyuki Sugita, "An Active Japanese Foreign Policy Impeded by a Frustrated Public in the Post-Cold War Era," *International Journal of Korean Unification Studies*, vol. 14, no. 2, 2005, pp. 182–94.

45 "Diet Enacts N. Korea Sanctions Law," *Kyodo News*, June 16, 2006; "Diet Passes Sanctions Bill," *The Japan Times Online*, June 17, 2006.

46 JCP, "JCP Opposes Bill to Deal with North Korea's Human Rights Violations," *Japan Press Weekly*, June 13, 2006, www.japan-press.co.jp/2006/2483/diet6.html (accessed March 30, 2011).

47 "Japan's Adoption of Anti-DPRK Law under Fire," *Korean Central News Agency*, June 26, 2006.

48 "Diet Enacts Laws to Augment War-Contingency Measures," *The Japan Times Online*, June 15, 2004.

49 Yukio Hatoyama, Secretary General, Democratic Party of Japan, *Statement Strongly Protesting the Launching of Missiles by North Korea*, Tokyo, July 5, 2006.

50 Japanese Communist Party, *North Korea's "Brinkmanship" Brings Instability into Asia*, Tokyo, June 25, 2006; Kazuo Shii, Chairman, Japanese Communist Party, *JCP Protests North Korea's Missile Launch*, Tokyo, July 5, 2006.

51 Kazuo Shii, Chairman, Japanese Communist Party, *UNSC Resolution on North Korea's Missile Launches is Reasonable: JCP Shii*, Tokyo, July 16, 2006; Social

Democratic Party, *Concerning Security Council Resolution Adoption Regarding the Missile Discharge by North Korea*, Tokyo, July 16, 2006 (in Japanese).

52 Social Democratic Party, *The North Korean Test Execution is Criticized*, Tokyo, October 9, 2006 (in Japanese).

53 Democratic Party of Japan, *Statement on Adoption by the UNSC of Resolution to Impose Sanctions on North Korea*, Tokyo, October 15, 2006.

54 Japanese Communist Party, *JCP Chair Urges North Korea to Accept UNSC Resolution 1718*, Tokyo, October 16, 2006.

55 "KCNA Assails Japan's Adoption of Anti-DPRK Law," *Korean Central News Agency*, February 3, 2004; "Law against DPRK Adopted in Japan," *Korean Central News Agency*, June 16, 2004.

56 "KCNA Blasts Japan's Financial Sanctions against DPRK," *Korean Central News Agency*, September 23, 2006; "Japan's Hostile Policy toward the DPRK Assailed," *Korean Central News Agency*, November 13, 2006.

57 "Japanese Militarists' Criminal Acts under Fire," *Korean Central News Agency*, December 23, 2006.

58 "KCNA Rebukes Japan's Moves to Go Nuclear," *Korean Central News Agency*, April 28, 2009.

59 "North Launch Spurs Lower House Censure," *The Japan Times Online*, April 8, 2009; "Upper House Condemns Launch, Seeks Sanctions," *The Japan Times Online*, April 9, 2009.

60 LDP, *Statement by the Liberal Democratic Party Regarding the Missile Launch by North Korea*, Tokyo, April 5, 2009, www.jimin.jp/jimin/english/news/news79.html (accessed March 30, 2011).

61 JCP, "North Korea's Rocket Launch is Regrettable: JCP Chair," *Japan Press Weekly*, April 6, 2009, www.japan-press.co.jp/2009/2617/fa_2.html (accessed on April 9, 2011).

62 The White House, Office of the Press Secretary, *Remarks by the President on North Korea*, Washington, DC, May 25, 2009.

63 LDP, *Statement by the Liberal Democratic Party Regarding the Nuclear Test and Missile Launch by North Korea*, May 26, 2009, www.jimin.jp/jimin/english/news/news81.html (accessed March 30, 2011).

64 Prime Minister of Japan and His Cabinet, *Statement by the Prime Minister of Japan*, Tokyo, May 25, 2009.

65 The White House, Office of the Press Secretary, *Remarks by President Barack Obama*, Prague, April 5, 2009.

66 US Department of Energy, National Nuclear Safety Administration, *Bacchus Subcritical Experiment Conducted at Nevada National Security Site*, Las Vegas, September 15, 2010, www.nv.doe.gov/library/newsreleases/Bacchus_Subcritical_Experiment_09162010.pdf (accessed on April 9, 2011).

67 "Lower House Condemns North's Nuke Test," *Asahi Shimbun*, May 27, 2009; "Upper House Adopts Resolution Condemning North Korean Nuclear Test," *Kyodo News*, May 27, 2009.

68 "Japan Decides on Additional Sanctions on N. Korea," *Kyodo News*, June 16, 2009.

69 "Kids at Pro-North High Schools Fret Tuition Waiver Snub," *The Japan Times Online*, March 10, 2010.

70 JCP, "Secure Right to Education for All Children," *Japan Press Weekly*, March 11, 2010, www.japan-press.co.jp/2010/2662/wellbeing1.html (accessed March 30, 2011).

71 "Policy of Discrimination against Koreans in Japan Blasted," *Korean Central News Agency*, March 13, 2010; "Japanese Authorities' Discriminate Education Policy Assailed," *Korean Central News Agency*, March 3, 2010.

72 "Abduction Minister Renews Resolve to Tackle Issue of Missing Japanese," *Kyodo News*, July 8, 2010.

73 "Kan Confers with Lee on North Korea," *The Japan Times Online*, November 24, 2010.
74 "Japanese Authorities' Discriminating Policy Flayed," *Korean Central News Agency*, December 2, 2010.
75 Anthony DiFilippo, "The North Korean Nuclear Issue in Disarray," *The Korea Times*, May 1, 2009.
76 "Aso Hints Japan Urging U.S. to get N. Korea Back on Terrorism Blacklist," *Kyodo News*, May 28, 2009.
77 "U.S. Thinking of Restoring N. Korea to Terrorist List," *The New York Times*, June 7, 2009.
78 Anthony DiFilippo, "North Korea as a State Sponsor of Terrorism: Views from Tokyo and Pyongyang," *International Journal of Korean Unification Studies*, vol. 17, no. 1, 2008, pp. 1–40.
79 United States Department of State, *Country Reports on Terrorism 2008*, Washington, DC, April 2009.
80 "U.S. Putting N. Korea Back on Terrorism List 'Necessary': Kawamura," *Kyodo News*, June 8, 2009; "Relist North: Saiki," *The Japan Times*, June 11, 2009.
81 DPJ, *Hatoyama Says "Only Natural" for US to Consider Putting North Korea Back on Terror List*, June 8, 2009, www.dpj.or.jp/english/news/index.html?num=16243 (accessed March 30, 2011).
82 DPJ, *Statement Following the Start of Procedures by the United States to Remove North Korea from the List of State Sponsors of Terrorism*, Tokyo, June 26, 2008.
83 "U.S. Double Standards Policy on Nuclear Issue under Fire," *Korean Central News Agency*, June 2, 2009; "U.S. Termed Chief Culprit of Nuclear Proliferation," *Korean Central News Agency*, June 11, 2009.
84 Office of the Press Secretary, The White House, *Letter from the President Regarding North Korea: Text of a Letter from the President to the Speaker of the House of Representatives and the President of the Senate*, Washington, DC, February 3, 2010.
85 "U.S. Spares N. Korea 'Terror Sponsor' Status," *Daily Yomiuri Online*, June 24, 2010.
86 DPJ, *Haku Questions Government Response on Abduction Issue*, February 4, 2010, www.dpj.or.jp/english/news/index.html?num=17685 (accessed March 30, 2011).
87 *Newsletter (No. 7) from the Headquarters for the Abduction Issue, Government of Japan*, Tokyo, November 2009.
88 Prime Minister of Japan and His Cabinet, Speeches and Statements by Prime Minister, *Joint Press Conference at the Conclusion of the Japan–Republic of Korea Summit Meeting (Summary)*, Tokyo, June 7, 2003.
89 Richard Cronin, "The North Korean Nuclear Threat and the U.S.–Japan Security Alliance: Perceived Interests, Approaches, and Prospects," *The Fletcher Forum of World Affairs*, vol. 29, no. 1, Winter 2005, p. 53.
90 Ministry of Foreign Affairs, *Press Conference 1 June 2004*, Tokyo, June 1, 2004.
91 "Diet Passes Amendment Allowing Sanctions on N. Korea," *Kyodo News*, February 9, 2004.
92 "Abe Says Ferry-Ban Could be Scrapped," *The Japan Times Online*, May 16, 2004.
93 "U.S. to Raise Abductions at G-8," *The Japan Times Online*, April 29, 2006; G-8 Summit 2006, *Chair's Summary*, St. Petersburg, July 17, 2006, http://en.g8russia.ru/docs/25.html (accessed March 30, 2011).
94 DPJ, *Statement Regarding Broadcast Directive Relating to the Abduction Issue*, Tokyo, October 27, 2006; JCP, "Government Orders to NHK of What to Air in Violation of Freedom of Press," *Japan Press Weekly*, November 8–14, 2006, www.japan-press.co.jp/2006/2503/press.html (accessed March 30, 2011).
95 Author interviews with representatives of the Liberal Democratic Party and the Democratic Party of Japan, July 28, 2006 and July 31, 2006.

96 Author interview with an LDP official, Tokyo, July 28, 2006.
97 LDP, *Meeting of the LDP Countermeasures HQ for the North Korea Abduction Issue*, Tokyo, December 10, 2004.jimin.jp/jimin/english/new/news44.html (accessed on April 9, 2011); LDP, *Resolution: LDP Countermeasures HQ for the North Korea Abduction Issue*, Tokyo, December 10, 2004, www.jimin.jp/jimin/english/news/news45.html (accessed March 30, 2011).
98 "Gov't Displeased with Yamasaki Visit to N. Korea, Says 'Undesirable,'" *Kyodo News*, January 9, 2007; "Yamasaki's Pyongyang Trip Draws Flak," *The Japan Times Online*, January 10, 2007; Hisane Misake, "Japanese Bigwig on Surprise Pyongyang Visit," *Asia Times Online*, January 12, 2007; Ministry of Foreign Affairs, *Press Conference, 12 January 2007*, Tokyo, January 12, 2007.
99 Author interview with an official from the New Komeito Party, July 27, 2006; New Komeito Party, *Speech at the Foreign Correspondents Club of Japan* (by Takenori Kanzaki, Chief Representative of New Komeito), Tokyo, August 26, 2005, www.komei.or.jp/en/news/2005/speech050826.html?kw=abduction (accessed on January 28, 2007).
100 Author interview with a DPJ official, July 31, 2006.
101 DPJ, *DPJ Diet Members Question Government Response to Abduction Issue*, Tokyo, December 10, 2004, www.dpj.or.jp/english/news/041214/02.html (accessed on March 30, 2011).
102 "SDP, Now Merely an Also-Ran, Has No One to Blame but Itself," *The Japan Times Online*, December 11, 2002.
103 Author interview with representative of the SDP, Tokyo, July 31, 2006.
104 "JCP Shii on Japan–North Korea Summit Talks," *Japan Press Weekly*, September 18, 2002, www.japan-press.co.jp/2002/2301/sii%20on%20jp-nk.html (accessed March 30, 2011).
105 Author interview with representative of the JCP, July 28, 2006.
106 See Prime Minister of Japan and His Cabinet, Speeches and Statements by the Prime Minister, *Policy Speech by Prime Minister Shinzo Abe to the 166th Session of the Diet*, Tokyo, January 26, 2007; Ministry of Foreign Affairs, *Policy Speech by Minister for Foreign Affairs Taro Aso to the 166th Session of the Diet*, Tokyo, January 26, 2007.
107 United Nations General Assembly, Department of Public Information, *General Assembly Adopts 46 Third Committee Texts on Human Rights Issues, Refugees, Self-Determination, Racism, Social Development*, New York, December 19, 2006.
108 "KCNA [Korean Central News Agency] Comments – Internationalizing of Abduction Issue is Product of Japan's Shamelessness," *The People's Korea*, February 12, 2005; "KCNA Accuses Japan of Working Hard to Evade Settlement of its Past Crimes," *Korean Central News Agency*, December 19, 2006.
109 Author meeting with official from the DPRK Ministry of Foreign Affairs, Pyongyang, January 8, 2009.
110 "Japan Cannot See in 21st Century as Long as Relations with DPRK Remain Unsettled," *Korean Central News Agency*, August 10, 1999; "Japan's Ambition for Reinvasion Blasted," *Korean Central News Agency*, January 31, 2007.
111 Peter Duus, "The Greater East Asian Co-Prosperity Sphere: Dream and Reality," *Journal of Northeast Asian History*, vol. 5, no. 1, June 2008, pp. 143–54; Bill Gordon, "Greater East Asia Co-Prosperity Sphere," http://wgordon.web.wesleyan.edu/papers/coprospr.htm (accessed April 1, 2011).
112 Richard Armitage and Joseph Nye, *The U.S.–Japan Alliance: Getting Asia Right through 2020*, Center for Strategic International Studies, Washington, DC, February 2007.
113 Anthony DiFilippo, *Japan's Nuclear Disarmament Policy and the U.S. Security Umbrella* (New York: Palgrave Macmillan, 2006), Chapter 8.

114 "Tok-Islet is Korea's: North and South Oppose Japan's Claim to Tok Islet," *The People's Korea*, April 2, 2005; "Japan's Claim to Tok Islet Flailed," *Korean Central News Agency*, February 13, 2006.

115 "Two Political Parties of North and South Issue Joint Statement," *Korean Central News Agency*, August 22, 2008.

116 Japan Ministry of Defense, *Defense of Japan 2009*, Tokyo, 2009, Chapter 1.

117 "Japan's 'White Paper on Defense for 2009' Slammed," *Korean Central News Agency*, July 28, 2009.

118 "All Koreans Called Upon to Remain True to the Idea of 'By Our Nation Itself,'" *Korean Central News Agency*, August 14, 2008; "Visits to 'Yasukuni Shrine' Assailed," *Korean Central News Agency*, November 4, 2008.

119 "Japanese Reactionaries' Visit to the 'Yasukuni Shrine' Flayed," *Korean Central News Agency*, May 1, 2009; "China Expresses Grave Concern over Japanese PM's Offering to Yakusuni Shrine," *Xinhua*, April 23, 2009; "South Korea Regrets Japanese PM's Offering at War-linked Shrine," *Yonhap News Agency*, April 21, 2009.

120 "Japanese Reactionaries' Scheme for Revival of Militarism Censured," *Korean Central News Agency*, November 1, 2009.

121 "Japan's Distortion of History Flayed," *Korean Central News Agency*, May 23, 2009.

122 Victor Cha, "What Do They Really Want? Obama's North Korea Conundrum," *The Washington Quarterly*, vol. 32, no. 4, October 2009, pp. 119–38; Jonathan Pollack, "Kim Jong Il's Clenched Fist," *The Washington Quarterly*, vol. 32, no. 4, pp. 153–73.

123 "Gates: N Korea Progress Sign of Dark Future," *ABC News*, May 30, 2009.

124 Morton Abramowitz and Steven Bosworth, *Chasing the Sun: Rethinking East Asian Policy* (New York: Century Foundation Press, 2006), p. 70.

125 Shi Yongming, "Challenging Talks," *The Beijing Review*, vol. 50, no. 1, January 4, 2007, pp. 10–11; Selig Harrison, "North Korea: A Nuclear Threat," *Newsweek International Edition*, October 16, 2006; Selig Harrison, "Getting Around Pyongyang's Hard-Liners," Nautilus Institute, Policy Forum Online, July 7, 2005, www.nautilus.org/fora/security/0555Harrison.html (accessed on April 9, 2011).

126 JCP, *JCP Chair Shii Issues Statement Welcoming Agreement of Six-Party Talks*, Tokyo, February 13, 2007, www.jcp.or.jp/english/jps_weekly07/20070213_shii_danwa.html (accessed on April 9, 2011); SDP, *About Agreement Document Announcement at Six-Party Talks*, Tokyo February 13, 2007, www5.sdp.or.jp/central/timebeing07/danwa0213.html (in Japanese) (accessed on April 9, 2011).

7 Conclusion

Separate concerns and rapprochement possibilities

By 2008, significant progress had been made between Washington and Pyongyang toward the goal of resolving the North Korean nuclear issue. This progress, unfortunately, was ephemeral. By the end of 2008, the six-party talks (China, the two Koreas, Russia, Japan and the United States) once again became ineffective; this time because of a verification dispute. By June 2009, US–DPRK relations had deteriorated to the point where Pyongyang concluded that the Obama administration "is little different from the preceding regimes in the hostile policy towards" the Democratic People's Republic of Korea (DPRK).[1] Although at least for a brief time bilateral relations looked more promising between Washington and Pyongyang, the same cannot be said for the relationship between Japan and the DPRK.

This chapter identifies, often in a summary fashion, the ongoing security-related problems that trouble the relationship between the United States and North Korea and between the DPRK and Japan, while also considering relevant South Korean, Chinese and Russian interests. This chapter also incorporates recent developments – i.e., largely during the first two years of the Obama administration – in outstanding security-related problems associated with the DPRK. This chapter concludes by stressing that peaceful coexistence and rapprochement must be built on the trust-building actions of the United States, Japan, North Korea and South Korea, which along with DPRK needs to discover the path to unifying the Korean Peninsula. All of this is contingent upon countries' resolve to dialogue, often bilaterally, with each other.

The history problems between Japan and North Korea

For North Korea, the "history problem" refers to the still unresolved issues that stem from the period 1910 to 1945, the time when Japanese imperial forces annexed the Korean Peninsula.[2] Pyongyang maintains that the resolution of this problem, which it sees as the most significant outstanding issue standing in the way of improving DPRK–Japanese relations, would conceivably include a large compensation package from Japan, possibly costing it as much as $20 billion.[3]

Pyongyang is unrelenting in its demand that Tokyo make amends for its brutal colonization of Korea.[4] For Pyongyang, the kidnapping of Japanese nationals pales in comparison to the past atrocities perpetrated by Japan during its imperialist heyday. According to Pyongyang, owing to Japan's colonization of the Korean Peninsula, it abducted or coercively removed over 8.4 million Koreans to serve as soldiers and forced laborers; of these, more than one million were killed. Moreover, Japanese forces, says Pyongyang, exploited 200,000 Koreans females by making them become *juugun inanfu*, that is, sex slaves or comfort women.[5]

Although Tokyo recognizes that historical problems with the DPRK have not been resolved, typically it has minimized their significance – or even worse denied them. Such was case when Prime Minister Shinzo Abe stated in early 2007: "There has been debate over the question of whether there was coercion [of comfort women] but the fact is, there was no evidence to prove there was coercion as initially suggested."[6] While outraging South Korea, China and Taiwan, victims also of Japan's imperialist past, Abe's comment caused Pyongyang to lash out at Japan. Within days after Abe's remark, the DPRK Foreign Ministry stated: "Abe has taken the lead in totally negating the crimes" [against the comfort women]. The DPRK Foreign Ministry also stressed: "No matter how desperately the Japanese authorities may try to whitewash the crime-woven past of Japan and cover up the crimes related to the 'comfort women' for the imperial Japanese army, the worst flesh traffic in the 20th century, they are historical facts that Japan can neither sidestep nor deny."[7]

Ongoing: the abduction issue

Since 2002, one position has dominated Japanese policymaking: North Korea committed heinous political crimes by kidnapping a number of Japanese nationals, and all of the abductees must be fully accounted for. This position on the abduction issue is so pervasive in Japan today that having a different view causes one to run the risk of being labeled a "traitor."[8] The Japanese government and media have been instrumental in fashioning this generally one-sided position on the abduction issue.[9]

Although normalized relations with the DPRK remains "high on the agenda" for some in the Japanese Ministry of Foreign Affairs, today there are problems that prevent this from occurring. Specifically, the abduction issue "has a life of its own" and this has caused Japan to be "trapped in a vicious cycle." Causing frustration among some officials in the Japanese Ministry of Foreign Affairs is that they recognize the abduction issue has been politicized or "overplayed," that public sentiment on this matter is not rational, and that these problems have adversely affected policymaking in Japan.[10] However, those in the Ministry of Foreign Affairs who recognize the consequences stemming from the politicization of the abduction issue, something that is flatly denied by some bureaucrats,[11] are not by far the dominant voice in the Japanese government.

Some on the far right in Japan want Tokyo to continue to prioritize the abduction issue, but for a reason different from its connection to popular sentiment. Convinced that it will not be resolved any time soon, these ultra-rightists see the abduction issue as a way for Tokyo to avoid making reparations to the DPRK for the past crimes perpetrated by Japan on the Korean people. They maintain that giving aid to the current autocratic government in the DPRK would be foolhardy, since it is the North Korean people and not a small select group associated with the DPRK's autocratic leader that should benefit from Japanese reparations.[12]

Many in Tokyo see Japan's defeat in the Pacific War as a historical line of demarcation – in other words, a way to largely ignore the past and focus on more recent times. Tokyo acknowledges that what Japan did before the war, in Korea, in China's Manchuria and elsewhere, was wrong. However, this was the distant past, a Japan quite different from today. Since the war, Japan has become a respected member of the international community. Excluding Taiwan, of all of the world's countries, Japan has established normal diplomatic relations with every one of them, except North Korea.[13] Many Japanese people stress – from officials within the Cabinet Office's Headquarters for the Abduction Issue to the average person[14] – that the DPRK's abductions of Japan's nationals occurred well after the end of the Pacific War, the point at which their country put itself on the road to redemption.

Tokyo has repeatedly indicated that it "places the highest priority on resolving the abduction issue,"[15] something strongly supported by the Japanese public. By 2008, over six million Japanese people had signed a petition urging their government to "rescue" the abductees, who Tokyo continues to maintain have been victims of "unprecedented state sponsored crimes."[16] Promoted aggressively by conservatives and nationalists,[17] Tokyo has often made it clear that normalized ties between Japan and North Korea are contingent on the resolution of the abduction issue.

The Japanese government's position is that North Korea is "obligated to prove" that the abductees are dead, maintaining that Pyongyang has not provided to Tokyo "acceptable evidence" that they are deceased. Thus, Tokyo bases its policy on the assumption that the unaccounted-for abductees are still alive – the exact opposite of what Pyongyang says. Moreover, Tokyo wants Pyongyang to send those who were responsible for the kidnappings to Japan – while the DPRK maintains that they have been executed – and believes that, since the abduction issue is a security problem, it should be addressed within the context of the six-party talks. Pyongyang, which has never wanted the abduction issue discussed at the six-party talks, has insisted: "all of the living abductees have already returned to Japan" and repeatedly stated that this matter had been settled in 2002 when Prime Minister Junichiro Koizumi and Kim Jong Il signed the Pyongyang Declaration.[18]

In Japan, private organizations working on the abduction issue, which have been very influential in formulating the nation's policy toward the DPRK, report considerably higher numbers of persons kidnapped by North Korea than the Japanese government. One such organization, the Investigation Commission on Missing Japanese Probably Related to North Korea (COMJAN), maintains that 35 Japanese people have been abducted by North Korea and that the DPRK may have kidnapped as many as 470 people.[19] The National Association for the Rescue of Japanese Kidnapped by North Korea (NARKN) maintains that North Korea abducted more than 100 Japanese people, plus many others from 11 countries besides Japan.[20] Holding the same position on the abduction issue as NARKN, the Association of the Families of Victims Kidnapped by North Korea (AFVKN) stated that the abduction issue is a "global problem, not just a problem for Japan."[21] Although the government of Japan, as noted in Chapter 6, officially maintains that the DPRK adducted 17 of its nationals, officials are not reluctant to state that 400 or more Japanese individuals may have been kidnapped by North Korea.[22]

Japan strongly opposed Washington's removal of the DPRK from the US list of states sponsoring terrorism, even though the Bush administration continued to emphasize the United States would not forget about the abduction issue.[23] Moreover, like Tokyo, the Japanese public had concluded that the DPRK was a rogue state that had to be dealt with sternly. Similar to what past surveys had demonstrated, after the Japan–DPRK working-level talks were held on the abduction issue in June 2008, more than 60 percent of the respondents to a *Nikkei Shimbun* poll opposed Tokyo easing economic sanctions on the DPRK in exchange for Pyongyang beginning a reinvestigation of the abduction issue.[24] Because Tokyo's hopes of having bilateral discussions with Pyongyang had been diminished by the fall 2008, it adopted the position that getting the DPRK to reinvestigate the abduction issue hinged entirely on sanctions, believing that they "may work on North Korea.[25]

The politicization of the abduction issue became clear late in the summer of 2009 when it was used to try to curry favor with Japanese voters for Prime Minster Aso and his Liberal Democratic Party (LDP), whose prospects for maintaining control of Japan's powerful lower house had become very bleak. Attempting to forestall the likelihood that he would be forced out of office after the elections were held in late August 2009, when the Democratic Party of Japan (DPJ) was expected to win by a big margin, Aso undertook an unprecedented political move. Cognizant of voters' interest in the unresolved abduction issue, Aso visited the place where North Korean agents had abducted Megumi Yokota in 1977, the first Japanese prime minister to ever do this.[26]

The landslide defeat of the long-dominant LDP by the DPJ in August 2009 and the assumption of Yukio Hatoyama to the office of prime minister did not change Tokyo's position on the kidnappings. In his speech given to the UN General Assembly in September 2009, Hatoyama declared: "In particular, regarding the abduction issue, constructive actions by the DPRK, including swiftly commencing a full investigation as agreed last year, will be an avenue towards progress in Japan–DPRK relations."[27]

In October 2009, Hatoyama called South Korean President Lee Myung-bak's Grand Bargain, a comprehensive assistance package offered to North Korea after it demonstrates its commitment to denuclearization (see below): "an eminently wise approach." Hatoyama told Lee that South Korea, like Japan, has been troubled by the abduction of its citizens by North Korea. According to Hatoyama, Lee responded: "that the abduction issue naturally forms a part of the comprehensive package."[28] Hatoyama later stated: "Japan's stance is to reach a comprehensive resolution of these [nuclear, missile and abduction] issues, a position we consider to be consistent with that behind the 'grand bargain' advocated by President Lee Myung-bak."[29]

Tokyo, which in November 2009 announced that Kim Jong Il supervised the agency that kidnapped Japanese citizens,[30] continues to directly tie the abduction issue to Japan's security. Writing as if the DPRK is again preparing to perpetrate abductions, Japan's Ministry of Defense pointed out in its 2009 White Paper that the kidnapping of the country's citizens "is a major threat to the lives and security of the Japanese public."[31]

Other outstanding problems between Japan and North Korea

Besides the unresolved historical and abduction issues, there are other major problems creating animus in the Japan–DPRK relationship, many of which have already been discussed in this book.

Pyongyang often complains about the continuous strengthening of the US–Japan security alliance and about the prospects of Japanese constitutional change and remilitarization. As we have seen, Pyongyang is not pleased with Japan's demonstrated commitment to missile defense and its deployment of spy satellites, both of which for the DPRK prove that Tokyo has become increasingly interested in launching a preemptive strike.[32] Pyongyang is aware that Japan, if it so chooses, can adapt some of the work from its space program to deliver nuclear weapons, should Tokyo decide to build them.[33]

Tokyo has been equally concerned about North Korea's policy commitment to *songun* (military first), which has resulted in Pyongyang spending many wŏn to build up the DPRK's military and to it demonstrating its commitment to missile and nuclear development. Regarding the latter, Japan's Ministry of Defense recently emphasized: "Concerns over North Korea's nuclear weapons and ballistic missiles have grown more serious."[34]

This work has shown in detail that problems involving Chongryon Koreans have been exacerbated in recent years and that, along with Beijing and Seoul, Pyongyang has been troubled by visits made by Japanese politicians to Yasukuni Shrine in Tokyo. It has also discussed the textbook controversy, in which Japanese nationalists and conservatives have succeeded in getting schoolbooks to minimize their country's imperial history.

Still another serious problem in the recent past, between Japan and the DPRK, has been North Korean ships suspected of entering Japanese waters. Tokyo has claimed that these suspicious ships (*fushinsen*) have been involved in drug smuggling, spying activities and kidnapping. Suspicions pertaining to illegal entry became a reality in December 2001, when the Japanese Coast

Guard was involved in a gun battle with a ship that had entered Japan's waters masquerading as a Chinese fishing vessel. Other than issuing warning shots, this was the first gun battle involving Japanese maritime forces since the Pacific War. Several months after the incident, the Japanese government confirmed that the sunken ship was a North Korean vessel. Then Chief Cabinet Secretary Yasuo Fukuda stated: "Now we can label it as a spy ship." Kim Jong Il apologized for the spy-boat incident, saying: "This will never happen again."[35] Nonetheless, the incursions of North Korean ships into Japanese waters has given Tokyo one more reason to maintain that the DPRK is a threat to Japan's national security.

Difficulties in normalizing Japan–DPRK relations

Pyongyang and Tokyo have understood for some time that normal diplomatic ties would benefit both countries and improve the security environment in Northeast Asia. When the Cold War ended, Tokyo and Pyongyang quickly seized the opportunity to begin normalization discussions. The first round of bilateral talks between Tokyo and Pyongyang occurred in late January 1991. Although they met frequently, Japan and the DPRK were unable to realize rapprochement. By November 1992, Japan and the DPRK were engaged in the eighth round of normalization discussions. However, negotiations stopped after reports came to light that North Korea had kidnapped a Japanese women to work as a Japanese language instructor in the DPRK. Missile testing by North Korea, the first DPRK nuclear crisis in the early 1990s, at which time Pyongyang threatened to pull out of the Nuclear Nonproliferation Treaty,[36] and the abduction issue, led to a prolonged interruption in normalization talks.

However, things changed in March 2000. The expectation that progress could be made in resolving the abduction issue led to Tokyo's announcement that it wanted to resume food aid to the DPRK, which Japan had stopped after Pyongyang launched the *Kwangmyŏngsŏng-1* in August 1998. Tokyo and Pyongyang eventually took part in the tenth and eleventh rounds of normalization discussions; however, they accomplished little. Things looked much better for the bilateral relationship when Prime Minister Koizumi announced in August 2002 that he would be visiting North Korea in September,[37] a trip that the Bush administration attempted to persuade him not to make.[38] The summit ended with the two leaders signing the Pyongyang Declaration and with a promise to resume normalization talks in October.

However, the twelfth round of Japan–DPRK normalization talks was not successful. Although Pyongyang recommended that discussions be held again in November, this never happened.[39] The October normalization talks went nowhere largely because Tokyo wanted to focus on the abduction issue, while Pyongyang was interested in settling the history problem.

In May 2004, Koizumi made his second trip to Pyongyang. During his one-day summit with Kim Jong Il, Koizumi indicated that he wanted to provide food aid – that had stopped in December 2001 after the North Korean vessel entered Japanese waters[40] – and pharmaceutical assistance to the DPRK.[41] After Koizumi returned from the summit he stated: "I will keep to my strong expectation that my visit to North Korea this time will serve as a turning point for realizing the normalization of relations between Japan and North Korea."[42] However, this proved to be wishful thinking.

In August 2004, via the United Nations' World Food Program, Japan gave about half of the 250,000 tons of food aid it had promised to North Korea. However, because of differences on the abduction issue, Tokyo did not provide the rest of the food aid that it had promised to the DPRK.[43]

The six-party talks held in September 2005 produced a Joint Statement in which the United States and the DPRK agreed to "take steps to normalize their relations." This joint statement also called on Japan and North Korea to work toward the goal of normalized relations, in accordance with the Pyongyang Declaration.[44] In late December, Japanese and DPRK officials met in Beijing and agreed to have three consultations – on the abduction issue, on the nuclear and missile problems, and on normalizing bilateral relations, which included the history problem – that would facilitate future normalization talks. During the December meeting, Tokyo stressed that "unless a variety of issues including the abduction issue are resolved, there can be no normalization of relations." For its part, Pyongyang again indicated that the kidnapping problem had been resolved when Prime Minister Koizumi visited the DPRK in September 2002.[45] Not long after this, the Japanese government reassured the Bush administration that the missile, nuclear and abduction issue first had to be resolved before Japan would normalize relations with the DPRK.[46]

After more than three years, Japan and the DPRK held normalization talks in Beijing in February 2006. However, prior to these talks the animosity between Tokyo and Pyongyang had been exacerbated when then Chief Cabinet Secretary Shinzo Abe stated that before the rapprochement process could begin between Japan and North Korea, the abduction issue, which "ranks No. 1," must be resolved. "If there is no progress toward resolving this issue, there will be no progress on other issues."[47] Pyongyang stressed just before the beginning of the DPRK–Japan normalization talks that Abe and then Foreign Minister Taro Aso were "typical hard-liners in the Japanese circle." Pyongyang pointed out that Abe, Aso and other conservatives had been placing priority on the abduction issue so that the public would be more supportive of it, thereby allowing Tokyo to eschew dealing with the history problem and the execution of the Pyongyang Declaration.[48]

The heightened mutual distrust and enmity between Tokyo and Pyongyang meant that the normalization talks held in February 2006 were unsuccessful. At the conclusion of the February talks, Song Il Ho, the North's negotiator in charge of Japan–DPRK normalization talks, pointed out that there remains a "huge difference of opinion regarding the abduction issue."[49] The Japanese side understood that, besides the abduction issue, Japan and North Korea have other major differences between them.[50] Making the success of these talks even more unlikely was that the Bush administration did not want Tokyo to normalize relations with North Korea until the nuclear issue had been resolved. Although Tokyo and Pyongyang have held bilateral discussions since the failed normalization talks in February 2006, including the task force meetings on normalization in March and September 2007, they have been unable to have formal discussions on rapprochement.

By 2006, the failure to resolve the abduction, missile and nuclear issues had taken their toll on the Japanese public's views of establishing friendly ties with North Korea. Not long before the normalization talks took place in October 2002, 66 percent of the respondents to a Japanese Cabinet Office survey supported normalizing Japan–DPRK relations. However, by 2005 public support in Japan for normalizing relations with the DPRK had fallen precipitously to 33 percent. Then, only 21 percent of the respondents wanted Tokyo to settle the past with North Korea – good news to Japanese nationalists whose hard-line positions toward the DPRK were becoming increasingly influential in Japan. Because of DPRK missile and nuclear testing in 2006, public support for normalizing Japan–North Korean relations declined to about 30 percent, while support for settling the past dropped to less than 19 percent.[51]

The paucity of trust building

Along with China, Russia and South Korea, the United States, Japan and the DPRK have concerns about the deteriorated security environment in Northeast Asia. Expectedly, separate countries with sometimes-different political perspectives and interests means that there will inevitably be security disagreements and problems. To improve the security environment of Northeast Asia, additional trust-building efforts are needed.

Like its predecessor, the Bush administration reasoned that the DPRK would collapse one way or another in the not-too-distant future.[52] Until this happened, the Bush administration insisted for several years that it must maintain a hard-line policy toward the DPRK. Perceiving US policy as hostile, Pyongyang's justified its *songun*-based reactions by maintaining that it needed to protect the nation's sovereignty.

During 2007, the Bush administration began abandoning its hard-line DPRK policy. Although the road was not smooth, Pyongyang eventually began disabling its plutonium-reprocessing facilities at Yongbyon in early November 2007.[53] Still, problems between North Korea and the United States did not end.

At first, Tokyo was somewhat reluctant to support the Bush administration's hard-line policy toward the DPRK in 2002. However, the Bush administration made it very clear to Tokyo that it did not want Japan to normalize relations with North Korea until there was a resolution to the nuclear dispute.[54] Soon, Tokyo fully supported Washington's hard-line North Korean policy and in little time adopted and maintained one of its own that has centered on the abduction issue.

The Bush administration's willingness to adopt a somewhat conciliatory DPRK policy for awhile put Tokyo in a difficult position with respect to the abduction issue. Tokyo, contrary to what it agreed to at the six-party talks in February 2007, continued to withhold Japan's share of the bill for energy assistance to the DPRK in exchange for North Korea's nuclear disablement work until progress has been made on the abduction issue. This eventually forced Washington to look to Australia, New Zealand and the European Union for replacement funds.[55]

Just as Tokyo largely avoided building trust with the DPRK, so did Pyongyang eschew this with Japan. However much Pyongyang had become tired of hearing about the abduction issue, particularly in light of the unresolved history problem, it avoided fully explaining why the reinvestigation that it agreed to undertake in August 2008 did not materialize, other than to say: "Japan has never cooperated with the DPRK in the settlement of the abduction issue."[56]

The failure of the six-party talks held in December 2008 to resolve the verification dispute pertaining to the DPRK's nuclear issue created a major leak in the small amount of trust building that had been created between Washington and Pyongyang. Pressed by conservative governments in Tokyo and Seoul, the Obama administration, which had signaled that the policies of the Bush team had exacerbated the DPRK nuclear issue, made clear that it would stick to the six-party framework, despite its limited success. Expecting too much too soon from the Obama government, Pyongyang pushed *songun* initiatives to the forefront and launched a satellite only two and half months into the new administration, subsequently detonated a second nuclear device and conducted missile tests, all during the first half of 2009.

The DPRK Foreign Ministry gave a detailed statement in late July 2009 explaining why Pyongyang would no longer participate in the six-party talks. The Foreign Ministry pointed out that because the core principle – the "spirit of mutual respect for sovereignty and equality" – stipulated in the joint statement of the six-party talks held in September 2005 had been abandoned, these multilateral discussions were no longer of any value. It indicated that the DPRK was the only non-aligned country in the six-party talks, the rest being either permanent members of the UN Security Council or involved in security alliances with the United States. Stressing that the DPRK had the "legitimate right" to launch the satellite that it tested in April, the Foreign Ministry's statement made clear that Pyongyang was not at all pleased with the hostile reaction by the UN Security Council. Maintaining that members of the six-party talks had been pursuing their "ulterior aims to disarm and incapacitate the DPRK," Pyongyang emphasized, as it had done similarly since the spring, that these multilateral talks had been "reduced to a platform for blocking even the DPRK's development of science and technology for peaceful purposes and curbing the normal progress of its economy."[57]

Just a few days earlier, Sin Soh Ho, the DPRK's permanent representative to the United Nations, had stated that the "six-party talks are gone forever.

We will never participate in the six-party talks." However, Sin emphasized at the same time that the DPRK wanted bilateral talks with the United States.[58] Pyongyang then decided to introduce an icebreaker. When Bill Clinton visited the DPRK in early August 2009 and met with Kim Jong Il, the Dear Leader decided to comply with the former president's request. Kim released the two American journalists who had been held there since their capture in March 2009 and sentenced to 12 years of hard labor after being convicted of entering the country illegally "for the purpose of making animation files to be used for an anti-DPRK smear campaign over its human rights issue."[59] Clinton's visit led to some speculation that the six-party talks could possibly take place in the future.[60]

The Obama administration stressed that Clinton went to Pyongyang as a citizen on a "private humanitarian mission" and not as a representative of the US government. Moreover, the Obama administration left no doubt that Pyongyang's release of the convicted American journalists was completely separate from the North Korean nuclear issue, and that US policy, as before Clinton's trip, remained unchanged – to enforce the sanctions imposed by the UN Security Council.[61] As it had for some time, the Obama administration continued to stress that bilateral discussions between Washington and Pyongyang could only occur within the context of the six-party talks.

After Clinton's visit, Pyongyang decided that it would begin to warm up to Seoul. Pyongyang made a number of goodwill gestures toward Seoul, including releasing a Hyundai employee and four South Korean workers that were being held by the North. Pyongyang also sent a delegation to Seoul to attend the funeral of former South Korean President Kim Dae Jung, participated in North–South discussions to arrange for meetings of families that had been separated for years by the Korean War and reopened its border, which restarted tourism and permitted South Korean firms to continue doing business in the DPRK.

Seoul has struggled with the question of the DPRK's nuclear weapons. Like some conservatives in the United States and Japan, in Seoul some believe that Pyongyang does not intend to give up its nuclear weapons. This group reasons that by the DPRK keeping its nuclear weapons Kim Jong Il can guarantee the existence of his autocratic regime and his family's firm hold on the reins of government. Others in Seoul believe that China, North Korea's closest ally, has not pushed Pyongyang as hard as it could have to get rid of its nuclear weapons because a collapse of the DPRK would instantly create a serious refugee problem for Beijing. Still others in Seoul believe that while Washington very much wants the DPRK to denuclearize, it has largely ruled out military action because of the problems it experienced in Iraq and Afghanistan. This has left Seoul with three courses of action from which it has had to choose. First, it can hope that the DPRK collapses, thus simply wait for the North's demise. Second, believing that Pyongyang will not disarm, Seoul can give aid to the DPRK as a ransom for South Korea's security. Third, Seoul can decide that it will not accept nuclear weapons in North Korea.[62] Led by its conservative President Lee Myung-bak, Seoul ultimately concluded that the third course was the best selection for South Korea, although, like the right in the United States, the collapse of the DPRK remains the preferred outcome.[63]

While Lee's government accepted the North's new conciliatory behavior, his policy nonetheless mirrored that of the Obama administration with respect to maintaining the integrity of the six-party framework. Conspicuously absent from Seoul's position since Lee assumed the presidency in February 2008 was the trust necessary to build strong relations with the North.

In August 2009, the Lee administration issued a document entitled *Policy of Mutual Benefits and Common Prosperity toward North Korea*. This document eliminated any doubts that may have been lingering concerning his government's position with respect to the DPRK. The policy paper made clear that the Lee administration, unlike previous South Korea governments, would not be automatically giving assistance to the North. The paper spelled out that the priority of the Lee government is not inter-Korean relations but denuclearization, which therefore underscored the South Korean president's commitment to "move in tandem with progress in the Six-Party Talks." While the Lee government indicated that it was willing to provide financial and other aid to the North, it made clear that assistance fully depends on Pyongyang's genuine involvement in the denuclearization process.[64]

A month later Lee proposed in New York City a Grand Bargain, a conditional offer – apparently built on the August policy paper – to Pyongyang that would provide both economic assistance and a security guarantee to North Korea. The proviso: "Once North Korea gives up [its] nuclear programs and ambitions."[65] Although the new DPJ Prime Minister Yukio Hatoyama called Lee's Grand Bargain "completely correct,"[66] the Obama administration did not publicly support it.

Bidding directly to the Obama administration in August 2009, the DPRK invited Stephen Bosworth, the US Special Representative for North Korea Policy, to visit Pyongyang. Putting aside that it had not been at all happy that Bosworth had remained in his position as dean at the Fletcher School of Law and Diplomacy in Massachusetts, and not devoted his full attention to the nuclear issue, Pyongyang believed that bilateral dialogue, and not the six-party talks, would be the only effective way to deal with Washington. Then, Kim Jong Il himself struck a conciliatory note, even though it had been played a number of times in the past by the DPRK. Broadcast on the Voice of Korea, formerly Radio Pyongyang, in August, Kim's statement maintained: "We can ease tensions and remove the danger of war on the peninsula when the United States abandons its hostile policy and signs a peace treaty with us."[67]

Although the Obama administration did not address Kim's call for a peace treaty, it did respond to remarks made a few days later by Sin Son Ho, the DPRK's permanent representative to the United Nations. In early September 2009, Sin sent a letter to the president of the UN Security council, who for that month was Susan Rice, the US permanent representative to the United Nations. In his letter, Sin stressed that his government rejected the latest UN Security Council Resolution 1874, which extended and strengthened sanctions imposed on the DPRK. Sin wrote that the DPRK's second nuclear test, which precipitated the resolution, would have never occurred had the Security Council responded the same way to its launching of a "peaceful satellite" in April as it did to the satellite tested by South Korea in August 2009. Stressing that the DPRK has "never objected to the denuclearization of the Korean Peninsula and to the world itself," Sin wrote in his letter to Rice that Pyongyang, however, does not accept the six-party framework that both stifles his country's economic development and violates its sovereignty. Sin's letter stated that denuclearization is contingent on Washington's nuclear policy with respect to his country. Reinforcing the international belief that Pyongyang has a predilection for provocation, attention was immediately given to Sin's remarks pertaining to the DPRK reprocessing fuel rods, weaponizing plutonium, both of which it had previously announced in June 2009, and that his country had recently moved from the experimental to the final phase of uranium enrichment.[68] Reacting to Sin's comments, Bosworth stated during his visit to Seoul that any North Korean nuclear activity, including highly enriched uranium "is a subject of concern, and one which we have to address."[69]

Significantly, speculation was rife that Pyongyang had begun making conciliatory moves because the DPRK was feeling the pressure of the toughened sanctions regime, which had been imposed on it by the UN Security Council and by Japan. However, Sin's letter to Rice made clear that the DPRK had repositioned *songun*, which had briefly taken a backseat in its foreign policy, alongside of conciliation. Although Pyongyang continued to exhibit irenic behavior, the repositioning of *songun* to the forefront of the DPRK's policy agenda lessened the plausibility that sanctions had led North Korea to making conciliatory gestures.[70]

Because mastering the uranium-enrichment process would give Pyongyang, which had denied for years that it had been involved in this work, a second way to produce nuclear weapons, Sin's comment in his letter to Rice that the DPRK was in the final enrichment stage created a brief international stir. Pyongyang had initially raised some concern on this same issue in June 2009 when, immediately after the UN Security Council unanimously passed Resolution 1874, the DPRK Foreign Ministry announced that it would begin to enrich uranium.[71]

While some thought Sin's comment was more DPRK bluster, more than a year later when Stanford University's Siegfried Hecker visited the Yongbyon nuclear site in November 2010, he was shown a uranium-enrichment structure that contained 2,000 centrifuges and a light-water reactor that was being built. Hecker maintains that the uranium-enrichment work seems not to be to produce nuclear weapons, though this could change in the future, but rather to produce low-enriched uranium, according to the North Koreans, for the light-water reactor that will generate energy.[72]

Since the end of the Cold War, successive US administrations generally have been very reluctant to agree to bilateral discussions with the DPRK, preferring instead to rely on sanctions.[73] The Obama administration has been no different. For months, it continued to stick to its position of refusing to have bilateral discussions with the DPRK, with Bosworth, while consulting with the Japanese in Tokyo in September 2009, saying that discussions between Washington and Pyongyang would not take place "in any form" until North Korea does what it agreed to do in these multilateral talks.[74]

However, back in Washington the State Department soon announced something very different, saying that the United States would be willing to meet bilaterally with Pyongyang. Hedging as best he could at first, US Assistant Secretary of State Philip Crowley indicated: "it's important to characterize it properly. It's a bilateral discussion that – hopefully within the Six-Party context – and it's designed to convince North Korea to come back to the Six-Party process and to take steps towards denuclearization." Crowley then went on to state straightforwardly: "if, through a bilateral process, we can bring them [the North Koreans] back to the Six-Party process, that is our objective."[75] Not long after this Kim Jong Il told China's special envoy to President Hu Jintao during a meeting in Pyongyang that the DPRK wants to resolve the nuclear issue through bilateral and multilateral discussions,[76] though he did not specifically state the six-party talks.

Shortly before Prime Minister Aso and his LDP suffered a crushing defeat to the DPJ in late August 2009, Pyongyang suggested, in a noticeable departure from the past few years, that it would be willing to warm up to Japan. However, according to a researcher in the DPRK Foreign Ministry, first Tokyo had to change its policy toward the DPRK.[77]

Pyongyang's dual-pronged policy – relying on *songun* and conciliation – caused South Korea's President Lee Myung-bak to comment: "The situation surrounding North Korea is fluid," a remark meant to convey his belief that in the DPRK hardliners and those predisposed to conciliatory diplomacy had been at odds about how to deal with the country's problems connected to the nuclear issue.[78] In any case, in September 2009, senior DPRK official Kim Yong Nam gave a not-too-common interview in Pyongyang to *Kyodo News*, Japan's major news agency. Kim stated: "If [Tokyo] respects the Pyongyang Declaration, seriously settles the unfortunate past based on it and resolves [other] issues of concern, while setting fruitful relations in political, economic, cultural and other areas that benefits both sides, [these actions] would not only match the wishes of the people in both countries but secure peace and stability in Northeast Asia."[79] Seeing the outgoing Aso administration as having been completely hostile toward the DPRK, the conciliators in North Korea became cautiously optimistic that Prime Minister Hatoyama's DPJ, which had announced after the August election that it wanted to improve Japan's relations with its Asian neighbors, would be willing to settle outstanding differences between Pyongyang and Tokyo.

In September 2009, Song Il Ho, the North's ambassador in charge of normalization talks with Japan, stated during an interview in Pyongyang that his government was hopeful that the incoming DPJ and its coalition partners would take "a step to seriously improve [North] Korea–Japan relations." Song stressed that, given the hostility of the Aso government toward the DPRK, mainly Japan's increased reliance on a sanctions regime, the agreement to improve bilateral ties, reached at the DPRK–Japan talks held in Shenyang in August 2008, was void and a new one would be necessary. Song stressed the importance of settling the past and maintained, as Pyongyang has done many times before, that the abduction issue had already been resolved. However, Song also indicated that the DPRK is willing to participate in an effort "that shows by what measures [the kidnapping problem] can be solved."[80] Shortly after this in New York, Pak Kil Yon, the DPRK's Vice Minister of Foreign Affairs told UN Secretary-General Ban Ki Moon that Pyongyang was willing to have bilateral talks with Tokyo that included the abduction issue.[81] Despite some promising talk from both sides, relations never did improve between Japan and the DPRK.

Visiting Seoul in November 2009, President Obama met with President Lee, who was trying to win US support for his Grand Bargain, which some in South Korea see as absolutely necessary because of Beijing's limited influence on Pyongyang and the reluctance of DPRK officials to accept denuclearization.[82] Although Lee stated during a joint press conference that he and the president of the United States "fully share the view that the North Korean nuclear issue requires a definite and comprehensive resolution, as I described in our grand bargain," Obama was more circumspect in his remarks and never mentioned the Grand Bargain. Emphasizing his commitment to the six-party talks, Obama announced that Stephen Bosworth would travel to North Korea in early December, and participate in bilateral discussions with officials there as part of his administration's plan to get the DPRK to accept the multilateral process as the best way to resolve the nuclear issue.[83]

Lee claimed when he met with Obama in Seoul in November: "the North Koreans haven't yet conveyed what they thought of the grand bargain." However, well before this meeting Pyongyang had called the Grand Bargain "ridiculous," saying it "is a pipedream to expect the DPRK will dismantle its nuclear program without the U.S. drop of its hostile policy toward the DPRK."[84]

Still dodging rapprochement

To help improve the security environment of Northeast Asia, Washington, Tokyo and Pyongyang, as well as Seoul, must be committed to the implementation of confidence- and trust-building efforts and to making reasonable concessions. Pyongyang is hardly averse to normalizing relations with the United States and Japan,[85] which have both established preconditions before giving serious consideration to rapprochement, making this more of an ideal beset by a torturous path than a near-term achievable goal. Pyongyang recognizes that normal relations with the United States and Japan would help its struggling economy. However, just because Pyongyang welcomes rapprochement does not mean that it would be willing to succumb to what it perceives as unreasonable demands or hostile policies.

Of late, the United States, the DPRK as well as Japan and South Korea have been much too eager to resort to a show of military power in the face of problems. For example, following the artillery exchange in November 2010 between the two Koreas that killed four South Koreans on Yeongpyeong Island in the Yellow Sea, the United States and South Korea immediately carried out war exercises, rejecting Beijing's proposal to hold an emergency six-party meeting to deal diplomatically with the heightened regional tension. War exercises were also held between the United States and Japan with – for the first time – South Korean observers present. Pyongyang, which in December 2010 fired artillery into the Yellow Sea, reacted harshly to the US–South Korean military exercises, which included the nuclear-powered vessel the USS George Washington, by saying: "If the U.S. brings its carrier to the West Sea of Korea at last, no one can predict the ensuing consequences."[86]

Like Tokyo and Seoul, Washington continues to have serious concerns about Pyongyang's nuclear objectives. This explains why successive US administrations have maintained a comprehensive sanctions regime on the DPRK beyond those imposed by the UN Security Council, while, like the Obama administration, they have drawn attention to North Korea's violation of proliferation norms.[87] However, the Obama administration's concerns about the DPRK's proliferation activities appear to be at least partly for public consumption.[88] If the Obama administration had been genuinely concerned about the possibility of DPRK proliferation activities it would have been far more willing to meet either in a bilateral or multilateral setting with Pyongyang.

Pyongyang also continues to have serious concerns about the objectives of the United States and its alliance partners. These concerns have given Pyongyang reason to justify *songun* and to repeat its claim that the DPRK's nuclear weapons serve as a deterrent to ensure the nation's sovereignty and to maintain peace in Northeast Asia.[89] However, although Washington and its Japanese and South Korean allies insist on seeing evidence of the DPRK's denuclearization and improved relations with Seoul before beginning the six-party talks,[90] Pyongyang stated in fall 2010 that, while it is "not begging," it would participate in multilateral or bilateral meetings.[91]

Indeed, Pyongyang, Washington and its Japanese and South Korean allies have a long way to go before they realize rapprochement. Complicating this problem, like in the past, too often the politics of "defector analysis" creates pejorative impressions of the DPRK.[92] At the same time, Pyongyang retains its usage of uncomplimentary labels, such as imperialist reactionaries when referring to the United States and Japan, while calling South Korea a "puppet" of the United States.

A peace treaty: the nucleus of rapprochement

Discussions between Washington and Pyongyang dealing with the creation of a permanent peace treaty that would replace the 1953 armistice agreement and officially end the Korean War – something that the DPRK has wanted for some time – would have an assuaging effect on Northeast Asia. A peace treaty and the international legitimacy affixed to it would immediately create conditions that, if diligently pursued, markedly improve the security environment in Northeast Asia. The Joint Statement that came out of the September 2005 six-party talks stated: "The directly related parties will negotiate a permanent peace regime on the Korean Peninsula at an appropriate separate forum."[93] However, during its first two years in office, the Obama administration, like its predecessor, showed neither an interest in a traditional peace treaty nor a willingness to begin discussions to normalize bilateral relations until after the DPRK has become satisfactorily committed to the denuclearization process. And yet, Washington wants the DPRK to get rid of its nuclear weapons and permanently end its activities to produce them.

Whether or not the six-party talks become an effective vehicle to get the DPRK to denuclearize is not important. What is important is that denuclearization occurs. The six-party framework is just one mechanism that can be used to do this. Bilateral talks between Washington and Pyongyang can also play an important part in the denuclearization process and could be the starting point for launching discussions on a peace treaty to replace the armistice agreement. Bilateral talks between Washington and Pyongyang that include serious discussions on a permanent peace treaty could open the diplomatic door wide enough to give the United States, South Korea, China, Russia and, to some extent, even Japan what they want, which is for the DPRK to complete the denuclearization process. At the same time, a peace treaty would give the DPRK what it has sought for some time. While Pyongyang has frequently stressed that Washington's hostile policy is a threat to the sovereignty of the DPRK, and since October 2006 has been the reason why it must maintain a nuclear deterrent, it has also indicated often that under the right conditions it will get rid of its nuclear weapons. The longer the delay in trying to accomplish this, the more difficult it will be.

Pyongyang has sometimes stated that nuclear disarmament and the denuclearization of the Korean Peninsula is the wish of the Great Leader, Kim Il Sung. In September 2009, the DPRK's Vice Minister of Foreign Affairs Pak Kil Yon told the UN General Assembly: "We have never denied the denuclearization of the Korean peninsula and the rest of the world. The denuclearization is the behest of President Kim Il Sung and nuclear-free world is a long cherished-desire [*sic*] of humankind." Vice Minister Pak went on to note: "The denuclearization of the Korean peninsula depends on whether or not the US changes its nuclear policy towards Korea. In order to realize the denuclearization of the Korean peninsula, the US administration must discard [the] old concept of confrontation and show the 'change' in practice, as it recently stated on several occasions."[94]

Significantly, just during the first two months of 2010, Pyongyang made several calls for a peace treaty to supplant the armistice agreement. Pyongyang stated in January 2010 that had a peace treaty been in place "the nuclear issue would have not surfaced." It went on to state that a peace treaty will be useful in eliminating the enmity between Washington and Pyongyang and will "positively promote the denuclearization of the Korean Peninsula at a rapid tempo." Pyongyang maintained that "a peace treaty would mark the beginning of confidence-building" and that such an accord is not "different from the issue of the denuclearization of the peninsula."[95]

However, if a peace accord is going have any chance of being acceptable to Washington, it must be conditional: a *quid pro quo* – the DPRK's denuclearization in exchange for a treaty that becomes permanent once Pyongyang completes the disarmament process. Thus, a peace treaty that entered into force immediately ending the Korean War would have to include a clause stipulating that the DPRK has one or perhaps two years from the date of signing to complete the denuclearization process, return to the Nuclear Non-proliferation Treaty as a nonnuclear weapons state and sign and ratify the Comprehensive Test Ban Treaty (CTBT). Barring unforeseen extenuating circumstances, if the DPRK failed to meet these conditions, the treaty would become invalid.

In addition to the United States and the DPRK, a conditional peace treaty that becomes permanent must also include South Korea and China as signatories – the four countries that were the principal combatants in the Korean War. Thus, besides bilateral and six-party discussions, four-party talks represent still another mechanism that can be used to hasten the denuclearization of the DPRK. Despite Pyongyang's historical reluctance to have Seoul sign a peace treaty, South Korea views the existence of nuclear weapons in the North as a threat to its national security. Because of its active involvement in the Korean War and because it sees DPRK's nuclear weapons as a security threat, plus the fact that nuclear weapons in North Korea violate the 1992 Joint Declaration of the Denuclearization of the Korean Peninsula signed by Pyongyang and Seoul, South Korea needs to be a signatory to a peace accord.

The Obama administration could make a peace treaty more appealing to Pyongyang by pledging to work with other countries to end all subcritical nuclear testing and by promising to send the CTBT to the US Senate for ratification no more than one month after the signing of the peace accord. In a speech given in April 2009, President Obama said: "my administration will immediately and aggressively pursue U.S. ratification of the Comprehensive Test Ban Treaty,"[96] something that the White House has not yet done. The imminent ratification of the CTBT by the United States would put pressure on China, which has not ratified the accord, to do so.[97]

Thus, at least some of the above suggests that a peace treaty, if properly implemented, would have collateral benefits that would help drive a peace process and facilitate the establishment of a peace regime on the Korean Peninsula.[98] Specifically, a conditional peace treaty that becomes permanent would provide Washington and Pyongyang with the opportunity to begin discussions to normalize bilateral relations. Such an accord would also create the requisite impetus and right political environment for the two Koreas to engage in serious bilateral discussions that address the future unification of the peninsula.

A conditional peace treaty would also substantially reduce tensions and hostilities – or ideally eliminate major differences and serious problems altogether – between North and South Korea that have long been associated with the disputed Northern Limit Line (NLL) that divides their territorial waters in the Yellow or West Sea. Although the NLL was not part of the 1953 Armistice Agreement, since 1999 sea battles between the two Koreas in the waters in its vicinity have claimed the lives of a number of military personnel from both sides.[99]

The tragedy in the Yellow Sea in late March 2010 that took the lives of 46 South Korean sailors on board the warship Cheonan significantly heightened tensions in Northeast Asia. Based on the South Korean-led international investigation that the Obama administration fully endorsed, Seoul insisted it had proof that a torpedo fired from a North Korean submarine caused the Cheonan to sink, leading President Lee Myung-bak to promise to "take resolute countermeasures" by working with the international community so that the DPRK would get comeuppance for its aggression. However, Pyongyang repeatedly maintained its innocence, charging that South Korea's claims were "sheer fabrication."[100] In addition to the problems that there were several very important unanswered questions pertaining to why the DPRK would attack the Cheonan and irregularities in the data,[101] neither China nor Russia accepted the international investigation. Despite Seoul and Washington's desire to have the UN Security Council once again sanction the DPRK, China's opposition prevented this; moreover, the Presidential Statement that did result did not directly blame North Korea for the sinking of the Cheonan.[102] Almost certainly, had a peace treaty been in place or even in the process of negotiation, the only plausible explanation for why any Korean warship would sink would be because of an accident. Had a peace treaty been in place, the deadly clash between North and South Korea in November 2010, which this time also included two civilian casualties on the South's Yeonpyeong Island, would not likely have occurred.

Even before the peace treaty becomes permanent, there is no reason why Seoul and Pyongyang could not begin work to expedite the economic reunification of the peninsula, given the sources of growth that remain dormant in North Korea.[103] It is in Pyongyang's short- and long-term interests to implement and complete the denuclearization process as specified in the peace treaty. For Pyongyang, a peace treaty would mean the end of internationally imposed sanctions, which should be removed when the accord is signed as an incentive to the North, improved relations with the South and normalized ties with the United States. Normalized relations with the United States would make available to the DPRK a number of economic opportunities, including funds from international lending institutions that can be used to help grow its beleaguered economy.

Japan–DPRK relations could also benefit from a permanent peace treaty that creates the foundation for an enduring peace regime on the Korean Peninsula. An improved security environment in Northeast Asia would create an atmosphere conducive to helping Japan and the DPRK address and resolve their bilateral differences. A sincere commitment by Pyongyang to undertake a thorough reinvestigation of the abduction issue would be welcomed by Tokyo and especially by the Japanese people. A thorough reinvestigation of the abductions issue would also be welcomed by the Obama administration, which has reattached the United States to a problem the Bush team jettisoned toward the end of its second term, so that it could push the denuclearization process forward.

However, Tokyo would need to reciprocate. Once Pyongyang demonstrates a genuine commitment to a reinvestigation, Tokyo should immediately begin easing sanctions on DPRK. Tokyo should continue to ease sanctions and as quickly as possible eliminate them as the reinvestigation proceeds in earnest. At the same time, Tokyo should immediately permit the Mangyongbong-92, the North Korean vessel, to enter Japan and transport Chongryon Koreans who want to visit the DPRK. Permitting the reentrance of the Mangyongbong-92 would indicate to Pyongyang that Tokyo is serious about improving conditions for Chongryon Koreans residing in Japan, as called for in the 2002 Pyongyang Declaration. In return, Pyongyang could immediately announce a moratorium on long-range missile launches, again consistent with the spirit of the Pyongyang Declaration.

To the DPRK the history problem is the most pressing problem that needs to be settled. Pyongyang has stressed that, although Tokyo has incessantly complained about the abduction issue, North Koreans criticize the DPRK Ministry of Foreign Affairs for not getting information on the deaths of their relatives during the time when Japan annexed the peninsula.[104] Since in the DPRK the colonization of the Korean Peninsula has left lasting scars, Tokyo has to demonstrate to Pyongyang that it wants to resolve the history problem in an equitable manner and make clear that previous attempts to sanitize Japan's past behavior were wrong.

After Pyongyang meets the conditional requirements of the peace treaty and with the improvement of the security environment in Northeast Asia, other important developments become possible. Already recognized as a leading global champion of nuclear disarmament, Japan could take the very bold step of endorsing a nuclear-weapons-free zone in Northeast Asia, a move that would take South Korea and Japan out from under the US nuclear umbrella,[105] the latter supported by more than 60 percent of the DPJ lawmakers in the lower house.[106]

A conditional peace treaty that becomes permanent would reasonably quickly put an end to the Cold War mentality that besets much of Northeast Asia, most especially as this pertains to the DPRK's relations with the United States, Japan and South Korea. This sustained mentality has been fed by hostile policies, military threats, missile and nuclear tests and sanctions.

Because a permanent peace treaty would eliminate this Cold War mentality in Northeast Asia, it therefore is the most practical and least costly way to address and resolve many of the region's security problems, while creating the conditions for future improvements and lasting peace.

Notes

1 "KCNA Slams U.S. Administration's Invariable Hostile Policy Towards the DPRK," *Korean Central News Agency*, June 1, 2009.
2 USC–UCLA Joint East Asian Studies Center, East Asian Studies Documents, *Treaty of Annexation* [Annexation of Korea by Japan], August 22, 1910.
3 Mark Manyin, *North Korea–Japan Relations: The Normalization Talks and the Compensation/Reparations Issue*, Congressional Research Service Report for Congress, Washington, DC, June 13, 2001.
4 "Japan's Redemption of Its Past Crimes Urged," *Korean Central News Agency*, July 29, 2009.
5 "Japan Urged to Take Practical Step for Settlement of Past," *Korean Central News Agency*, January 17, 2005; "Indelible Crimes of Japan," *Korean Central News Agency*, August 14, 2008; Tim Beal, "Multilayered Confrontation in East Asia: North Korea-Japan," *Asian Affairs*, vol. XXXVI, no. III, November 2005, pp. 339–60.
6 "No Government Coercion in War's Sex Slavery: Abe," *The Japan Times Online*, March 2, 2007.
7 "Japan Urged to Pay for Crimes Related to 'Comfort Women' for Imperial Japanese Army," *Korean Central News Agency*, March 7, 2007.
8 Conversation with researcher at The Japan Institute of International Affairs, Tokyo, July 29, 2009.
9 Amii Abe, "Taboo in Japan: Can Japan Think Strategically about North Korea," *Policy Forum Online*, Nautilus Institute, April 9, 2009, www.nautilus.org/publications/essays/napsnet/forum/2009–10/09029Abe.html (accessed on April 5, 2011).
10 Author interview with an official in Ministry of Foreign Affairs, Asian and Oceanian Affairs Bureau, Northeast Asia Division, Tokyo, July 28, 2009.
11 Discussion with Deputy Director General of The Japan Institute of International Affairs, Tokyo, July 29, 2009.
12 Author meeting with researchers from the Institute for International Policy Studies, Tokyo, July 30, 2009.
13 Wada, Haruki, "Japan–North Korean Relations – A Dangerous Stalemate," *The Asia-Pacific Journal*, vol. 25-2-09, June 22, 2009.
14 Author meeting with official from the Headquarters for the Abduction Issue, Tokyo, Japan, July 24, 2009 and author discussion with Japanese college student at Ikebukuro Nishiguchi Kōen (Ikebukuro West Gate Park), Tokyo, July 28, 2009.
15 Headquarters for the Abduction Issue, Government of Japan, *For the Return of All of the Abductees: Points of Contention with the North Korean Position* (Tokyo: Headquarters for the Abduction Issue, July 2008).
16 Ministry of Foreign Affairs, *Abductions of Japanese Citizens by North Korea* (Tokyo: Ministry of Foreign Affairs, 2008).
17 Takashima Nobuyoshi, "The North Korean Abductions and the Rewriting of Japanese History," *Japan Focus*, February 2003, www.japanfocus.org (accessed April 1, 2011); Gregory Clark, "Abduction Issue – Rightwing's Political Football," *The Japan Times Online*, February 27, 2004.
18 Author interview with officials in Headquarters for the Abduction Issue, Tokyo, July 14, 2008; Ministry of Foreign Affairs, *Abductions of Japanese Citizens by North Korea*, Tokyo, 2008.

19 Author interview with official of COMJAN, Tokyo, July 14, 2008; COMJAN, *Introduction of COMJAN*, Tokyo, n.d.
20 NARKN, *North Korean Abduction Victims Worldwide*, Tokyo, August 2006; AFVKN and NARKN, *Worldwide Abductions Perpetrated by North Korea in 12 Countries*, Tokyo, December 2006.
21 Author interview with AFVKN official, Tokyo, July 14, 2008.
22 Author interview with official in the Japanese Ministry of Foreign Affairs, Tokyo, July 30, 2007; author interview with officials in Headquarters for the Abduction Issue, Tokyo, July 14, 2008.
23 United States Department of State, *On the Record Briefing: Special Envoy for the Six-Party Talks Ambassador Sung Kim, Assistant Secretary of State for Public Affairs Sean McCormack, Assistant Secretary of State for Verification, Compliance, and Implementation Paula DeSutter, and Acting Assistant Secretary of State for International Security and Nonproliferation Patricia McNerney on North Korea*, Washington, DC, October 11, 2008.
24 Survey data from The Maureen and Mike Mansfield Foundation, www.mansfieldfdn.org (accessed April 1, 2011).
25 Author interview with official from the Headquarters for the Abduction Issue, Tokyo, Japan, July 24, 2009; Government of Japan, Policy Planning Division, *Headquarters for the Abduction Issue, News Letter (No. 6) from the Headquarters for the Abduction Issue*, Tokyo, June 22, 2009.
26 "Aso Visits Site Tied to Abduction," *The Japan Times Online*, August 2, 2009.
27 Ministry of Foreign Affairs of Japan, *Address by H.R. Dr. Yukio Hatoyama Prime Minister of Japan at the Sixty-Fourth Session of the General Assembly of the United Nations*, New York, September 24, 2009.
28 Speeches and Statements by Prime Minister, *Joint Press Conference by Prime Minister Yukio Hatoyama of Japan and President Lee Myung-bak of the Republic of Korea*, Seoul, October 9, 2009.
29 Speeches and Statements by Prime Minister, *Joint Press Conference by Prime Minister Yukio Hatoyama of Japan, Premier Wen Jiabao of the People's Republic of China and President Lee Myung-bak of the Republic of South Korea following the Second Japan-China–ROK Trilateral Summit*, Beijing, October 10, 2009.
30 "Kim Jong Il Oversaw Abduction Agency," *Asahi Shimbun*, November 3, 2009.
31 Japan Ministry of Defense, *Defense of Japan 2009* (Tokyo: Ministry of Defense, 2009), p. 3, www.mod.go.jp/e/publ/w_paper/pdf/2009/Part1-overview-chap1.pdf (accessed on April 5, 2011).
32 "Japan's Projected Missile Test-fire Blasted," *Korean Central News Agency*, July 23, 2008; "KCNA Blasts Japan's Moves to Become a Military Power," *Korean Central News Agency*, September 5, 2008.
33 "DPRK Foreign Ministry Spokesman on Japan's Rocket Test-Fire," *Korean Central News Agency*, September 10, 2001; Selig Harrison, *Korean Endgame: A Strategy for Reunification and Disengagement* (Princeton, NJ: Princeton University Press, 2002), pp. 231–44.
34 Japan Ministry of Defense, *Defense of Japan 2009* (Tokyo: Ministry of Defense, 2009), p. 3, www.mod.go.jp/e/publ/w_paper/pdf/2009/Part1-overview-chap1.pdf (accessed on April 13, 2011).
35 "Japan Says North Korea Boat in Sea Battle was a Spy Ship," *The New York Times*, October 5, 2002; "N Korea 'Spy Ship' a Hit with Tourists," *BBC News*, June 2, 2003; Richard Samuels, "New Fighting Power! Japan's Growing Maritime Capabilities and East Asian Security," *International Security.* vol. 32, no. 3, Winter 2007/08, pp. 84–112.
36 Leon Sigal, *Disarming Strangers: Nuclear Diplomacy with North Korea* (Princeton, NJ: Princeton University Press, 1998); Joel Wit, Daniel Poneman and Robert

Gallucci, *Going Critical: The First North Korean Nuclear Crisis* (Washington, DC: Brookings Institution Press, 2004).

37 "Chronology of Major Events in Japan–North Korea Relations," *The Japan Times Online*, September 18, 2002; Manyin, *North Korea–Japan Relations: The Normalization Talks and the Compensation/Reparations Issue,* June 13, 2001; Mark Manyin, *Japan–North Korea Relations: Selected Issues*, Congressional Research Service Report for Congress, Washington, DC, November 26, 2003; Ministry of Foreign Affairs, *Announcement by the Chief Cabinet Secretary on Food Aid to North Korea*, Tokyo, October 6, 2000.

38 Bruce Cumings, "Decoupled from History: North Korea in the 'Axis of Evil,'" in Ervand Abrahamian, Bruce Cumings and Moshe Ma'oz, *Inventing the Axis of Evil: The Truth about North Korea, Iran, and Syria* (New York: New Press, 2004), pp. 70–71.

39 Ministry of Foreign Affairs, *12th Round of the Japan–North Korea Normalization Talks (Evaluation and Outline)*, Tokyo, October 2002; Ministry of Foreign Affairs, *Japan–North Korean Relations*, Tokyo, May 2004.

40 Manyin, *Japan–North Korea Relations: Selected Issues*, November 26, 2003.

41 Prime Minister of Japan and His Cabinet, *Japan–North Korea Meeting*, Tokyo, May 22, 2004.

42 Ministry of Foreign Affairs, *Press Conference by Prime Minister Junichiro Koizumi after the Japan North Korean Meeting*, Pyongyang, September 22, 2004.

43 "Yokota Furor Spells End to Food Aid for North Korea, Machimura Says," *The Japan Times Online*, December 11, 2004; "Suspension of Food Aid to N. Korea to Continue," *The Japan Times Online*, January 30, 2006.

44 Ministry of Foreign Affairs of the People's Republic of China, *Joint Statement of the Fourth Round of the Six-Party Talks*, Beijing, September 19, 2005.

45 Ministry of Foreign Affairs, *Governmental Consultations between Japan and North Korea* (December 24–25, Beijing), Tokyo, December 26, 2005.

46 "Japan Assures U.S. on Plans for N. Korea," *The Japan Times Online*, January 8, 2006.

47 "Japan List Abduction Top Priority in Talks with DPRK," *Xinhua News Agency*, November 8, 2005.

48 "KCNA Urges Japan to Honestly Approach DPRK–Japan Inter-Governmental Talks," *Korean Central News Agency*, February 3, 2006.

49 "North Korea Says 'Huge Difference of Opinion' Remains in Abduction Issue with Japan," *Mainichi Daily News*, February 7, 2006.

50 "DPRK–Japan Talks Conclude without Major Progress," *Xinhua Online*, February 8, 2006.

51 "66% of Japanese Favor Links with North Korea," *The Japan Times Online*, December 22, 2002; Government of Japan, *Public Opinion Survey on Diplomacy by the Cabinet Office of Japan*, Tokyo, October 2005 and October 2006, the 2005 and 2006 surveys accessed on the Maureen and Mike Mansfield Foundation website, www.mansfieldfdn.org (accessed April 1, 2011).

52 Central Intelligence Agency, Office of Asian Pacific and Latin American Analysis, *Intelligence Report*, Washington, DC, January 21, 1998; Mike Chinoy, *Meltdown: The Inside Story of the North Korean Nuclear Crisis* (New York: St. Martin's Press, 2008), pp. 138–39.

53 "KCNA Report on Visit to Area of Nyongbyon by Those Concerned and Nuclear Experts," *Korean Central News Agency*, November 30, 2007.

54 Anthony DiFilippo, "Kojireta Kankei no Nichicho Kokko Seijohka," *Kitachosen o Meguru Hokutoh Ajia no Kokusai Kankei to Nihon*, henshuusha Yoichi Hirama, Yone Sugita (Tokyo: Akashi Shoten, 2003), pp. 66–84 ("The Troubled Relationship: What Normalized Relations Would do for Japan and North Korea," in

Japan and Northeast Asian International Relations Involving North Korea, eds. Yoichi Hirama and Yone Sugita [Tokyo: Akashi Shoten, 2003], pp. 66–84).

55 "Australia, NZ, EU Invited to Aid NK," *The Korea Times*, October 31, 2008.
56 "KCNA Slams Japan's Dishonest Stand Towards Issue of Fulfillment of Its Commitment," *Korean Central News Agency*, October 22, 2008.
57 "DPRK Foreign Ministry Spokesman on Unreasonable Call for Resumption of Six-party Talks," *Korean Central News Agency*, July 27, 2009.
58 "Pyongyang Willing to Resume Dialogue with the United States: N. Korean Amb. To U.N.," *Kyodo News*, July 24, 2009.
59 "KCNA Detailed Report on Truth of Crimes Committed by American Journalists," *Korean Central News Agency*, June 16, 2009.
60 Kim Ji Soek, "Yi Myung Bal Dae Tong Ryong Nam Buk Kwan Kye Puleora" ("President Lee, Salvage the Relationship between North and South Korea") *Hankyoreh*, August 4, 2009.
61 The White House, Office of the Press Secretary, *Press Briefing by Press Secretary Robert Gibbs*, Washington, DC, August 6, 2009.
62 Kim Dae Jung, "Buk Haek 3 Ka Seol kwa Uri 3 Ka Seol" ("Three Hypotheses of Nuclear Power and Three Hypotheses of South Korea"), *Chosun Ilbo*, July 5, 2009.
63 Michael Green, "The Perilous Case of Kim Jong Il," *National Interest*, September/October 2009, Issue 103, pp. 36–42.
64 Republic of Korea, *Policy of Mutual Benefits and Common Prosperity toward North Korea*, Seoul, August 17, 2009.
65 *Meeting with H.E. Lee Myung-bak*, Council on Foreign Relations, New York, September 21, 2009, www.koreasociety.org/culture_policy_society/culture_policy_society/lee_myung-bak.html (accessed April 1, 2011).
66 "S. Korea, Japan Say No Aid until N. Korea Disarms," *The Mainichi Daily News*, October 11, 2009.
67 "North Korea Opens Border; Again Calls for U.S. Treaty," *The New York Times*, September 1, 2009.
68 "DPRK Permanent Representative Sends Letter to President of UNSC," *Korean Central News Agency*, September 4, 2009.
69 "US to Talk with NK Only in Six-party Framework," *The Korea Times*, September 6, 2009.
70 Anthony DiFilippo, "Nuclear Faceoff: United States vs. North Korea," a two-part Op-ed Article, *The Korea Times*, September 21, 2009 and September 24, 2009.
71 "DPRK Foreign Ministry Declares Strong Counter-measures against UNSC's 'Resolution 1874,'" *Korean Central News Agency*, June 13, 2009.
72 Siegfried Hecker, "A Return Trip to North Korea's Yongbyon Nuclear Complex," Center for International Security and Cooperation, Stanford University, November 20, 2010.
73 Don Oberdorfer, *The Two Koreas: A Contemporary History* (Reading, MA: Addison-Wesley, 1997), pp. 249–336.
74 "No Immediate Plan for U.S., N. Korea Talks: Nuke Envoy Saiki," *Kyodo News*, September 7, 2009.
75 US Department of State, *Daily Press Briefing*, Washington, DC, September 11, 2009.
76 "DPRK Top Leader Meets Chinese Presidential Envoy," *Xinhua*, September 18, 2009.
77 "N. Korea Urges Japan to Drop 'Hostile Policy,' Sanctions after Election," *Kyodo News*, August 12, 2009.
78 "NK Leadership Shows Signs of Internal Row," *The Korea Times*, September 12, 2009.

79 "N. Korea's No. 2 Says Pyongyang Seeks 'Fruitful Ties' with Hatoyama Gov't," *Kyodo News*, September 10, 2009.

80 "Japan, N. Korea Need a New Accord to Improve Ties: North Envoy," *Kyodo News*, September 11, 2009.

81 "N. Korea Says Abductions to be Discussed with Japan: U.N. Source," *Kyodo News*, September 28, 2009.

82 Han Sung Joo, "Yuk Ja Hoe Dam Un Chin Cha Tokee Inka?" ("Is the Six-party-Talks a Real Rabbit?"), *Donga Ilbo*, October 13, 2009.

83 The White House, *Remarks by President Barack Obama and President Lee Myung-bak of Republic of Korea in Joint Press Conference*, Seoul, November 19, 2009.

84 "KCNA Dismisses S. Korean Chief Executive's 'Proposal' as Rubbish," *Korean Central News Agency*, September 30, 2009.

85 Gavin McCormack, *Target North Korea: Pushing North Korea to the Brink of Nuclear Catastrophe* (New York: Nation Books, 2004).

86 "KCNA: Who is to Wholly Blame for Armed Clash in the West Sea of Korea," *Korean Central News Agency*, November 27, 2010.

87 US Department of State, *Existing Sanctions and Reporting Provisions Related to North Korea*, Washington, DC, October 11, 2008; US Department of State, *U.S. Department of State Designation of North Korean Nuclear and Missile Entities*, Washington DC, September 8, 2009, www.state.gov/r/pa/prs/ps/2009/sept/128698. htm (accessed April 1, 2011); Department of Defense, *Nuclear Posture Review Report*, Washington, DC, April 2010.

88 For a discussion of proliferation and exaggerated claims see, Francis Gavin, "Same as It Ever Was: Nuclear Alarmism, Proliferation, and the Cold War," *International Security*, vol. 34, no. 3, Winter 2009/10, pp. 7–37.

89 United Nations General Assembly, *Nuclear Weapons, Irrational Doctrines Justifying Their Use, Non-proliferation Treaty Non-compliance Block Nuclear Disarmament, Iran Tells First Committee*, Sixty-third General Assembly, First Committee, New York, October 13, 2008; "End to U.S. Nuclear Threat to DPRK Called For," *Korean Central News Agency*, October 22, 2008; "UFG Termed Test Nuclear War against DPRK," *Korean Central News Agency*, August 24, 2009; "U.S. Hostile Policy Toward the DPRK Censored," *Korean Central News Agency*, September 28, 2009.

90 US Department of State, *Trilateral Statement of Japan, Republic of Korea and the United States*, Washington, DC, December 6, 2010.

91 Author interview with DPRK ambassador to North Korea's permanent mission to the United Nations, New York, October 21, 2010.

92 For examples of defector analysis, see Helen-Louise Hunter, *Kim Il-song's North Korea* (Westport, CT: Praeger, 1999); Bradley Martin, *Under the Loving Care of the Fatherly Leader: North Korea and the Kim Dynasty* (New York: Thomas Dunne Books, 2004); Andrei Lankov, "Pyongyang Strikes Back: North Korean Policies of 2002–8 and Attempts to Reverse 'De-Stalinization from Below,'" *Asia Policy*, no. 8, July 2009, pp. 47–71; John Park, "North Korea, Inc.: Gaining Insights into North Korean Regime Stability from Recent Commercial Activities," United States Institute of Peace, Working Paper, April 2, 2009.

93 Ministry of Foreign Affairs of the People's Republic of China, *Joint Statement of the Fourth Round of the Six-Party Talks*, Beijing, September 19, 2005, www. fmprc.gov.cn/eng/zxxx/t212707.htm (accessed on April 1, 2011).

94 *Statement by H.E. Mr. Pak Kil Yon, Vice-Minister of Foreign Affairs, Chairman of the Delegation of the Democratic People's Republic of Korea at the 64th Session of the United Nations General Assembly*, New York, September 28, 2009; "DPRK Stand on World Peace and Security Clarified," *Korean Central News Agency*, October 1, 2009.

95 "DPRK Proposes to Start of Peace Talks," *Korean Central News Agency*, January 11, 2010; "US Urged to Make Decision to Replace AA by Peace Treaty," *Korean Central News Agency*, January 21, 2010.
96 The White House, Office of the Press Secretary, *Remarks by President Barack Obama*, Prague, April 5, 2009.
97 South Korea and Russia have already signed and ratified the CTBT.
98 Anthony DiFilippo, "North Korea's Denuclearization and a Peace Treaty," *North Korean Review*, vol. 7, no. 1, Spring 2011, pp. 7–20; Anthony DiFilippo, "The Peace Deal Obama Should Be Making," *Foreign Policy*, February 1, 2010, www.foreignpolicy.com/articles/2010/02/01/the_peace_deal_obama_should_be_making (accessed April 1, 2011); Anthony DiFilippo, "The Peace Deal Obama Should Make: Toward a U.S.–North Korea Peace Treaty," *The Asia-Pacific Journal*, 7-4-10, February 15, 2010, www.japanfocus.org/-Anthony-DiFilippo/ 3304 (accessed April 1, 2011).
99 John Barry Kotch and Michael Abbey, "Ending Naval Clashes on the Northern Limit Line and the Quest for a West Sea Peace Regime," *Asian Perspectives*, vol. 27, no. 2, 2003, pp. 175–204.
100 "Seoul Vows Retaliation after Confirming N.K. Torpedo Sank Warship," *Yonhap News Agency*, May 20, 2010; "National Defence Commission Issues Statement," *Korean Central News Agency*, May 20, 2010.
101 Anthony DiFilippo, "N. Korean Culpability or Fuzzy Politics?" *The Hankyoreh*, June 15, 2010; Seunghun Lee and J.J. Suh, "Rush to Judgment: Inconsistencies in South Korea's Cheonan Report," *The Asia-Pacific Journal*, 28-1-10, July 12, 2010, www.japanfocus.org/-JJ-Suh/3382 (accessed April 1, 2011).
102 United Nations, Security Council, *Statement by the President of the Security Council*, New York, July 9, 2010.
103 Goohoon Kwon, "A United Korea? Reassessing North Korea Risks (Part 1)," Global Economics Paper No: 188, Goldman Sachs, New York, September 21, 2009.
104 Author meeting with researcher in the DPRK Ministry of Foreign Affairs, Pyongyang, January 8, 2009.
105 Yuasa Ichiro, "Strategy for a Northeast Asia Nuclear Weapon-free Zone as a Step to 'Common Security,'" *Policy Forum*, Nautilus Institute, December 9, 2010, www.nautilus.org/publications/essays/napsnet/forum/strategy-for-a-northeast-asia-nuclear-weapon-free-zone-as-a-step-to-common-security/ (accessed April 1, 2011).
106 "Many in DPJ want Japan to Cut Link to U.S. Nukes," *The Japan Times Online*, October 11, 2009.

Selected bibliography

Abe, Amii. "Taboo in Japan: Can Japan Think Strategically about North Korea," *Policy Forum Online*, Nautilus Institute, April 9, 2009, www.nautilus.org/publications/essays/napsnet/forum/2009–10/09029Abe.html (accessed on April 7, 2011).

Abramowitz, Morton and Bosworth, Stephen. *Chasing the Sun: Rethinking East Asian Policy.* New York: Century Foundation Press, 2006.

Akaha, Tsuneo. "Japan's Policy Toward North Korea: Interests and Options," in *The Future of North Korea*, ed. Tsuneo Akaha. London: Routledge, 2002, pp. 77–94.

Akiyama, Masahiro. "A Discussion of the Current Security Issues in Japan: Security Guidelines, the Constitution, Legislative Reviews, and the Missile Threat," MIT Securities Studies Program, Seminar Series, March 15, 2000.

Armitage, Richard and Nye, Joseph. *The U.S.–Japan Alliance: Getting Asia Right through 2020*, Center for Strategic International Studies, Washington, DC, February 2007.

Ashizawa, Kuniko. "Tokyo's Quandary, Beijing's Moment in the Six-Party Talks: A Regional Multilateral Approach to Resolve the DPRK's Nuclear Problem," *Pacific Affairs*, vol. 79, no. 3, Fall 2006, pp. 411–32.

Babson, Bradley. "The International Financial Institutions and the DPRK: Prospects and Constraints," North Pacific Policy Papers, #9, University of British Columbia, March 14, 2002.

Beal, Tim. "Multilayered Confrontation in East Asia: North Korea-Japan," *Asian Affairs*, vol. XXXVI, no. III, November 2005, pp. 339–60.

——. *The Struggle Against American Power.* London: Pluto Press, 2005.

Becker, Jasper. *Rogue Regime: Kim Jong Il and the Looming Threat of North Korea.* New York: Oxford University Press, 2005.

Berger, Thomas. *Cultures of Antimilitarism: National Security in Japan and West Germany.* Baltimore, MD: Johns Hopkins University Press, 1998.

Bolton, John. *Surrender is Not an Option: Defending America at the United Nations and Abroad.* New York: Threshold Editions, 2007.

Carlin, Robert and Weeks, John. "Negotiating with North Korea: 1992–2007," Center for International Security and Cooperation, Stanford University, January 2008, pp. 1–51.

Cha, Victor and Kang, David. *Nuclear North Korea: A Debate on Engagement Strategies.* New York: Columbia University Press, 2003.

——. "What Do They Really Want? Obama's North Korea Conundrum," *The Washington Quarterly*, vol. 32, no. 4, October 2009, pp. 119–38.

Chae, Kyung-suk. "The Future of the Sunshine Policy: Strategies for Survival," *East Asian Review*, vol. 14, no. 4, Winter 2002, pp. 3–17.

Chang, Gordon. *Nuclear Showdown: North Korea Takes on the World*. New York: Random House, 2006.

Cheon, Seongwhun. "North Korea and the ROK–U.S Security Alliance," *Armed Forces & Society*, vol. 34, no. 1, October 2007, pp. 5–28.

Chinoy, Mike. *Meltdown: The Inside Story of the North Korean Nuclear Crisis*. New York: St. Martin's Press, 2008.

"Comrade Kim Jong Il Defies Revisionism: On Marx, Engels, Lenin, and Stalin." Excerpted from *Respecting the Forerunners of the Revolution is a Noble Moral Obligation of Revolutionaries*, Pyongyang, 1996.

Cronin, Richard. "The North Korean Nuclear Threat and the U.S.–Japan Security Alliance: Perceived Interests, Approaches, and Prospects," *The Fletcher Forum of World Affairs*, vol. 29, no. 1, Winter 2005, p. 51–73.

Cumings, Bruce. "Decoupled from History: North Korea in the 'Axis of Evil,'" in eds. Ervand Abrahamian, Bruce Cumings and Moshe Ma'oz, *Inventing the Axis of Evil: The Truth about North Korea, Iran, and Syria*. New York: New Press, 2004.

——. *North Korea: Another Country*. New York: The Free Press, 2004.

——. "The North Korea Problem: Dealing with Irrationality," *Current History*, September 2009, pp. 284–90.

——. *The Origins of the Korean War: The Roaring of the Cataract*, vol. 2. Princeton, NJ: Princeton University Press, 1990.

DiFilippo, Anthony. "Can Japan Craft an International Nuclear Disarmament Policy?" *Asian Survey*, vol. 40, no. 4, July/August 2000, pp. 571–98.

——. *The Challenges of the U.S.–Japan Military Arrangement: Competing Security Transitions in a Changing International Environment*. Armonk, NY: M.E. Sharpe, 2002.

——. *Cracks in the Alliance, Science, Technology, and the Evolution of U.S.–Japan Relations*. Aldershot: Ashgate, 1997.

——. "How Tokyo's Security Policies Discount Public Opinion: Toward a New Agenda," *Pacifica Review: Peace, Security & Global Change*, vol. 14, no. 1, February 2002, pp. 23–48.

——. "Hubris, Intransigence, and the North Korean Nuclear Crisis," *Japan Focus*, January 8, 2007.

——. *Japan's Nuclear Disarmament Policy and the U.S. Security Umbrella*. New York: Palgrave Macmillan, 2006.

——. "Kojireta kankei no nichicho kokko seijohka," *Kitachosen o Meguru Hokutoh Ajia no Kokusai Kankei to Nihon*, henshuusha Yoichi Hirama, Yone Sugita. Tokyo: Akashi Shoten, 2003 ("The Troubled Relationship: What Normalized Relations Would do for Japan and North Korea"), in *Japan and Northeast Asian International Relations Involving North Korea*, eds. Yoichi Hirama and Yone Sugita. Tokyo: Akashi Shoten, 2003, pp. 66–84.

——. "N. Korean Culpability or Fuzzy Politics?" *The Hankyoreh*, June 15, 2010.

——. "North Korea as a State Sponsor of Terrorism: Views from Tokyo and Pyongyang," *International Journal of Korean Unification Studies*, vol. 17, no. 1, 2008, pp. 1–40.

——. "The North Korean Nuclear Issue in Disarray," *The Korea Times*, May 1, 2009.

——. "Nuclear Deterrence and Animosity in Japan-North Korean Relations: Steps to Coexistence," *Pacific Focus*, vol. XXI, no. 1, Spring 2006, pp. 137–74.

——. "Nuclear Faceoff: United States vs. North Korea," two-part Op-ed Article, *The Korea Times*, September 21, 2009 and September 24, 2009.

——. "Opposing Positions in Japan's Security Policy: Toward a New Security Dynamic," *East Asia: An International Quarterly*, vol. 20, no.1, Spring 2002, pp. 107–35.

——. "The Peace Deal Obama Should Be Making," *Foreign Policy*, February 1, 2010, www.foreignpolicy.com/articles/2010/02/01/the_peace_deal_obama_should_be_making (accessed on February 1, 2010).

——. "The Peace Deal Obama Should Make: Toward a U.S.–North Korea Peace Treaty," 7-4-10, *Asia-Pacific Journal*, February 15, 2010.

——. "Security Trials, Nuclear Tribulations and Rapprochement in Japan–North Korean Relations," *Journal of Pacific Asia*, vol. 11, spring 2004, pp. 7–31.

——. "Targeting Chongryun?" *Policy Forum Online*, Nautilus Institute, October 11, 2007, www.nautilus.org/fora/security/07076DiFilippo.html (accessed on October 11, 2007).

——. "U.S. Policy and the Nuclear Weapons Ambitions of the 'Axis of Evil' Countries," *New Political Science*, vol. 28, no 1, March 2006, pp. 101–23.

Dionisopoulos, P. Allan. "Revisionist Tendencies in Post-occupation Japan," *The Western Political Quarterly*, vol. 10, no. 4 December 1957, pp. 793–801.

"Does Pyongyang Really Want Peace?" In *North Korea: Uneasy, Shaky Kim Jong Il Regime*. Seoul: Naewoe Press, 1997, pp. 11–14.

Downs, Chuck. *Over the Line: North Korea's Negotiating Strategy*. Washington, DC: American Enterprise Institute Press, 1999.

Drifte, Reinhard. *Japan's Quest for a Permanent Security Council Seat: A Matter of Pride or Justice?* London: Macmillan, 2000.

Duus, Peter. "The Greater East Asian Co-Prosperity Sphere: Dream and Reality," *Journal of Northeast Asian History*, vol. 5, no. 1, June 2008, pp. 143–54.

Eberstadt, Nicholas. *The End of North Korea*. Washington, DC, American Enterprise Institute, 1999.

——. "The Persistence of North Korea," *Policy Review*, Hoover Institution, Stanford University, no. 127, October and November, 2004.

Frank, Ruediger. "The Political Economy of Sanctions against North Korea," *Asian Perspective*, vol. 30, no. 3, 2006, pp. 5–36.

Fukuoka, Yasunori. "Koreans in Japan: Past and Present," *Saitama University Review*, vol. 31, no. 1, 1996.

——. *Lives of Young Koreans in Japan*, trans. by Tom Gill. Melbourne: Trans Pacific Press, 2000.

Funabashi, Yoichi. *The Peninsula Question: A Chronicle of the Second North Korean Nuclear Crisis*. Washington, DC, Brookings Institution Press, 2007.

Garwin, Richard and von Hippel, Frank. "A Technical Analysis of North Korea's Oct. 9 Nuclear Test," *Arms Control Today*, November 2006.

Gause, Ken. "Can the North Korean Regime Survive Kim Jong Il?" *The Korean Journal of Defense Analysis*, vol. 20, no. 2, June 2008, pp. 93–111.

Gavin, Francis. "Same as It Ever Was: Nuclear Alarmism, Proliferation, and the Cold War," *International Security*, vol. 34, no. 3, Winter 2009/10, pp. 7–37.

Goodkind, Daniel and West, Loraine. "The North Korean Famine and Its Demographic Impact," *Population & Development Review*, vol. 27, no. 2, June 2001, pp. 219–38.

Haggard, Stephan and Noland, Marcus. *Famine in North Korea: Markets, Aid, and Reform*. New York: Columbia University Press, 2007.

Hagström, Linus. "Normalizing Japan: Supporter, Nuisance, or Wielder of Power in the North Korean Nuclear Talks," *Asian Survey*, vol. 49, no. 5, September/October 2009, pp. 831–51.

Han, Chung Sook. "Il Bon kwa 6 Cha Hoe Dam" ("Japan and the 6-party Talks"), *The Hankyoreh*, October 23, 2009.

Han, Sung Joo. "Yuk Ja Hoe Dam Un Chin Cha Tokee Inka?" ("Is the Six-party-Talks a Real Rabbit?"), *Donga Ilbo*, October 13, 2009.

Harrison, Selig. "Getting Around Pyongyang's Hard-Liners," *Policy Forum Online*, Nautilus Institute, July 5, 2005, www.nautilus.org/fora/security/0555Harrison.html (accessed September 29, 2006).

——. *Korean Endgame: A Strategy for Reunification and Disengagement*. Princeton, NJ: Princeton University Press, 2002.

Hecker, Siegfried. "A Return Trip to North Korea's Yongbyon Nuclear Complex," Center for International Security and Cooperation, Stanford University, November 20, 2010.

Heilbrunn, Jacob. *They Knew They Were Right: The Rise of the Neocons*. New York: Doubleday, 2008, pp. 228–80.

Hicks, George. *The Comfort Women: Japan's Brutal Regime of Enforced Prostitution in the Second World War*. New York: Norton & Company, 1994.

Ho, Jong Ho, Kang, Sok Hui and Pak, Thae Ho. *The US Imperialists Started the Korean War*. Pyongyang: Foreign Languages Publications House, 1993.

Hughes, Christopher. *Japan's Remilitarization*. London: Routledge, 2009.

——. "'Super-sizing' the DPRK Threat: Japan's Evolving Military Posture and North Korea," *Asian Survey*, vol. 49, no. 2, March/April 2009, pp. 291–311.

Hughes, Llewelyn. "Why Japan Will Not go Nuclear (Yet): International and Domestic Constraints on the Nuclearization of Japan," *International Security*, vol. 31, no. 4, Spring 2007, pp. 67–96.

Hunter, Helen-Louise. *Kim Il-song's North Korea*. Westport, CT: Praeger, 1999.

Ishiguro, Yoshiaki. "A Japanese National Crime: The Korean Massacre after the Kanto Earthquake of 1923," *Korea Journal*, vol. 38, no. 4, Winter 1998, pp. 331–54.

The Japan Institute of International Affairs. *Resolving the North Korean Nuclear Problem: A Regional Approach and the Role of Japan*, JIIA Policy Report, Tokyo, July 2005.

Jin, Saeng So. "The Self-Identities of *Zainichi* Koreans," The College of William & Mary, Spring 2000, www.wm.edu/so/monitor/spring2000/paper1.htm (accessed on August 29, 2007).

Johnston, Eric. "The North Korea Abduction Issue and Its Effect on Japanese Domestic Politics," Japan Policy Research Institute, JPRI Working Paper 101, June 2004.

Jo, Song Baek. *The Leadership Philosophy of Kim Jong Il*. Pyongyang: Foreign Languages Publishing House, 1999.

Kagan, Robert. "Benevolent Empire," *Foreign Policy*, Summer 1998, pp. 24–35.

Kang, Jungmin and Hayes, Peter "Did North Korea Successfully Conduct a Nuclear Test? A Technical Analysis," *The Asia-Pacific Journal: Japan Focus*, October 22, 2006.

Kaplan, Eben. "The Proliferation Security Initiative," *Backgrounder*, Council on Foreign Relations, October 19, 2006.

Kaplan, Robert. "When North Korea Falls," *The Atlantic Monthly*, October 2006, pp. 64–73.

Kashiwaaki, Chikako. "The Politics of Legal Status: The Equation of Nationality with Ethnonational Identity," in *Koreans in Japan: Critical Voices from the Margin*, ed. Sonia Ryang. London: Routledge, 2000, pp. 13–31.

Kihl, Young Whan, "Staying Power of the Socialist 'Hermit Kingdom,'" in *North Korea: The Politics of Regime Survival*, eds. Young Whan Kihl and Hong Nack Kim. Armonk, NY: M.E. Sharpe, 2005, pp. 3–33.

Kim, Dae Jung. "Buk Haek 3 Ka Seol kwa Uri 3 Ka Seol" ("Three Hypotheses of Nuclear Power and Three Hypotheses of South Korea"), *Chosun Ilbo*, July 5, 2009.

Kim, Hong Nack. "Japanese–North Korean Relations under the Koizumi Government," in *North Korea: The Politics of Regime Survival*, eds. Young Whan Kihl and Hong Nack Kim. Armonk, NY: M.E. Sharpe, 2005, pp. 161–82.

Kim, Ilpyong. "Kim Jong Il's Military-First Politics," in *North Korea: The Politics of Regime Survival*, eds. Young Whan Kihl and Hong Nack Kim. Armonk, NY: M.E. Sharpe, 2005, pp. 59–74.

Kim, Il Sung. Excerpted from *The Creation of the People's Liberation Army*, speech presented at the review of the Korean People's Army, February 8, 1945.

——. *For a Free and Peaceful New World*, speech given to the Inter-Parliamentary Conference, Pyongyang, 1991.

——. *The Life of a Revolutionary Should Begin with Struggle and End with Struggle*, speech made at a banquet given by the Central Committee of the Workers' Party of Korea and the Government of the Democratic People's Republic of Korea. Pyongyang: Foreign Languages Publishing House, 1990.

——. *Revolution and Socialist Construction in Korea*. New York: International Publishers, 1971.

Kim, Ji Soek. "Yi Myung Bal Dae Tong Ryong Nam Buk Kwan Kye Puleora" ("President Lee, Salvage the Relationship between North and South Korea"), *The Hankyoreh*, August 4, 2009.

Kim, Jong Il. "The Democratic People's Republic of Korea is a Juche-Oriented Socialist State with Invincible Might," *Rodong Sinmun* and *Minju Joson*, September 5, 2008, republished in *Study of the Juche Idea*, no. 81, February 2009 by the International Institute of the Juche Idea, Tokyo, 2009.

——. *On the Juche Idea*, Document sent to the National Seminar on the *Juche* Idea to commemorate the 70th birthday of Kim Il Sung, March 31, 1982, published by *The People's Korea*, 1998, www1.korea-np.co.jp/pk/062nd_issue/98092410.htm (accessed on April 7, 2011).

——. *The Songun-Based Revolutionary Line is a Great Revolutionary Line of Our Era and an Ever-Victorious Banner of Our Revolution*. Pyongyang: Foreign Languages Publishing House, 2007.

Kim, Jong-In. "In the Course of Mounting Tension between North Korea and Japan: Difficulties for *Zainichi* Korean Women to Live in Japan," *Voices from Japan*, no. 18, Winter 2007, pp. 44–46.

Koh, Byung Chul. "'Military-First Politics' and Building a 'Powerful and Prosperous Nation' in North Korea," *Policy Forum Online*, The Nautilus Institute, April 14, 2005, www.nautilus.org/fora/security/0532AKoh.html (accessed on April 7, 2011).

Kotch, John Barry and Abbey, Michael. "Ending Naval Clashes on the Northern Limit Line and the Quest for a West Sea Peace Regime," *Asian Perspectives*, vol., 27, no. 2, 2003, pp. 175–204.

Krauthammer, Charles. "The Unipolar Moment," *Foreign Affairs*, vol. 70, no. 1, 1990/91, pp. 23–33.

Kunihiro, Masao. "The Decline and Fall of Pacifism," *The Bulletin of the Atomic Scientists*, vol. 53, no. 1, January/February 1997, pp. 35–39.

Kwon, Goohoon. "A United Korea? Reassessing North Korea Risks (Part 1)," Global Economics Paper No: 188, Goldman Sachs, New York, September 21, 2009.

Lankov, Andrei. "Pyongyang Strikes Back: North Korean Policies of 2002–8 and Attempts to Reverse 'De-Stalinization from Below,'" *Asia Policy*, no. 8, July 2009, pp. 47–71.

Lebovic, James. "Perception and Politics in Intelligence Assessment: U.S. Estimates of the Soviet and 'Rogue-State' Nuclear Threats," *International Studies Perspectives*, vol. 10, 2009, pp. 394–412.

Lee, Myonwoo. "Japanese-North Korean Relations: Going in Circles," in *North Korea and Northeast Asia*, eds. Samuel Kim and Tai Hwan Lee. Lanham, MD: Rowman & Littlefield Publishers, 2002, pp. 89–108.

Lee, Seunghun and Suh, J.J. "Rush to Judgment: Inconsistencies in South Korea's Cheonan Report," *The Asia-Pacific Journal*, 28-1-10, July 12, 2010.

Lie, John. *Zainichi (Koreans in Japan): Diasporic Nationalism and Postcolonial Identity*. Berkeley: University of California Press, 2008.

Liem, Channing. *The Korean War (6.25, 1950 – 7.27, 1953) – An Unanswered Question*. Pyongyang: Foreign Languages Publishing House, 1993, reprinted in *The People's Korea*, 1998,www1.korea-np.co.jp/pk/054th_issue/koreanwar/98080502.htm (accessed on April 7, 2011).

Li, Li. "Launching Another Crisis," *The Beijing Review*, vol. 49, no. 29, July 20, 2006, pp. 10–11.

Lynn, Hyung Gu. *Bipolar Orders: The Two Koreas Since 1989*. London, Zed Books, 2007.

MacArthur, Douglas. *Reminiscences*. New York: MacGraw-Hill, 1964.

Maki, John. "The Constitution of Japan: Pacifism, Popular Sovereignty, and Fundamental Human Rights," *Law and Contemporary Problems*, vol. 53, no. 1, Winter and Spring 1990, pp. 73–87.

Martin, Bradley. *Under the Loving Care of the Fatherly Leader: North Korea and the Kim Dynasty*. New York: Thomas Dunne Books, 2004.

McCormack, Gavan. "Difficult Neighbors: Japan and North Korea," in *Rethinking Historical Injustice and Reconciliation in Northeast Asia: The Korean Experience*, eds. Gi-Wook Shin, Soon-Won Park, and Daqing Yang. New York: Routledge, 2007, pp. 154–72.

——. *Target North Korea: Pushing North Korea to the Brink of Nuclear Catastrophe*. New York: Nation Books, 2004.

Miyagi, Yukiko. "Foreign Policy Making under Koizumi: Norms and Japan's Role in 2003 Iraq War," *Foreign Policy Analysis*, vol. 5, 2009, pp. 349–66.

Morris-Suzuki, Tessa. *Exodus to North Korea: Shadows from Japan's Cold War*. Lanham, MD: Rowman & Littlefield, 2007, 231–45.

——. "The Forgotten Victims of the North Korean Crisis," *Japan Focus*, March 15, 2007.

——. "The Forgotten Victims of the North Korean Crisis," *Policy Forum Online*, Nautilus Institute, March 13, 2007, www.nautilus.org/fora/security/07022MorrisSuzuki. html#sect2 (accessed on May 23, 2007).

——. "Japan's 'Comfort Women': It's Time for the Truth (in the Ordinary, Everyday Sense of the Word)," *Japan Focus*, March 8, 2007.

——. "Japan's Hidden Role in the 'Return' of Zainichi Koreans to North Korea," *ZNet*, February 7, 2005.

Noland, Marcus. "The Economic Implications of a North Korean Nuclear Test," *Asia Policy*, no. 2, July 2006, pp. 25–39.

——. "The (Non) Impact of U.N. Sanctions on North Korea," *Asia Policy*, no. 7, January 2009, pp. 61–88.

"North Korea's Foreign Trade Remains Bleak [June 1995]." In *North Korea: Uneasy, Shaky Kim Jong Il Regime*. Seoul: Naewoe Press, 1997, pp. 63–66.

Nye, Joseph. *Soft Power: The Means to Success in World Politics*. New York: Public Affairs, 2004.

Oberdorfer, Don. *The Two Koreas: A Contemporary History*.Reading, MA: Addison-Wesley, 1997.

Oh, Kongdan and Hassig, Ralph. *North Korea Through the Looking Glass*. Washington, DC: Brookings Institution Press, 2000.

Okonogi, Masao. "The Ideology and Political Leadership of Kim Jong Il," in *North Korea at the Crossroads*, ed. Masao Okonogi. Tokyo: Japan Institute of International Affairs, 1988, pp. 1–21.

Oros, Andrew. *Normalizing Japan: Politics, Identity, and the Evolution of Security Practice*. Stanford, CA: Stanford University Press, 2008.

Pak, Chi Young. *Korea and the United Nations*. Boston: Kluwer Law International, 2000.

Park, John. "North Korea, Inc.: Gaining Insights into North Korean Regime Stability from Recent Commercial Activities," United States Institute of Peace, Working Paper, April 2, 2009.

Park, Kun Young. "Nuclear Politicking on the Korean Peninsula: A Highly Enriched Uranium Program Coming Out of the Pandora's Box," *Korea Journal*, Summer 2009, pp. 99–118.

Park, Myung Rib. "Yuk Sa Sok Ui Hankook Munjewa Buk Hae Munje" ("Korean and North Korean Nuclear Problem in History"), *The Hankyoreh*, September 20, 2009.

Pollack, Jonathan. "Kim Jong Il's Clenched Fist," *The Washington Quarterly*, vol. 32, no. 4, October 2009, pp. 153–73.

Pritchard, Charles. *Failed Diplomacy: The Tragic Story of How North Korea Got the Bomb*. Washington, DC: The Brookings Institution, 2007.

Pyle, Kenneth. *Japan Rising: The Resurgence of Japanese Power and Purpose*. New York: Public Affairs, 2007.

Quinones, C. Kenneth. "Dealing with Pyongyang: In Search of a More Effective Strategy," *International Journal of Korean Unification*, vol. 14, no. 1, 2005, pp. 1–30.

Reeves, Richard. *President Nixon: Alone in the White House*. New York: Simon and Schuster, 2001.

A Report of the Project for the New American Century. *Rebuilding America's Defenses: Strategy, Forces and Resources for a New Century*, Washington, DC: September 2000.

Richelson, Jeffrey. *Spying on the Bomb: American Nuclear Intelligence from Nazi Germany to Iran and North Korea*. New York: W.W. Norton, 2006.

Rozman, Gilbert. "The North Korean Nuclear Crisis and U.S. Security in Northeast Asia," *Asian Survey*, vol. 47, no. 4, July/August 2007, pp. 601–21.

Ryang, Sonia. "The North Korean Homeland of Koreans in Japan," in *Koreans in Japan: Critical Voices from the Margin*, ed. Sonia Ryang. London: Routledge, 2000, pp. 32–54.

——. *North Koreans in Japan: Language, Ideology, and Identity*. Boulder, CO: West-view Press, 1997.

——. "The Tongue that Divided Life and Death: The 1923 Tokyo Earthquake and the Massacre of Koreans," *Japan Focus*, September 3, 2007.

——. "Visible and Vulnerable: The Predicament of Koreans in Japan," in *Diaspora without Homeland: Being Korean in Japan*, eds. Sonia Ryang and John Lie. Berkeley: University of California Press, 2009, pp. 62–80.

Samuels, Richard. "New Fighting Power! Japan's Growing Maritime Capabilities and East Asian Security," *International Security*, vol. 32, no. 3, Winter 2007/08, pp. 84–112.

——. *Securing Japan: Tokyo's Grand Strategy and the Future of East Asia*. Ithaca, NY: Cornell University Press, 2007.

Sato, Isao. "Comment: Revisionism During the Forty Years of the Constitution of Japan," *Law and Contemporary Problems*, vol. 53, no. 1, Winter and Spring 1990, pp. 97–104.

Scoblic, J. Peter. *Us vs. Them: How a Half Century of Conservatism Has Undermined American Security*. New York: Viking, 2008.

Shen, Dingli. "North Korea: The Chinese View," *Le Monde Diplomatique*, November 2006.

Shi, Yongming. "Challenging Talks," *The Beijing Review*, vol. 50, no. 1, January 4, 2007, pp. 10–11

——. "Relations at a Crossroad," *The Beijing Review*, vol. 50, no. 11, March 15, 2007, pp. 10–11.

Sigal, Leon. *Disarming Strangers: Nuclear Diplomacy with North Korea*. Princeton, NJ: Princeton University Press, 1998.

——. "Try Engagement for a Change," *Global Asia: A Journal of the East Asia Foundation*, vol. 1., no. 1, September 2006, pp. 50–57.

Smith, Hazel. *Hungry for Peace, International Security, Humanitarian Assistance, and Social Change in North Korea*. Washington, DC: United States Institute of Peace, 2005.

——. "North Korean Shipping: A Potential for WMD Proliferation?" East-West Center, *Asia Pacific Issues*, no. 87, February 2009.

Snyder, Scott. *China's Rise and the Two Koreas: Politics, Economics and Security*. Boulder, CO: Lynne Rienner, 2009.

Soh, Chunghee Sarah. "The Korean 'Comfort Women' Tragedy as Structural Violence," in *Rethinking Historical Injustice and Reconciliation in Northeast Asia: The Korean Experience*, eds. Gi-Wook Shin, Soon-Won Park, and Daqing Yang. New York: Routledge, 2007, pp. 17–35.

Song, Hesuk. "Target of Scapegoating: Why does Discrimination towards Koreans Persist in Japan?" The Association of Korean Human Rights in Japan, Tokyo, 2003.

Stares, Paul and Wit, Joel. *Preparing for Sudden Change in North Korea*, Council Special Report No. 42. New York: Council on Foreign Relations, January 2009.

Stone, I. F. *The Hidden History of the Korean War, 1950–1951*. Boston: Little, Brown, 1988.

Stueck, William. *The Korean War: An International History*. Princeton, NJ: Princeton University Press, 1995.

Sugita, Yoneyuki. "An Active Japanese Foreign Policy Impeded by a Frustrated Public in a Post-Cold War Era," *International Journal of Korean Unification Studies*, vol. 14, no. 2, 2005, pp. 171–94.

Swaine, Michael with Runyon, Loren. "Ballistic Missiles and Missile Defense in Asia," National Bureau of Asian Research, vol. 13, no. 3, June 2002, pp. 58–63.

Takao, Yasuo. *Is Japan Really Remilitarizing? The Politics of Norm Formation and Change*. Victoria: Monash University Press, 2008.

Takashima, Nobuyoshi. "The North Korean Abductions and the Rewriting of Japanese History," *Japan Focus*, February 2003.

Takesada, Hideshi. "Military Trends in North Korea," in *North Korea at the Cross-roads*, ed. Masao Okonogi. Tokyo: Japan Institute of International Affairs, 1988, pp. 73–76.

Valencia, Mark. "The Proliferation Security Initiative: A Glass Half Full," *Arms Control Today*, June 2007.

Vorontsov, Alexander. "North Korea's Military-First Policy: A Curse or a Blessing?" Center for Northeast Asian Policy Studies, The Brookings Institution, Washington, DC, May 26, 2006.

Wada, Haruki, "Japan-North Korean Relations – A Dangerous Stalemate," *The Asia-Pacific Journal*, vol. 25-2-09, June 22, 2009.

——. "Re-Examining Alleged Abduction of Japanese," from *Sekai*, January and February 2001, accessed on December 18, 2007, www.kimsoft.com/2001/wada.htm (accessed on December 18, 2007).

Whelan, Richard. *Drawing the Line: The Korean War, 1950–1953*. Boston: Little, Brown and Company, 1990.

Wit, Joel Poneman, Daniel and Gallucci, Robert. *Going Critical: The First North Korean Nuclear Crisis*. Washington, DC: Brookings Institution Press, 2004.

Yang, U-ja. "Highlighting Multiple Discrimination: Survey Report by *Zainichi* Korean Women on Ourselves," *Voices from Japan*, no. 18, Winter 2007, pp. 41–44.

Yoshimi, Yoshiaki. *Comfort Women: Sexual Slavery in the Japanese Military During World War II*, trans. by Suzanne O'Brien. New York: Columbia University Press, 2000.

Yuasa, Ichiro. "Strategy for a Northeast Asia Nuclear Weapon-free Zone as a Step to 'Common Security,'" *Policy Forum*, Nautilus Institute, December 9, 2010, www. nautilus.org/publications/essays/napsnet/forum/strategy-for-a-northeast-asia-nuclear-weapon-free-zone-as-a-step-to-common-security/ (accessed April 1, 2011).

Zhang, Hui. "Assessing North Korea's Uranium Enrichment Capabilities," *Bulletin of the Atomic Scientists*, June 18, 2009.

Zhou, Yongsheng. "Closing of an Era," *Beijing Review*, vol. 49, no. 34, August 24, 2006, pp. 10–11.

Index

www.ingramcontent.com/pod-product-compliance
Ingram Content Group UK Ltd.
Pitfield, Milton Keynes, MK11 3LW, UK
UKHW020356010325
455677UK00021B/488